BLACK PORTSMOUTH

Revisiting New England: The New Regionalism

SERIES EDITORS

Lisa MacFarlane
University of New Hampshire

Dona Brown
University of Vermont

Stephen Nissenbaum
University of Massachusetts at Amherst

David H. Watters
University of New Hampshire

This series presents fresh discussions of the distinctiveness of New England culture. The editors seek manuscripts examining the history of New England regionalism; the way its culture came to represent American national culture as a whole; the interaction between that "official" New England culture and the people who lived in the region; and local, subregional, or even biographical subjects as microcosms that explicitly open up and consider larger issues. The series welcomes new theoretical and historical perspectives and is designed to cross disciplinary boundaries and appeal to a wide audience.

Richard Archer, *Fissures in the Rock: New England in the Seventeenth Century*

Nancy L. Gallagher, *Breeding Better Vermonters: The Eugenics Project in Vermont*

Sidney V. James, *The Colonial Metamorphoses in Rhode Island: A Study of Institutions in Change*

Diana Muir, *Reflections in Bullough's Pond: Economy and Ecosystem in New England*

James C. O'Connell, *Becoming Cape Cod: Creating a Seaside Resort*

Christopher J. Lenney, *Sightseeking: Clues to the Landscape History of New England*

Priscilla Paton, *Abandoned New England: Landscape in the Works of Homer, Frost, Hopper, Wyeth, and Bishop*

Adam Sweeting, *Beneath the Second Sun: A Cultural History of Indian Summer*

Mark J. Sammons and Valerie Cunningham, *Black Portsmouth: Three Centuries of African-American Heritage*

Pauleena MacDougall, *The Penobscot Dance of Resistance: Tradition in the History of a People*

Robert and Viola Opdahl, *Rise and Sing: A Shaker Musical Legacy*

BLACK PORTSMOUTH

Three Centuries
of African-American Heritage

MARK J. SAMMONS AND VALERIE CUNNINGHAM

University of New Hampshire Press

DURHAM, NEW HAMPSHIRE

Published by University Press of New England
Hanover and London

University of New Hampshire Press
Published by University Press of New England,
One Court Street, Lebanon, NH 03766
www.upne.com
©2004 by Mark J. Sammons and Valerie Cunningham
Printed in the United States of America
5 4 3 2 1

Support for the publication has been provided by The Otto Fund, a charitable giving partnership of the Greater Piscataqua Community Foundation.

Portions of this text are from the *Portsmouth Black Heritage Resource Book* (copyright 1996, 1998), and are used with permission of the Portsmouth Black Heritage Trail, Inc., board of directors.

Library of Congress Cataloging-in-Publication Data
Sammons, Mark.
Black Portsmouth : three centuries of African-American heritage / Mark J. Sammons and Valerie Cunningham.
   p.   cm. — (Revisiting New England)
Includes bibliographical references and index.
ISBN 1-58465-289-6 (pbk. : alk. paper)
   1. African Americans—New Hampshire—Portsmouth—History. 2. African Americans—New Hampshire—Portsmouth—Social conditions. 3. African Americans—New England—History. 4. Portsmouth (N.H.)—History. 5. Portsmouth (N.H.)—Race relations. 6. New England—History. 7. New England—Race relations. I. Cunningham, Valerie. II. Title. III. Series.
F44.P8S25 2004
305.8'96X073'07426—dc22   2004007172

CONTENTS

PREFACE

❧

WHEN MY FRIENDS AND COLLEAGUES ask me why I put two authors' names on a book I appear to have written entirely on my own, a book into which I have poured countless hours of research and thirty years of experience in public history, the answer comes with ease and gratitude. The very core of the book—the documentary evidence of the Black presence in Portsmouth—is Valerie Cunningham's work. This has been a monumental thirty-year task of searching local archives, sifting out hundreds of minute and elusive references that together make the story told here. She has spent countless hours tutoring me in the nuances of interpreting race— I am, after all, a guest in this territory—and reviewing and refining every word I have written. Continuing the spirit of the last thirty years, Valerie is researching a new area of Black history; she has spent the last year amassing photographic evidence of the local Black presence. This effort brought all the illustrations to the present volume. Valerie is in every way the originator, guiding spirit, and coauthor of this book.

Mark J. Sammons

This work originated in 1996 with short walking tours to sample Black history sites in Portsmouth. Questionnaires seeking guidance from the audience revealed a hunger for information about all periods and subjects: status, gender, work, spiritual life, resistance, slavery, freedom, and community.

People were astonished and eager to learn more about our town's Black history, to comprehend and correct their understanding of the past and its impact on the present. Some white people, horrified by the acts of their ancestors, engaged in constructive and informative dialogue about such topics as the boundaries of inherited guilt and quotidian opportunities to challenge casual racism.

Other conversations signaled interesting levels and qualities of discomfort with certain subjects and interpretations of Black history. Guides (all of them white) at the several local historic-house museums proved willing, even eager, to interpret slavery's presence, if occasionally tentative, unsure. A very few proposed that calling a "slave" an "enslaved person" was grammatically cumbersome at best and incorrect at worst, proposing that enslavement had occurred once, at the moment of capture or sale. These few were stung by the notion that enslavement had been an ongoing daily act. This belied the guides' emotional investment in the colonial merchants whose lives they interpreted. It also revealed a lifelong habit of viewing slaves as a class rather than as humans with individual personalities, experiences, and rights. It reveals the ease with which the trivial can distract us all from the larger significance of human experience.

Because the narratives in this book are about

the human experience, we often use words like "Black," "Jewish," "Hispanic," and "enslaved" as adjectival modifiers of individuals and groups, of men and women, of Africans and Americans, rather than using these words solely as nouns. Our goal is to remind ourselves and the reader of the distinction between status and humanity. Terms that place status above humanity are subtly but fundamentally bigoted, out of place in a work based in humanist scholarship.

We use the word "white" in lowercase type to indicate race. We capitalize the word "Black" because, in the context of American history, it indicates a complex ethnicity far beyond race.

Our use of such language will no doubt attract charges of "political correctness," a term meant solely to defame common courtesy. Those who are troubled by courtesy may wish to examine the roots of their uneasiness.

Special Thanks

Many people in and around Portsmouth have contributed to this project in many ways. We thank Professors David Watters and John Ernest of the University of New Hampshire for encouraging us to venture into this project and for their tireless and tactful advice. We thank Ellen Wicklum and Mary Crittendon of University Press of New England for their patient guidance along the unfamiliar route to publication, and William Hively for his thoughtful editing.

We thank the Greater Piscataqua Community Foundation for sponsoring a regionwide conversation on the meaning of diversity in an increasingly fragmented nation. This visionary committee brought the present authors together. We extend special thanks to its then-director Angela Matthews for many encouraging words. A summer's project has sprawled into an eight-year partnership and labor of love.

For volunteering to conduct pilot tours with some of the information herein, and canvass the public on their response, we thank Geraldine Copeland, Carole Arterbery, Kelvin Edwards,

Arianna Freeman, Tulani Freeman, Douglas Glover, Susan Kisslinger, and Roberta Ransley. We thank T. J. Wheeler and the Blues Bank Collective, and also the Reverend Pat Bowen and the people of South Church for providing a public forum in which to test our ideas.

For adopting focused research topics, for testing and critiquing interpretations, for encouragement, and for helping in innumerable ways we thank Charles DeGrandpré, Judith Harris, Arthur Hilson, Sandra Pettiford Lee, T. J. Wheeler, Cynthia Thomas, Algene Bailey, Jeffrey Bolster, Leigh Donaldson, Thomasina Downing, Royalene Edwards, Sheila Reed Findlay, Vernis Jackson, Marcia Jebb, Chris Remignanti, Jennifer Stiefel, and Geraldine Palmer.

For providing a congenial setting for meetings we thank the Reverend Doctor Arthur Hilson and the people of New Hope Baptist Church, and the Reverends Robert and Jennifer Stiefel and the people of Christ Episcopal Church.

For help in locating items in archives and libraries we thank Susan Grigg, Jane Porter, Kevin Shupe, Nancy Noble, and Roberta Ransley. For sharing random findings while working on other projects, thanks go to Ronan Donahoe, Nancy Burns, Elizabeth Nowers, Richard Winslow, Cynthia Thomas, and Jody Fernald.

For their availability to consult on areas of special expertise we thank Richard Candee, Jim Dolph, Robert Olson, Jim Garvin, John Ernest, Jeff Bolster, David Watters, and Nancy Lukens.

For sharing their experience interpreting Boston's Black history we thank Kenneth A. Heidelberg and Suzanne Muscato-Lalley of the African Meetinghouse Museum.

For their generosity in sharing institutional archives and their research findings we thank Ursula Wright, Nina Mauer, and Peter Michaud, all of the Society for the Preservation of New England Antiquities at Langdon House; Barbara Engelbach and Joyce Volk of the Warner House Association; Nancy Goss and Barbara Ward of the Colonial Dames and Moffatt-Ladd House; Andy Melville; Donna Belle Garvin of the New Hampshire Historical Society; Jim

Garvin of the New Hampshire Division of Historical Resources; and Laurel Ulrich.

For their help and encouragement at the beginning of this project we thank Dennis O'Toole, Kathleen Shea, Funi Burdick, Jack Casey, Judith Crouse, and Cheryl Gove, all of Strawbery Banke Museum.

For invaluable help in locating and preparing illustrations we thank Lynn Sanderson of the Whalley Museum and Library, Tom Hardiman of the Portsmouth Athenaeum, David Smollen of the New Hampshire Historical Society, and Jane Fithian, volunteer graphic designer.

We offer special thanks to the board of directors of the Portsmouth Black Heritage Trail, Inc., for permission to use portions of their guide resource book.

For inspiration and encouragement, and for infinite patience with the time this has taken from family life we offer our deepest gratitude to Augusta and Clarence Cunningham and to David Scott Allen.

Mark J. Sammons and Valerie Cunningham

BLACK PORTSMOUTH

CHAPTER I

The Seaport

◆)§℈(◆

Since her after-school job at the library in the 1950s, Valerie had been puzzled by references in antiquarian tomes to Black people in colonial Portsmouth. Schoolbooks never mentioned Blacks in New England.

That schoolgirl's growing interest in history flowed into an appreciation of African art and jazz, and she studied their history. Family and friends debated art, music, and race relations at home and church, as did visitors at the nearby guesthouse for Black tourists where Valerie had a summer job.

She came to understand that the occupations of the local Black people she knew were not reflective of their character or intellect but a circumstance of race-based restrictions. These well-educated, articulate, and responsible people, these pillars of the community, lived middle-class lives on the hourly wages of laborers and domestics.

Amid local de facto segregation they began to press for compliance with recent Supreme Court decisions regarding civil rights. They organized a local branch of the National Association for the Advancement of Colored People.

The teenager wondered if those Black colonists had been just as smart and dignified and persistent, and wondered who they really were. And so her search began.

Valerie grew up, married, moved away. She was reading race history and in 1967 stumbled across Lorenzo Greene's *The Negro in Colonial New England*. It showed her where to look for evidence. When from time to time she returned to the area she could hardly wait to resume her search.

Upon moving back to Portsmouth Valerie approached the clergy in town asking to see old church records. She started with Saint John's Episcopal Church, where ancient volumes were pulled from closets. She spent hours paging through them. The task seemed hopeless. Pages of terse and repetitive entries recorded births and baptisms, marriages, deaths, financial expenditures—hard to read and nothing relevant. For hours she squinted at the crabbed handwriting scratched with a quill.

Then, an entry made in December of 1807 made Valerie stop and reread it: "To Venus—a Black—$1." Yes! Here was a name that hadn't

Alexander "Skipper" Moore, a Spanish-American War veteran, enjoyed exploring the waters of the Piscataqua region in his boat after he retired from military service. Another hobby was reading and talking about Portsmouth history. Much credit goes to Moore for repeating the stories he knew about slavery in Portsmouth, telling them so often that they could not be forgotten by those who heard them. *Photograph courtesy of Geraldine M. Palmer.*

gotten into the local history books. One name was enough to make her keep looking. And looking. And looking.

The purpose of this book is to contextualize the lives of a selection of Black people who lived in Portsmouth in the last three centuries. Whites successfully purged from memory and knowledge the historical presence of Black people in New England in a gradual process that started after the Revolution and eventually enabled them to prosecute abolition and the Civil War from a position of moral superiority over Southerners. This collective white amnesia leads directly to the diffuse and unarticulated assumption that the few Blacks in small-town New England today are modern arrivals without precedent.[1] But this is not the case.

The stories that follow provide a cumulative account of Black people in Portsmouth. They show how the individual experiences of Black people—any people, really—in a small town have always been part of larger regional patterns, closely connected as well to national and international events.

The little port of Portsmouth is nestled in a corner of New Hampshire's minute Atlantic seaboard. It sits a couple of miles from the ocean on the banks of a tidal estuary called the Piscataqua River, which forms the boundary between New Hampshire and Maine. New Hampshire and Maine originated as one vast land grant to two men who split their territory along the river, initiating separate histories, both of which promptly encompassed Africans. In the 1650s Maine was absorbed into Massachusetts, of which it remained a province until 1820, when, through politicking related to slavery, it became a state. The separate political histories of Maine and New Hampshire notwithstanding, the river has always served as a unifying influence, binding the river basin's many towns into a single cultural region, locally known by the river's name, the Piscataqua.

Portsmouth is a quirky little city of somewhat over twenty thousand people, swelling to perhaps fifty thousand during business hours. It puts on a convincing urban face. It was something of a city in the early republic, when it ranked among the new nation's dozen largest population centers. But the very definition of urbanism left Portsmouth behind as other cities underwent growth so explosive that the old seaport city could be defined only as a town. In proud denial of this new reality, it was reincorporated as a city in the 1850s.

Portsmouth markets itself, and is widely perceived, as a colonial seaport town. It is a microcosm of the oldest New England seaports and follows their typical patterns in history, commerce, and cultural identity. On the heels of an epidemic that decimated the Native population, Europeans arrived in 1623, and in the following decades their several hamlets coalesced into the villages at the core of today's Rye, New Castle, Dover, and Portsmouth. In the 1650s, with chamber-of-commerce zeal for self-promotion, the riverbank village dropped its descriptive original name of Strawberry Bank in favor of the more marketable name Portsmouth.

For all practical purposes Portsmouth is New Hampshire's only seaport. The depth and swift tidal currents of the harbor prevent it from freezing. Today it supports limited commercial fishing, light industry, and technology firms numerous enough to adopt the eager nickname "the e-coast." In the last quarter of the twentieth century Portsmouth emerged as New Hampshire's cultural capital.

Though abutted by four New Hampshire towns, in many ways Portsmouth's nearest neighbor is the town of Kittery, Maine, directly across the river. They share settlement stories and a harbor. An early center at Kittery Point grew up around a cove at the mouth of the river, but that village's growth wound down when ships grew too large to be accommodated. When a United States naval shipyard was founded in Kittery in 1800 on an island in the river opposite the center of Portsmouth, a second center, Kittery Foreside, prospered along the back channel behind the island. Another center, Kittery Depot, flourished and faded with the railroad. Fourth and fifth centers, neither of them residential, have emerged since the 1970s off Interstate 95 along U.S. Route 1, and around a new post office. A constant stream of goods and people, both Black and white, flows across the river on today's three steel bridges even as they did from the beginning of settlement, on wherries and ferries. Kittery recurs in the stories that follow with only occasional distinction from Portsmouth.

Portsmouth consists of a small, dense waterfront district of commercial and residential sections with industrial areas just upstream and Victorian-era residential districts extending westward for a scant mile. Beyond are scattered postwar residential suburbs. These suburbs, outlying commercial strip developments, and light-industrial zones form a modestly scaled version of the widespread American phenomenon of a "ring city" around an old city core. The whole is interspersed with salt creeks; extensive bogs surround the populated core. These bogs and creeks contain and compress the town and contribute to an urban density out of character with the actual population.

Today's landscape is a layering of several centuries. The downtown area, where much of our story plays out, has several slight knolls, scarcely perceptible to the modern pedestrian. Viewed from small seventeenth-century wooden boats these knolls seemed impressive enough to be dignified with the names of Spring Hill, Church Hill, Meetinghouse Hill, Windmill Hill. To these we might add, in modern coinage, Sheraton Hotel Hill and City Hall Hill. Market Square occupies a yet-unnamed central high ground. The land-based stroller starting on high ground at the city parking garage will experience these as mere ripples in the landscape. Nonetheless, several are crowned by prominent buildings today—two churches, a Victorian ward hall (currently the children's museum), a hospital recycled into a city hall, and a hotel.

In the first centuries of old-world occupation, the town crystallized along the lines of an inherited hierarchical sense of order. Primary thoroughfares formerly called highways connected hills to waterfront and hinterland. The highways were bisected by secondary ways called streets. A web of tiny passages called lanes threaded the interstices between streets; many lanes dead-end at salt creeks or the riverbank. Early seats of political and religious authority crowned the hills. Mansions gathered round them or on highways or overlooking their own-ers' waterfront source of wealth.

Waves of rebuilding have scarcely altered the first centuries' accumulation of public thorough-fares in the old center. Depending on one's mood, this ancient system lends quaintness, walkability, or a confounding traffic pattern. Either way, the streets shape quotidian motion through the city center and invite the reader to repopulate them with the Black and white people who once trod there.

New Hampshire is one of several states some-times described as the whitest state in the na-tion. This evaluation implicitly minimizes the presence and contributions of Black, Native, and other nonwhite people. In a state where diver-sity is often measured as subtle nuances in con-servative political outlook, it's easy to see New Hampshire as relentlessly white. It's easy to see Portsmouth the same way.

The whites who comprise 96 percent of New Hampshire's population are of various Eu-ropean ancestry. The state's population also in-cludes Latin, Asian, Black, and Native Ameri-can people, each less than 2 percent of the state's population. Concentrations of people of color occur in three major cities: Manchester, Nashua, and Portsmouth.[2] In this oddly pastel corner of the continent, it's easy to forget that the vast majority of migrants from the Old World to the New World came from Africa. As a result people of African descent remain the numeri-cally dominant non-Native population in large sections of southern North America as well as in the Caribbean, Central America, and most of eastern South America.[3] Given its location on an outer fringe of North America, Portsmouth was once a remarkably cosmopolitan and diverse place.

In accepting the dominant myth of a homo-geneous population, Portsmouth's white citizens often simply overlook local ethnic and racial di-versity. Natives were increasingly pressured by racial prejudice to accommodate to the growing European population's culture. Thus the major-ity overlooks their continuing presence. The first European immigrants were not solely Bri-tish. At least one Mediterranean household, the Amazeen family, was among them, and early Anglo immigrants brought a handful of Scan-dinavian indentured servants almost at the out-set. Simultaneously, Africans were brought here, unwilling immigrants who constituted the sec-ond significant wave of old-world colonists to come to New Hampshire.

Portsmouth's maritime economy and its sta-tus as colony capital until the Revolution brought continuing diversity. In the eighteenth century Scots-Irish trickled into Maine and inland New Hampshire. In the early nineteenth century Portsmouth's population mix was enlivened with the occasional Euro-Caribbean, Jew, Hawaiian, and Irish, the latter at first trickling in via the lumbering districts of Canada and Maine.

As in so many eastern seaboard cities, eth-nic neighborhoods—Irish, Italian, and Rus-sian Jewish—were established sequentially in Portsmouth from the midnineteenth to early twentieth centuries; modest numbers of Cen-tral European, French-Canadian, Greek, and other immigrants also came to town. The ethnic composition of the population diversified fur-ther during World War II and the Cold War, with influxes of workers for the Portsmouth Naval Shipyard and Pease Air Force Base. Since the 1970s Asian, Gay, and Hispanic residents have added to the mix. In close parallel to the state mix, Portsmouth's population is 93.5 per-cent white. But with a Black population of 2.7 percent, it has the state's largest proportional presence of Black people today. With a slightly wavering presence of 2 percent to 4 percent since the eve of the Revolution, Portsmouth has been New Hampshire's Black capital for most of its history.[4] Asians are almost as numerous at 2.4 percent. Less than 2 percent each of Pacific Islanders, Latins, others, and Natives make up the remainder of the population.

From an early date the seaport's population diversified in other ways too. Curiously for New England, religion was merely a secondary mo-tive for the settlement of coastal New Hampshire. This led to early indifference, ambivalence, and sometimes outright unclarity about religious affairs, from which sprang a subtly nuanced diversity. The Puritan church and its Congregational descendant quickly became the dominant orthodoxy here by accident of growth, not by design as in Massachusetts and Connecticut. The Puritans enjoyed official political ascendancy only during a thirty-year period in the seventeenth century when fledgling New Hampshire asked to be taken under the wing of Massachusetts. The Anglican Church appeared briefly at the outset, fizzled, and was established anew in Queen's Chapel in the eighteenth century. In 1711 the local Puritan congregation split. A few decades later a regional type of Calvinist Baptists branched off, and soon other Reformed denominations sprang up. Catholicism attained permanent numbers and a parish only in the second quarter of the nineteenth century, and Greek Orthodoxy and a Jewish synagogue were established in the twentieth century. Religious heterodoxy has a long tradition in Portsmouth.

This, then, was the modestly varied population, sometimes vigorously divided, among whom Portsmouth's colonial Africans and later African-Americans lived and live today.

Portsmouth's colonial reputation notwithstanding, the city's built environment dates mostly from the nineteenth and twentieth centuries. Today's population ignores the abundant physical evidence in favor of a more charming myth. They hold that the city froze in time around 1815 with the exhaustion of the hinterland's accessible timber reserves, the sharp diminution of international maritime trade in the War of 1812, and a fire that swept away fifteen downtown acres in 1813. These were serious setbacks, but the city revived. The foundations of the myth of stasis were laid in 1823 during the bicentennial celebration of the settlement of New Hampshire.

As declining international maritime trade was succeeded by coal importation Portsmouth found new sources of prosperity—which we'll see excluded Blacks from participation—in bank-

ing, insurance, the railroad, steam-powered industry, and beer brewing. The Portsmouth Naval Shipyard expanded with each successive war. With returning prosperity Market Square was partly rebuilt and almost entirely remodeled in up-to-date Victorian styles. As population growth resumed new neighborhoods sprang up on the hitherto agrarian lands fringing the colonial core. This created, in a single generation, a West End of closely packed freestanding houses, in a period when the local Black population's numbers leveled and sagged.

In spite of this growth, and responsive to the growing visibility of non-Anglo immigrants in Portsmouth as in every New England city, old white families nursed a notion of loss and memory. Reminders of a preimmigrant past were presaged in the 1823 bicentennial observances by a reverent exhibit of ancestral portraits. There followed a series of Old Home Days beginning in the 1850s, reunions that appear not to have included or recognized Blacks, not surprising since the Supreme Court had just found that Blacks in America were not citizens.

Historical preservation of the physical environment began with a history-minded private renovation of the Moffatt-Ladd mansion in 1862 and continued with the foundation of a string of historic-house museums in the first half of the twentieth century. These became repositories of the portraits and elegant objects of the town's oldest white families. Starting in the early twentieth century Portsmouth citizens refurbished their nineteenth-century buildings to endow them with an imaginary eighteenth-century appearance, transfiguring even the Victorian-style North Church (1854) and high school (1855). In the late 1950s resistance to urban renewal awakened and with colonial-revival zeal founded Strawbery Banke Museum as a northerly Williamsburg. In recent years the museum expanded its narrative to encompass three centuries including immigrants and some Black history. Though urban renewal swept hundreds of colonial buildings from Portsmouth's North End, the unrelenting colonial self-imagery pastes incongru-

All participants in the 1923 Pageant of Portsmouth posed for a panaramic photograph. The section shown here includes some of the people who appeared in the "Negro Court" scene. Names listed in the program: Dr. John H. Neal, Harry E. Philbrook, Albert E. Rowe, Albert O. Foster, Haywood Burton, A. Leslie Ramsay, Robert Harris, Anderson Scott, W. D. Blanks, P. R. Allen, Rev. George B. Riley, Jesse Hood, Gustava Allen, Ardella Cooper, Finnegan Cooper, Robert Cooper, Katherine Farmer, Blanche Hagen, Christobel Harris, Patience Hinton, Ida Moore, Blanche Ramsay, Sophie L. Scott, Herbert Tatcher, Frances Tilley, Katie Tilley, Marjorie Watkins, and Bertha Williamson. Some of these actors also sang in the Pagent Chorus and appeared in other scenes. *African American Resource Center.*

ous colonial ornament on virtually all the city's suburban ranch houses and McMansions.

Like the white paint that signifies colonial to the modern mind, the early story of Portsmouth's people is too easily assumed to have been all white. Through all this colonial-revival sentimentality the historical presence of Black people surfaced only rarely. Essays, both reminiscent and historical, written in the 1850s by newspaper editor Charles W. Brewster make fleeting references to Black colonists. In an 1853 historical parade a Black cook was included on a parade float of a ship. The 1923 tercentennial pageant included a portrayal of the colonial-era Negro Court. Though Black people played the pageant's Black roles, rather than whites in blackface makeup, the script was suffused with contemporary racist stereotypes, scarcely a useful insight into the historical Black presence. In the early twentieth century a costumed mannequin portraying a Black person kneeling to work at the kitchen fireplace was installed in one historic-house museum, acknowledging the early presence of enslaved people there, but was removed some decades later as whites became ashamed of their history of racism. The city's recollection of its Black history was put aside and forgotten.

Colonial mythology, preserved mansions, and self-congratulatory pageants notwithstanding, Portsmouth's downtown was in fact a gritty sailor town through the first three-quarters of the twentieth century. Industrial and waterfront workers and the shipyard's fluctuating population of sailors added sometimes-lurid color to the local scene. Though the waterfront's red-light district was suppressed by the 1920s and its rotting piers buried under a park beginning in the 1930s, downtown was still known for its after-hour bar fights twenty-five years after World War II ended.

Transformation began in the 1970s when the affordable downtown gained an active visual- and performing-arts population. A community block grant funded a pedestrian-friendly reconfiguration and beautification of Market Square. As traditional small businesses abandoned the old center for outlying commercial strips, downtown Portsmouth carved out a new economic niche and identity by commodifying waterfront ambiance, a walkable historic environment, meeting places such as cafés, cultural activities, and proximity to the natural splendor of the ocean, islands, and nearby mountains.

These charms and amenities attracted tourists, high-tech businesses, civilian workers, and new residents. Portsmouth's traditional blue-collar population found itself recontextualized, and today these old-timers view the revitalization and recolonization of Portsmouth's downtown with an ambivalence ranging from pride to indifference to hostility. Demolition of the North End and gentrification of the South End have long since displaced low-income families including some Black families, all of whom once found affordable housing there. People of color remain invisible to the white population.

A far-reaching transformation occurred with the establishment during the Cold War of the 509th Bomb Wing and Pease Air Force Base at the conjoined borders of Portsmouth, Greenland, and Newington. It brought new Black residents to the area as the Air Force led the armed forces in racial integration. In 1991, just as New Hampshire's economy sagged, the base closed. Some twelve hundred civilian jobs were lost, and over three thousand military personnel and their families left the area. The abandoned base was converted into an office and industrial park that by early 2003 employed nearly five thousand people.[5] The base's closure ended a forty-year tradition of bringing new Black people to the city. The Portsmouth Naval Shipyard managed to stay off the short list of base closings through the 1990s. Its relentless pursuit of efficiency as a survival strategy brought a 50 percent drop in its workforce from 1989 to 1999, when it employed thirty-four hundred men and women. Even at its reduced level, the shipyard is the second-largest employer north of Boston as of 1999, after Maine's Bath Iron Works, though few Black workers are found among its employees.

Documenting local Black history is daunting. With the notable exception of a Revolutionary-era petition for the abolition of slavery in New Hampshire few Black-authored documents are available from colonial Portsmouth. Other early Black-authored documents—correspondence, for example—are unknown; if they existed they were carried away, lost, discarded, or destroyed. They may yet exist with the race of their author unidentified. Not until the nineteenth and twentieth centuries did Black Yankees leave a surviving record in their own terms, though Portsmouth examples are scarce.

Modern knowledge of colonial Africans is found almost solely in records written by non-Black people. Culling meaning from archival snippets is difficult. White record keepers, with no interest in the Black experience, mention nonwhites only in terse terms. The references are found mostly in legal, business, and church records and occasionally in newspaper articles, diaries, or reminiscences. In the latter sources the actions or appearance of Black people are often misinterpreted or described in barbed, critical, fearful, or ridiculing language.

Mrs. Newlywed's New Wench Cook

This stereograph reflects the "genteel" racism of early-twentieth-century white society. Portraying Black people as docile, irresponsible, and incompetent was commonplace in the postemancipation years. The images seeped into the national psyche and have persisted in various forms to the present. *African American Resource Center.*

White literature treated Black people as incidental or, in expanded misinterpretations of resistance, as childlike or humorous. Sometimes this style is dubbed "genteel racism," as if racism in any form is ever genteel. Genteel racism was comprised of writing in dialect and of characterizing Black people as lazy, stupid, or acting inappropriately—as if they were true citizens or white. Infrequently this literary genre unwittingly tells a tale of Blacks outwitting whites in contravention to white assumptions. The style assumed, defined, and promoted differentiation and a conviction among whites of their own supremacy.[6] Such records form an improbable lens. They tell of Black presence, activity, and the status allowed them by a dominant white society. When carefully parsed these documents provide tantalizing glimpses into Black thought. Through them we can see something of the early Black experience; we can begin to reconstruct their stories.

The white tradition of telling history through stories of empowered men acting on the public stage is an unworkable model for conveying Portsmouth's Black history. Since power was denied to early Black people, a different approach is needed to make sense of what we find. Beginning in the 1960s and '70s social historians, particularly women's historians, developed new modes of inquiry and probed new sources for information. By analyzing the minutiae of many individual lives they found meaningful patterns of cultural experience. In their example we find a way to interpret Black lives in early Portsmouth.

However, something like this model had been under way among Black writers since the nineteenth century. As early as the 1840s, even as genteel racism was emerging as a literary style, Black Americans were writing autobiographies, and collecting and publishing biographies of other Black people. This biographical tradition found meaning in narratives of how ordinary Black people founded institutions, served their country, led communities, or pursued civil rights.

Many of these works used the format of collected short biographies. Examples include William Cooper Nell's *Colored Patriots of the*

BEACON BEAM

An old negro in a South Carolina town was arrested for stealing chickens, and as he bore a rather bad reputation it was quite hard to secure counsel for him. At last a young lawyer, who had known Rastus for a long time, took his case, to the great joy of the old fellow. At his trial the judge asked him:

"Are you the defendant?"

The old fellow was perplexed for a moment, and then replied:

"No, sah, dat's de defendant, sah," pointing proudly to his counsel, "I'se de man wot stole de chickens."

A more recent expression of "genteel racism," appearing in the *Beacon Press,* privately published as a free "Official Guide Book" to Portsmouth, dates to September 1968. Such racial and ethnic humor was used in comic strips and as space fillers by national and local publications into the 1970s. *African American Resource Center.*

American Revolution and *Services of Colored Americans in the Wars of 1776 and 1812.* Use of collective biography to convey military history persists in the numerous contemporary works about Black soldiers in World Wars I and II including, for example, many titles on the single subject of Tuskegee airmen.

Nineteenth-century published Black autobiographies surprise modern white Americans by their abundance. These range from the *Narrative of the Life of Frederick Douglass, an American Slave, Written by Himself* to the humble *Life of James Mars, a Slave Born and Sold in Connecticut,* published in 1868. Olive Gilbert's 1850 autobiography, *The Narrative of Sojourner Truth,* enjoyed renewed popularity beginning in the 1970s for its account of northern slavery, religious awakening, and women's history issues. Famous across lines of race is Booker T. Washington's *Up from Slavery.*

Works with a more analytical approach expanded this tradition, illustrating their cases through incidental biography and autobiographical material. W. E. B. DuBois' *The Souls of Black Folk* is monumental not for its length but for its probing analysis of the Black experience in America, including his recognition of the entwined but opposite pulls of Blackness and Americanness. One chapter famously critiques the messages promulgated by Booker T. Washington.

Recent Black history writings by both Black and white authors tend toward a convergence of historical narrative, analysis, and collective biography. Lynne Olson uses vivid literary portraits of numerous women in *Freedom's Daughters: The Unsung Heroines of the Civil Rights Movement from 1830 to 1970.* Gregory S. Bell's *In the Black: A History of African Americans on Wall Street* is an unexpected narrative enlivened with unfamiliar names. Cornel West and Henry Louis Gates Jr. have created a collection of one hundred biographies (ten per decade) in *The African-American Century: How Black Americans Have Shaped Our Country* to show how the twentieth century transformed Black Americans, and Black Americans transformed twentieth-century America.

The present work continues in this long tradition of telling Black history through collective biography. We interpret the stories of some fifty people in such detail as is available. We also refer to perhaps four hundred more individuals, mostly Black, some white, mostly local, and mostly by name, but some of their names have been lost to history.

In addition to gathering our stories around the lives of individuals, we've organized them into chronological and topical sections. "Colonists" covers the seventeenth and eighteenth centuries, when most of the subjects of this book lived in enslavement. "Early Americans" addresses the experience of circumscribed freedom in the decades from the Revolution through the early nineteenth century. "Abolition" describes Black abolitionists and events leading up to and through the Civil War. "Community" describes the people who created institutions, or-

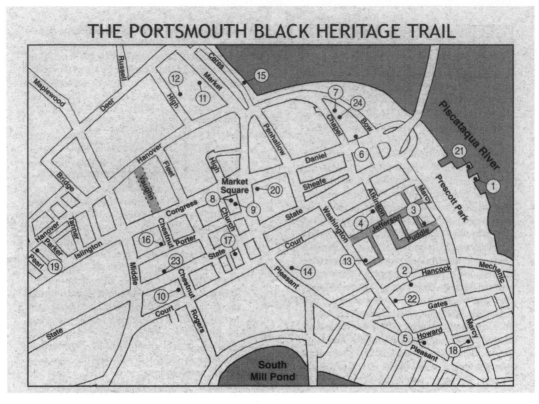

THE PORTSMOUTH BLACK HERITAGE TRAIL

Key

1. Wharf, Prescott Park
2. Stoodley's Tavern, Hancock St.
3. Sherburne House, Strawbery Banke Museum
4. Pitt Tavern, Strawbery Banke Museum, Court St.
5. Site of *Gazette* printing office, Pleasant St.
6. Macphaedris-Warner House, Daniel St.
7. St. John's Church, Chapel St.
8. North Church, Market St.
9. Site of town pump, by east front of North Church
10. Site of Negro burial ground, Chestnut St. extending westward between Court and State Sts.
11. Moffatt-Ladd House, Market St.
12. Site of Whipple house, 127 High St.
13. Penhallow House, Strawbery Banke Museum, Washington St.
14. Langdon House, 143 Pleasant St.
15. Ceres St. waterfront
16. Site of the Temple, Chestnut St.
17. South Church, 292 State St.

18. South Ward Hall, Marcy St.
19. Pearl Street Church, corner Hanover & Pearl Sts.
20. 14–16 Market St.
21. Navy Yard (viewed from Prescott Park)
22. 171 Washington St.
23. Rockingham Hotel, 401 State St.
24. St. John's Parish Hall, Chapel St.

Sites beyond area shown on map:
Langdon slave cemetery, 1035 Lafayette Rd. (Rte. 1), adjacent to Christ Church
New Hope Baptist Church, 263 Peverly Hill Rd.
Portsmouth Plains, area near intersection of Middle Rd. and Islington St.

Additional points of interest:
Emmanuel Church of Christ, Bartlett St.
Middle Street Baptist Church, Court St.
North Cemetery, Maplewood Ave.

Some of the many people and incidents in this book are also cited in the Portsmouth Black Heritage Trail. Its map is included here to help readers orient themselves to the city's landscape. *Map design by Christopher Remignanti and Mark J. Sammons. Portsmouth Black Heritage Trail.*

ganized community, and served in patriotic contexts in the first half of the twentieth century. "Civil Rights" addresses mid-twentieth-century activism that brought white Portsmouth into step with new national-level court decisions and legislation. "Living with Diversity" is a coda synopsizing the last quarter of the twentieth century. Collectively, the intimate stories reveal patterns that characterized their times.

Though our narrative is purportedly a local history, our themes are regional and national.

This book invites ordinary and often extra-ordinary people out of their forgotten obscurity—women and men, working and fighting, resisting and accommodating, praying and playing—into visibility and the life of modern memory. Portsmouth's past isn't what it used to be.

CHAPTER 2

Colonists

Sitting on the back doorstep of the house at the dusty corner of Horse Lane, Bess enjoyed the spring sun. She looked down the slope behind the house, her eyes following the line of the fence that edged the side street, toward the master's pottery shop. Woodpiles surrounded the rosy brick kiln that stood like a three-story wine bottle against the glare reflecting off the Puddle Dock inlet beyond. She saw the pale form of Samuel Marshall and the mahogany-colored Adam and Mercer moving among the sheds preparing for the spring production of kitchenware.

Bess turned her attention to the cool clay jar around which her warm arms were wrapped. It had not been produced here, in Marshall's workshop, but far away. She closed her eyes, tipped her nose to its wide mouth, and drew one last long, deep breath of the sweet-sour perfume that lingered in it. She was momentarily transported. Her girlhood in the West Indies had been harsh, and her sale away from her parents while a girl had wrenched her with grief then, and still did when she let herself think about it. But the warm sun on her shoulders and the ris-ing scent of tamarind brought pleasant recollections of her mother, of the extravagant tropical wildflowers, the occasional opportunity to slip away unnoticed to play in refreshing water. Though it had been oppressively hot in those islands, now she thought of the softness of the breezes that had rustled the trees rather than stinging like a whip, as did New Hampshire's winter winds. Her mouth watered at the thought of sipping tamarindo, deliciously sour, sweetened with sugar or molasses, brown from the sticky gum of those odd seedpods from the feathery trees.

The crack of an ax on firewood startled Bess from her brief reverie, and she looked up to see the men starting the onerous process of preparing several cords of wood for the upcoming firing. She looked down at the pot in her hand, so unlike the local wares in shape and subtly different in texture and color. She supposed slaves had made it somewhere down in the islands as other forced Black workers had no doubt harvested and packed its contents for shipment. Bess sighed, reached for a trowel, and began filling the empty tamarind jar with dirt, then deftly tucked in the little plant, tamped the earth, and set it on the back doorstep to nurture till the sun brought on its pretty blooms in the short New Hampshire summer. Wiping her hands on her apron Bess turned and went into the house to tackle the never ending task of cleaning out the fine gray clay dust tracked in by the men.

Bess, origin unknown, lived a century after the first Africans came to Portsmouth. She was no pioneer in the traditional sense of the word, as this was a well-settled town by the eighteenth century. Instead, like all the Black and white people in Portsmouth, she was a colonist living in a distant political outpost of the British Empire.

But the Black colonists were unwilling colonists. They came neither in search of opportunity nor under finite terms of indenture. Among them we'll meet all kinds of people. Many were skilled artisans like potters Adam and Mercer Marshall, a cooper named Nero Wheelwright, a plowman named Pomp, and printer Primus Fowl. We'll meet women like farmworkers Hannah and Nanne, and free Black people like Violet Dearborn, her husband Newport Stiles Freeman, and their children. We'll encounter leaders of the Black community assembled in a royal court that included King Nero, Viceroy Willie Clarkson, Sheriff Jock Odiorne, and Deputy Pharaoh Shores. We'll meet Revolutionary War participant Prince Whipple and twenty men bold enough to publicly challenge the institution of slavery. We'll glimpse Fortune and the Franco-African Jean Paul, who reclaimed their freedom. Some of these people lived beyond the end of slavery in New Hampshire and bravely faced new challenges and forged new institutions in freedom.

The Origins of American Slavery

Long after the abolition of slavery in the United States, it is hard to understand how so virulent an institution came into being. Slavery was an ancient and varied institution in Europe, Africa, and Asia. The word's origin in reference to Slavic peoples indicates an earlier tradition of slavery in Europe.

There was an earlier tradition of slavery in western Africa too. People there were sometimes enslaved as punishment for crimes, or sold by family members to pay debts, or taken as war captives. African slavery reduced the status of the individual, though not always for a lifetime. It did not cause geographic displacement, complete family separation, or suffering under sometimes fatal conditions. Nor was it based on race.[1] Individuals knew why and how they had come to their status as slaves. They experienced dismay and disruption of their lives and plans while remaining in a familiar culture with familiar languages and a predictable fate.[2]

Upon learning of African participation in the slave trade modern whites perk up. Apparently this old news eases a sense of inherited guilt or seems somehow to transfer their own shame to modern Black Americans.

New-world slavery was unlike slavery anywhere else. It was extraordinarily ruthless. During the seventeenth century western European nations created a profitable Atlantic economic system built on European capital, American land, and harsh labor. This system created a demand of incomprehensible scale, and conditions of unprecedented brutality.

Europeans in America were unwilling to submit to the working conditions necessitated by their agriculture and their exploitation of natural resources. Failing in attempts to enslave Natives, whose Caribbean populations were decimated by European disease in the decades after 1492, they turned to Africa. The first enslaved Africans imported to the New World were brought to the Caribbean by 1505. The traffic did not cease for three and a half centuries. An estimated 2.5 million Africans were brought to the islands alone, making the West Indies the birthplace and longtime epicenter of American slavery. Slaves there and on the adjacent mainland harvested mahogany, rosewood, logwood (for dye), spices, chocolate, coffee, cotton, and sugar; and they manufactured molasses and rum. But the West Indies were not the sole destination of the slave trade. At least 10 to 12 million Africans—and likely several million more—were forcibly brought to the Americas to produce pitch, tar, and turpentine, to raise tobacco, cotton, rice, indigo, and other crops, or to quarry salt, gold, silver, copper, and other minerals. These numbers do not include the unknown numbers of those who perished in fortified holding grounds called factories on the west coast of Africa or during transport across the sea. This was the largest forced movement of people in human history.[3] Africa was the greatest single source of immigrants to the Americas.

The system was used in all European colonies throughout the Americas—Dutch, British, Portuguese, Spanish, and French—and in most instances continued as those colonies attained independence. Through the nineteenth century various countries abolished first the trade, then the institution. Slavery finally ended in the Americas with emancipation in Brazil in 1888.

Because of slavery the population and wealth of the Americas today are an extension of Africa. The majority of people in the Americas today are nonwhite, of African and Native descent. Because of slavery Brazil has the largest Black population outside Africa, and South Carolina the largest in the States. While the political, ecclesiastical, and educational institutions of North and South America grew out of European culture, the population and to a very large degree the wealth of the Americas are extensions of Africa. Africans and their descendants have been major contributors to the total capital of the Americas, significant even in Portsmouth.

Transport

The Euro-American version of slavery was a voracious market-driven system that placed no value on life. White demand transformed West Africa. Eager for wealth, coastal Africans increasingly organized raiding parties to kidnap and sell others.[4] The captives were inexorably marched or traded toward the African coast. Gathered into chained gangs or coffles, many died from beating and dehydration in their captors' haste to reach the coast.

On the coast, gangs of captives were crowded into fortresses called barracoons or factories where more lives were lost to malnutrition and disease, especially dysentery. Fear was heightened by the arrival of heavily armed white traders with red faces, stringy hair, and their steaming deck-top cauldrons, evidence seeming to confirm a widespread belief in white cannibalism.[5]

On the transatlantic voyage—the Middle Passage—tremendous numbers of captives were packed into low-ceilinged holds. Seasickness, dehydration, starvation, rape, and malnutrition contributed to disease and despair, to many deaths and some suicides.[6] The dead were tossed overboard, and sometimes the living too after Britain outlawed the international slave trade north of the equator in the 1830s.[7] Arrival in the Americas meant release from the ship's confinement into the terrors of sale, separation from their countrymen, and dispersal toward expected cannibalism.

Perpetual Enslavement

Slavery in America was an ongoing act. It was not a finite transition at the moment of capture. For captive individuals it continued daily with imprisonment in an African fortress, suppression of shipboard revolts, resale, statutory limitations, punishment in manacles, whipping, or exemplary execution. Enslavement continued in the daily stripping away of native name and culture, in forced and uncompensated work, in monitoring, in the owner's intermittent decision to ignore or retaliate against resistance. It continued in periodic recapture of runaways. These were a part of slavery in Portsmouth as elsewhere.

The daily repetition of enslavement made

whites uneasy. Everywhere slavery existed owners created a web of laws—usually fraught with contradictions—to control owners and slaves alike. New Hampshire was no exception to fear and the legislative impulse.

In all periods white attempts to justify slavery were defensive; whites understood that slavery had no defense. Justifications were few and almost solely economic. Biblical citations as defense would not, for the most part, appear until several centuries later.[8] Whites knew that the system debased the enslaver as much as the enslaved. Some owners succumbed to morality and freed their slaves, a reminder to other owners that they daily bore the burden of willfully sustaining the system in the face of their own moral understanding, their wealth and other resources, and their power to refrain from participating in it. Enslavement was a conscious and perpetual act by all slave owners every day of their lives.

Nonslaves

Distinguishing slavery from other socially and legally circumscribed statuses unnecessarily confounds antiquarians and modern apologists alike. They ask defensively how the status of a slave was any different from that of the children, apprentices, wives, poor, prisoners, and soldiers who were also dependent upon and bound by law to yield their productivity to a master.

Children were dependent by virtue of helplessness and in adolescence by presumed inability to support themselves. But they lived with the knowledge and expectation of independence upon attaining their majority.

Apprenticeship and indentured servitude were nothing like slavery. These were documented and contractual obligations of fixed duration. The apprentice's productivity was absorbed as compensation for the master's lost time in training him, and as they became better it served as a kind of tuition—indeed supplemental tuition payments were sometimes part of the contract. It was a mutual two-way agreement with obligations incumbent on the master, and at foreordained conclusion the apprentice could choose for himself his next move.

Wives were in the curious position of *femme covert*, both legally free and legally invisible under the protective wing of the husband. They could own property, even businesses, though the husband administered these on the woman's behalf. If widowed, *femme sole*, direct control of a woman's property reverted to her, though the husband's property was divided among offspring, with a portion reserved for (but not owned by) the widow during her independent life.

Nor were paupers like slaves. The poor benefited from government-mandated and town-funded support. In extreme cases the town paid families to take in paupers for a year at a time or put them in an almshouse. Any value of the pauper's productivity did not accrue to either the pauper or the caretaking household but rather to the town as partial repayment for their care.

Prisoners, of course, knew their reduced status had good reason. Their productivity accrued to the county or state, again in partial support of themselves, and for most a sentence was temporally finite.

Similarly soldiers served in a broadly agreed-upon cause. Though service was sometimes obligatory, unwilling, or fatal, it was presumed finite and usually paid.

None of these limitations of status was permanent, race-based, or automatically transferred to the next generation. Slavery, by contrast, was not compensated, was not rationally punitive for transgression, and was presumed permanent and hereditary. The enslaved were not heirs to the family wealth to which they contributed. They were alienated from the bonds and benefits of kinship in the extended families in which they lived.

The relatively abrupt appearance of slavery in the midst of older social relationships confounded Euro-Americans. White culture, law, and polity dealt with the conundrum of how humans could be property by equating slaves to animals—sentient, productive, but property nonetheless—an outlook that proved to be a grossly inadequate analogue. When slaves exercised their humanity and independence with back talk, by ignoring or pretending not to understand directives, by running away, or by assaulting their oppressors, owners and whites in general did not see evidence of normal human yearnings. They saw instead confirmation of their equation of slaves with animals. It was a way whites coped with what they knew to be wrong. The enslaved were trapped.[9]

The Origins of an Afro-American Culture

Africans throughout the Americas contributed to the creation of a new culture. This came about through three main factors. One was the merger of diverse western African traditions that otherwise would not likely have flowed together. Another was the adaptation of inherited African cultures to enslavement. Third was the African response to the prevailing Euro-American culture that surrounded them, whether by rejection, assimilation, or adaptation.

The results were a distinctly African-American culture.[10] We'll see it in eighteenth-century Portsmouth in the stories of annual coronations, clothing styles, and other details of local daily life. Conversely Euro-American culture absorbed African features in foodways, health practices, religious expression, music, language, and self-identity.

Portsmouth and the Slave Trade

The earliest-known Black person in Portsmouth was brought directly from Africa in 1645. A Massachusetts slave trader named Captain Smith brought several African captives to New England from Guinea on Africa's western coast to be sold as slaves. Smith sold one of his captives to a "Mr. Williams of Piscataquak." The captive's name and exact origin remain unknown. During his time here, this African was probably an unwilling laborer in Mr. Williams's house-

hold, barnyard, timber stand, or boat.[11] There was at that date no urban economy to which to apply his labor.

By the end of the seventeenth century the scattered hamlets originally called Strawberry Bank were coalescing into the coherent townscape of Portsmouth. Local merchants had entered trade in the Caribbean islands—known in colonial New England as the West Indies. Among a prospering mix of farmers, artisans, merchants, and mariners, there was wealth and demand enough for Portsmouth to enter the slave trade too. In 1682 William Fitzhugh of Virginia corresponded with members of the Cutts family regarding prices he would pay for enslaved boys, girls, men, and women (three thousand to five thousand pounds of tobacco each) should Cutts be able to procure some for him.[12]

White traders found increased opportunity to trade in human cargo when in 1696 Parliament repealed the monopoly it had previously granted to the Royal African Company. Any British trader could now legally attempt to enter this lucrative field.[13] Piscataqua involvement continued, with some slaves brought home. By 1708 Governor Dudley reported to the British Board of Trade and Foreign Plantations that there were seventy slaves in New Hampshire. This was a sizable number in the context of the tiny colony. These Black people must have been very visible in the small and circumscribed white population.

Governor Dudley also said there was no New Hampshire involvement in the slave trade at that date. If he wasn't misinformed or for some reason lying, he must have made this statement during a brief lull in the local trade. Through the next several decades New Hampshire ships carried many Africans to the Caribbean, Virginia, and Portsmouth.

If the revocation of the Royal African Company's charter had not been sufficient incentive to enter the slave trade, another inducement occurred in 1713. England and Spain were on highly competitive terms and forbade or narrowly limited their citizens' right to trade in one

another's colonies. Nonetheless England negotiated with Spain a contract to supply forty-
eight hundred enslaved Africans to Spanish
America every year. The arrangement would
stretch thirty years to 1743 before expiring.[14]

Between 1728 and 1745 Portsmouth captains
named Samuel Morse, Dickerson, John Major,
Joseph Bayley, and John Odiorne mastered
ships owned by Pierce Long, Joshua Pierce,
John Rindge, and J. & S. Wentworth bound
for Guinea, Virginia, and Barbados. Their cargoes typically included from one to a dozen enslaved people along with other merchandise.
The trade could be risky; Africans boarded
Captain Dickerson's ship off the Guinea coast
and murdered him.[15]

The West Indies had a considerable economic impact on Portsmouth. Local merchants
traded in the British colonies there—Barbados,
Jamaica and Antigua, British Honduras (Belize), and British Guiana (Guyana)—and sometimes illegally in Spanish, Dutch, and French
colonies. By the mid–eighteenth century some
Portsmouth merchants even owned sugar plantations in the British West Indies and in De-
merara in South America. It appears that as a
result of this activity many who were ultimately
enslaved in Portsmouth passed through or were
born in the West Indies. Successive generations
were born in Portsmouth while a steady flow of
new workers arrived. Imports to Portsmouth
made it convenient for less traveled whites to buy
slaves. Certainly white people whose business
took them no farther than the larger slave ports
of Boston or Newport saw examples enough of
the potentials of slavery.

Because Portsmouth was at a remote edge of
the Atlantic trade system, ships entering the
Portsmouth-Kittery harbor, if carrying any enslaved Africans, usually had only one or two
aboard.[16] An impressive exception occurred in
1755 when a vessel owned by John Moffatt, the
Exeter, carried a larger number:

An Inventory of Sundrys belonging to the
Cargo of the Snow *Exeter* Benjamin Russell

Late Master Deceased. Presented to our view
& Taken by us ye subscribers, September ye
6th 1756.
  Twenty Men Slaves
  Seven More Boy Do [ditto]
  Ten Boy Do Fifteen Women Do
  Two Women girl Do Seven girl Do
  —Sixty one Slaves

In addition to listing these sixty-one men,
women, adolescents, and children, this inventory itemized the personal effects of the deceased
captain, the provisions, and cargo including tobacco, wine, beef, rice, corn, rum, pitch, tar, and
turpentine.[17] The enslaved were just another
commodity.

Such large human cargoes were probably
destined for sale by ones, twos, and threes along
the eastern seaboard or for wholesale disposition at ports with high demand. Import records
from colonial Portsmouth do not survive to tell
whether this large-scale instance was a one-of-
a-kind venture or one of many.

Recurrent advertisements suggest that at least
small numbers were regularly imported and
sold. "Likely Negro Boys and Girls just imported from Gambia, and to be sold on board
the Sloop *Carolina* lying at the Long Wharff in
Portsmouth. Enquire of Mr. Traill or of Mr.
Harrison on board said Sloop," reads one of at
least forty-four advertisements for enslaved
people that appeared in the Portsmouth newspapers during the eighteen years between 1757
and 1775.[18]

By midcentury Portsmouth merchants knew
slave trading in wider markets might make
them rich. A local newspaper article in 1758
greedily reported that the "riches taken from
Senegal in Gum, Gold, Slaves and other effects
is supposed to be worth near £70,000."[19] A subsequent article expressed the hope among local
merchants of gaining control of "the island of
Goree, a little Eastward of Gambia which we
have strong hopes of, by the Advices, sent Home
by Commodore Marsh, by the Nassau, the most
valuable port of the coast of Guinea will be open

to us only, that is, the Gum trade."[20] Monopolizing a gum port was desirable, but Goree was also a major slave-processing location. Local merchants knew what they were after.[21]

Plantation and mine owners elsewhere were eager to buy mature young men who could endure heavy work. Britain's 1713 deal to supply forty-eight hundred slaves annually to Spanish America stipulated that none of the annual cargo would be under the age of ten years, none over forty years, and nine-tenths were to be sixteen years or older. For their own purchase New England buyers favored younger captives. In 1779 twenty enslaved Portsmouth men mentioned they were all brought from Africa to Portsmouth as children.[22] Local buyers preferred males, so African men outnumbered African women in colonial Portsmouth. The local preference for buying children was perhaps based on the assumption they could be easily trained in the ways of the buyer's household or trade.

The work assigned to the enslaved followed the work and gender roles of their master or mistress: craftsman, waterfront laborer, mariner, farmer, gardener, dairymaid, cook, housekeeper, seamstress, or laundress. Those owned by the elite probably worked on their outlying farms, in-town gardens, on their wharves and perhaps occasionally as house servants to bolster their owner's status.

In New England, Black individuals were fewer in number and lived more thinly scattered among whites than in the slave compounds of the South and Indies. In most colonial Portsmouth households there were no Black people, and in a few only one or two. As a result, most spent their days isolated from one another among white people.

The sparse numbers notwithstanding, occasions for contact with other Africans were possible and important. Given that the institution of slavery was in many ways a function of white wealth, concentrations of slaves—as of capital— were a significant feature of seaports, including Portsmouth. The port's compactness meant most Black people lived within a few blocks of one another. When they negotiated free time from their owners they could readily visit one another. Segregated seating at churches provided another opportunity for socializing. Socializing led to affection and—when allowed by masters—marriage. Colonial Portsmouth's few free Black residents could move around town freely, visiting one another and those who remained enslaved.

At the outset communication could be difficult if the enslaved had been taken from diverse African nations and tribes. The interrelationship of West African language groups and cultures eased this until the eventual acquisition of English as a common language. As with immigrants today this acquired English was sometimes restructured according to African syntax.[23] Through this social intercourse Portsmouth's colonial Black people got to know one another, created a community and institutions, and built enduring families against all odds.

While the enslaved were allowed little control over many aspects of their lives, they had more control than modern people assume. Slavery obviously proceeded from great inequalities in power: masters had technology, literacy, numeracy, brutality, laws, and police power on their side. But the enslaved did not accept their enforced condition passively. They negotiated constantly for rights that became customary and needed ongoing protection. They pressed for privileges such as the right to make a sea voyage, to visit loved ones, to work a small garden patch and sell its produce. Some negotiated with their owners to purchase their own freedom with money earned at independent work. Some, lacking permission, tried to earn money anyway: "Any Person or Persons who employ Pomp Rose R——e (so called), a [illegible] Negro that goes about cutting of Wood or other work, are desired not to pay him anything for his Labour, but to his Mistress, madame Sarah R—— of Portsmouth."[24]

When negotiation was rebuffed there were other means, both subtle and direct. Some refused to work, others feigned misunderstanding or incompetence. Some freed themselves simply by leaving. While Euro-Americans viewed Black people as "slaves" by nature, clearly the enslaved did not. Slavery was never a natural condition.

Cities and Numbers of Africans in Early New England

Because of complex factors of geography, economy, culture, and transportation technology, North America's first cities emerged mostly on the Northeast's coasts and major waterways. Wealth and population were concentrated in these cities, which were crossroads of international goods, ideas, and people. Most New England slavery was found in and around these cities, or on farms within easy access of major navigable waterways. The latter include Narragansett Bay in Rhode Island, the lower Connecticut River Valley of Connecticut and Massachusetts, Boston Harbor, and the estuarine system of Great Bay and the Piscataqua River.[25]

As an effect of this early pattern, when freedom came much later most Black people found themselves in or near coastal cities. Cities provided work and the opportunity to socialize with one another, so coastal cities like Portsmouth continued to see the region's greatest concentrations of Black people.

Relevant population records from before the Revolution are few and scattered, but they provide glimpses of the local Black population. Between Governor Dudley's 1708 report of 70 slaves in New Hampshire and the eve of the Revolution seventy years later there was a manifold increase in numbers. In 1775 there were 656 slaves in New Hampshire, when the colony stretched inland well beyond its original sixty-mile boundary. Yet most of the total population, including the enslaved, were in the southeast in and around the original coastal settlements.[26] By contrast, there were over 5,000 slaves in Massachusetts, 3,700 in little Rhode Island—where they constituted at least 6 percent of the total population—and over 6,400 in Connecticut.

Statistics too easily become mind numbing and impersonal. Whether spoken of by the million or the shipload or as scattered individuals, all those in bondage were individuals whose expectations, hopes, families, and identities were stolen and withheld from them. The theft of anyone's freedom was no less tragic or severe because that person was geographically isolated from thousands or millions of others. In 1695 Nathaniel Keen of Kittery beat his enslaved woman to death; to claim that slavery was less heinous in New England or New Hampshire or Portsmouth merely because it was of a lesser scale than elsewhere is a false and unacceptable notion.

Sale of Enslaved People

Portsmouth's historic Stoodley's Tavern is a local patriotic icon.[27] It was a gathering place of patriots during the months preceding the outbreak of the Revolutionary War. Tradition holds that it was to this building that Paul Revere came on December 13, 1774, with the news that the British were sending man-of-war shiploads of troops from Boston to secure the arms at His Majesty's Castle of William and Mary (now Fort Constitution) in New Castle.[28] A mob hastened to the fort, intimidated its tiny garrison into surrender, and whisked the arms away to secret storage before the British arrived. This minor act of defiance—one among many contemporary ones like it in the colonies—looms large in New Hampshire's iconography because it was the sole revolutionary military action to occur on New Hampshire soil.

But Stoodley's Tavern is equally a symbol of oppression. Only a decade earlier it was the site of public slave auctions: "To be sold at public vendue at the house of Mr. James Stoodley, Innholder in Portsmouth on Wednesday the seventh day of July at six of the clock afternoon, three Negro Men and a Boy. The conditions of the sale will be cash or good merchantable items."[29] Five years later another advertisement

This eighteenth-century warehouse is typical of those once lining the wharves in Portsmouth. The small flat-bottomed boat is a replica of a gundalow, a local form of sail-powered barge used to carry supplies up and down the swiftly moving Piscataqua River. *Photography by Tulani Freeman. Portsmouth Black Heritage Trail.*

announced, "To be sold at public vendue at the house of captain James Stoodley, Innholder in Portsmouth on Friday next at 2 o'clock Afternoon One Negro Man, has been with the English 2 years, Negro Girl about 17, . . . a few hogshead of West India rum . . . few bags of cotton wool. . . . "[30]

Method and Location of Slave Sales in Portsmouth

Sales of newly arrived African children, women, and men took place in a variety of ways and locations in Portsmouth. Some were offered for view and sale at taverns. Some were auctioned. For example, in November and December of 1760 John Stavers advertised an upcoming sale of several Black people at his tavern, named the Earl of Halifax, which once stood on today's State Street: "To be sold . . . a few Negroes, lately imported in the snow *Gen. Townshend* . . . from the West Indies . . . at Stavers Tavern."[31]

Some advertisements invited direct application to the owner or inquiry at the printer's office for direction to the owner. Some Africans were sold from shipboard or at dockside, probably through warehouses similar to the eighteenth-century Sheafe Warehouse that survives today in Prescott Park. Others were sold through private sales and trades.

Private sale by direct application to the owner or by inquiring at the newspaper office for direction to the owner seems to have been the most common mode. Advertisements for such sales appear in most issues of the weekly *Gazette* in the 1770s.

Of the several dozen slave sale advertisements that appeared in Portsmouth newspapers from 1757 to 1775, only a few others specify public auctions.[32] Whether additional auctions occurred prior to these remains unknown because Portsmouth did not have a newspaper in which to advertise them until 1756. The Portsmouth-produced *New Hampshire Gazette* advertisements may record the end of an earlier practice; slavery in New Hampshire peaked in the 1760s.[33]

The enslaved, separated from other Africans or anyone who spoke their language, lived among whites whose intimidating authority was enforced by the evidence of their wealth, by their ability to write an unfamiliar language, and by impressive technologies like huge oceangoing ships, intricate navigation devices, machines, and firearms.[34] Awed or not, newly arrived individuals were led through the degradation of enslavement to despondency, sometimes to infanticide and suicide.[35]

Auction

Our temporal and cultural distance from the eighteenth century makes it difficult and distasteful to imagine an auction of human beings. Stoodley hosted various types of public gatherings in his third-floor ballroom or great room, but it was probably impractical to haul bulky bales of cotton and huge barrels of rum upstairs only to be hauled down again. Goods were likely displayed on the ground floor or in the rear yard, and the auction could have been held anywhere in the building that was convenient for the numbers who showed up.

Local men or women, callous to what they were participating in, gathered on that hot July evening in 1762 or brisk April afternoon in 1767. They inspected and evaluated what interested them, whether the West India goods or the people offered for sale. They judged health, strength, age, short-term and long-term usefulness, tried to discern the personalities of those exhibited for sale, and calculated their cash value. They contemplated what they had on their farm, in their workshop, in their warehouse, or collectible debts owed them that they might convert to payment for whatever or whomever they purchased. Perhaps the bidders ordered up some meat, bread, and cheese while they waited for their choice to come up to bidding. Certainly they socialized over a drink, without which little transpired in eighteenth-century New England.

The experience of the enslaved would be quite different. They had probably arrived at Portsmouth on commercial speculation within

To be Sold at Public Vendue, At the House of Mr. James Stoodly, Innholder in Portsmouth, on Wednesday the seventh Day of July current, at Six of the Clock Afternoon, Three Negro Men and a Boy: The Conditions of Sale will be in Cash, or good Merchantable Boards. Portsmouth, July 1. 1762.

TO BE SOLD at Public Vendue, On Tuesday the 22d of April Instant, at Two o'Clock Afternoon, at the House where the late Mr. *Thomas Beck* lived, in the road leading to Rye, near Mr. *John Langdon's*; — ONE yoke of OXEN, several Steers; Cows; Sheep; 1 good Horse; several Calves; with sundry other Things, Wearing Apparel, &c. ALSO, A likely Negro GIRL.

TO BE SOLD (Cheap for Cash or good Lumber) By *William Pearne*, At his Store near the Hon. Mark Hunking Wentworth's, Esq; — Good COTTON WOOL, by the bag or smaller Quantity— Good Muscovado Sugar by the Hogshead or smaller Quantity—Choice good old Rum— Good Lignumvitæ by the tun or hundred weight; together with several sorts of English Goods. —Also one NEGRO MAN about Twenty Years of Age.

Negro women, men, and children are mentioned along with imported items, livestock, and "sundry other things" for sale or trade in the *New Hampshire Gazette* during the eighteenth century. These ads appeared on July 2, 1762 (*top*), and April 3, 1767 (*middle* and *bottom*). Courtesy Portsmouth Athenæum.

the last two weeks and were no doubt confused, demoralized, and terrified. The man who had "been with the English for 2 years" had probably been in Barbados, Jamaica, or another British colony before being brought to Portsmouth. This surely signaled newspaper readers that he could probably speak some English and would know the expectation of uncompensated labor. Perhaps, if he shared a common African language with the seventeen-year-old girl, he had apprised her of the actual nature of her fate.

They felt the humiliating sting of being studied like merchandise. Then the voice of the auctioneer rose, and the viewing and discussing of merchandise was joined by bidding. Arrangements for payment were discussed at a side table, and there was a commotion of carting goods away. Eventually the people themselves came up for sale and were, in a reversal of increased crowding during capture and transport, now scattered and taken away individually to fates unknown.

Enslaved People in Stoodley's Household

The probating of James Stoodley's estate in 1779, following his death, generated an inventory that listed two servants he owned, "a Negro Man Named Frank £20" and "a Negro Wench Named Flora, £100."[36] The disparate cash values placed on these two suggest that Frank may have been old and able to do less work while Flora was in her prime. There is no clue to when Stoodley purchased them. Perhaps he bought them at an auction in his own tavern.

James Stoodley was a member of North Church, where he owned an expensive pew for himself. He owned additional seating for Frank and Flora in the upper gallery where the church set aside seating for Black people, both enslaved and free. In the post-Revolutionary era Flora would marry Siras Bruce, a freedman by then employed by John Langdon. These scant facts are all that records reveal of Frank and Flora.

White Fears, Regulation, and Legislation

In 1730 at a justice of the peace court held at Sherburne's tavern in Portsmouth, Edward Hilton told the justice how his servant Sambo said he'd like to split out Hilton's brains and bury him in the swamp.[37] Sambo now faced trial and punishment for his brief inability to keep his mouth shut through constant and cumulative degradation. Hilton's fears were part of a broader white fear of an institution they had created but seemed almost unable to control.

Courts of all levels heard the myriad small cases and lawsuits between Yankees. Among them were occasional cases like Sambo's involving slaves and their owners. They stemmed from the web of regulatory statutes passed by the legislature or emerging from decisions of higher courts.

New Hampshire's colonial governments— Portsmouth was the capital of the province— tried to legislate relationships between owners and those whom they enslaved. Whether provincial or town laws, some protected slaves, but most focused on control to allay white uneasiness.[38] All were meant to align people and conduct with hierarchical assumptions about social order.

Protective Legislation

In 1641, when Massachusetts governed New Hampshire, a court decision in Boston disallowed enslavement of any but those who had been seized in "just wars." This presumably was meant to minimize random kidnapping of Native Americans and of Africans.

This decision was brought into effect in 1645 when a Boston court was tracking down a number of "negroes which Capt Smith [had] brought fraudulently & injuriously taken and brought from Guinny, by Capt Smith's confession, & the rest of the company." One had been sold by that Massachusetts trader to a "Mr Williams of Piscataquak" (possibly New Hampshire's lieutenant governor Francis Williams). He was ordered to "forthwith send ye neger which he had of Capt Smith hither, that he may be sent back without delay, & if you have anything to aledge why you should not returne him, to be disposed of by the court, it will be expected you should forthwith make it appear, either by yourselfe or your agent but not to make any excuse or delay in sending of him."[39]

This is the earliest recorded presence of an African in the Piscataqua region. His name and fate are unknown. Ultimately the Massachusetts law protected few or none. As slavery burgeoned, the law was forgotten.

When Nathaniel Keen of Kittery beat his enslaved woman to death in 1695 he was charged with murder. White indifference to the life of an enslaved Black person is evident in the reduction of charges against Keen to cruelty and his eventual release from confinement after paying a fine. Ambivalence about the relative value of people's lives repeatedly played out in parallel form through the late twentieth century, when American court decisions regarding punishment for murder continued to be reduced because the victim was Black, ethnic, a prostitute, or Gay.

Physical abuse of slaves led to additional protective legislation. In 1718 the New Hampshire General Assembly forbade "Inhumane Severities, which by Evil masters or Overseers may be used towards their Christian Servants." This act would free any servant or enslaved person who was maimed by his master.[40] The act implies the need to deal with recurrent brutality.

Legislation eventually discouraged murder of slaves and servants: "If an owner shall willfully kill his Indian or Negro servant or servants he shall be punished with death."[41] In eighteenth-century Anglo-America the term "servant" was understood to mean servant for life or slave when referring to a Black person. New Hampshire was the only New England colony to pass such a law.[42]

A combination of tradition, common-law court decisions, and legislation outlined a rough patchwork of rights of enslaved and free Black people. The enslaved could own personal property, they could testify in court, and their murder was punishable. These slim protections of 1718 came two years after a series of severe legislative acts.

Restriction

Most race-related legislation narrowed rather than protected rights. As the population of enslaved Black people in Portsmouth grew in the late seventeenth and early eighteenth centuries, so did white anxieties. Legislation circumscribed and controlled the enslaved.

Anxiety was transmuted to fear by news of events in New York. In the night of April 6, 1712, a group of enslaved people there set fire to a building and killed nine of the whites who came to fight the fire, then escaped. Eventually seventy enslaved people were arrested and forty-three tried. Twenty-five were convicted. Of these, thirteen were hanged, one was starved to death in chains, three were burned at the stake, one was broken on the wheel, and six committed suicide to escape execution by whites. The fate of one person was not specified. The New York Assembly passed a new slave code restricting movement and stripping the enslaved of any remaining rights. New York's example was soon followed in neighboring colonies. Pennsylvania opted to place high duties on imported slaves to discourage the growth of the institution.[43]

The New Hampshire Assembly responded with a series of acts in 1714. One forbade concealing or transporting runaway apprentices, servants, or enslaved people.[44] Generations later acts of kindness or conscience would again be criminalized in two federal fugitive slave acts.

Because of fear of insurrection or "conspiracies, outrages, barbarities, murder, burglaries, thefts and other notorious crimes and enormities, as sundry times have of late been perpetrated and committed by Indians and other slaves within several of her Majesty's plantations in America" the Assembly forbade further importation into New Hampshire of any "Indian, Servant, or Slave" and levied a tax on all enslaved males or females of whatever age.[45] Notwithstanding this legislation, importation of enslaved people to New Hampshire continued and increased.

The Assembly also instituted a selective race-based curfew. "Whereas great disorders, insolencies and burglaries are oft times raised and committed in the night time by Indian, Negro and Molatto Servants and Slaves to the Disquiet and hurt of her Majesty, No Indian, Negro, or Molatto Servant or Slave is to be from Home after 9 o'clock."[46]

The penalty was ten stripes. Whipping in colonial Portsmouth was usually administered at the pump on The Parade by the east front of North Church. The penalty was to be administered to the delinquent, not to his master. Free Black people registered with justices of the peace or town clerks and kept copies of their freedom papers as protection against charges of curfew violations or kidnapping as an escapee.

The curfew seems to have been loosely enforced, and violations persisted. Fifty years later, in 1764, rising political tensions prompted a reminder. "All Masters and Owners of any Indian, Negro or Molatto servants or slaves are hereby notified that the justices of the peace within the town of Portsmouth are determined to cause to be strictly executed the law of this Province entitled An Act to Prevent Disorders in the Night therefor whoever shall think it necessary to send out any Indian, Negro, or Molatto servant or slave after 9 o'clock at Night will do well to give such servant or slave a ticket whereby he may escape punishment inflicted by the law aforesaid."[47] The 9:00 P.M. curfew was again promulgated through the press in 1771.[48] By this time the legislature was meeting in the new 1762 State House in Portsmouth's central square.[49]

The enslaved quickly learned to bypass curfews and written passes, sometimes called tickets. Ebenezer Sawyer of Wells, perhaps in town on business, found that his "Negro fellow named Pomp" had gone missing and advertised in the local paper for him. "N.B. said Negro before his Elopement precur'd a counterfeit pass changing his own Name and his Masters. . . ."[50]

In 1718 New Hampshire forbade Blacks from serving in the militia. This probably stemmed from a fear of arming Black men, perhaps combined with incredulity of their capabilities. White fears of rebellion persisted for the duration of the institution of slavery. In 1807 the owners of the Portsmouth-built slave ship *Mendor* carried three blunderbusses, one musket, four pistols, cutlasses, and ammunition for protection against the enslaved they were carrying.[51] This was probably also true of many slave ships, including the nineteenth-century Portsmouth-built *Nightingale,* captained by the "Prince of the Slavers," Francis Bowen.[52]

Avoiding Public Expense

Like all New England towns, Portsmouth had a colony-mandated tax-financed welfare system to care for the indigent, a practice derived from Elizabethan prototypes. White culture made it difficult for free Black people to make a living, then blocked access to public poor relief and discouraged private assistance. The Town of Portsmouth did this in 1731 by passing the cost to anyone with whom free Black people boarded: "If any free negroes or indians come into this town . . . those who entertain them for seven days . . . shall support them if they come to want."[53]

The resolve went on to exempt the town from the expense of caring for the children of enslaved people by explicitly transferring responsibility for their care to owners who assented to such unions. "And every person that shall marry a Negro or indian so coming into any Negro or indian of theirs, the master or mistress assent to such marriage shall support persons so as to free the town of any charge."[54] Because of this, white owners withheld assent, even as clergy railed against extramarital relations. Black families were illegitimatized.

White Confusion, Separation, and Differentiation

By the eve of the Revolution, cumulative law and practice in New Hampshire, as throughout the colonies, had created a legal paradox. Sometimes the enslaved were treated as property, sometimes as people. Like personal estate, enslaved individuals were bought, sold, valued in tax tables, bequeathed, and probated. Yet their humanity was recognized in that they could own property, be charged and tried for crimes, and bear witness. Murdering a slave was a criminal act. Sometimes their legal status was betwixt and between: they were prohibited from serving in the militia (required of white males) but were repeatedly called upon by their masters to serve in all of America's wars up through the Civil War. This confusion haunted legal codes throughout America as long as slavery existed.[55]

Throughout the colonies, as laws governing servants evolved in the 1600s and 1700s, they steadily distinguished servants by race and applied differing restrictions to them. White servants, whether indentured for a fixed number of years or opting for employment as a hired hand, were often exempt from curfews, had fewer limits on their mobility, and had access to poor relief if they fell on hard times. They also had the knowledge that their servant status would change with expiration of indenture or by negotiating different employment. With this came the opportunity to dream of and work toward greater prosperity. Thus white servants understood that they were free to strive for prosperity and status by accumulating and managing at least part of the value produced by their labor.

The effect of this distinction in law was for white servants to differentiate and dissociate themselves from Black slaves, and view themselves as superior solely by virtue of race. By the 1830s white servants would reject the traditional language of servant and master because it was associated in their minds with slavery and Blackness. They began adopting such terms as laborer, worker, or employee for themselves. For the master they adopted a New York term, "boss," unaware that it was a Dutch word for master. Thus distinctions in law cultivated distinctions in society and divided natural political allies who might otherwise have banded together to press for better conditions for all laborers regardless of race.

These laws and related developments laid the groundwork for a persistent feature in American culture. In the absence of a hierarchical nobility, and with money's displacement of various seventeenth-century determinants of rank, poor whites learned to use race as a way of feeling they were at least one rung higher than someone else. Through the ensuing centuries this technique of race-based differentiation persisted, and its logic of supposed superiority was readily adapted to set apart and scorn other marginalized or unpopular groups. It would be applied successively to Catholic, Irish, Mediterranean, Jewish, Gay, Latin, Mexican, and Native Americans. Fear, economic desperation and miserliness, contempt for racial or ethnic difference—all would shape white perceptions of and debate about status in America indefinitely.

One Negro Man £200, One Ditto Woman £50: Location, Labor, Value

No doubt the narrow lanes of the Puddle Dock neighborhood of Portsmouth were breathless and dusty on that August afternoon in 1744 when a Black man and woman sat in the back ell of the Sherburnes' house wondering about their fate. The house was probably still in mourning, the mirrors draped, and Mary Sherburne, newly widowed by the death of her husband Joseph, dressed in mourning too.

Her husband's family had built the place around 1696 and enlarged it in 1702, shortly after which Joseph and Mary had moved in to raise their family, to operate a small shop amid its huge beams and diamond-paned windows, and to oversee shipping from their little wharf across the lane.

Forty years later, upon Joseph's death, the court appointed someone, probably a family acquaintance, to go through the house itemizing and assigning a cash value to everything in it. This was a necessary step in settling the estate. The deceased died intestate, that is, without a last will and testament. In such instances estates were divided between the heirs. Following a formula prescribed by law, an estate was divided equally among the children, with one-third of the total temporarily held back for the widow's lifetime use but not her legal ownership. While Mary must have been anxious to know how her third would play out, the family's enslaved man and woman must have been considerably more anxious. Like the house, furniture, other lots, and outlying farmland, they were appraised and assigned to an heir. They must have wondered if the children, grown now, would keep them or sell them to strangers.

Evidently, the inventory taker didn't bother asking their names; he certainly didn't record them. To him they were merely more personal estate. He wrote on the inventory:

One Negro man   £200
One   ″   woman £50.[56]

Relationships, Authority, Location, and Work

The inventory is the only known scrap of evidence recording the existence of those two Black people in the Sherburne household. A few generalizations about their lives can be inferred from this limited information.

Relationships of master and household were partly shaped by a strong New England tradition of absorbing servants and apprentices into the household. It was a paternalistic relationship, with the male head of household standing in as parent. He provided guidance and admonition, urged church attendance if he was pious, taught necessary skills, and assigned work.

In the context of this traditional relationship, New England's enslaved Black people, like white servants and indentured apprentices, usually lived in the same house as their masters, worked beside them, ate the same or similar food at the same or adjacent tables, and were taken to their owner's church.[57]

Servants—especially hired hands in agrarian households—shared bedrooms and even beds with family members, particularly with children, who were low in the family hierarchy. The still lower status assigned to the enslaved was expressed differently. They slept separately and in the lowest-status places: back bedchambers or even in a cellar, attic, ell, or shed. Although all the rooms in New England houses were below freezing on winter nights, cellar dampness and drafty corners made New England's slaves particularly vulnerable to illness, especially if there was no one of the same gender, race, and status with whom to share a bed for warmth. As the Sherburnes' house had only a crawl space beneath the first-story floorboards, the two enslaved people probably slept under the house's steep gables. Separate slave-quarter buildings were virtually nonexistent in New England.

The tasks of the enslaved paralleled the tasks of their master and mistress. The late Joseph had been a mariner, shopkeeper, and merchant, and held various minor town and colony offices including justice of the peace, whence his epithet "esquire." In addition to this house, Sherburne owned two lots in the glebe.[58] He also owned 15 acres of mowing and pasture land near the town animal pound, half a right to land in Rochester, 354 acres in Barrington, and one right to land in Kingswood. The work of Sherburne's man may have included sailing, unloading merchandise at the wharf, stocking store shelves, maintaining the house, and agricultural labor or logging on the outlying lands.

The enslaved woman likely worked beside Mary Sherburne and Mary's mother-in-law at all the tasks related to maintaining a household: procurement, preservation, preparation, and presentation of food; cleaning, sewing, gardening, and stocking the store shelves during the men's absence. They probably processed flax and wool from their country properties.

Placing a Cash Value on People

White owners, buyers, town governments, and probate courts had an informal method of appraising the cash value of human beings. Valuations varied according to an individual's sex, age, health, strength, and the fluctuating economy. The Sherburnes' enslaved man was valued at £200. The inventory lists no single household item of comparable value. The remote and probably undeveloped 354 acres in Barrington were valued at only £170. A half-right of land in nearby Rochester was valued at £150. The nearby 15 acres by the pound were cleared for mowing and pasturage and valued at £400. This house on Puddle Dock, along with its wharf and garden, were valued at £700. At £200 the man was highly valued.

The Sherburnes' Black woman was valued at £50. This may reflect age or—just as likely—a lower economic value placed on female work in eighteenth-century culture, whether by free or enslaved persons, Black or white. At £50 she was nonetheless among the most highly valued possessions. The most expensive objects in the Sherburne house were the canopy beds with their costly bolsters, pillows, and handmade textiles. Two beds with their textiles were valued at £25 and £50 respectively. The family silver collectively surpassed the woman's cash value; two silver cans, six large spoons, one pepper box, and one salt cellar (37 oz.) added up to £60.8.0. Of

value equal to the Black woman was the family pew in "Mr Fitches Meeting House" (North Church), valued at £50. Ownership of a pew suggests these enslaved people spent Sundays in the back gallery of North Church.

While their high value suggests they were young, healthy, and skilled, their names, arrival date, and fates remain unknown. The Sherburne house survives on its original site, providing a physical link to their presence in Portsmouth.[59] Sophisticated archaeological work has enabled the reconstruction of the back garden down to such details as the placement of fence posts, garden paths, and raised beds, with pollen analysis providing clues to the genera and species of plants raised there or in the region. Map analysis has enabled a sketchy reconstruction of the wharf opposite the front of the house. Such details aid our envisioning the environment in which these two Africans lived and labored. Archaeology has even recovered shards of contemporary ceramics they saw or handled in their daily routines.[60]

Skilled Craftspeople

Many slaves were distributed through the ranks of Portsmouth's middle-class artisans. Craftsmen must have been attracted to the prospect of trained help who—unlike apprentices—would not become competitors or linger to seek the hand of the master's daughter and his inheritance. Following is a sampling of Black artisans in colonial Portsmouth households.

Adam, Mercer, and Bess Marshall

Adam, Mercer, and Bess were part of the mid-eighteenth-century household of Samuel Marshall, who lived on the southwest corner of Jefferson Street and Horse Lane from about 1736 until 1749.[61] Marshall was a potter, producing utilitarian kitchenware from the local gray clay,

Enslaved Africans and Black Americans were considered personal property under white law and were valued or appraised accordingly, whether in advertisements, inventories or bills of sale. This bill of sale records goods received by Edmund Quigley on March 15, 1755, including a Negro man named Bristol and a Negro woman named Kate. *New Hampshire Historical Society.*

the iron content of which oxidizes and turns the wares a reddish brown when fired. He probably trained his enslaved men in many or all the tasks of his trade.

They dug and weathered clay to rot away organic impurities. They milled and kneaded it for uniform texture, and made pots on the wheel,

the most skilled step in the process. They purchased or quarried fine sand and milled it into a powder, which, mixed with powdered lead oxide and water, made a creamy glaze. The dry pots were dunked, dried, gingerly stacked in the kiln, and its door bricked.

Meanwhile they assembled and split many

cords of wood. They stoked the fire for most of a day, raising temperatures gradually with hardwood then soft, judging the temperatures by the color of the glowing pots as the silica in clay and glaze foamed and fused into a glassy waterproof surface. After gradually lowering the temperature by shifting back to hardwood, they would finally cover the fuel openings and let the kiln cool for a few days. Unloading the kiln could involve prying loose wares that had toppled and fused to one another, leaving hazardous razor-sharp edges. They then packed the wares with straw in barrels or crates and distributed them to local shopkeepers and housewives, or loaded them onto boats at the family's wharf on Puddle Dock and shipped them up and down the Piscataqua to adjacent towns.

While Adam and Mercer worked with Samuel Marshall at these tasks, Mrs. Marshall and Bess did household tasks. They worked in the garden between the house and pottery works, sewed, did laundry, and cleaned. The latter tasks were made burdensome by pervasive clay dust and life at the intersection of two unpaved streets busy with traffic headed to the long wharves on the river and the shops and little wharves along Puddle Dock. The women also bought foodstuffs, varied by a modest gathering from the small urban garden they maintained amid the clay dust and woodpiles. Bess gained considerable knowledge and skills for these tasks, as well as for the preservation, preparation, and presentation of food. Among their routine cooking and serving utensils was red kitchenware manufactured by Samuel, Adam, and Mercer.

Bowls were among the many manufactures of the Marshall pottery workshop. Most of these were destined for kitchen use in Piscataqua-area homes. By this period the local white middle class was adopting the practice of transferring their traditional one-pot meals to individual plates. But Africans in New England continued eating from a shared bowl, as white Yankees had long done. This may signal a withholding of

This tamarind jar was excavated at Strawbery Banke Museum from the Marshall pottery-making site. Tamarind seedpods were transported from their native East Africa and cultivated in the West Indies for their refreshing sweet-sour flavor. *Photography by Robert Burth. Collection of Strawbery Banke Museum.*

sufficient utensils, or just as likely represent the cultural persistence of once parallel European and western African traditions of eating from shared bowls.[62]

The urban diet included exotic foodstuffs delivered by sea trade and rarely traded inland. Among the unexpected features of the colonial Portsmouth diet were tamarinds. These come from a feathery-leafed tree native to tropical Africa that grows wild throughout Sudan. In the sixteenth century it was introduced to tropical America for cultivation, long before English settlers brought apple trees and wheat to North America. The tree produces a flat, fuzzy, tan, hand-shape seedpod from which a sour, brown, gooey paste is extracted. It is used in cooking or mixed with water and sugar for a refreshing sweet-sour drink still popular in the West Indies.[63]

The consumption of tamarinds in colonial Portsmouth certainly illustrates the cosmopolitan nature of a seaport. This taste was not limited to world-traveled and prosperous white sea captains. The appetite came with Black people from Africa via the West Indies. Archaeologists have located tamarind jars in the context of solely Black communities on the rural South Shore of Massachusetts, evidence of a taste likely paralleled in Portsmouth's urban Black population.[64] Archaeological investigation has turned up a couple of tamarind jars in Portsmouth, too, one of them at the Marshall house site, where contextual evidence hints that it had been reused as a flowerpot. There is no way of knowing whether the jar and its contents were purchased by the white Marshalls or Black Marshalls, or came into the house secondhand and empty. But by whatever means the jar came to Portsmouth and into the Marshalls' possession, the jar was likely made—and its contents harvested and packed—by enslaved workers in the West Indies.

Sometime after the Marshalls sold their house in 1749, subsequent owners sold the bottom half of the lot including its wharf rights. The pottery works were eventually demolished, and in the 1790s a new house was built over the site. The Marshall house itself was demolished in the mid–twentieth century.

The only tangible evidence of Adam, Mercer, and Bess's lives is archaeological fragments at Strawbery Banke Museum, which encompasses the Marshall site. The collection includes pottery fragments, no doubt partly the collective work of Adam, Mercer, and their owner. The collection also includes the tamarind jar found at the Marshall site. Mercer's and Bess's fates remain unknown. Adam lived to be very old and, one day while home alone, fell into the fire and burned to death.[65]

Nero, Cato, and Jane Wheelwright

Nero was a cooper. Coopers made kegs, barrels, hogsheads, buckets, piggins, and any staved containers. There was art to it and plenty of geometric mystery, as there were virtually no straight edges in any of the pieces and most pieces curved in sections of ovoid solids. No doubt Nero found satisfaction in mastering the trade, in spite of reaping no pay for his work, whether excellent or indifferent.

There was tremendous demand for coopered containers. They were sold locally for storage or shipping farm produce such as pickled meat and fish. Vast quantities of barrel staves were exported from every northern New England port blessed with river access to inland lumber supplies. Staves were shipped in bundles called shooks and sold in Atlantic ports where wood was short or labor applied to more profitable activities. At those ports the staves were assembled into barrels, filled with local produce or manufactures, and reexported. In the West Indies sugar, molasses, rum, coffee, and chocolate were exported in barrels made of imported staves. Barrels from Piscataqua staves carried these goods to British colonies everywhere and, via the mother country, to the farthest corners of the earth.

When Nero's master died, the master's widow Demaris inherited ownership of Nero. Nero continued coopering while Demaris owned the business. She made the business decisions—probably with practical advice from Nero—and thus gained the title of cooperess. His unpaid labor kept them both adequately.

Demaris's property, including her business, with Nero and his skills, must have made her attractive in the marriage market. Eventually Demaris married Jeremiah Wheelwright. What was hers—there were apparently no children with claims on her late husband's estate—became his; Nero got a new master and a new last name.

Portsmouth was so small a town that Nero probably knew that Jeremiah Wheelwright already owned a Black man of his own, a man named Cato. Could Nero have heard that Wheelwright had paid the £200 purchase price for Cato with £100 worth of shingles plus a Black girl named Jenny valued at another £100, whom he simply traded off to a new owner in Somersworth, a long day's walk northward? Had Nero heard how Cato had suffered a hernia while working for Wheelwright? Wheelwright had sued the man from whom he'd bought Cato, claiming he'd been sold faulty merchandise. Wheelwright might have gotten away with the sham if some sailors hadn't sworn in court that Cato had been fine when they last saw him just before the sale. Wheelwright lost his lawsuit. This litigious white man would now be Nero's master.[66]

The reconfigured Wheelwright family apparently continued to live off Nero's coopering skills and the unpaid labor of the Black domestic woman Jane. If Cato were still part of Wheelwright's household, Nero would likely have had to teach him the cooper's trade. Demaris surrendered the title of cooperess as Jeremiah took over the business management and the title. Nothing indicates Jeremiah knew anything of the hands-on aspects of the cooper's trade.

The household moved to a new place on Jose's Lane, an incomplete street running down to the river, now Jefferson Street. By her new husband Demaris bore a daughter Mary and a son John.

By 1786 Nero and Jane were getting along in age when Jeremiah, mindful of his mortality and perhaps ill, made out a will. He died later that year. Jeremiah Wheelwright's last will and testament bequeathed Nero and Jane to a nearby neighbor, Dr. Hall Jackson, stipulating that while Jackson would technically own them, Nero and Jane were for the use of the Wheelwrights' now grown and married daughter, Mary Wheelwright Oram. The reason for this peculiar arrangement is obscure; perhaps it was a way of protecting Mary's property from acquisition by her husband, Oram. Son John acquired the house from his parents' estate.[67]

When Jeremiah Wheelwright's estate was probated and inventoried later that year, Nero and Jane were listed among the other personal property: "Nero, a Negro Man 30—. Jane, a Negro Woman 20—."

At £30 and £20 these people were the highest-valued personal possessions in his estate. The most expensive items—all the beds, bedding, bedsteads, and their curtains combined—added up to only £21.9.6. Nero and Jane were surpassed in value only by real estate, two plots of land with houses valued at £175 and £20 respectively. The total estate was valued at £388.4.5.[68]

While Demaris and then her second husband had been the business managers, held the title of cooper, and received the profits, Nero was the craftsman whose skill kept the family solvent.

A Tailor

William Ham, a tailor, bought a lot on Washington Street at the corner of Jefferson Street and in 1791 built a house that stands there still. An enslaved man whose name is unknown to us was part of his household, recorded a year earlier in the 1790 U.S. census. Surely Ham trained this man as a tailor. Apparently Ham's expansion into a new house was too much for his modest revenue to support during the lingering post-Revolutionary economic depression, when the port's streets were described as full of weeds for lack of traffic. Four years later Ham sold the house to Joseph Brown, a sea captain.[69]

In 1821 Ham (or perhaps a son of the same name, also a tailor) still lived nearby on Pitt (now Court) Street and kept a shop on State Street, but no Black man lived with him then.[70] Perhaps Ham sold him when he sold the house on Washington Street just before the economy picked up, or sold him during the economic depression of 1815–20, or freed him, or found he had run away in the changing spirit of the times. While mechanized spinning and then weaving were introduced to the region during this very period, sewing was not yet mechanized. In these same years men's fashion shifted to ever more tailored silhouettes and structure. The services of an accomplished slave must have been valuable and his loss regretted by Ham.

Hopestill Cheswell

Hopestill Cheswell was a housewright and carpenter from Newmarket, New Hampshire, born about 1712. He made a significant mark on colonial Portsmouth's landscape. Apparently the son of Richard Cheswell, a Black man, and an unknown white woman, his white maternity made him free.[71] A biracial man whom whites would identify as Black, he was unlikely to have been admitted to apprenticeship even though free, making his training a puzzle. Perhaps a grandparent trained him or he had an innate gift for this. Portsmouth's mid-eighteenth-century growth provided ample employment for housewrights and carpenters.

Hopestill built—or at least framed—the Bell Tavern that once stood on Congress Street.[72] It was reputedly built in 1743. "That it was strongly made, the test of a century and a quarter has shown," noted a Victorian-era chronicler approvingly.

The local white population, including the patron for whom the tavern was constructed, clearly treated Hopestill as Black: "On the completion of the work there was, according to the custom of the day, a merry gathering to commemorate it. Though Hopestill had performed an important part of the work, he did not venture to approach the board, until it was decided by the company that he should be permitted to come in and partake with them on the joyful occasion." The relationship in this instance is particularly curious, as the hesitant white patron for whom the tavern was built, Paul March, was Hopestill's half brother.[73]

The tavern figured prominently in Portsmouth's public life. Along with the port's other

central taverns it was much frequented when the colonial Assembly was in session, especially after 1762, when the new capitol, a few yards away in the square, was ready for occupancy. In later years the tavern was owned by Colonel William Brewster, whose enslaved servant Nero was repeatedly elected king at the annual Negro Coronations, and festivities related to this event are presumed to have occurred in the tavern's extensive backyard or field. At the time of the American Revolution, the tavern was owned by John Greenleaf and was one of several gathering places of patriots.

Mid-nineteenth-century antiquarian Charles Brewster cites a letter he received from someone in Wolfboro who had stayed in the building in the 1810s. The letter's author observed: "It was not a beautiful structure—an architect would not hold it up as a model. I don't think its proportions are exactly laid down in the books. It had no stately columns, pillars, dome or tower. But it had a history, and hallowed memories which are more significant and enduring." Its construction by Hopestill Cheswell, and its presumed role in the annual Negro Coronations, add additional layers of "hallowed memories," though the building does not survive today.

On Pleasant Street, opposite the Governor John Langdon house, once stood the Reverend Samuel Langdon house, built by the minister of North Church about 1749. In 1859 the elderly Captain Daniel Fernald reminisced about this house. According to oral traditions Fernald had heard, the house was built by one Hopestill March, a biracial man of Dover. This was probably the same Hopestill Cheswell, housewright from Newmarket, the confusion over surname arising from Cheswell's half brother's last name.

Hopestill Cheswell has also been linked to the construction of the Purcell house, also known as the John Paul Jones house, home of the Portsmouth Historical Society.[74] The Langdon and Purcell houses are classic examples of the many mid-eighteenth-century mansions built for Portsmouth's elite.[75] Both houses have two ample stories plus gambrel roofs. They are heavily framed, in the way of the place and time, and are arranged four rooms per floor flanking a center hall. Within, the stairways are characteristic of Portsmouth opulence with low risers, deep treads, and balusters repeating three different designs per tread. The main rooms are wainscoted, the fireplace walls fully paneled with pilasters framing the fireplaces. Typically such buildings were built by a professional team, all of whom hewed framing timbers, then turned to specialties like joinery, carpentry, turning, glazing, and masonry, with some specialists like carvers hired from outside the regular crew. The housewright was often a designer, craftsman, and supervisor. The exact nature of Hopestill's work on these buildings remains to be discovered. Great as his impact seems to have been on the look of the colonial town, no other Portsmouth buildings by Hopestill are known to survive today.

Cheswell's success as a housewright enabled him to amass more than one hundred acres during the years between 1733 and 1749, which, in a traditional New England way, he farmed while practicing his trade. In 1749 he acquired part ownership of a sawmill and stream in Durham, and part of a fall and mill privilege at Wadleigh's Falls, surely to provide his need for timber. Like others in his town Cheswell petitioned for road improvements and joined with neighbors in creating new rights-of-way. He and his wife, an illiterate white woman named Catherine Keniston, named their son Wentworth Cheswell, perhaps for Hopestill's mother, sometimes theorized to be a Wentworth, or perhaps in honor of Royal Governor Benning Wentworth. Their son attended Dummer Academy and became a schoolmaster, landowner, pew owner, patriot, member of the committee of safety, and long-time officeholder in Newmarket.[76]

Primus Fowle

Primus worked in the Portsmouth printing office of Daniel Fowle. We can only wonder how Primus felt if he knew the content of advertisements he printed that read: "To be sold: A strong healthy Negro Boy about eleven years old. In country $2\frac{1}{2}$ years, can be well recommended to a Gentleman's Family, a farmer or tradesman. Any good master who desires to purchase and will pay cash, may enquire at the printing office of the New Hampshire Gazette."[77]

This colonial Portsmouth printing business started in 1756. Daniel Fowle brought his press and family from Boston to reestablish his business here. His family consisted of himself, his wife, Primus, and two enslaved women. The white Fowles had no children of their own. Beginning that same year Fowle published the *New Hampshire Gazette,* various government documents, and no doubt numerous handbills or broadsides not specifically attributable to him but a staple of eighteenth-century presses. Sometimes Fowle published in partnership with Robert Fowle, presumed to be his brother. They worked from a wooden house with printing office that once stood at the corner of Howard and Pleasant Streets.

Primus worked for more than fifty years as a printer and lived more than ninety years.[78] In addition to operating the press, Primus's tasks must have included mixing ink, inking type, and the tedious and unpleasant task of cleaning type.

A nineteenth-century account notes that Primus was illiterate, remarkable if true given a lifetime surrounded by the printed word. There are numerous examples of literate slaves in Portsmouth and elsewhere. Daniel Fowle, knowing the power of literacy, must have made the conscious decision to withhold from Primus the knowledge of reading in spite of the potential value of that skill to typesetting.

A description written by one who remembered him tells a bit about Primus's appearance and personality. Primus was permanently bent forward at a forty-five-degree angle from his half century of leaning forward to pull the press's lever.

Primus grew attached to the mistress of the house. In his grief at her death Primus called her

Primus Fowle operated this press for Daniel Fowle at the office of the *New Hampshire Gazette*. Its hand-pulled lever, wooden screw, and stone bed impressed one sheet at a time against inked type. The press was sold at auction in 1890. *Courtesy Portsmouth Athenæum.*

an old fool for dying. His attachment to her made him certain of his entitlement to a prominent place in her funeral procession. In eighteenth-century Portsmouth these were hierarchically organized, with a family's servants and slaves walking to the left of the white survivors. During Mrs. Fowle's funeral procession, Primus took the place of honor on the right. His master whispered to him to switch places. Primus did not move. Daniel Fowle touched him and whispered his request again. Primus loudly sputtered a directive to his master to go to the other side, and called him a "mean jade."[79] Victorian antiquarian Charles Brewster, with white perspective, remembered Primus as an "old peppery Negro."[80] Primus's startling remark was

seared into the memory of white mourners and passed from generation to generation.

This anecdote shows both Primus's attachment to his late mistress and his overt defiance of white expectations of propriety and his white master's claim to status. It also reports in no uncertain terms what he thought of Daniel Fowle. It is a rare and informative glimpse into the relationship between an enslaved African and his New England mistress and master.

Primus lived through the Revolution, presumably helping his master remove the printing business temporarily to the neighboring town of Greenland for greater safety from confiscation should Portsmouth be occupied as Boston was, or burned by the British navy as Portland was. Daniel Fowle died in 1787 and bequeathed his property, including his "servants," to a former apprentice named John Melcher.[81]

John Melcher lived on Paved (now Market) Street very near Market Square, and Robert Fowle lived next door or within a few doors on the same side of the same street.[82] Primus went to live in one of their households (the records are a bit confusing about whether he lived with Melcher or Fowle), where he continued at the printer's trade.[83]

By the end of the century Robert's printing shop was in one of "a long string of very old one-story buildings owned by Robert Fowle. . . . John Melcher was apprenticed to him. He occupied one part as a dwelling house, had a woman, a relative, with him, and an old negro man named Primus (whom I well remember) to wait on him."[84]

Unlike the deaths of most of Portsmouth's Black residents, Primus's demise in May of 1791 was announced in the *Gazette*. "In this town, Primus a Negro late the property of Daniel Fowle Esquire, deceased, his funeral will be tomorrow at six o'clock P.M. from the dwelling house of the Printer thereof, where his acquaintances may attend and pay funeral obligations."[85] The "Printer thereof" was John Melcher. Clearly a connection between Primus and Melcher had been retained, whether he lived with Melcher or Fowle.

Primus's friends and acquaintances probably assembled at the Melcher dwelling on Market Street in keeping with regional burial tradition. These might have included his contemporaries, elderly Black men brought from Africa to Portsmouth as boys, some now freed, others still enslaved. There would have been members of the Negro Court or the African Society. Primus's acquaintances also included the white neighbors, apprentices, tradespeople, schoolboys, and Market Street passersby who had befriended him on their way to the baker, the barber, the schoolhouse, and other destinations within a block or two. But from this distance we don't know how conventions of time and place and race worked on such an occasion. Surely among Primus's less fond acquaintances were the "roguish boys" who "grieved" him, probably teasing him because of his color, age, and stooped posture.

In his last years Primus "was borne down with pain," which he may have alleviated with rum. Both are mentioned in a poem about him that appeared in the *Gazette* a week after the announcement of his death. The poem is unsigned.

Epitaph on the Death of Primus

Under these clods, old Primus lies
At rest and free from noise,
No longer seen by mortal eye
Or grieved by roguish boys;
The cheerful dram he loved 'tis true
Which hastened on his end.
But some in paved-street well knew
He was a hearty friend,
And did possess a grateful mind
Though borne down with pain,
Yet where he found a neighbor kind
He surely went again;
Too often did the mirth of some
His innocence betray,

By giving larger draughts of rum
Than he could swill away,
But now he's dead, we sure may say
Of him, as of all men,
That while in silent graves they lay
They'll not be plagu'd agen.[86]

Primus was in his nineties when he died. Apparently giving him too much to drink had been the adults' way of "grieving" him. Decades before the temperance movement this poet perceived drink as having "hastened" Primus's death. If in that heavy-drinking era Primus's drinking was sufficient to warrant notice, perhaps he was treating extreme or acute pain or depression.

Obituary, commemorative poem, and later reminiscences show that Primus was well known in Portsmouth. Age, cheerfulness, friendliness, innocence, dedication to the white people he unwillingly found himself amidst, and a quick tongue gave Primus prominence and remembrance beyond the usual limitations of bonded servitude.

Craftswomen, Craftsmen, and Local Myth

Early records tell more about men, but enslaved women certainly acquired enormous bodies of knowledge and skills assigned to females by regional culture. They were highly technical skills on which all of society depended for survival. No one could live without the farm and garden produce, the dairying, and the food preservation and preparation wrought by women. Childcare was a constant and critical need amidst the hazards of fireplaces and wells. In New Hampshire's climate of deadly winters, in which unprepared people still freeze to death every year, the production of textiles, clothing, and bedding was critical to the survival of all. In addition the beginnings of a cult of cleanliness associated with intellectual refinement engendered an ever increasing battle against grime rising from messy trades, unpaved streets, urban livestock, and insects. Black women learned and practiced these

Romanticized representations of Black women providing child care for white families have been repeated throughout American history in every region of the country. The foreground figures in this disturbing scene are Sarah Walker Rolfe Thompson and her husband Benjamin Thompson (later known as Count Rumford). In the background is Dinah, whom baby Sarah later remembered as "a favorite slave." Thompson is saying good-bye before he abandons them in Concord, New Hampshire, in 1775 for Boston, then for England. The reminiscence painting was commissioned by the elderly daughter, Countess Sarah Rumford, in 1850. Benjamin Thompson's Farewell, *oil on canvas, by D. G. Lamont, 1850. Gift of Timothy W. Woodman, courtesy of the New Hampshire Historical Society.*

William Pitt Tavern was the site of a violent interaction between the enslaved James Stavers and a zealous patriot. Originally built in 1766, the restored tavern is part of Strawbery Banke Museum. *Photography by Brad Randolph. Portsmouth Black Heritage Trail.*

skills daily in colonial Portsmouth, a body of crafts that ought not to be overlooked.[87]

Local modern myth envisions adult male slaves and holds that slavery in colonial Portsmouth was limited solely to the acquisition of house servants as status symbols in the homes of the white elite. This notion probably originated innocently enough in the historic-house museums, all mansions of the colonial elite. More problematic, the assumed or implied absence of slavery outside this narrow context minimizes the Black historical presence, eases tender white consciences by seeming to exempt northern enslaved workers from hard labor, and denies their capital contribution to the colonial economy. Only recently has interpretation of slavery in these houses begun to extend beyond the walls to mention Black labor in gardens, in workshops, on outlying farms, and aboard ships. Emphasis on the region's slave labor in the role of house servants obscures their major, perhaps primary, productive role in New England.[88] The enslaved were at once capital and capital producers.

Fortune and James: Invisibility

Fortune liberated himself at age sixteen. James was caught in the cross fire of Revolutionary ill will, later forced to steal, and yet somehow remained invisible. Fortune and James probably never met one another. Consecutive encounters with or ownership by John Stavers linked them and other Black men. Stavers was a sometime sailor and longtime tavern keeper in Portsmouth.

Fortune was part of the Stavers household when John Stavers and his second wife Katherine operated a tavern on Portsmouth's Queen (now State) Street. Fortune walked out on slavery in 1764. James was part of the Stavers household when they operated in a new tavern they had built in 1766 on Pitt (now Court) Street. During the turmoil of the Revolution the Staverses would find it politically astute to change the name of their business from the Earl of Halifax Tavern to the William Pitt Tavern. The impressive three-story tavern still presides over lower Court Street. Perhaps Fortune and James were bought by Stavers at one of the auctions he hosted in his earlier State Street tavern.[89] Their stories follow.

Tavern Work

Given New England tradition it is likely that all in the Stavers household, Black and white, adults and the seven children, worked together at tasks assigned by Mr. and Mrs. Stavers. Operating a large tavern in a busy seaport and capital city generated much work. Both taverns were near the midpoint of the short four-block walk from the waterfront to the State House, and the second tavern was the terminus of the Boston to Portsmouth stagecoach route. Business was likely brisk with captains and sailors, travelers, and—when the courts and legislature were in session—with people from the hinterlands of the province of New Hampshire. The Staverses had licenses to lodge guests, serve food, and dispense alcoholic beverages. The business brought by these licenses generated considerable work for Fortune and James and the rest of the household.

All the domestic tasks involving food, drink, heat, light, storage, cleaning, and care of livestock were immensely magnified in a commercial setting. The tavern hosted occasional military enlistments and drew crowds for auctions, concerts, monthly Masonic meetings, exhibitions of curiosities, dances, and banquets. Stavers also advertised stallions standing at stud, and some of the work of dealing with feisty stallions must have fallen to Fortune and James. Caretakers of horses were called ostlers or hostlers, a skill that would sustain some of Portsmouth's Black men in post-Revolutionary freedom.

Fortune

On May 11, 1764, John Stavers ran an advertisement in the *New Hampshire Gazette.* "Ranaway—Negro Boy named Fortune, Age 16, wearing a Red Jacket and Canvas Trowsers. . . ."[90]

What incident triggered Fortune's departure will never be known: perhaps an argument, a scolding, or a blow. The latter is not improbable given Stavers's earlier violence toward an enslaved African. Before John settled down to marriage and tavern keeping in Portsmouth, he had been a sailor. In 1752, when in the capacity of mate on board the *Princess Dowager* sailing from Saint Christopher (Saint Kitts, West In-

dies) under Captain Nathaniel Warner, Stavers beat the captain's Negro servant, for which the captain subsequently took Stavers to court.[91] Given this history, it is quite possible that Fortune's self-liberation was precipitated by Stavers's turning on him violently.

Such a blow would have been merely a trigger. The underlying cause for Fortune's departure, of course, was the condition and nature of enslavement. The tasks at the tavern may seem routinely domestic, but slavery was never benign. While white youths were formulating visions of their future, Fortune had no choices or hope of improved status.

Without his owner's action or permission to earn money and buy his freedom, Fortune could not hope that his talent, intelligence, or hard work could improve his condition. Enslavement was clearly intolerable to the adolescent. Others had rebelled; early Portsmouth newspapers frequently advertised runaways. The number would increase in the 1770s, when white people failed to apply the rhetoric of independence to Black people.

Running away in 1764 was problematic. There was no sizable community of free Blacks in which a fugitive could hide unnoticed (as there would be by the eve of the Civil War a century later). The combined thirteen colonies had only a few thousand free Black people. Whether Fortune was successful, recovered and sold, or reenslaved elsewhere is unknown; no more is heard of him after his disappearance was advertised.

James

James was caught in the political cross fire of the Revolution. On Wednesday January 29, 1777, in the midst of the Revolution, a mob of patriots who believed John Stavers remained loyal to the Crown government assembled in front of Stavers's tavern. Unlike his locally born wife Katherine, John was born in England and came to Portsmouth as an adult after a career at sea. Stavers's origins, perhaps even a lingering accent, may have contributed to the air of disloyalty enthusiastic patriots attributed to him. At any rate, the fervor of the times sucked John and James into the whirlwind.

One member of the mob began chopping down Stavers's tavern sign. Stavers sent James out to drive them away. Apparently James seized the implement from the ax man, Mark Noble, and hit Noble on the head with it, probably using the blunt end or broad side of the ax, as it rendered Noble unconscious without killing him. But for a moment Noble was believed to be dead, and the cry of murder went up. John Stavers was arrested immediately, taken before the Portsmouth Committee of Safety, and then remanded to the New Hampshire Committee of Safety in Exeter—to which the government had moved upon outbreak of war—for a gang trial of fifteen suspected Loyalists. A few, including Stavers, were released for lack of evidence; most were imprisoned.

In all this commotion James was not arrested, nor was he charged with potentially deadly assault. Apparently James was terrified of retribution; oral tradition later reported that James was found several days later hiding in the cellar, up to his chin in a water cistern.[92] A few days later, on February 3, Mark Noble wrote to the New Hampshire Committee of Safety saying he understood that no harm had been meant by the "bad blow" he had received and that he hoped Stavers would be released, by which he meant John Stavers, not James.

The entire incident—whether as recorded in the New Hampshire Committee of Safety records or retold in later reminiscence—is traditionally defined in terms of its free white participants. It appears that two mechanisms were at work. The first was public preoccupation with the Revolutionary War. When releasing John Stavers, the Committee of Safety summed up the mood of the moment when they advised him to be careful "in these times of Jealousy & danger." Ignoring James's actions as representing his master, not himself, hints of a second

mechanism: lack of status of the enslaved. Their identities were often simply absorbed into their masters'. Their voice was rendered nonexistent in the Revolutionary political debate.

Later in the war years James's story continued in another direction. The November 1778 minutes of the New Hampshire Court of Sessions record the conviction of two women—Sarah Giles and Jane Cooper—for receiving goods stolen from John Stavers.[93]

On July 31, 1777, James had stolen goods from his master John Stavers and sold them to Sarah Giles. Six months later, on November 25, 1777, James stole again, this time relaying the goods to Jane Cooper. These were not thefts of little things that could be spirited out of the tavern in a pocket or under a coat. The scale of the thefts is startling, and the deed must have taken hours, even if done in incremental bits of time. To Sarah Giles, James relayed twelve gallons of rum, two bushels of corn, two bushels of salt, forty pounds of pork, and four gallons of cherry brandy. To Jane Cooper, James relayed three gallons of rum, thirty pounds of salt pork, one bushel of Indian corn, one bushel of salt, one pound of tea, eight pounds of sugar, and one ruffled shirt.

Stavers did not charge James with the theft. Instead he charged Sarah Giles and Jane Cooper through the local justice of the peace, Samuel Penhallow. The value of the stolen goods was so high that the case exceeded the justice's jurisdiction and was referred to the Court of Sessions in Exeter. If this had been an act of resistance by James against his enslavement surely Stavers would have charged and punished James directly.

An additional factor was at work. Both women threatened James, apparently with violence and at gunpoint. They "with Force and Arms did presume privately to buy and receive of and from one James a Negro Servant or Slave belonging to John Stivers [Stavers] of said Portsmouth, Innholder, knowing him the said James to be the Servant & Slave of the said John Stivers, certain Goods, Wares & Merchandize & Provisions. . . ."[94]

The women entered pleas of innocent, but a jury found them guilty. They were fined double the value of the stolen goods, and—in keeping with the legal procedures of the time—paid everyone's court costs.

Why James wasn't prosecuted as a participant is unclear. Evidently he convinced Stavers that his actions had been unwilling and forced. Though Black people could and did sometimes bear witness in court, and were prosecuted for crimes, they were as often considered invisible under the cloak of their owners' authority. Black invisibility before the law seems likely in this case since James is not even listed among the summoned witnesses.

Why the women made James steal for them is unknown. They were farmers' wives, married to William Giles and Philip Cooper, both yeomen of Portsmouth. Perhaps the chaotic economy of the Revolutionary War had created desperate shortages in their homes; perhaps these had been compounded by the absences of husbands away at war. Perhaps the women were spiteful about Stavers's rumored political stance. Perhaps they were merely dishonest.

If James had been free he could successfully have reported the coercion to the authorities. Enslaved, he had no reason to believe this would work. If he was African-born and had witnessed a court session there, he would have seen in American law a mix of parallels and contrasts.[95] West African justice was founded in family and community obligations. Like the African captives' arbitrary and unwilling enslavement in an American artificial family, American law might have seemed to James to be founded solely in coercion.[96] James's experience of being ignored by the law provides an illustration of the paradoxical legal status of enslaved people.

A Curiosity

Another African person is known to have passed through John Stavers's tavern. In 1764 an advertisement appeared in the local paper: "To be seen at Mr. John Stavers's, A white Negro Boy About Nine Years old, born in Virginia, his Father and Mother both Black, his Wool quite white, his Eyes and Noses most wonderful to see; price Six Shillings Old Tenor—may be seen any Hour from Six in the Morning, until Ten at Night. Any gentlemen or ladies, that have a desire to have him brought to their Houses, by applying to the Owner at the Sign of the Earl of Halifax, shall be duly attended on."[97]

Evidently the child's owner was staying for a while at Stavers's tavern, perhaps making an itinerant living by exhibiting the boy for a fee. The commercial exploitation of this child's rare physical appearance occurred in the context of an eighteenth-century tradition of public entertainments held at taverns. Portsmouth taverns were venues for traveling exhibitions, performances, and concerts; Stavers hosted these in his third-floor great room. This exhibition, appallingly exploitative in modern eyes, was merely a passing novelty to eighteenth-century white American society, perhaps exciting scientific curiosity in a few highly educated sorts. It was a prelude to the common nineteenth-century practice of commercial exhibition of freaks of nature in the context of circuses.

Hannah, Pomp, Nanne, Violet, Scipio: Agricultural Work

Some slaves in colonial New Hampshire were put to agricultural work. The area's thin and infertile soil could not support large-scale farms, so the application of slave labor to agriculture was on a smaller scale than elsewhere. Among New Hampshire slaves agricultural work was likely a more significant employment than yet documented, as the regional economy was mostly agricultural, rural tradesmen were also farmers, and the urban elite often owned outlying farms.

A Rural Slave Burial Ground

Among the tidal creeks that thread Portsmouth's extensive hinterland of rolling coastal lowlands,

Simple stones mark graves in the Langdon slave cemetery. The markers are small, not inscribed, and made of readily available local stone. *Photography by Gene Hill, Jr. Portsmouth Black Heritage Trail.*

Sagamore Creek reaches deep into the rural periphery. Portsmouth's Langdon family for several centuries owned much of the land on the south side of this creek's upper reaches. Much of the north bank of the creek belonged to another branch of the Langdon family.

On a bluff on the south side of the creek is a small and ancient burial ground with toppled walls and uninscribed burial markers.[98] Oral tradition says the burial ground was for the Langdon family's enslaved people. No corroborating written evidence verifies this tradition, but the physical evidence is consonant. The small stones are made of readily available local stone rather than the imported and engraved slate that figures prominently in white burial grounds. The family record of slave ownership makes it probable that these are indeed the burial markers of those farmworkers.

People Enslaved by the Langdons

Members of the Langdon family bought Black men and women at intervals, starting by the late 1600s and continuing to the eve of the Revolution.

On June 16, 1699, Captain Tobias Langdon of Portsmouth bought from Christopher Possell, a tanner in Hampton, an unnamed Black youth about sixteen or seventeen years of age.[99]

On September 10, 1718, Captain Tobias Langdon bought a "Negro Slave Named Hannah."[100] In 1724 Tobias Langdon, a wheelwright by trade, bequeathed to his son John Langdon Sr. "all my Chattel undisposed of By the will, Be it Cattle Stock Goods utensills whatsoever to me Belonging & all my Slaves."[101] On February 26, 1742/43, John Langdon Sr. (1708–80), yeoman (farmer) of Portsmouth, bought of Jacob Tilton of Newmarket "a Negro Servant Slave named Pomp" about fourteen years of age, and Tilton did "warrant Said Servant to be Sound and wel in Helth."[102] Some bills for clothing an enslaved man named Pomp also survive. On December 6, 1776, and again on July 23, 1779, John Langdon Sr. bought shoes for Pomp. If this was the same Pomp purchased in 1742/43, he would have been in his forties by this time.[103] (The Gregorian calendar was introduced in 1582 but the Julian calendar remained in use in England, and thus New Hampshire, until 1752. During this period the Julian calendar was twelve days behind the Gregorian one, resulting in the "1742/43" year.)

The Langdons held women in enslavement too. On August 6, 1763, Joseph Langdon conveyed ownership of "one certain Negro Female Slave for Life named Nanne" (whom he had bought from his late brother Tobias) to Sarah Langdon of Portsmouth, widow of Tobias. He did this not for money but "in consideration of

Hay making and other seasonal farmwork continued to be available to Black men, as shown in this twentieth-century Portsmouth scene. *Gift of Richard Candee, courtesy of the African American Resource Center.*

the Love & Good Will that he bears to Sarah Langdon." Knowing that this gift was coming to her, the previous day Sarah Langdon provided for Nanne's possible freedom should she outlive Sarah.[104] March 1, 1773, Mary Langdon (wife of John Langdon Sr.) bought from Elizabeth Lear of Portsmouth for £25 "a Negro Wench, named Violet" in six annual payments.[105]

Africans on the Farm

The boys, men, and women mentioned above likely lived and worked on the Langdon farm or moved seasonally from the farm to a house in town, according to where their labor was wanted.[106] The people inherited by John Sr. from Tobias may have been trained wheelwrights like their former master. This skill must have been invaluable on a farm, where New England's legendary rocks and ruts wrought havoc on the wheels and iron tires of farm carts, wagons, and wheelbarrows.

In 1755 John Langdon Sr. rented out Pomp, by this time about twenty-five years old, and sometimes six oxen to a Mr. Clarkson for hauling dung and perhaps for plowing.[107] If Mr. Clarkson was the owner of Will Clarkson, the two Africans might have hauled dung and plowed together. Will Clarkson, when owned by Peirse Long, was viceroy to Portsmouth's Af-

rican king, Nero Brewster,[108] and was a signer of a 1779 petition to the legislature asking for an end to slavery.[109] Working together in the fields provided opportunity for interaction among Africans even on outlying farms.

Recurrent rental of Pomp with oxen suggests he was a teamster. Oxen were the prevalent draft animals of colonial New England, critical for many agrarian tasks: stone clearing, plowing, manuring, harvesting, lumbering. Pomp grew up with the Langdons and likely trained the teams himself, directing the oxen with the traditional oral commands. After a lifetime's uncompensated labor for the Langdon family, Pomp was no doubt buried under an unmarked stone in the Langdons' rural slave burial ground.

Enslaved women like Mary Langdon's Violet probably worked beside their mistresses at textile production, in the garden and buttery, and at other tasks characteristically assigned to farm women in that time. Perhaps they took surplus garden produce by broad canoe or cart to sell at the market house on Spring Hill.[110]

The Langdons were not alone in applying slaves to farmwork. Scattered newspaper advertisements provide indirect evidence of a wider practice. On August 19, 1757, James Dwyer advertised in the *New Hampshire Gazette* for a runaway described as a "Negro man servant named Scipio, about thirty five Years old, about Five Feet Eight Inches high, well set, and of a yellowish complexion; had on one of his Hands a Scar. Said Negro was born and brought up among the English; he understands Husbandry, mows well, and affects to be thought a Man of Sense."[111]

On January 21, 1757, the same paper advertised "To be sold a strong healthy Negro Boy about eleven years old. In country two-and-a-half years, can be well recommended to a Gentleman's Family, a farmer or tradesman. Any good master, who desires to purchase, and will pay cash, may enquire of the printer. . . ."[112] In 1776 a twenty-five-year-old man was advertised for sale because his employer didn't have work enough to make owning him worth the expense of maintaining him. The advertisement noted that the man for sale "understands farming business well."[113]

Scipio's understanding of husbandry (livestock management) and skill at mowing (done with a scythe in field or salt marsh) suggests a lifetime of agricultural work. The advertisement for the eleven-year-old assumes a market for agricultural work. Just as Langdon bought Pomp when young, this youngster was offered for sale in a local white culture that preferred training boys to the owner's standards, which made them valuable long-term investments.[114]

Advertisements regarding the enslaved often name virtues, flaws, or features of identification. Such details carry evidence of the world and condition in which these enslaved people lived.

Scipio, the aforementioned thirty-five-year-old runaway "of a yellowish complexion," was perhaps a child of both Black and white ancestry. Scipio also bore a scar on his hand, perhaps from an accident with an agricultural edged tool or from an injury inflicted by livestock, or perhaps evidence of violent punishment inflicted by an owner or a court "among the English" in North America or the West Indies.[115] Scipio was arrogantly mocked for imagining himself "a Man of Sense," illustrating the white assumption of inferior intelligence among Black people. Scorn, injury, and mockery together indicate a degradation that may have inspired Scipio to run away.

The advertisement for the eleven-year-old boy notes that he had been in the country two and a half years. This probably signaled familiarity with the expectations of his enslaved status and an ability to speak English. Others were newly imported, not "seasoned" to their status, as whites called subjugation, and unable to speak English. That this boy was taken from Africa at age eight is a stark reminder of the complacency with which whites viewed enslavement, even of children.

Further Reflections

The Langdons' two private family burial grounds—one for whites, the other for Blacks—were part of a rural tradition that supplemented the several public burial grounds around the perimeter of the compact center of Portsmouth. Whether the general tradition had dynastic or merely practical implications, the Langdons' ground expressed a patriarchal and familial perception of those whom they enslaved by providing them a private burial ground on family land even though the separate grounds differentiated by race. The number of stones suggests generations of use, or perhaps use by several branches of the Langdon family. If the latter is true, it hints of family and community among the enslaved who were forced to work in agriculture, a Black clan or community comprehending the various branches of the white Langdon clan.

Quamino, Prince, Nero, a Negro Girl, Cato, Peter, John Jack, and Phyllis: The Role of Slavery among the White Colonial Elite

The historical limitation to white men of the power to record, interpret, and especially preserve history inadvertently emphasizes the presence of slaves in mansions of the mercantile elite to the exclusion of their presence in the homes of artisans and farmers, on ships, and on the waterfront. Nineteenth- and twentieth-century New England historians often dismissed slaves as merely status symbols of the elite. This overlooks the capital-producing labor of most slaves in the region. It also overlooks the elite's ownership of farms, wharves, and other loci of productive labor where their slaves were in all likelihood put to work. New England's elite—merchants, ministers, town officers, clergy—were often called away by their professions; their slaves likely played major productive roles during these absences.[116]

In Portsmouth, the narrow slave-as-status-symbol interpretation was sustained and promulgated by historic house-museum guides. It was an easy assumption to make if a guide was aware of no other slaves in the colonial town while entertaining an exaggerated sense of the importance of the patriarch of the historic house the guide cherished and helped to preserve. This sense of slavery's limited role is false, but some slaves did indeed work as house servants of the mercantile elite. No doubt their presence in these mansions enhanced the owner's status in the eyes of other whites. This function of slavery, including the mechanisms of elevated status, merits closer examination.

Slaves are documented in connection with many of colonial Portsmouth's impressive mansions, several of which survive. By way of a sample, the successive owners of a single mansion, the Macpheadris-Warner house, housed a surprising number of enslaved people.

This brick house stands on the northeast corner of Daniel and Chapel Streets. Scottish immigrant merchant Archibald Macpheadris built it in 1715–19. After him the mansion was occupied successively by the households of Royal Governor Benning Wentworth and then by merchant Jonathan Warner through the rest of the eighteenth century.

The Macpheadris Household

In 1726 Archibald Macpheadris purchased two males from Captain Samuel Moore. One was named Prince, the other Quamino.[117] Later in the same year Macpheadris acquired a boy named

Nero from the West Indies.[118] An inventory of 1729 lists "2 Negro boys and 1 Negro girl" without giving their names. The inventory taker may have mistaken a young boy for a girl, or there may have been others in the household. The New England preference for purchasing children and training them to the owner's liking persisted in domestic contexts as in other settings.

Quamino was probably an Akan name; it is certainly from western Africa in what today is Ghana. The name means a male child born on Saturday.[119] Quamino's African name was a rare survivor and a sign of resistance amid a culture whose dominant members usually renamed those whom they enslaved.

The Wentworth Household

Benning Wentworth's rental and occupancy of Macpheadris's mansion may represent a relatively brief interlude when there were no slaves in the house. Contemporary documents mention slaves in many other branches of the Wentworth family, and this ownership played out in the existence of many Black people with the surname Wentworth.[120] Many others of the Portsmouth governing and Anglican oligarchy also held slaves. Though there is no documentation, it seems unlikely that Benning did not own slaves.[121] Anecdotes alluding to slaves at Wentworth's later country mansion at Little Harbor seem to have originated around the turn of the twentieth century.[122] Given the fractured paper trail, it is likely no contemporary evidence will ever come to light.

The Warner Household

Later in the eighteenth century, beginning around 1760, Jonathan Warner lived in the brick mansion with his wife Mary, Archibald Macpheadris's daughter.[123] They too kept slaves. One was Cato, who would later sign a petition to the legislature in 1779 requesting an end to slavery. Their biracial slave Frank died in 1779 when he fell from a ship.[124] Another, Peter, would also sign the petition, and afterward he was married to Dinah Pearn on July 6, 1786, by the North Church minister.[125]

A fourth was John Jack. At an unknown date John Jack married a free woman named Phillis, who in 1792 bought land, apparently with a house on it, in Greenland, New Hampshire. They had three children; although a son died, two daughters continued to live there until they sold the property in 1845.[126] In 1796 John Jack, apparently free by then, and Phillis harbored the fugitive slave Ona Judge.

Cato, John Jack, and Peter are said to have lived in the upstairs of a wooden kitchen ell extending from the back of the brick house.[127] As bedchambers followed the hierarchy of the rooms below, assignment to a room above the kitchen symbolized the low status forced on these men in the white household, though they were prominent in the Black community.

The Role of Slavery among the White Elite

Macpheadris, Wentworth, and Warner were among the town's most politically influential people. Macpheadris and Warner were members of the Royal Governor's Council. Wentworth was the royal governor and a relation of Macphaedris's wife. All were wealthy. Their world was hierarchical, and they were acutely status-conscious.

Many mansions like the Macpheadris-Warner house overlooked their owner's source of wealth (wharves, ships, and warehouses). In a hierarchically organized landscape others were clustered around the hilltop seats of power (churches and capitol) or lined the main "highways" that connected wealth and power. These locations were part of a matrix of symbols indicating status, used to create a gulf between the powerful rich and lesser ranks of society. Though not large by today's standards, these painted mansions tow-

ered over their neighbors, an effect sometimes heightened by a cupola.[128] The grand houses had sumptuous interiors and were outfitted with gleaming furnishings and textiles, books, and opulent clothing. Such owners also had comfortably furnished pews in their churches, conspicuously located near the pulpit. They attended exclusive activities such as private balls, concerts, and theatrical events, and were members of a cooperative library. Altogether these mansions were outward and visible proclamations of their owner's status and refinement.

This was in deliberate and stunning contrast to Portsmouth's side-street and back-lane world of smaller, unpainted homes and shops for middling-level artisans, shopkeepers, and poor laborers. This other and larger world comprised homes of modest interiors, no slaves or a few assigned to strictly practical work, occupancy of plain cheap or free pews, and coarse public entertainments. Occupants of these homes were excluded from the rarefied world of the elite by education, dress, bearing, manner, and even by language.

Unlike agrarian and artisanal slaves, those in the mansions of the elite were also symbolic of their owner's status. At any given time in eighteenth-century Portsmouth there were a dozen or two such grand families. The surnames of the enslaved—which changed with ownership—include those of all the local elite: Hall, Warner, Moffatt, Shores, Frost, Whipple, Brewster, Rogers, Rindge, Newmarch, Gardner, Tuckerman, Sherburne, Wentworth, Clarkson, Odiorne, Hubbard, Gerrish.[129] Their owners gained from these enslaved servants the generation of capital value and, at least in the owners' eyes, social aggrandizement.

What was the African point of view? Africans were certainly familiar with the concept of status and status symbols, though the specific symbology of western Africa was in most ways visually different. Those who spent their days in these mansions could and did decode the unwritten language. They were well placed to watch the impact of the white men's status symbols on one another, noting how the symbols worked to intimidate and exclude white tradesmen or laborers. When such men or women came to a mansion to apply for work, they waited in garden chairs lined up in the tall stone-colored hallways, reminders that though they were physically in the building they were symbolically outdoors, still outside the social circle. The appearance of the master of the house from behind a closed door might give a glimpse of a brilliantly colored and alien world beyond. If the master or mistress arrived by descending the stairs, he or she would be silhouetted against the arched stair-landing window, a deliberate allusion to windows above pulpits whence scripture was interpreted and town government moderated. Anyone who glimpsed the bedchamber would see in its canopy a deliberate parallel to the canopies over pulpits, judges' benches, the governor's seat in church and the capitol, and their authority that emanated from kingly thrones.[130] The associations were not lost on those who glimpsed them. Subtler refinements were understood only by others educated to connoisseurship by their own education, wealth, and access to this coded system. Evidence of understanding was a ticket to admission. Interestingly, Black people in these households learned and understood this symbology better than any white laboring people in town. They might have been amused by its effects or perhaps indifferent to it, but they comprehended and absorbed it. In freedom some would successfully duplicate it in their own homes, if on a modest scale.

Although enslaved throughout capture, sale, and ongoing bondage, those who worked in these houses were first and foremost people, not "slaves," let alone symbols. Thinking of them as merely slaves or merely status symbols trivializes their lives and is racist. They held the truth in their minds and hearts; they were free people unwillingly held captive.[131]

Some antiquarians try to sidestep internalized guilt by suggesting that the character of slavery was somehow related to the scale of slavery. This argument irrationally claims that where there were fewer slaves, as in New England, slavery was not as severe, demoralizing, or immoral as elsewhere. Slavery was, of course, as immoral and every bit as demoralizing in New England as elsewhere. A Kittery slave named Tony saw in the Anglo-American justice system a permanent escape from this misery. He murdered his master's young daughter (by throwing her down a well) not only to cause his master irreparable grief but so that he himself would be freed from bondage by execution. He was duly tried, convicted and, on July 29, 1756 executed.[132] In asking why he hadn't simply committed suicide, Tony's captors completely missed the symbolism of his act.

Whites at that time claimed no moral ground for slavery and justified it almost solely in economic terms. Whites sometimes freed their African servants, demonstrating that it was always within their moral ken and legal power to do so. Every sale, every resale, every law, every punishment, every day of holding these people as chattel was an ongoing act of enslavement. Far from symbols that aggrandized the white owners, slaveholding degraded them.

Venus: Decoding Clues

Church records of baptisms, marriages, and funerals provide many clues to the presence, lives, and status of Portsmouth's early Black population. The enslaved were often required to attend their master's church. In the century from 1742 to 1841 over one hundred names of Black people, enslaved and free, appear in the Saint John's Church records. Similar information is found in the records of North Church and South Church.

Individual entries are often tantalizing and frustrating for their lack of detail. An example is an 1807 entry in the Saint John's records: "Contribution Xmas day—Venus—a Black—$1."

This entry records a gift to Venus, following an old Anglican Christmas custom of charitable giving at Christmas.

In 1807 a dollar was equivalent to two days' pay for an unskilled white man. It was equal to what a woman could earn in four or more days. It was a sizable gift.

But who was Venus, and what can reasonably be surmised about her? Venus's name indicates that she was formerly enslaved. The charity gift indicates that she was free in 1807, no longer maintained by an owner.

Importation of enslaved African people to Portsmouth had tapered off thirty years earlier during the Revolution. If Venus was imported rather than born here, she was probably no younger than forty, and possibly elderly.

Her association with Saint John's strongly suggests that her former owner was a parishioner.[133]

Venus's lack of a last name suggests she was on her own, no longer enslaved by a white family, and not married. The Christmas gift, of course, indicates she was poor. Venus's single status and poverty suggest that she was marginally employed or not at all.

Evidently Venus was not quite poor enough to be cared for from the town poor-relief fund nor sheltered at town expense in the almshouse. Venus probably lived a marginal existence, perhaps lodging with other poor people. Urban poverty at that time meant living at the fringes of the compact part of town or retreating to a nearby rural area.[134]

Venus certainly sat in the Negro pews that were features of almost all of Portsmouth's churches.

What's in a Name?

This woman's name—Venus—tells a tale. She was stripped of her original name and given this name upon enslavement. The renaming symbolically detached Venus from any other time, place, culture, or family she had known. In white eyes, this act rendered these past connections illegitimate. This detachment reinforced her chattel status.

Venus's name is drawn from classical mythol-ogy. Knowledge of classical antiquity was evidence of education and refinement. Seaports like Portsmouth were contact points between European culture and the American hinterlands. Educated people were acutely aware of the symbolic significance of knowledge of antiquity and its literary and aesthetic prototypes. For a century they copied Roman decorative motifs for their houses and furnishings as a sign of intellectual refinement. By 1807 erudite Americans were rediscovering Greek prototypes. By then even the women of Portsmouth were wearing Grecian gowns, as were elegant women throughout the extended western European world. Portsmouth examples of enslavement names drawn from classical antiquity include Venus, Caesar, Cato, Pompey, Cyrus, Scipio, Primus, Titus, and Nero. Other Portsmouth owners gave names drawn from literary or poetic sources: Romeo, Fortune, Flora, Dinah, Phyllis, or Candace. Still others gave place-names, perhaps indicative of place of birth or purchase: Boston, Newport, and London. Whatever the source, new names disconnected their bearers from their origins.

When such names appear in early records they identify a Black person; sometimes they are the historian's only clue to color. The few colonial Black people with biblical, Christian, or Anglo names easily slip by unidentified.

The names given to Blacks signaled a lack of status in white society. Upper-class white people in this period didn't draw their children's names from classical and poetic sources; they preferred biblical or saints' names. But white people often used classical and poetic names for pets, and place-names for stud livestock. Drawing names for pets, livestock, and slaves from common sources separated the enslaved from humanity in the minds of their owners and classified them as animals, childlike, of inferior intellect, and easier to abuse. The practice had the same social function as the later use by whites of the term "boy" for Black, Jewish, and Gay men, or "girl" for grown women to separate, exclude, and isolate them at the bottom of society.

A few Africans in Portsmouth, as elsewhere in New England, managed to retain their African names. Local examples include Quamino (Macpheadris), Quam (Sherburne), Kittindge (Tuckerman), Cuffe (Whipple), and perhaps Garrott (Colton), Juba (Plummer), and Quint. Persistence of African names may represent occasional white indifference or assertive and successful refusal by some captives to accept any but their real name. The name Prince is sometimes interpreted as white mockery and sometimes as Black insistence on acknowledging highborn status back in Africa.[135]

In later freedom, Black parents would give their children conspicuously Biblical or Anglo names—Rebecca, Candace, Richard, Esther, William, Robert—that signaled separation from slavery, acculturation to the predominant Anglo-centric culture, and identification with citizenship in the new republic.

Though Venus's identity cannot be precisely pinned down, the simple phrase written with a quill pen, "Contribution Xmas day—Venus—a Black—$1," reveals a great deal about Venus when placed in historical context. In brief, there is much in her name.

North Church People: Status and Religion

Many of colonial Portsmouth's enslaved Africans were in some way associated with one of the port's several churches. The Black Sherburnes, Frank and Flora Stoodley, Prince Whipple and Dinah Chase, Peter Warner and Dinah Pearn, are a few among many.[136] Their presence raises many questions about their status and its expression in church, about religious perceptions and the interplay of traditions. Scattered documentary clues enable interesting speculation.

Houses of worship were outward expressions of a Christian perception of social rank as part of a divinely ordered hierarchy of creation. The pulpit's significance—or rather the significance

of what transpired there—was proclaimed by its central location, height, and rich ornament with canopy overhead.[137] From the 1600s through the mid-1800s churches of most New England denominations seated churchgoers according to social rank, the method of placement gradually shifting from assignment to purchase.[138] Pews representative of the highest rank were close to the pulpit, the lowest farthest from it. Private pews gave rise to the practice of numbering pews for easy record keeping.

Throughout New England some pews were set aside as general seating for special groups. Details varied according to town, location, date, and circumstances. Regional variants included free seats reserved for adolescents, Native Americans, the poor, widows, the hard-of-hearing, and Black people.

Portsmouth was no exception to these regional customs. Negro pews were features of the old North Meetinghouse that stood on Market Square from 1711 to 1854. That three-story wooden building, later remodeled and then entirely replaced, followed the characteristic spatial organization of New England meetinghouses. The pulpit and main door were on opposite broad sides of the building with balconies above the door and at each narrow end. North Church had two tiers of balconies.

Apparently North Church required slave owners to purchase pew space for their enslaved people as for themselves.[139] The Negro pews here were high above the front door in the upper balcony on the east wall.

Negro pews were probably a feature of the colonial South Church in the South End, of the Anglican Queen's Chapel, and of the brick Saint John's Church that replaced it in 1807. Oral tradition holds that in Saint John's Church the pews were identified with brass labels engraved "Negro" and remained in place into the twentieth century. Such labels were commonplace throughout urban New England, and they were no doubt found in Portsmouth's other early houses of worship too.

Rank, Location, Change, and White Ambivalence

In a system that expressed social rank or "dignity" in terms of proximity to the pulpit, the placement of Negro pews against the back wall of the balcony declared Black people's low status in white eyes. This is verified in the occasional white reference to these seats by extremely degrading terms.[140]

A few New England churches placed Negro pews in the side balconies, a location typically reserved for adolescents and unmarried young adults. This highly visible location brought the controlling gaze of all churchgoers. In many churches monitors were assigned to watch the behavior of adolescents. Placing Black people in a location corresponding to adolescents reveals white perception of Black people as childlike, untrustworthy, or given to inappropriate behavior. These became enduring assumptions in white culture.

In North Church people in the Negro pews could look in one direction to the pulpit, whence scripture was interpreted and town meetings moderated, and glance the other direction out the windows to see the Pleasant Street Parade with the town pump that doubled as a whipping post. Their view encompassed three authorities that shaped local life and defined their position in it: church, town, and courts.

Through the nineteenth century the Quaker and Universalist doctrine of the equality of all people in the eyes of God was gradually absorbed into the thinking of New England's major Protestant denominations. From the 1840s to the 1930s churches gradually shifted to free seating. Old pew numbers and labels became relics of an abandoned practice. This transition occurred in an increasingly democratic but persistently racist and segregated society that left Black and white churchgoers in an especially ambivalent relationship.

White embarrassment engendered by the combination of free seating and segregation diminished without resolution when Black churches were established and drew Black people away from the predominantly white churches. This happened in Portsmouth in the 1890s when People's Baptist Church was established.

Withholding the Message and Its Effects

From an early date some white New Englanders objected to the conversion of slaves to Christianity. The complainants' reasons varied. Some whites felt Africans were not intelligent enough to comprehend Christianity. Others didn't want to put themselves in the position of enslaving baptized Christians. Such owners were highly likely to leave their enslaved people behind when they went to church.[141] A self-emancipated southern slave who found safe harbor in Portsmouth and nearby Greenland, New Hampshire, later reflected on how her Virginian owner had given her no religious instruction and spent his Sundays in card playing and drinking wine.[142]

Tavern keeper James Stoodley's ownership of a pew in North Church for Frank and Flora in addition to his own pew indicates that he opted to take them to his church.[143] If purchase of seats was widely required as a precondition to bringing one's slaves to churches, miserliness might have provided whites an additional motive for leaving the enslaved behind on Sundays. Most estate inventories of slave owners who had pews for themselves don't list Negro pews.

Certainly many of Portsmouth's enslaved were at home unattended on Sundays. In some New England cities they spent Sundays at informal markets, selling and buying produce from the personal garden plots they had negotiated from their owners. This was likely the case in colonial Portsmouth too, where local market houses—and memory of Africa—provided a model of how to proceed.

The pious were scandalized to learn of working, buying, and selling on the Sabbath. Boston's colonial selectmen complained of the enslaved coming into town on Sundays "with corn, apples, and other fruit of the earth to the great disturbance of the public peace and scandal of our Christian profession."[144]

Such Sabbath markets provided Black women an opportunity to exercise their traditional West African role of trading. They also allowed unsupervised socializing.[145]

Churches in New England

The preceding pages are about expressions of white status and control in architectural context. Religion itself provides a window into the remarkable survival, adaptation, and transformation of African spiritual traditions in the New World. Looking at religion provides insight into the adjustment of Christianity to these and to the institution of slavery.[146]

Though the presence of royal governors in New England made the Church of England (Anglican) the legally established religious denomination in New England, organized parishes were for the most part found only in capitals and a few port cities. The prevalent religious force in colonial New England was Calvinism, most remembered for its defining doctrine of predestined salvation or damnation. The Pilgrims and Puritans introduced this radical Reformed branch of Protestantism, giving it nearly a century's head start over the Anglicans. By virtue of its prevalent numbers, Calvinism became the regional orthodoxy. From it the region's Congregational, Baptist, and Unitarian denominations evolved, providing a unified heritage to a diversifying religious landscape.

In the ideal Calvinist model the family patriarch was responsible for the moral education and conduct of his entire household. His responsibilities included promoting church attendance, leading family prayers, catechism, guidance, and admonition. From New Hampshire's beginning, Calvinist control of government and population was weaker than elsewhere in New

England. After the 1690s Calvinism's influence very gradually weakened throughout New England. Through the 1700s and into the 1800s male church membership declined. Though church attendance remained fairly high, increasing numbers of people gave only nominal attention to other religious matters.

Some owners required church attendance of those they held in bondage. A few gave them scriptural names, though this was not a common source of names assigned to the enslaved.[147]

When catechizing the enslaved, masters and clergy alike tended to emphasize scriptural passages dealing with obedience. Whether overtly conscious or unconscious of the message, whites presented Africans with a specially tailored version of Christianity suited to the maintenance of the status quo. As the first local doubts about the legitimacy of slavery were publicly voiced in the 1770s, a letter to the editor in the local newspaper justified the institution with scriptural passages.[148] This was an early example of a practice that would, in the South, become a frantic scramble by the 1840s.

Those slaves exposed to New England religion received it as did all Yankees; through a didactic, rational, and dry style, whether Anglican or Calvinist. The principal mode was hour-long sermons, psalm singing, and the reading of scripture chapters, which the Calvinists augmented with long extemporary prayers. Churchgoers attended two services each Sunday.

Isolated in remote galleries, hidden from view, subjected to long abstract sermons in complex language, enslaved churchgoers sometimes responded with little interest. Some played quiet games or snacked during church.[149] From 1750 to 1771 North Church appointed three consecutive overseers of the Negro pews to minimize such pastimes.[150]

Euro-American churchgoers didn't understand much of Christian doctrine, as the very existence of slavery suggests. Language barriers and an alien style were obstacles for some African hearers. It was difficult for some to see a relationship between Africa's traditional emotive, participatory, and antiphonal religious style and New England's dry and didactic religious style.[151]

Black Church Members and African Tradition

Not all the Christian message was ignored or uncomprehended by the enslaved. Among those who learned English well were some who read scripture willingly, understood and embraced Christianity, and applied for and were admitted to full church membership.

Of the Black church members who can be traced in eighteenth-century Portsmouth 64 percent belonged to North Church, 23 percent to South Church, and 13 percent to Queen's Chapel, roughly parallel to the distribution of the white population. Most joined as adults, a limitation of Calvinist tradition.[152] The number of Black people associated with Portsmouth churches rose at the end of the century, when an American-born generation was reaching adulthood and manumission increasing.

Religion in seventeenth- and eighteenth-century western Africa was not monolithic, any more than were culture or language in that vast region. West African religions were varied.[153] Many traditions shared participatory features. They included responsive music, dance, ecstatic spirituality, and trances.[154] These may have contributed to overall American and New England religious style.

In the 1730s and '40s a religious awakening or revival swept parts of Britain and British America. In addition to the revivalists' radical message of freewill access to salvation, its preachers veered away from a hierarchical theology, were inclusive, and introduced free pews. They found Black American listeners particularly responsive to their message. The revival's itinerant preachers used responsive music and an excited and emotional preaching style. It is possible that the more responsive the Black listeners became,

the more excited the preachers became, gradually drawing the Anglo preachers closer to an African expression of spirituality.[155] This African style is still discernible in Black churches and white evangelical churches throughout modern America.

No Portsmouth resources record how African residents responded to the evangelical preachers who came here. George Whitefield, one of the major British evangelicals, preached in Portsmouth in 1745 and again in 1770 a month before his death.[156] Though Whitefield found Portsmouth people "unresponsive," Black New Englanders generally responded enthusiastically to his preaching. Phillis Wheatley, enslaved in Boston, wrote an elegy on Whitefield's death that was promptly published and offered for sale in Portsmouth by October 1770. A local advertisement for the publication excerpted a verse:

> He leaves this earth for Heaven's unmeasur'd
>   height:
> And worlds unknown receive him from our
>   sight;
> There Whitefield wings, with rapid course
>   his way,
> And sails to Zion, through vast seas of day.[157]

The advertisement notes with some awe that Phillis had been in the country only nine years "and yet would have done honor to a[n Alexander] Pope or Shakespere." Language was not a barrier for her.

Notwithstanding Whitefield's judgment of Portsmouth as "unresponsive," evangelical churches sprang up in the provincial capital. An Independent Congregational Baptist church had been founded by the year 1757, and an anti-Calvinist Sandemanian church was founded in 1764.[158] Jeremiah Wheelwright owned a wall pew in the independent church called "Mr. Drown's Meetinghouse."[159] Perhaps he required the attendance of his enslaved people Cato, Nero, and Jane. The only known Black member of this independent church was "Dinah," recorded through her excommunication and subsequent readmission.[160]

The late-eighteenth-century shift from Calvinist focus on eternal damnation toward a more optimistic hope of salvation coincided with increasing Black church membership. Ancestor-centered West African religious belief in rebirth into one's own family back in Africa was gradually displaced by a roughly parallel belief in eternal life in a Christian heaven.

While masters and clergy promulgated scriptural passages emphasizing obedience, the enslaved noted scriptural passages that implied the afterlife was a promised land where earthly injustices would be corrected.[161] They increasingly interpreted this in terms of righteous Blacks prevailing over iniquitous whites. The anticipation may have taken concrete form before the eyes of those who attended and viewed the annual Maundy Thursday foot-washing ceremony at Queen's Chapel four days before Easter, where they would have seen their masters humbled, washing the feet of their servants, perhaps even of their slaves.[162]

Nero Brewster, Willie Clarkson, Jock Odiorne, Pharaoh Shores: Black Coronations, Internal Status, and Social Control

"Died, on Monday last, at Col. William Brewster's, NERO, late King of the Africans, in this town, aged 75. — A Monarch, who, while living, was held in reverential esteem by his subjects—consequently, his death is greatly lamented."[163]

One of the sights of late colonial Portsmouth was the procession of the Negro Court each June. Arrayed in brilliant clothes, the region's Black population assembled, then processed out of the city center to the outskirts and returned some hours later with festive music and boisterous gunfire to a grand celebration of their newly elected monarch and his court.

This annual rite was not limited to colonial Portsmouth. In Salem, Boston, Providence, New Haven, and at least fourteen other New England towns, as well as in other American colonies, Black society chose one of its own as a community leader at an annual election.[164] In colonies where white governors were elected to office, Black leaders were usually called Negro governors. In colonies where white governors were appointed by the Crown, Black leaders were called Negro kings. The latter was the case in New Hampshire.

"Negro Election Days" were quite impressive throughout New England. There were local variations of detail, but they shared general features. The Black population assembled from all over the capital and neighboring towns. They dressed in their best clothing, often favoring brilliant colors. The day began with a procession led by the current Black governor or king. He, his officers or court (sometimes on horseback and with dress swords), and the crowd all proceeded with lively music and gunfire to the site of the elections, usually in a broad open space capable of accommodated their numbers, sometimes under and around a large a tree. After last-minute politicking came the elections. Then all processed to the home of the elected leader for an afternoon and evening of refreshments, drinking punch, music, dance, and general merriment.[165]

In colonial New Hampshire's version the procession went to Portsmouth Plains on the outskirts of town, probably following a route out Middle Street and Middle Road. For many years Nero, owned by Colonel William Brewster, was elected king. Willie Clarkson (owned by Peirse Long) was elected viceroy. Jock Odiorne was elected sheriff and Pharaoh Shores his deputy.[166] The postcoronation festivities must have been at the Bell Tavern in Congress Street, a business owned and operated by Nero's owner. It had a spacious yard two hundred feet deep, large brick stables, and an excellent garden,[167] providing ample room for such a gathering.

King Nero Brewster and his court were held in high regard by the rest of the Black population. As happened elsewhere in colonial America, King Nero served as social leader and justice for minor crimes. For example, when Prince

Jackson (owned by Nathaniel Jackson of Portsmouth's Christian Shore neighborhood) was charged with stealing an ax, he was brought before King Nero. Prince was found guilty and sentenced to twenty lashes. These were publicly administered by the king's viceroy, Willie Clarkson, at the town pump, by North Church. When Prince was later charged with larger thefts, he was prosecuted by the white county court.

White Participation and Perceptions

The traditional white tellings of Negro Coronations assume that all-powerful whites allowed these events to take place. In reality, restrictive white law failed to control interaction among Black Americans, who were creating their own social order.[168]

The law also failed to control whites. At first glance white participation appears to have been entirely as passive observers. But whites participated by failing to exercise an authority theoretically capable of preventing the event. They overtly supported it by granting free time and making loans of clothing, uniforms, swords, guns, and even horses. The king's owner condoned these lapses when he hosted a large celebration at his own expense.[169] Lastly, whites recorded the elections in their writings. These seemingly minor levels of participation carry interesting meanings.

White writings portray Negro elections in language that combines sentiment, amusement, and sometimes mockery. Whites found the institution harmless and misinterpreted it as inept mimicry of their own institutions. This signals the inability of whites to understand what they were seeing.

Whites also saw their own status reflected in Black elections. A century later Portsmouth's native son Thomas Bailey Aldrich mentioned that in colonial times "the rank of the master was the slave's rank. There was a great deal of ebony standing around on its dignity in those days."[170] Aldrich snidely voiced an otherwise accurate measure of King Nero's owner, Colonel William Brewster, as a prominent citizen.[171]

The white notion that Black elections in some degree reflected white status no doubt encouraged an owner's willingness to finance his enslaved person's participation though it might entail considerable expense. An owner's largesse was noted by other whites and—to them—demonstrated his status among them.[172] It was no doubt noted by Black people too, who might view the generous white man as a good person to work for if circumstances ever permitted.

The assignment of minor criminal cases to the jurisdiction of Black courts enabled white authorities to escape Black censure or retaliation, as in the case of the stolen ax. But whites told tales geared to undermine the courts' legitimacy. A white-narrated anecdote tells of the Black court hastening justice to avoid delaying dinner; the tale recurs in the mid–nineteenth century and again in the city's 1923 tercentennial pageant. Obviously it was meant to portray Blacks as inept. Its origin, however, is in a standard white middle-class antilawyer convention. The same convention is discernible in other eighteenth-century narratives of white injustice in Portsmouth, in nineteenth-century humor, and even in Alexander Pope's early-eighteenth-century poetry.[173] The dinner story articulates white ambivalence toward both lawyers and Black people in their midst.

Lastly, participation in this Black institution involved men, women, and children of all ranks, white and Black. This temporarily collapsed the usually rigid boundaries the white male elite tried to maintain between classes, sexes, ages, and races.[174] The cyclical, ceremonial, and temporary implosion or inversion of rank was a carefully monitored and ritualized feature of western European culture manifest at May Day, at Mardi Gras, and in Christmas lords of misrule and mummers. The seventeenth-century Puritans had relentlessly tried to eradicate these irreverent manifestations from their New England Eden. And yet here was a new variant among their eighteenth-century descendants.

Black Participation and Perspectives

White assumptions notwithstanding, the origins of Black elections were African. This fact was obscure to white New Englanders. Most whites didn't travel enough to discover that coronations were not a localized quirk, as reported by most nineteenth-century chroniclers.

Black elections were held in North and South America and the West Indies. Though far-flung, they were similar to one another in their festivity and features because they stemmed from a shared origin.[175] The event took its general form from celebrations like the spring Odwira festival of the Ashanti people who lived in an area then known as Guinea, modern Ghana. This was a ritual of social purification in which negative social forces were purged, chief and community sanctified, and ancestors honored.[176]

In western Africa leadership was not necessarily hereditary as in the European model; it was sometimes elective. In colonial America white people failed to recognize that the institution in their midst was not a naive imitation of their own institutions; it was an African tradition adapted to the conditions of American slavery.[177]

The music that seemed crude and cacophonous to Euro-American ears was an evocation of complex West African rhythms and sounds made with such instruments as were available locally. Random gunfire (rather than salutes in unison) harked to another West African tradition.

The colorful clothing—a phenomenon noted throughout the Americas—was long perceived by whites as uninformed mismatching, as an unseemly or comical inability to dress properly. In reality it was a deliberate evocation of African aesthetics. Hand-me-down garments were transfigured as patterns were juxtaposed and colors heightened by contrast. The details of this ongoing sartorial transformation are well documented, particularly in advertisements for runaways. Fortune ran away in a red jacket. Cromwell, aged forty-five, ran away from Henry Sherburne Jr. wearing a blue cloth coat and breeches, and a scarlet cloth jacket with metal buttons.[178] Jean Paul, a French Creole, ran away in 1764 wearing an earring, a red handkerchief on his head or in his pocket, a blue jacket, striped overalls, and large buckles on his half boots.[179] Scipio ran away from James Dwyer of Portsmouth in 1757 wearing "a Saxon blue Frize Jacket Lin'd with baize, slash sleeves and small Metal Buttons, a brown Fustian Jacket without sleeves, a pair of scarlet everlasting Breeches."[180] Stephen Hall, of mixed ancestry, ran away barefoot—desperation rather than an Africanism, given that it was December.[181] The colors, patterns, kerchiefs, and earrings evoked African aesthetics with American garments; they were neither wholly African nor wholly American, but African-American.[182]

Trials and the administration of punishment were a normal feature of West African society. Their appearance in colonial Negro Courts simply adapted an African tradition, though certain features of African justice—like punishment for adultery or sentences of enslavement—were perverted or obviated in America.[183]

Elections served the Black population in additional ways. Though the conditions of New England slavery worked against community, election days enabled, shaped, and celebrated Black community. Election gatherings transmitted African cultural values to a new generation. The election in many New England towns of individuals from royal or princely background, or of those who were African-born and could recite some of their lineage, shows that elections were explicitly Afrocentric events.[184] In Portsmouth, king, viceroy, sheriff, and deputy were all African-born.[185] Through shared celebration and shared respect for office, elections helped forge Africans from disparate tribes into a single Afro-American community. Elections prepared individuals for leadership roles in a free society, which, unknown to the participants, lay in the not too distant future. Precedent for this was set in 1779 when King Nero, Viceroy Willie, Sheriff Jock, and Deputy Pharaoh were among the twenty Black men who signed a petition to the New Hampshire state legislature seeking the abolition of slavery.

While Negro Coronations had elements that white society considered useful for social control, they were an African-American tradition of cultural significance and social value in their own right. They celebrated and honored the African-Americans' own autonomous leadership class.[186]

A Tradition Ends

Black elections in New England peaked around 1790, then gradually died off.[187] One reason for the decline was increasing attack from the white male power base. This happened as the event was extended from one day to several days, which intensified revelry, drinking, and gambling. White clergy and officials, who had uncomfortably endured the temporary collapse of boundaries, found this magnification unsettling. They felt that their own social order was particularly threatened by the bad example the Black elections set for those whom the white elite considered to be the "lower orders" of whites, who participated at the fringes of Black coronations. White leaders pressured all whites to disapprove the events. When the states of Connecticut and Massachusetts moved their white elections (to which their Black elections had always been connected) to autumn and winter, the associated Black elections withered because the change severed the calendar connection to spring festivals like Odwira.[188]

Another reason was that the generation that had come from Africa was dying off. Locally, King Nero Brewster died in 1786; it is unknown whether Portsmouth's Black coronations survived his death.

Post-Revolutionary manumission propelled young Black men and women into migratory job searches that broke community continuity and undermined the persistence of local traditions like coronations. In this same era, marginally employable whites found themselves competing with newly free Black people for low-level employment, and the whites didn't like it. Modern-style racism was emerging. It is possible that this racism combined with elite condemnation to convert fringe participation by whites in the Black coronations to hostility toward Black coronations. The white elite fostered racist attitudes among marginalized whites by connecting bad behavior among white youths with the Black presence, as when a local newspaper editorial complained of white and Black youths participating in the evils of Christmas sports.[189]

As free citizens Black Americans could not fight such hostility through their votes, because in most states free Black men could not vote. Meanwhile, the energies of the increasingly free Black population of New England were redirected to fighting for liberty, education, and justice. In this environment, Black elections faded from the American scene.

The Unnamed, Unrecorded Dead: Health, Medicine, Death, Burial

In colonial Portsmouth segregation applied in death as in life. Portsmouth established a "Negro Burying Ground" on what was then the edge of the compact part of downtown. It occupied the west side of Chestnut Street between State and Court Streets. While some farm families like the Langdons buried their enslaved people in segregated grounds on their own land, this plot was available for all burials of Africans. It was not a gesture of generosity, but a feature of segregation and limitation to satisfy white expectations.

The Negro burial ground was carved from one of two parcels of land called the glebe donated to the town in 1640 for the support of the ministry. One parcel was a twelve-acre area a little beyond the outer edge of the 1640s waterfront hamlet (though encompassed by today's much expanded downtown).[190]

In 1705 the town decided to improve the church's income by dividing one of its two

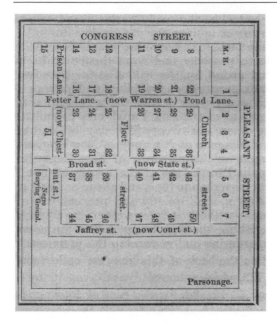

A "Negro Burying Ground" was included in the division of the glebe and appears on this 1705 lot map reprinted in Charles W. Brewster's *Rambles About Portsmouth*, 1859.

glebes into lots and renting them on long-term leases. A diagram was entered in the town record book showing proposed lot divisions. Part is marked "Negro Burying Ground."[191] Whether the map indicates an existing or new use is unclear; its active use is confirmed by a documentary reference fifty-five years later.[192]

Separate African burial grounds (or separate areas within general burial grounds) were features of many American communities.[193] In September 1991, for example, the African Burial Ground in New York City was discovered largely intact.[194]

Age and Causes of Death

Little information is available on the longevity and causes of death of colonial Portsmouth's Black population. Of twenty-one traceable cases eight died under the age of 20. Of adults, six died between ages 21 and 40, three between 41

and 50, four between 51 and 88. Recorded causes of death among adults are varied. They include consumption (tuberculosis); atrophy (complete physical deterioration); fits; fever; lockjaw (tetanus); rickets (bone deterioration from lack of vitamin D or sunlight); jaundice (excessive bile in blood, accompanied by yellowing); dropsy (abnormal accumulation of fluids in body cavities and tissues); palsy (paralysis, sometimes with tremors); palpitation of the heart; and mortified hernia.[195]

These known causes of death are too few in number to allow statistically significant generalizations. Of the eleven known causes of death, four are related to unhealthy living conditions (tuberculosis and rickets) or work (tetanus and hernia). The remainder are as equally attributable to old age as to heightened vulnerability due to bad living conditions.[196]

Some deaths were lingering, others sudden: "Last Tuesday Evening, Mr. Thomas Hart of this Town, sent his Negro Man, about Twenty-seven Years of Age, on an Errand to a Neighbor's House, being then in a State of Health, who was taken in a Fit about ten Minutes after he entered the House, and exper'd in 12 Hours. He was a very valuable Servant."[197] John Toby died an avoidable death, one recurrent even in modern New England: "We hear from Kittery, that on the 24th ult. was found dead about a mile from his House, John Toby a Mulatto. The Coroner's Inquest gave it as their Opinion That he froze to Death the weather being then extremely cold."[198]

African Medicine

What is conspicuous by its absence is death from smallpox, even though smallpox recurrently took white lives and disfigured survivors in colonial Portsmouth since 1692.[199] Europeans and Euro-Americans turned to quarantine—whence Pest Isle in Portsmouth Harbor—to hope, and to prayer to avoid this disease.

A tenth-century Arab physician first distinguished smallpox and measles from one another, and the medical practice of inoculation against smallpox had been in use in the Middle East for many centuries by the time Portsmouth was settled.[200] The practice of inoculation (sometimes called variolation from the Latin word for smallpox) appears to have spread across Islamic North Africa and down into West Africa. There it was adapted in hopes of protection against the yaws, a tropical disease with visual similarity to smallpox in the form of skin lesions.[201]

In eighteenth-century Boston, Reverend Cotton Mather learned of inoculation from his enslaved Coromantee man from West Africa. Carefully transcribing this man's speech patterns, Mather described how pus from a sick person was scratched into the skin of a healthy person. "I have since met with a considerable number of these Africans who all agree in one story: that in their country grandy-many die of the small-pox. But now they learn this way: people take juice of small-pox; and cutty-skin, and put in a drop; then by an by a little sicky-sicky, then very few little things like small-pox; and no body die of it; and no body have small-pox any more."[202] The inoculated person contracted a very mild case of the disease, recovered in three weeks, and thereafter was neither contagious nor vulnerable to the full-blown disease.[203]

Mather apparently conveyed the knowledge of inoculation from his Black informant to Dr. Zabdiel Boylston—or Boylston learned it from another African—for he was practicing the procedure by 1721.[204] Boylston first tested the technique on three people: his six-year-old son, a thirty-six-year-old Black man, and a Black child of two-and-a-half years age.[205]

Coincidentally the practice of inoculation was introduced from Constantinople (Istanbul) to Britain by Lady Mary Wortley Montague, the British ambassador's wife there, in the same year Boylston began practicing it in Boston.[206] The ancient Arab knowledge did not jump from Constantinople to England and thence to Boston in a single year. From the wording of Mather's Black informant—"in their country

grandy-many die of the small-pox but now they learn this way"—inoculation was relatively new but already established in West Africa. Africans carried it to Boston and taught it to whites like Mather. Boylston's early tests on Black people suggest additional African connections. Boston's Black community showed superior resistance in the city's smallpox outbreak of 1752, suggesting inoculation was established and widely practiced by them when it had yet to gain acceptance by whites.[207]

It took forty years for knowledge of inoculation to reach Portsmouth's white population. In 1764 Portsmouth physician Dr. Hall Jackson introduced it to his city. He quarantined the newly inoculated during the mild phase of the disease. Through the ensuing decades Jackson inoculated hundreds of people during brief three-week quarantines on various islands in the Piscataqua River. In April and May of 1778 the recently arrived Reverend Ezra Stiles of North Church had his family, household, and "my negro servant Newport" inoculated by Dr. Hall Jackson, among six hundred inoculations by three doctors in Portsmouth that spring, of whom about four hundred were residents of Portsmouth.[208]

In 1798 a British doctor, Edward Jenner, adapted inoculation effectively. He discovered that inoculation with cowpox pus would protect against smallpox (a variant procedure distinguished by the name vaccination, derived from the Latin word for cow). Encouraged by the successful precedent of inoculation, vaccination reached Boston in only two years (July 1800), and by October Dr. Lyman Spaulding was vaccinating people in Portsmouth.[209]

The procedure was already common knowledge among Black people throughout the New World. Throughout the Americas white observers had occasionally noted slaves inoculating their children but misinterpreted what they saw as infanticide by despairing parents to save their children from a life of enslavement. While those white observers missed both the moral and medical lessons, Portsmouth's Black popu-

lation probably practiced inoculation well before Hall Jackson introduced it to the town's
white public, given its use among Blacks across
three continents.

Africans brought a complex repertoire of
medical procedures, beliefs, rites, charms, and
protections, and adapted them to their new-
world setting. These were by no means inferior
to white European medicine, which was comprised of folklore, ossified wisdom inherited
from the classical world, and a century or two of
haphazard experiment that was just laying the
foundations of modern scientific procedure. Professional Euro-American medicine used leeches,
bleeding, and dangerous toxins, while white
folk medical practice relied on traditional herbal
remedies and protective superstitions, and attributed health and disease to climate, fog, and
imbalanced humors.[210]

In the context of ineffective medicine, some
whites overcame their disregard for Black culture and valued the mystery attached to the
medical practices of marginalized or "exotic"
peoples like Native Americans and Africans.
New England newspapers sometimes printed
Black folk remedies, and individuals sometimes
sought out an itinerant Black "doctoress"[211]
or adopted traditional African protections from
illness or evil.

For example a nineteenth-century anecdote,
set before 1813, tells of a white man resorting
to an African folk practice to shake off a be-
witchment associated with an uninhabited and
"haunted" seventeenth-century residence on lower
State Street lately occupied by attorney John
Samuel Sherburne.[212]

Witches or spirits would turn the unwary
passerby into a horse for the night, the tales
went, leaving the victims in the morning with
the marks of horseshoe nails on their hands and
feet and bridle sores in the mouth. One stormy
night a passerby

saw a woman walking before him with a lighted
lantern at her side. He had nearly overtaken

her, when she disappeared, but the light still
moved on before him and he was powerless to
turn from it, and before morning was led by it
into an alder swamp near the Pound, worried
and greatly fatigued. It at last occurred to him
that the woman who had preceded him with
the light was a witch, and that if he could turn
any one of his garments he had on inside out,
he would get rid of her influence. So after
great exertion he succeeded in getting his coat
off, and, turning the sleeves, put it on again,
when the light immediately disappeared and
he succeeded in getting out of the swamp into
South road.[213]

The mid-nineteenth-century chronicler of
this anecdote—at the height of the temperance
movement—wryly noted that neighbors thought
this story was a cover-up of a night spent gambling in a local tavern.

Of greater interest is that protection from
malicious spirits by turning one's clothes inside
out originated in West Africa, where belief in
spirits was strong.[214] This was one of a wide
range of West African folk protections from
evils that also included carrying talismans for
protection from disease.

While it might seem odd that African protections and medicine should be absorbed into
a religiously Calvinist or Puritan culture, it was
an easy transfer. Euro-American folk superstitions and fears were parallel to African beliefs
and included equivalent protective actions. The
educated scoffed at them as meaningless; even
theologians dismissed them as harmless super-
stition. Professional medicine often couldn't do
much better, so the protections and folk medical
practices persisted for generations.[215]

Burial Customs, Black and White

Churches of Calvinist derivation did not view
last rites or burial as sacramental. Their burial
ceremony was stark. The Calvinist theology of

predestined damnation for most souls saw nothing to celebrate. Tolling of the church bell announced a death in a well-known code that indicated gender and age of the deceased. The deceased was laid out at the home for a couple of days. Mirrors were draped. Friends were notified and gathered in mourning clothes. A minister might say a prayer. The family lined up by rank or kinship relation to the deceased (with servants or slaves on their left) and led a procession of relatives and friends to the burial place. The coffin was lowered into the ground without further words. The rattle of dirt on the coffin was the most memorable sound. The following Sunday's sermon might extract lessons from the life and death of the deceased, directly addressing surviving family from the pulpit.

The Anglican/Episcopal (Queen's Chapel/ Saint John's) burial tradition was more focused on salvation and its funeral style quite different. Burial was conducted from home or church, and the minister read scripture and said prayers at the graveside. Nonetheless, its hopeful texts were delivered in solemn style.

Black individuals who were members of a local church were probably buried according to the traditions of their adopted denomination. Unchurched Africans may have been buried according to the rites of their master's denomination or turned over to the Black community for burial according to its own customs.[216] Surely non-Christian Africans owned by unchurched white families were buried according to local Black custom.

Local records have not yielded any clues to the nature of colonial Portsmouth's Black funerals. Scattered clues from other New England towns, taken collectively, probably represent norms for New England, including Portsmouth. These burials expressed West African religious tradition and belief.

In West African tradition the deceased was expected to be reborn into his clan. This prospect was occasion for celebration. Seventeenth-century West Africans believed the deceased

would be honored by and take delight in merriment associated with this transition. Funeral processions were accompanied by music, first passing each house in a village to provide the corpse an opportunity to signal any malefactors. At the grave family and community made offerings and celebrated the prospect of rebirth.

Some of these customs carried over to New England. Euro-Americans were startled—and sometimes irritated—by meandering funeral processions, music, and celebration. In eighteenth-century Boston a series of laws and statutes were passed to stop Black funeral processions from wending about the town and to enforce less raucous observances.[217] In Hartford Zephaniah Swift remarked, "The funeral rites of a slave are performed by his brethren with every mark of joy and gladness—They accompany the corpse with the sound of musical instruments—They sing their songs and perform their dances around the grave and indulge themselves in mirth and pleasantry."[218]

Such distinctively African customs were steadily veiled in New England mannerisms. From the outset Euro-American clothing displaced African clothing. Then, as Africans were Christianized, celebration of rebirth into an African clan was transmuted into celebration of rebirth in heaven. Conversion and membership in local churches promoted adoption of the white burial styles favored by those churches. Time and locally born generations increasingly separated New England's Black people from African prototypes. But the change was a prolonged process. In nearby Salem, Massachusetts, in 1797 and 1809 the (white) Reverend William Bentley commented with satisfaction that Black funerals were increasingly sedate, indicating that the abandonment of African precedent was still in progress, if nearly complete.[219]

Portsmouth's Black funerals were probably accompanied by music, song, dance, mirth, and pleasantry. These features may have been muted but discernible as late as the 1789 funeral of a prominent individual like King Nero.[220]

In the American South a dense and segregated population of Black people enabled survival of the celebratory character of African funerals. To this day some New Orleans funeral processions thread the town en route to the burial site accompanied by solemn music and return accompanied by celebratory music.

Discontinuance of the Negro Burying Ground

The nucleated seaport town continued to grow outward toward the once peripheral Negro burial ground. In 1758 Gregory and Sarah Purcell built a large gambrel-roofed mansion near the ground's northwest corner.[221] By 1760 downtown Portsmouth had expanded to the Negro burial ground. What once had been remote wasteland suitable—in white eyes—only for the burial of a marginalized people was becoming desirable for development. In 1760 the Town of Portsmouth was preparing to build its first market house. An appointed committee evaluated a spot near the "Negro Burying Yard" but rejected it "supposing said Place not so Convenient as some other which might be Agreed on."[222] The market house was eventually built at the corner of Market and Bow Streets, but pressure for development of the Negro burial ground neighborhood was under way.

Use of the Negro burial ground appears to have been discontinued in the 1790s when most of the glebe's long-term rents were converted to something like permanent sale.[223] It appears the Negro burial ground was out of use by 1797, the year Prince Whipple was buried in the North Burial Ground. Sixteen years later J. G. Hale's 1813 map of Portsmouth shows wooden houses, several outbuildings, and a fire engine shed standing on the site of the former Negro burial ground.

What became of the old graves is unknown. During the laying of a drainpipe in the burial ground's vicinity construction workers turned up a full skeleton and a sufficient number of skulls to fill a sugar barrel. The early-twentieth-century antiquarian who noted this doesn't say at what date he saw this, nor does he comment on what became of the newly exhumed bones.[224] A turn-of-the-century widening of Chestnut Street turned up remains of coffins.[225] Together, these suggest that if any attempt was made to move remains to a new resting place, it was not thorough. Whether the effort was hampered by inadequate burial markers (as at the Langdon slave cemetery) or racist indifference, or whether no attempt at removal was made, is unknown.

The clustering of several Black burials near a back corner of Portsmouth's North Burial Ground suggests Portsmouth may have adopted a common regional practice of spatial segregation within a mostly white public burial ground, affirming the continuing white need for differentiation and evidence of separation and superiority.[226]

Whatever the details, the discontinuation of the Negro burial ground represents an early move by white authorities to cleanse the New England narrative of the historical presence of Black people.

The Cotton and Hunking Families: Family, Women, Marriage

Creating a family under the conditions of slavery was a challenge. The earliest discernable Black *family* in Portsmouth was recorded in 1717 when Joseph and Nancy and their two children Eleazor and James (all owned by William Cotton) were baptized by the Reverend John Emerson of South Church. Later that year Reverend Emerson also baptized Tony and his three children, Caesar, James, and Samson, held in slavery by Colonel Hunking.[227]

The absence of Tony's wife from the record hints at one difficulty of maintaining a marriage in slavery. His wife may have belonged to another owner, or been sold away, or succumbed to the unhealthy environment of attic or basement living.

Forging a family required an accommodation of African precedents to New England realities. West African communities were built around extended families. Many distantly related people kept track of a shared common ancestry. Unity was strong, and communities were stable. Elders arranged marriages between clans, taking into account suitability. Premarital play among the betrothed was allowed, perhaps partly to measure compatibility. Bride-wealth payments proved the ability of the husband to take good care of brides.[228] Polygamy was allowed to men of wealth and high rank.[229] A bride moved from her clan of birth into the clan of the husband, where she was governed by her husband and the clan patriarch, and accommodated her role to the husband's senior co-wives.[230] Stern justice limited unsanctioned sexual activity.

White New England culture urged enslaved Africans to adopt and adhere to white Protestant marriage practices, notably to monogamous, faithful, patriarchal unions sanctioned by justices or ministers. White society simultaneously set up a series of obstacles to these ideals, creating in its midst a scenario it found troubling.

First, whites made marriage impossible for half the Black male population by importing more males than females.[231] Portsmouth had a ratio of roughly two Black men to every Black woman. With an unofficial prohibition on interracial unions, half the Black male population had no option of marriage within Protestantism's monogamous expectations.

Second, by removing responsibility for child rearing from the parents, New England's white society removed one of the most powerful motives to keep a marriage intact during stressful times. Children of enslaved people belonged not to the parents but to the mother's owner. A 1731 Portsmouth bylaw explicitly assigned responsibility for married Black or Indian people to their owners and, by implication, the off-spring of such unions.[232] Owners had no incentive to approve marriage if it would incur child-rearing expenses. By removing responsibility for a child from its parents, white society perverted the marriage bond among the enslaved. A child's status of free or slave followed the mother's status, further perverting the parent-child bond. White men who forced themselves on enslaved women found themselves enslavers and sometimes sellers of their own children. The white father's conscience might be eased by an institutionalized white outlook in which a white woman could give birth to a Black child but a Black woman could not give birth to a white child. A biracial child was called "mulatto" or "yellow." Mulatto is a term of scorn originating in a Spanish word for mule, a cross between a horse and donkey, indicative of belonging to neither group.[233] Classified as Black, a biracial child was forced to endure white scorn, starting with that of its white parent.

Third, New England's white society physically isolated married slaves in the separate households of their owners. Life in rooms shared by others must have minimized the opportunities for private conjugal visits. The perennial possibility that one spouse or the other might be sold out of town added stress. Life shared in marriage was impossible, corrupting the institution.

While white New Englanders raged against adultery, they rarely applied their own laws and customs to the enslaved. Owners of males willingly overlooked extramarital sexual activity to avoid the potential expense that might be brought by formal marriage. In certain circumstances destitute offspring would become the financial responsibility of the father's owner. Better not to know the father's identity. As a result adultery among the enslaved was not subject to either African or Yankee restraints or social networks. Relative to the way kinship and marriage functioned in western Africa, the captives had been transported from civilized Africa to savage America.[234]

Marriage and Alternatives

Prior to 1760 few Black marriages are recorded in local church records. From 1760 to 1810 about one hundred marriages of Black couples are recorded in Portsmouth's church records.[235] Change was under way.

Some chose ministerial weddings because they had adopted local religion and wished to follow its principles. Others may have chosen this route to pacify their owners. But a ministerial marriage challenged as much as pacified. It demanded of a slave owner that he recognize the validity of the marriage by his own religious standards.[236]

The enslaved developed new types of relationships. Some entered common-law marriages, in which they simply declared themselves married and conducted themselves accordingly, to whatever degree was practical.[237] This might be accompanied by the gift of some symbolic token of endearment from the man to the woman.[238]

Where men greatly outnumbered available women and the conventions of marriage were frustrated, some enslaved men and women turned to extramarital sexual activity. The white owners of male slaves were especially willing to overlook this activity because the expenses of child rearing would fall on the mother's owner if the father were unknown. The white clergy and the pious excoriated and scorned this sexual activity as promiscuous. They misinterpreted it as characteristic of Africans, though it was a situation created by whites.[239]

Multiple relationships had a West African precedent; polygamy was allowed to men of wealth and rank. For men taken from such cultures multiple partnerships were an opportunity to create or imply status in new circumstances that attempted to deny all status.[240]

Black men who were granted or purchased their freedom sometimes bought freedom for their wife or bride-to-be. This happened in Portsmouth, for example, when Richard Mullinaux bought Nan Appleton in 1799.[241] Such a purchase, while reminiscent of bride-wealth

payments, brought the ability to live and love as they pleased.[242] Only in such a rare situation of freedom for both spouses could Africans in early New England know their families were secure.

A New Status for African Women in America

Adaptation to new situations brought a new status to Black women, notably a level of independence from their husbands and a modest freedom from traditional patriarchies. Whether married or not, enslaved women often raised their children in the absence of the children's father because of the obstacles imposed by enslavement. The children of the enslaved were likely to bear their mother's last name rather than their father's, until sold to another owner. As a result Black women in America were in many regards independent of their husbands in a way unknown among West African or white women.

A tier of female supervision interceded between enslaved women and their master. Though technically owned by the white mater, enslaved women appear to have received direct supervision not from him but from the mistress of the household, as did white hired girls. White women were allowed to own property and personal estate, though their fathers or husbands technically administered these. For example, on March 1, 1773, Mary Langdon (wife of John Langdon Sr.) bought from Elizabeth Lear of Portsmouth a woman named Violet.[243] In such instances both the African and Anglo patterns of patriarchy were displaced.

Delivered from West Africa's patriarchal social structure, African women found little reason to adopt a Christian variant of subordination. An informal matriarchal and matrilineal society emerged among enslaved African women in America, including in New England.[244]

The creation of new forms of relationships between the sexes was not peculiar to Portsmouth or New England but existed throughout the

Americas. These new relationships were neither African nor Euro-American nor characteristic of Black people. They were an enslaved people's adaptation to imposed circumstances.

Revolutionary Petitioners: Politics and Freedom

One of Portsmouth's icons of American independence is the colonial mansion known today as the Moffatt-Ladd House. In 1776 its occupant, William Whipple, was part of the Congress in Philadelphia that wrote the Declaration of Independence, which he signed.

Local tradition holds that Whipple commemorated the momentous event by planting horse chestnut trees in front of the house. The trees grew with the new nation. One tree survives at the southeast corner of the house and is treasured as a living monument to the Revolutionary era. While tradition assumes William Whipple planted and nurtured those chestnut trees, these tasks likely fell to one of the enslaved men in his household, Prince or Windsor.[245]

Word of the Declaration raced up the eastern seaboard ahead of the printed copies distributed to the various colonies. Like all towns, Portsmouth was abuzz, and when the paper copy arrived a crowd gathered to hear the electrifying document read from the balcony of the State House in the seaport's central square. Black men and women no doubt hovered at the edge of the crowd forming opinions of their own.

The bold gesture of white colonists against an oppressive government resonated quite differently among slaves. Those in the households of Portsmouth's politically active white families—like Frank Stoodley, a slave at the tavern to which Paul Revere conveyed urgent news in December 1774—were well situated to hear the rationale, rhetoric, and progress of white independence. They listened closely, absorbed all, and interpreted what they heard in their own terms.

In the midst of the Revolutionary War Prince Whipple and Windsor Moffatt were among a group of twenty Black men who made their own bid. Three and a half years after the white Declaration of Independence, on November 12, 1779, a group of slaves submitted a petition for their own freedom to the New Hampshire state legislature.

"To the honorable Council and House of Representatives of said State now sitting at Exeter in and for said State," the petition solemnly begins. It then continues with the names of the petitioners. "The petition of Nero Brewster, Pharaoh Rogers, Romeo Rindge, Cato Newmarch, Cesar Gerrish, Zebulon Gardner, Quam Sherburne, Samuel Wentworth, Will Clarkson, Jack Odiorne, Cipio Hubbard, Seneca Hall, Peter Warner, Cato Warner, Pharaoh Shores, Windsor Moffatt, Garrott Colton, Kittindge Tuckerman, Peter Frost and Prince Whipple, natives of Africa, now forcibly detained in slavery in said State most humbly sheweth that the God of Nature gave them Life and Freedom upon the terms of the most perfect Equality with other men."

They drew up and signed their petition at Portsmouth on November 12, 1779, just as Whipple and others had signed the Declaration.[246]

Origins and Authorship of the Petition

Other than the names and bits of biographical information about those who signed the petition, little is known about its origins. Certain signatures—notably those of King Nero Brewster, Viceroy Willie Clarkson, Sheriff Jock Odiorne, Deputy Pharaoh Shores—suggest the text was composed at a meeting convened by the Negro Court. King Nero's name at the very beginning suggests that he presided over the meeting, perhaps that he wrote the text, and certainly expresses his status as the Black community's titular head and spokesman.

The petition is closely reasoned, and its prose adheres to the canons of literary elegance for its time. Similar petitions from Boston were written in a much more vernacular language.[247] The text declares that all twenty signers were born in Africa and taken away in childhood; they had had their lifetimes to learn English. Their names show that they had spent their lives among the city's white elite. Given African-born Boston poet Phillis Wheatley's mastery of the language under identical circumstances there is no reason to assume the petition was put into words by a sympathetic white author. Whatever the minutiae of the petition's authorship, its existence shows the effective operation of a Black social and political culture in Revolutionary-era Portsmouth.

Revolutionary Rhetoric

The petition's rhetoric shows that the men had fully absorbed and understood the philosophies of the era. They used moral and religious arguments, invoking the inherent free equality granted all by the "God of Nature" who "gave them Life and Freedom upon the terms of the most perfect Equality with other men." Their nuanced phrasing even signals a knowledge of the rationalist Deism circulating at the time.

They used characteristic eighteenth-century political arguments, equating the "private tyranny" of slavery with the same "public" or political tyranny the Revolutionary leaders were trying to throw off. The petitioners carefully balanced political pleas, reason, and challenges.

The petitioners appealed to local religion too, with a subtle understanding of how white readers would react. They contrasted their "Native country where (though ignorance and un-Christianity prevailed) they were born free" to this country "where (though knowledge, Christianity and freedom, are their boast) they are compelled and their unhappy posterity to drag on their lives in miserable servitude!"

They did not complain, they said, they just wanted to know in what source their captors found authority to hold them. "We would wish to know," they queried, "Is it from the sacred volumes of Christianity?" "Is it from the volumes

of the law?" "Is it from the volumes of nature?" To each question they answered that they could not be sure but were told—presumably by those who enslaved them—the answer was negative. They slyly confessed that they were unsure, because knowledge of religion had been "hid from our minds," and all they knew of law was that it was "founded in reason and justice," hinting that the white man's law of reason might be unreasonable, irrational, and unjust.

Anticipating arguments, the petitioners doubted the financial loss that manumission might inflict on their owners, who, after all, had enjoyed lifetimes of virtually free service, "as we have most of us spent our whole strength and the prime of our lives" in their service.

They appealed to the heart with images of the bereaved mother, her "cheek wet for the loss of a child torn by the cruel hand of violence from her aching bosom!" and the infant's sighing in vain "for the nurturing care of its bereaved parent." They bluntly excoriated the victimization of "the ties of nature and blood" in the service of their owners' "vanity and luxury."

As a whole, the petition of 1779 follows a carefully constructed rationale.

A Recent British Court Case

The petition's allusions to Christianity and law may have been meant to remind legislators of an argument that British law annulled a slave's condition if he was baptized a Christian. This legal interpretation, ignored in America, stemmed from a 1749 British law case.[248]

More important, knowledge of a recent British law case that might have annulled slavery throughout Britain and its empire may have been kept secret from the petitioners. News that a decision was imminent had been announced in the *New Hampshire Gazette* in 1772.[249]

The case was heard before William, Lord Murray, first earl of Mansfield, chief justice of King's Bench.[250] An African, ultimately named James Somerset, had been enslaved in Africa and resold in Virginia to Charles Stewart, who brought him to London. While in London James ran away; he was recovered and delivered to a ship captain to be held on board awaiting the ship's departure for Jamaica, where James was to be sold. Three friends applied to the court for issuance of a writ of habeas corpus, and James Somerset was brought before the court to present his suit for liberty.

A hearing and judgment ensued. In 1772 Lord Murray found that slavery was so "odious" that it could exist only if there were a specific written law allowing it. No such law existing in Britain, Somerset must be free. In effect, any enslaved person who set foot in Britain would become free. Theoretically slavery had never existed in Britain. It had, of course, but importation of slaves to Britain rapidly slowed to a stop, and the decision was a major step toward the end of slavery there. This decision technically applied to the entire British Empire, but apparently it was suppressed and certainly ignored by white slaveholders everywhere.[251] Because Murray's decision implied that slavery never had a legal existence in Britain, it is sometimes misinterpreted today as saying that slavery never had a historical existence in Britain.

Mansfield's decision was published in America, though apparently not in Portsmouth. Nonetheless information about it circulated. Fragmentary knowledge of Mansfield's decision became entwined with an earlier debate about the freedom of a baptized slave. A 1774 advertisement in the *New Hampshire Gazette* alludes to these. The ad tells of Pompey, who ran away from Captain Benjamin Littlefield of nearby Wells, Maine, after consulting a justice about the decision. Pompey "says he was baptized in London and that he is become a free Negro having obtained the opinion of David Sewall, Esq."[252] One of Boston's three slave petitions explicitly cited Lord Mansfield's decision.

Though white Americans ignored Mansfield's decision, slavery was hard to reconcile with the rhetoric of independence. By 1774 advertisements in the Portsmouth newspaper for slave sales were diminishing, and advertisements for runaways were increasing.[253]

The Portsmouth petition of 1779 was a bold address to the respected leaders of the enslaving community. The petitioners described themselves as aged. Their productive years had been stolen from them; they had everything to gain for their posterity.

Outcome

The petition was transcribed into the records of the House of Representatives at its next session, on April 25, 1780. Upon reading and considering the petition the legislature "Voted. That the petitioners be heard thereon before the General Assembly on the first Friday of their next session, and that they in the meantime cause the substance of the petition and order of court thereon to be published three weeks successively in the New Hampshire Gazette that any person or persons may then appear and shew cause why the prayer thereof may not be granted." It was "Sent up for concurrence" by John Langdon, Speaker, and In Council [the governor's Council] the same day read and concurred," and signed by "J. Pearson, Sec'y."[254]

As instructed by the legislature the petition was published in its entirety in the *Gazette* on July 15, 1780. White response to this extraordinary document is summed up by the editorial disclaimer that it was printed "for the amusement" of its readers.

The House voted to postpone a hearing on the petition. A hearing was never held, and there was no further legislative action on it.

Though the legislature never entertained arguments on behalf of the petition, the petition's message was ultimately comprehended by some of the petitioners' owners. Ten years later six petitioners were free and independent family heads: Peter Warner, Pharaoh Shores, Jock Odiorne, Prince Whipple, Cesar Gerrish, and Romeo Rindge.[255] Other petitioners, however, remained enslaved. For most slaves in Portsmouth an-

Petition to the New Hampshire Government
1779

To the honorable Council and House of Representatives of said State now sitting at Exeter in and for said State:

The petition of Nero Brewster, Pharaoh Rogers, Romeo Rindge, Cato Newmarch, Cesar Gerrish, Zebulon Gardner, Quam Sherburne, Samuel Wentworth, Will Clarkson, Jack Odiorne, Cipio Hubbard, Seneca Hall, Peter Warner, Cato Warner, Pharaoh Shores, Windsor Moffatt, Garrott Colton, Kittindge Tuckerman, Peter Frost and Prince Whipple, natives of Africa, now forcibly detained in slavery in said State most humbly sheweth that the God of Nature gave them Life and Freedom upon the terms of the most perfect Equality with other men;

that Freedom is an inherent right of the human species not to be surrendered, but by consent, for the sake of social life;

that private or public tyranny and slavery are alike detestable to minds conscious of the equal dignity of human nature;

that in power and authority of individuals derived solely from a principle of coercion against the will of individuals and to dispose of their persons and properties consists the completest idea of private and political slavery;

that all men being amenable to the Deity, for the ill improvement of the Blessings of his Providence they hold themselves in duty bound, strenuously to exert every faculty of their minds to obtain that blessing of freedom which they are justly entitled to from the donation of the beneficent Creator;

that through ignorance and brutish violence of their countrymen, and by the sinister designs of others (who ought, to have taught them better) and by the avarice of both, they, while but children and incapable of self-defense, whose infancy might have prompted protection, were seized, imprisoned and transported from their native country where (though ignorance and un-Christianity prevailed) they were born free, to a country where (though knowledge, Christianity and freedom, are their boast) they are compelled and their unhappy posterity to drag on their lives in miserable servitude!

Thus, often is the parent's cheek wet for the loss of a child torn by the cruel hand of violence from her aching bosom! Thus, often, and in vain, is the infant's sigh for the nurturing care of its bereaved parent. And thus do the ties of nature and blood become victims, to cherish the vanity and luxury of a fellow mortal! Can this be right? Forbid it gracious Heaven!

Permit again your humble slaves to lay before this honorable assembly some of those grievances which they daily experience and feel. Though fortune hath dealt out our portions with rugged hand, yet hath she smiled in the disposal of our persons to those who claim us as their property; of them, as masters, we do not complain, but from what authority they assume the power to dispose of our lives, freedom and property we would wish to know.

Is it from the sacred volumes of Christianity? There we believe it is not to be found but here hath the cruel hand of slavery made us incompetent judges, hence knowledge is hid from our minds!

Is it from the volumes of the law? Of these also, slaves cannot be judges but those, we are told, are founded in reason and justice. It cannot be found there!

Is it from the volumes of nature? No! Here we can read with others, of this knowledge slavery cannot wholly deprive us. Here we know that we ought to be free agents! Here we feel the dignity of human nature. Here we feel the passions and desires of men, though checked by the rod of slavery. Here we feel a just equality. Here, we know that the God of Nature made us free!

Is their authority assumed from custom? If so, let that custom be abolished which is not founded in nature, reason nor religion.

Should the humanity and benevolence of the honorable assembly restore us to that state of liberty of which we have been so long deprived, we conceive that those who are our present masters will not be sufferers by our liberation, as we have most of us spent our whole strength and the prime of our lives in their service. And as freedom inspires a noble confidence and gives the mind an emulation to view in the noblest efforts of enterprise, and as justice and humanity are the result of your deliberations, we fondly hope that the eye of pity and heart of justice may commiserate our situation and put us upon the equality of freemen and give us an opportunity of evincing to the world our love of freedom, by exerting ourselves in her cause, in opposing the efforts of tyranny and oppression over the country in which we ourselves have been so long injuriously   enslaved.

Therefor, your humble slaves most devoutly pray for the sake of injured liberty; for the sake of justice, humanity, and the rights of mankind; for the honor of religion; and by all that is dear, that your honors would graciously interpose in our behalf and enact such laws and regulations as you in your wisdom think proper, whereby we may regain our liberty and be ranked in the class of free agents and that the name of slave may not more be heard in a land gloriously contending for the sweets of freedom; and your humble slaves as in duty bound will ever pray.

Portsmouth November 12th, 1779

Seneca Hall	Pharaoh Rogers
Peter Frost	Will Clarkson
Zebulon Gardner	Windsor Moffatt
Peter Warner	Romeo Rindge
Prince Whipple	Jack Odiorne
Quam Sherburne	Garrett Colton
Cato Warner	Cato Newmarch
Nero Brewster	Cipio Hubbard
Samuel Wentworth	Kittindge Tuckerman
Pharaoh Shores	Cesar Gerrish

State of New Hampshire:
In the House of Representatives,
April 25, 1780.

New Hampshire Provincial Papers, *ed. Nathaniel Boulton,* 18.705–7.

other fifteen to twenty years passed before they were freed, and some in New Hampshire waited sixty years or were never freed.

Prince Whipple: Revolution and Freedom

Prince Whipple is buried in Portsmouth's North Burial Ground on Maplewood Avenue. His grave is marked with emblems of veteran's service in the Revolutionary War.[256] Much of what is known about this Black veteran of the Revolution derives from oral tradition, recorded—errors and all—decades later. A few written documents substantiate, correct, or disprove these traditions.

Prince had been a free person in Africa. At an unknown date he came to America when a child.[257] Though local tales are full of additional but unverifiable detail, they are likely accurate in saying Prince left Africa as a free youth and was unwillingly enslaved.[258]

Prince ended up in the ownership of sometime sea captain William Whipple and his wife Katharine Moffatt. They lived in her father's three-story mansion set on a high turf terrace looking across the street and down the steep riverbank to their warehouses, wharves, and the

The *New Hampshire Gazette* published the 1779 petition of 20 enslaved Africans in Portsmouth with a dismissive prefatory remark. *Courtesy Portsmouth Athenæum.*

river.[259] Another enslaved man in the household appears to have been Windsor Moffatt, who had come into the family via Katherine. Cuffee, or Cuff, thought to be a relation of Prince's, probably lived in the house too but reputedly was given by William to his brother Joseph Whipple, at about the time the two white Whipples ceased operating a business together.[260]

Black and White Whipples in the Revolution

William Whipple had earlier served in the New Hampshire militia and would serve in the Revolution. Though New Hampshire law forbade Black men from serving in the militia, Prince would witness some important events of the Revolution in William's company. In 1775, as a series of skirmishes flared on the eastern seaboard, William was appointed to the rank of colonel of the First New Hampshire Regiment. Prince likely accompanied him during some of his early assignments.[261]

In 1776 William Whipple was one of New Hampshire's representatives to the Continental Congress and spent much time in Philadelphia. Independence was declared in July, and a state of war was officially entered. Congress had much work to do; it convened again that autumn. Whether Prince accompanied William is undocumented.

By December of 1776 the British, overseeing their campaign from winter headquarters in New York, had advanced their troops and Hessian mercenaries through New Jersey and established outposts in Princeton and Trenton. In response to this approaching hazard Congress left Philadelphia in early December and reconvened in Baltimore on December 20. The congressmen found an uneasy safety in their new location, 130 miles from Trenton. William Whipple—and Prince, if William took him on this trip—was in Baltimore when Washington received last-minute reinforcements and was able to execute the now famous surprise Christmas evening crossing of the Delaware River to rout the British in the Battle of Trenton on the morning of December 26.[262]

In 1777, with war accelerating, William was back in New Hampshire. William Whipple went to Exeter to attend a special session of the New Hampshire legislature, which convened there for security should the British seize Portsmouth. Exeter was a prosperous market town on the fall line at the head of the Piscataqua estuary. The legislature appointed Whipple to the rank of brigadier general. He was assigned to the First New Hampshire Brigade and instructed to participate in the effort to drive British general Burgoyne out of New York.[263] William took Prince with him. Prince was again with General Whipple at Saratoga 1777 and in the Rhode Island campaign of 1778.[264]

A local tradition that William Whipple freed Prince upon departure for war is wrong.[265] Prince remained enslaved by Whipple seven years longer. He was not manumitted until February 26, 1784.[266] The inaccurate tradition originated with a white antiquarian who may have wished to improve the founding father's reputation at a time of increasing white abolitionism.

After the war, Prince's status began a gradual transformation. Curiously, Prince was allowed the rights of a freeman on February 22, 1781, three years before he was actually manumitted.[267] What this meant—granted the rights of a freeman, yet remaining legally enslaved—is puzzling. It was likely related in some way to Prince's marriage, which appears to have taken place on the same day Prince was granted these rights. Perhaps it in some way assured the legal legitimacy of the marriage. Prince married a Black woman, Dinah Chase, manumitted at age twenty-one, on February 22, 1781, the day of her marriage, by her former owner, Reverend Chase of Newcastle.[268]

After his manumission in 1784 Prince Whipple enjoyed full freedom for only twelve years; he died in 1796. He was remembered as a "large, well-proportioned man, and of gentlemanly manners and deportment." Even nineteenth-century white antiquarians recalled that among the Black population he was regarded as a leader.[269] Prince Whipple's life and family in freedom are discussed in a subsequent chapter.

Africans in the Revolution

Artists Thomas Sully (in 1819) and Emmanuel Leutze (in 1851) both depicted a Black man among the crowd of men in their heroically scaled paintings of George Washington's Christmas evening crossing of the Delaware River.[270] Portsmouth legend wrongly claims the Black man was Prince Whipple. If Prince was with William Whipple at the Congress in Baltimore, William was highly unlikely to have sent him 130 miles on his own into potential enemy territory, especially when the British were offering emancipation in exchange for defection. Portsmouth is not alone in promoting a story of local Black involvement at that event of mythic importance. Other New England towns offer claimants for the same honor, such as Prince Estabrook of Lexington (later of Ashby), Massachusetts.[271]

The legend of Prince Whipple's presence at that fateful winter crossing originated in the book *Colored Patriots of the American Revolution.* Published in 1855, it is a pioneering work by Black historian William C. Nell. The error occurred during Nell's efforts to reconstruct the story when the principal players were all dead and gone. It suggests that the tale was already established and circulating in Portsmouth at that date, perhaps among Prince's descendants. It may represent a merger of general recollections of Prince's accompanying William in various Revolutionary campaigns and of the Whipples' presence in the mid-Atlantic region at the Continental Congress. While there is a thread of possibility that Nell recorded an accurate family narrative, documents and documentary gaps argue heavily for its improbability.

Beyond questions of its veracity, the tale symbolizes and emphasizes something much more important: Black participation in the Revolution. Nell published when northern whites were joining the abolitionist cause. White and Black abolitionists alike represented an ending to the institution of slavery as a necessary step in fulfilling the Revolutionary vision of freedom. It was important to remind their audience of the very real historical participation of Black men in the Revolution. Black people had helped win freedom for white people who then denied it to them or—as in the Whipple case—postponed it for years.

Though Prince Whipple probably was not there, many Black men were among Washington's six thousand troops who crossed the icy Delaware River during that nighttime squall. Hessian private Johannes Reuber, serving the British in Colonel Johann Gottlieb Rall's regiment, wrote in his diary of the American forces gathering across the river as including "black Negroes and yellow dogs." While the diarist used race and cowardice to defame the American enemy, his remark confirms even the British military knowledge of the presence of Black men among the American forces amassing on the banks of the Delaware.[272]

Washington had argued against allowing Black men to serve in the Continental Army. Many colonies and states had long-standing statutory or customary prohibitions of Black participation in state militias. New Hampshire forbade Black service by a statute of 1718. Such laws were based on white disbelief in Black initiative and effectiveness in battle. Statutes and traditions notwithstanding, urgent need eventually prompted Washington cautiously to approve the participation of *free* Black men in the Revolution. Rhode Island and Massachusetts subsequently mustered all-Black regiments.

At least 180 Black men from New Hampshire served in the Revolution. Most served in the Continental Army, some in the militia, navy, or aboard privateers. This was a significant proportion of New Hampshire's total enslaved population of about 630 men, women, and children.

While most of New Hampshire's Black population lived in Portsmouth, a disproportionately high number of New Hampshire's Black soldiers in the Continental Army came from rural areas. The reasons are unclear. Perhaps rural white populations were more lax about enforcing subordinate status for Black people. Certainly the tensions of the times made urban whites more wary; during the Revolution Portsmouth newspapers reprinted old curfew laws regarding slaves. Alternatively, Portsmouth's Black men may have been serving in proportional numbers in the navy and aboard privateers, for which fewer records survive than for the Continental Army.

The Black service record is parallel to the white record. Some were wounded, some died of illness, some died in action, and a few deserted. Overall, Black soldiers tended to serve longer than white soldiers, some through the entire war. Ignoring this evidence of good service, New Hampshire prohibited Black participation when it revised its militia statutes in the 1780s.

Some Black men who served in the Revolution remained enslaved, and their owners kept their pay. Others were manumitted upon enrollment or at the war's end. Some received their pay, pensions, or land grants on schedule. Others spent years beseeching the government for their pay. Applications for pensions provide a useful source of information about when and where they served.[273]

Manumitted Black men and women found themselves in a hostile white society unwilling to create a place for them. Even with later abolition, Black people would find the ideals of the Revolution were withheld from them.[274]

Free Black People in an Era of Slavery

Thus far this has been a narrative of people in enslavement. The region's colonial population included free Black people too. When and where the first free Black people settled in Portsmouth remains unknown, but the presence of free Blacks is implied in a 1731 Portsmouth ordinance that exempted the town poor-relief funds from caring for them should they become indigent.[275]

There were several routes to freedom, though numbers show they were unavailable to most. A very few Black people arrived from Africa as freemen—as oral tradition implies was the intent of Prince and Cuffee Whipple—and remained here as freemen.

Birth to a free mother, white or Black, was another source of free people of color in the colonial population. Housewright Hopestill Cheswell is an example. By contrast Scipio Dwyer remained enslaved, probably because he had a free white father and enslaved mother.

Another route to freedom was direct manumission by an owner. In the midst of the Revolution in 1778 Ezra Stiles, minister of Portsmouth's North Church, freed his slave Newport.

Sometimes direct manumission was granted after a fixed amount of time. For example, in 1791 Joanna Severett's will stated that after her death her "Negro woman" was to serve her sister "twenty years and then be free" (though she gave her "two servant boys" to her brother John without conditional freedom).[276] Many late-life manumissions appear in the Portsmouth records.

A few exceptional cases freed those young enough to have the prospect of years of freedom, as when the minister of nearby New Castle freed Dinah Chase at age twenty-one. Romeo Rindge, a signer of the 1779 petition for freedom, is listed as an independent head of household in the 1790 census.[277] Romeo's former owner, Daniel Rindge, who died in 1812, left Romeo provisions and an annual allowance from his estate. "As it is my intention that my former servant Romeo Freeman shall not want a comfortable living I hereby encumber my whole estate with such a sum in addition to what he the said Romeo may be able to earn by his labor as will in the opinion of my executor be sufficient for that purpose."[278] Over the ensuing years this bequest provided shoes, firewood, clothing, and medical expenses, which carried Romeo and his wife through his final illness and funeral.[279]

Some of the enslaved purchased their freedom. This required a master who was agreeable to the idea of such a sale and required that the owner allow the slave some time of his own for independent moneymaking labor. Years of work and hope could be stymied by a capricious refusal to fulfill the pledge. Nonetheless, a handful of people purchased their freedom by this means. In the midst of the Revolutionary War Violet ("widow of Boston") bought her freedom from Abraham Dearborn on March 25, 1778.[280]

Once free, some purchased a fiancé or spouse out of bondage into freedom, as did Black mariner Richard Mullinaux, who purchased from William Appleton nineteen-year-old Nan, whom he married a week later.[281]

In the turbulent 1770s, another possibility for release from slavery came as a reward for faithful patriotic service in the Revolution. This worked irregularly, as described above in the case of Prince Whipple.

Self-Emancipation: A Sample Case

Self-emancipation was another possibility. White owners perceived this act as "running away." The colonial-era *New Hampshire Gazette* carried many advertisements for runaways. Surely some successfully presented themselves elsewhere as free, or disappeared into protective free Black families.

One who emancipated herself is Ona Marie Judge (sometimes rendered in the diminutive Oney and the alternative spelling Jud), who hid successfully in Portsmouth and environs. Since childhood the biracial, fair, and freckled Ona had been Martha Washington's slave, for whom she served as a housekeeper and expert seamstress. In 1796, near the end of Washington's second term as president, Ona fled the presidential household at Philadelphia, then the nation's capital. George Washington, incredulous that the prospect of a lifetime in slavery was reason enough to flee, at first believed the twenty-two-year-old Ona had been seduced and abducted by a Frenchman. Washington expected this imagined villain would impregnate and abandon Ona to eke out a living at needlework. Ona, meanwhile, had found her way to Portsmouth.

Years later Ona said she had come on a ship captained by John Bolles, which she long kept secret lest he be punished. Washington eventually learned that Ona was in Portsmouth, probably through a "Miss Langdon" (perhaps Elizabeth Langdon), a sometime visitor of the Washingtons, who had recognized Ona in the Portsmouth streets.

On behalf of Washington, Secretary of the Treasury Oliver Wolcott located a ship embarking from Portsmouth for Philadelphia and by letter called for Ona to come to him, as if to employ her.[282] Through their correspondence Wolcott learned Ona thought well of the Washingtons yet had run away to be free. Wolcott told Ona she would be free upon George Washinton's death. Ona doubted this, as she believed

Eight DOLLARS Reward.

RUN away the 19th last. from *James Dwyer* of *Portsmouth*, a NEGRO MAN named *Scipio*, about forty Years of Age, a Subtle well set Fellow, five Feet ten Inches high, speaks good English, he carried with him 4 woollen check Shirts, one white ditto, 2 new under Jackets, one white lapelled Jacket bound with black, one new blue Kersey lapelled Jacket lined with red Baise and trimed with Metal Buttons, a brown Coat with Metal Buttons, one pair of black Plush Breeches, one pair of blue Cloth ditto. 2 pair of Yarn Stockings, 2 pair of worsted ditto, a new Hat, a new Worsted Cap and 2 pair of Shoes, &c. &c. &c.

Whoever apprehends said NEGRO, and brings him to his Master, shall receive Eight DOLLARS Reward and all necessary Charges paid by   JAMES DWYER.

N. B. All Masters of Vessels and others, are cautioned against secreting or carrying off said Negro, as they would avoid the penalty of the Law. †§† It is supposed he is in Company with Seneca, a Negro Man of Mr. Hale's.

Portsmouth, August 20*th,* 1764.

Six DOLLARS Reward.

RUN away from his Master Samuel Hall of Portsmouth, on Tuesday last a NEGRO MAN named Seneca, a thick set Fellow, about Thirty six Years of Age, and five Feet eight Inches high, with a Scar over his left Eye: He took with him one great Coat, five Jackets, three pair of Breeches, one pair of Trowsers, six pair of Stockings, two pair of Shoes, two Hats and Caps and three Shirts; Whoever will take up said NEGRO, and bring him to his said Master, shall have SIX DOLLARS Reward and all necessary Charges paid.

N. B. All Masters of Vessels and others are forbid carrying off said Negro, as they will answer the Penalty of the Law.

If he will return of his own Accord his Fault shall be forgiven.   *July* 16*th.*

When slaves freed themselves, the owners' runaway notices reveal much about both the owner and the fugitive slave. The colonial-era *New Hampshire Gazette* has many such advertisements. Details of clothing and physical descriptions provide clues about the lives of people for whom little other documentation exists. In these examples, the owner of Scipio (who ran from the same owner 7 years earlier) suspects his servant has taken off with the other escapee, Seneca. Both owners remind shipmasters of a law against transporting escaped slaves. Offers of generous rewards for the capture of these men—and a promise of forgiveness—indicate that both workers were highly valued by their owners. It is likely that if the escapees returned they would be able to negotiate some improved privileges. *Courtesy Portsmouth Athenæum.*

Washinton's will called for her bequeathal to his granddaughter, Eliza Custis. Nonetheless, Wolcott convinced Ona to go back to the Washingtons. A day's delay in the ship's departure gave Ona's friends time to convince her to stay in Portsmouth.

At some point Ona married a Black sailor, named John Staines, and had a child by him. Ona later told how Washington twice sent his nephew Burwell Bassett to Portsmouth, the first time to persuade Ona to return, the second time to bring home by force both her and her child, whom Washington still owned under the laws of the time. On his second visit to Portsmouth Bassett stayed with John Langdon, and either Langdon or a Black employee of his, Siras Bruce, alerted Ona to flee before midnight and hide, which she did.

Having successfully eluded reenslavement by the Washingtons, Ona eventually lived out her life in Greenland, a rural town on the western border of Portsmouth. She at first lived with Phyllis and John Jack, described in earlier in this chapter as formerly enslaved by Jonathan Warner. Ona later recalled that although she endured many hardships in New Hampshire she never regretted her freedom. Ona's story shows the persistence of pursuit and the intricacies of eluding reenslavement.[283]

Among free Black men and women in eighteenth-century Portsmouth, many probably experienced one of these routes to freedom—arriving free, direct manumission, self-purchase, self-emancipation—and were looking for a safe place in which to start a new life.

Documenting Freedom

Freed Black men and women were careful to document their new and tenuous freedom to protect themselves from counterclaims or capture and enslavement by unscrupulous slave dealers. For example, a free biracial woman named Leisha Webb recorded that she and her eight children by her husband "Negro Ceasor, a slave," were free persons.[284]

Violet Dearborn's and Newport Stiles's stories converge. In March of 1778 the aforementioned Violet, the widow of Boston, managed to purchase her freedom from Abraham Dearborn. They duly entered the act, price, and date in the town records: "Rec'd of Violet the widow of Boston, fifteen pounds lawful money in full for her time and that she is free from me and from mine."[285]

Three months later Newport was freed by his owner, the Reverend Ezra Stiles, and they recorded the manumission with both Samuel Penhallow, justice of the peace, and with the Town of Portsmouth.[286] Reverend Stiles had moved to Portsmouth from Providence in May of 1777 with his seven children and enslaved man "Newport my servant," aged twenty-nine. Stiles came to take the post of minister of North Church, where he served from 1777 to 1778.[287] Newport may have been the boy whom Stiles had years earlier preordered or "reserved" by sending a keg of rum aboard an Africa-bound trading ship.[288] Stiles afterward left Portsmouth to become president of Yale College.

Five months later Violet and Newport (who had by this time adopted the surname Freeman) were married, having first lawfully posted their intentions. Their banns and marriage, performed by the Reverend Samuel Haven, were recorded in the town records.[289]

Two years later Newport and Violet took their freedom papers and their infant son Jacob to the town clerk and recorded the free status of all three of them.[290] They afterward moved to Newport's earlier place of residence, Providence, Rhode Island. Some years later Violet returned to Portsmouth, perhaps widowed and ultimately impoverished. She died at the Portsmouth alms-house in 1818.[291]

Such incidents of freedom notwithstanding, before the American Revolution there were only a few thousand free Black people in all thirteen colonies combined. The American Revolution and the post-Revolutionary end of slavery in several northern states would create the first sizable numbers of free Black people in American history.

The Long-Range Impacts of the Slave System

By 1800 Black people had been part of the Portsmouth scene for over 150 years. Though many were still enslaved, increasing numbers were being freed, and a few had been free for a generation.

They had resisted enslavement in a variety of ways and negotiated a variety of small privileges, each no doubt a victory larger than the actual prize. They had adapted their diverse heritages to one another and to their new circumstances and passed these transfigured Africanisms to their heirs and into white culture. They had forged culture and community, institutions and family against all odds.

Three centuries of essentially free labor had been applied to the extraction of immeasurable riches from the natural resources of the New World. This vast wealth had accumulated among Europeans and Euro-Americans. According to the polity of one place or another, the wealth had concentrated in government, nobility, church, or general mercantile society.

This white prosperity had funded a mid-eighteenth-century consumer revolution in Europe and America.

White Yankees meanwhile supported the institution of slavery elsewhere. Portsmouth's export to the West Indies of utilitarian foodstuffs, livestock, barrel staves, lumber, even house frames freed island acreage for the more lucrative production of slave-cultivated crops. The West Indies are still burdened by an inherited legacy of a nonfarming or monoculture economy and the near absence of a middle class. Since World War II the old island economy of white landowners and Black laborers has been translated into a white vacationing class and a Black service class. The white assumption that Black people are servants, that servants are Black, is a searing vestige of centuries of slavery.

Colonial Yankees spent their fortunes on mansions, elegant furnishings, public buildings, and entertainment. The material heritage is as much a monument to the wealth created by compulsory Black labor throughout the hemisphere as to the white builders' grandeur. Whites bequeathed fortunes to successive generations who invested them for vast returns.

Euro-American slavery altered West African nations too. The constant infusion of valued trade goods into western Africa—gold, cowrie shells, textiles, vast quantities of alcohol, and especially weapons—changed local cultures. Competitive European alliances gave rise to new African governments and endless wars to sustain them. Subsequent creation of European and American colonies in Africa introduced new strata of power and class. European activity in Africa forever armed the continent, lending new levels of violence to its political life. The legacy of slavery is everywhere evident in the modern world.

CHAPTER 3

Early Americans

◀§℘▶

Dinah Gibson stayed still that night in 1825. She glanced toward the shadow of the house at the top of the slope where she had been brought to Kittery, as an enslaved eighteen-year-old back in the 1760s. She had seen much since then, including the tempestuous Revolution and the halting freedom that started in the 1780s when slavery began to come undone in Massachusetts and its province of Maine.

Dinah turned her head and looked at the river. The last ferry of the evening had disappeared into the dark silhouette of Portsmouth on the opposite shore, a many-steepled shadow against the star-pricked sky.

In Portsmouth, where she visited so often, Dinah knew of many who had been freed only in the infirmity of old age, a freedom that abandoned them to certain poverty. Dinah, freed when still relatively young, had found her way, hiring herself out for cooking. She had gained quite a reputation in Kittery and Portsmouth, especially for her sweet treats, spiced with unexpected combinations taught her years ago by some of the elderly women who remembered African ways.

Dinah had married in her fifties, late in life but enjoyable while it lasted. John didn't have a skilled trade and found that white folks would hire him only for menial tasks. But by combining their resources, Dinah and John had made do better than they could have alone. Then John was gone.

Dinah reflected on how old age had crept up on her. She kept on working, but through the kindness of the Rice family she found herself back in their home in Kittery. She lived there, not as a slave anymore, but as something between a boarder and pensioner. Dinah still crossed to Portsmouth for work, though in her eighties now she regretted that the special entertainments for which her skills were prized were often nighttime affairs, or afternoon events that stretched into night by the time she had cleaned up.

Dinah shifted to a new position and gave a great thrust with her arms. But they were weak now, and the movement sent a lightning bolt of pain through her hip; she was unable to lift herself. She wondered if anyone would be aware she wasn't back yet. She murmured one of the comforting prayers the minister at North Church had taught her. She called out, but there were no houses near enough for anyone to hear her. She shivered and tightened her shawl against the shrieking February wind, looking up and down the frozen lane where a patch of ice had caught her unawares.

Dinah Gibson was part of a population of Black people who recovered their freedom between 1785 and 1845, as slavery in New England diminished and disappeared. Life in New England—many generations for some—had forged them into Yankees, albeit with distinctive features stemming from a distinctive history. Like Dinah they all faced the challenge of making a living, building lives, and sustaining communities in restricting circumstances.

The opportunities of freedom were diminished for many by old age, limited education, and manumission into poverty. Throughout the nineteenth century all found that the opportunities of free life were limited, as race replaced enslaved status as a white criterion for exclusion from the social, economic, and political life of the larger community. For the first half of the century even New England's free Black citizens lived in fear of being kidnapped into southern slavery.

In the 1780s, almost as soon as the Revolutionary War was over, Black abolitionists were reenergized. Picking up where resistance and rejected petitions had left off, Black activists did their best to keep the white mind conscious of the contradiction of slavery in the midst of newly won independence. Progress came first to the northern states via Black resistance and activism.

Dismantling Slavery

The formal end of slavery in the United States began in Vermont, which was never organized as a colony. Vermont was carved out of overlapping claims by adjacent colonies/states when it declared itself a republic in 1777. In 1791 it was admitted to the United States as the first state added to the original thirteen. It entered as a free state, without the institution of slavery. Slavery was expressly forbidden in chapter 1, article 1, of its constitutions of 1777, 1786, and 1793.[1]

Massachusetts was the next place to see change. That state optimistically ratified a new constitution in 1780 while the Revolution was still in progress. That same year, in an incident initiated by a blow with a hot kitchen shovel, Elizabeth Freeman (Mum Bett or Mumbet) and Brom, both enslaved by Colonel and Mrs. John Ashley of Sheffield in the extreme western part of the state, successfully sued for their freedom. They were the first to do so under the new state constitution.[2] Perhaps a memory of her forthright boldness inspired Elizabeth's famous grandson W. E. B. DuBois.

A series of lawsuits and countersuits in the central Massachusetts town of Barre played out in 1781–83. They revolved around Quock Walker, his recent owner Nathaniel Jennison, and Seth and John Caldwell, heirs of a former owner to whom Quock had fled from Jennison. The suits culminated in a state Supreme Judicial Court instruction to the jury that slavery was incompatible with the new state constitution.[3]

Clearly the highest courts in the commonwealth would not support slave owners in such suits. As word of the successes achieved by Mum Bett, Brom, and Quock spread across Massachusetts and the province of Maine (part of Massachusetts until 1820), the enslaved began demanding pay or walking out on their masters, and the institution of slavery crumbled, if slowly.[4]

Citing the new state constitution became a critical tool in advancing other rights of Black residents of Massachusetts. In 1780, while Mum Bett was pressing her claim at the other end of the state, Paul Cuffe, a free Black Bostonian, indirectly argued for the right to vote. Alluding to the wartime cry of no taxation without representation, and citing the new state constitution, Cuffe requested that he and his brother be excused from paying taxes, because they had "no voice or influence in the election of those who tax us."[5] Massachusetts is the only state where slavery ended in response to judicial decisions.

In 1780 Pennsylvania set a precedent of legislating gradual abolition, a model followed by several other northern states. The Pennsylvania legislature passed an act requiring that Black and mulatto children born after 1780 be freed after serving their mother's owner for twenty-eight years. Other northern state legislatures passed variations on this gradualist model, sometimes including special provisions forbidding Black in-migration or requiring that freed Blacks leave the state. Gradual emancipation had the evil effect of pressuring freed parents of enslaved minors to linger for years in quasi-enslaved condition awaiting the emancipation of their children.[6]

Connecticut passed a gradual emancipation act in 1784. Its legislature waited over sixty years before finally abolishing slavery in 1848, when only a few elderly people remained enslaved and regional antislavery sentiment was building.[7]

Also in 1784 Rhode Island's legislature passed a gradual emancipation act. It freed only the children of slaves, boys when they reached the age of twenty-one, girls at eighteen. Soon after, the state's legislature forbade Rhode Islanders from participating in the slave trade. This statute was rendered a dead letter by failure to convict those charged with violating it.[8]

New Hampshire's first moves were ambiguous. Its constitution of 1784, like its Massachusetts model, included a bill of rights that stated that "all men are born equally free and independent" and other phrases about liberty and rights. But this did not have the effect in New Hampshire it had had in Massachusetts. Slavery continued in New Hampshire for decades.

In the New Hampshire tax code of 1784 slaves were to be taxed as property. A 1789 revision of that code stipulated that "slaves cease to be known and held as property."[9] Some owners may have responded to the ambiguous wording by freeing their slaves, though no clearly related cases are documented. The revised code was understood by most New Hampshire slave owners not to abolish slavery but merely to exempt this particular type of property from taxation. The United States census records show that in the following year, 1790, there were 157 slaves in New Hampshire.[10] It took fifteen years for slavery to dwindle to extinction in Portsmouth. Elsewhere in New Hampshire the institution lingered, in a few instances to 1840, the last census listing of an enslaved person in New Hampshire.[11] Not until 1857 would the legislature abolish slavery in New Hampshire.[12]

By 1790, the year of the first United States census, no slaves were enumerated in Maine, Massachusetts, and Vermont. New Hampshire had 157 slaves. Connecticut had 2,648. Rhode Island had 958. New York had 21,193, New Jersey had 11,423, and Pennsylvania 3,707. The remainder of the country's 694,207 slaves were in the nation's six southern states, the greatest concentration of them in Virginia.[13]

Individual emancipation and gradual abolition notwithstanding, white Yankees promoted slavery by indifference to its persistence and its expansion elsewhere, and by consuming slave-produced products.

A Nation in Motion, Cities in Change

For free people the opening decades of the nineteenth century were ones of tremendous excitement, change, apprehension, and optimism. Twenty years of economic confusion and depression that began with the war gave way around 1795 to a twenty-year boom. A generation reached adulthood who had scarcely or never known colonial life. They sought new fortunes in international trade, seaport commerce, investment, water-powered industry, or the newly opened Midwest. Small towns in northern New England lost population as young adults migrated to burgeoning coastal cities, to the new mill villages, or emigrated westward. In the Midwest diverse eastern populations were mixed and negotiated new polities and cultures. Most movement, however,

This view from Bow Street to Ceres Street shows what had been Portsmouth's eighteenth-century market house as it looked in the mid–nineteenth century. No doubt Dinah Gibson and the Whipple women shopped here, and Pomp Spring likely sold baked goods from his cart along these streets. The spring for which the hill is named still flows beneath the brick building on the left, built shortly after the fire of 1806. *Courtesy of Whalley Museum and Library.*

was within regions, and regionalism remained a characteristic of American culture.

This rising tide lifted Portsmouth too, which enjoyed growth parallel to that enjoyed by other seaports. Its population rose from 4,720 to 6,934 between 1790 and 1810. In 1801 the city built a new market house, and the central intersection on which it stood acquired the name Market Square. Prosperity combined with clearance when a large urban fire in 1803 provided an opportunity to rebuild the north side of Market Square in elegant neoclassical style. Another extensive urban fire in 1806 prepared the way for rebuilding part of the waterfront with towering brick commercial buildings that contained warehouses, countinghouses and shops, and required construction of an elegant new Saint John's church.

Then New England seaports lost ground during a fifteen-year series of economic catastrophes. These began in the first decade of the new century when President Jefferson sought to keep the United States out of foreign war by placing an embargo on the nation's own coasts. Then the War of 1812 disrupted trade. The war's end in 1815 brought a national depression that lingered to about 1820. A summer of frosts wrought by an Indonesian volcanic eruption

destroyed most of New England's crops in 1816.[14] All New England seaports had trouble during these years. The largest and those with the best harbors—notably Boston, Providence, and Portland—made the quickest recovery and forever left the region's smaller ports behind.[15]

Portsmouth suffered with the rest. In the midst of the War of 1812 the port endured the added blow of a catastrophic fire in December of 1813 that consumed acres of buildings in the central area and left hundreds homeless. Rebuilding took more than a decade, and the costs associated with a specially passed law requiring construction in brick sparked considerable class resentment. The neoclassical taste for achieving elegance through simplicity proved an economic virtue; the burnt area is still distinguishable by the austere brick architecture built over it.

Portsmouth's population growth stagnated, creeping up by only 1,000 in the next thirty years. The city enjoyed a small burst of growth between 1840 and 1850, then stagnated again, hovering around 9,500 for the next fifty years.

Black people participated in the region's motion and the city's intermittent stagnation. The appearance of out-of-town free Blacks among the Portsmouth poor-relief bills shows that rural New Hampshire's small numbers of young

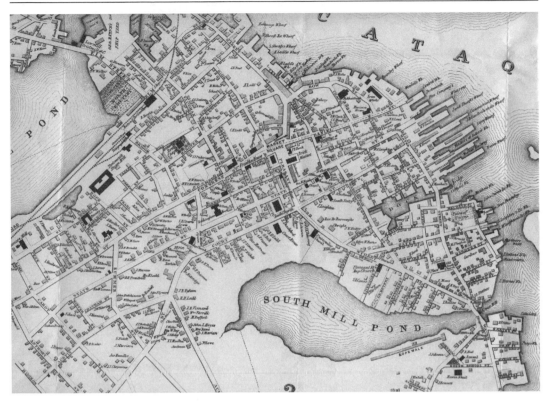

Charles W. Brewster's map of Portsmouth, 1850. The Federal-era's elite suburbs and Victorian era's West End occupy the lower left quarter of this map.

Black adults were leaving their hometowns in search of work and not succeeding. The rapid appearance and disappearance of new names in city directories shows that Black people were coming to and going from Portsmouth as were whites.

From 1700 to the Revolution the African-born portion of New England's Black people gradually decreased from about 70 percent to 30 percent. Because direct importation to New England had stopped at the Revolution, the percentage of the African-born was rapidly dwindling by 1800.[16] The great majority of the Black population was American-born.

During this period American cities began to undergo a change in land use. The colonial pattern of a wealthy core, with a utilitarian and poor perimeter surrounded by agricultural hinterlands, gradually shifted to land use sorted by

function. The elite built new suburban mansions on the edges of the compact centers, still a walkable distance from the core. Investment-funded enterprises like banks and insurance offices gathered around central locations. Commerce gathered along adjacent streets. Larger vessels favored the deepest part of any port. New industry at first clustered around inland waterpower but after 1840 along railroad lines that delivered coal for steam power to the cities. Thereafter, for the first time in American history—probably in Western history—old city centers became less fashionable for residence and thus less costly places to live.

Portsmouth was gradually reorganized along these lines. A new generation of elite families built fashionable neoclassical mansions on the port's approach roads, stately rows of them rising along Islington and Middle Streets. Insurance companies, banks, shops, and emporiums crowded Market Square and the streets feeding into it. After 1810 Portsmouth's involvement in international shipping declined, and the shallow waterways of the South End saw particularly rapid decline. After 1840 the local economy quickened with the arrival of railroad and steam. Factories with adjacent workers' houses sprang up along the rails, giving rise to a new West End neighborhood. The city's population rose, then hit a plateau. Parallel to these shifts in the topographical locus of wealth was the decline in value of Portsmouth's old waterfront neighborhoods, particularly the North and South Ends that sandwiched the commercial center. They became affordable havens.

Exclusion

Slavery's word origin in reference to Slavic peoples notwithstanding, colonial whites equated slavery and Blackness. The next generation of whites were uneasy and confused by a free Black population in their midst and continued to identify them as a slave class.[17] The whites' loss of implicit superiority and the advent of full citizenship for Blacks were unacceptable to whites. Where law had been removed as a differentiator, race remained and became more important to whites. They emphasized inherited assumptions of their inherent superiority in all matters from court to culture to conduct. They cast Blacks as inherently inferior in all matters from intelligence and self-discipline in the public realm to self-control in the private realm. By obstructing Black access to full citizenship and success, whites thought they saw their assumptions fulfilled in Black failure and poverty. Whites portrayed the occasional Black success as a novel aberration, not as a demonstration of inherent capacity.[18] Precedents for this are visible in colonial Portsmouth laws that cut off free Black people from poor relief.

White reliance on science to "prove," clarify, and classify fundamental racial differences was intermittently confounded by a number of factors. These included the anomaly of "white Negroes" like the one exhibited as a curiosity at Stavers's tavern in 1764, unthreatening in its day and context. Whites were disoriented when sometimes an individual's complexion changed completely over a number of years. Assumptions of a natural race-based slave class were inverted when Algerians enslaved white Yankee sailors captured when they ventured into the Mediterranean trade.[19]

White laborers considered free Black workmen undesirable competitors, while skilled artisans would not accept them into apprenticeship. Employment options were limited to tasks so menial and subservient that virtually no whites would do them. Under these conditions it was difficult for Black men to assemble the skills, tools, and funds to establish businesses of their own. Some Black-owned businesses had to rely almost solely on the patronage of Black customers, a limited market in Portsmouth. Black Americans in freedom found that work life involved a constant search for short-term employment.[20]

In the face of such hostility a few must have thought about returning to Africa. But a lifetime stood between them and their homelands. It would have been immensely difficult to locate a childhood home—if it survived—on so vast a continent. Those brought as children had forgotten most of their first language. Africa would have been a foreign place to any who made it back. Also, return to Africa would have placed returnees in danger of again being captured and sold into new-world slavery, a trade that continued to 1888. In any case few even had the option of returning. By the 1800s most free Blacks had been born in America and had no personal experience of Africa. With neither savings nor wealth, the only practical alternative was staying in America to live a free variant of a life that had become familiar.

The hostile environment of free Black Americans was noted. In 1831 French traveler Alexis de Tocqueville described Black Americans as "deprived of their rights in the midst of a population that is far superior to them in wealth and knowledge, where they are exposed to the tyranny of the laws and the intolerance of the people."[21]

What de Tocqueville was witnessing was the emergence of modern racism in America. European immigrants of the seventeenth and eighteenth centuries had not arrived with a concept of class based on race. They had not even perceived themselves as white but rather described themselves by nationality or perhaps by church affiliation. Even today Europeans don't generally describe themselves as white. Slavery first brought the distinctions of "free" and "slave"; manumission solidified the distinctions of white and Black. In America, whites are white only because of the Black presence.

As slavery eroded in the decades following the Revolution, free Black men acquired some of the political rights of white men, in some states including the right to vote. As racism emerged Black suffrage was repealed, followed in turn by the expansion of the white electorate beginning in the 1820s, when land ownership requirements for suffrage were eliminated. New Jersey, for example, removed the right to vote from its Black citizens in 1807. Connecticut narrowed its Black electorate by blocking new Black voters starting in 1818. New York removed property ownership requirements for the white electorate but retained them for Black voters. Pennsylvania disfranchised Black voters in 1838. As the Old Northwest was organized into states, Ohio, Illinois, Indiana, Michigan, Iowa, and Wisconsin did not allow Blacks to vote and made their participation in public affairs and access to public resources illegal. Some states entirely barred Black people from entering their territory. The only places where Black suffrage was never repealed once granted were Massachusetts, Maine, Vermont, and New Hampshire.[22]

With or without laws, a pattern of economic and physical intimidation of Blacks by whites enforced a race-based class system throughout the nation through the nineteenth and most of the twentieth centuries. The Supreme Court's Dred Scott decision of 1857 would in effect declare Black Americans noncitizens.

White ambivalence about the place of mixed-race individuals grew as race was ever more sharply defined. Stigmatization or acceptance of "mulattos" varied by region and by the degree of the mixed-race individual's accommodation to white expectations. Wentworth Cheswell of Newmarket, one-quarter Black, was recorded as white in the U.S. census but was remembered only three years after his death as "yellow," pejorative slang for mixed race.[23]

Later non-Anglo immigrants found themselves on the receiving end of ethnic hostility from whites of Anglo Protestant origins. They learned that over a generation or two their children and grandchildren could adopt Yankee ways sufficiently to blend in and evade hostility. But color was a permanent identifier.

Uninterrupted access to the vote in New Hampshire notwithstanding, the pattern of marginalization persisted. In 1854 a Portsmouth newspaper reported: "A Black Loafer: Within a few days, a large Black man, not young nor beautiful, has made unbidden calls in several entries and kitchens in this city, walking in without knocking—sometimes alarming the inmates, when they happened to be women only—but not stealing any thing as we learn. He is represented as being impudent; —and we should judge a little insane or slightly intoxicated. He ought to be arrested as a vagrant and sent to the Almshouse; or sent home, as it is said he does not belong in the city, but in a neighboring town."[24]

This news item synopsizes the condition to which many Black men were reduced in freedom. It also speaks of white expectations of theft, insanity, and drunkenness, and hints at a profound white fear of interaction between Black men and white women, all in response to an unattached and harmless, if intrusive, Black man who was perhaps hoping for nothing more than a gift of food.

Many of Portsmouth's Blacks spent their declining years at the almshouse. By 1830, when Portsmouth's population was only slightly over 1 percent Black, 30 percent of the almshouse residents were Black.[25]

Numbers and Location of Black People in Portsmouth

The United States census of 1790 enumerated most individuals anonymously under the name of the head of the household, sorting them into only four categories: free white males of sixteen years and upward, including heads of families; free white males under sixteen years; all other free persons; slaves. Black members of a household, enslaved or free, were listed on the back of the census form, segregated even on paper.

How the numerous individual census takers interpreted the third category is unclear and probably was inconsistent among them and among regions. Options included using this category for all people unrelated to the head of household, for free Black people, or for other nonwhites. Nonwhite was a vaguely defined white perception that in New England encompassed biracial, Native, Asian, Polynesian and sometimes Mediterranean and Irish people, all of whom were present in the early republic and soon in Portsmouth too. "All other free persons" probably enumerates free Black people more than any others, but certainty is possible only where the double-sided form was used as intended or in instances in which names of known Black people are listed as head of household, as with "Prince Whipple . . . 5."

The 1790 census of Portsmouth listed 26 enslaved people and 76 people under "all other free persons." If all were Black in that particular year, there were 102 Black people in Portsmouth.[26] Over the next half century Portsmouth's total Black population rose and fell in slightly delayed parallel with the city's total population.[27]

The eighteenth century's wildly imbalanced gender distribution evened out in the natural conditions of married life in freedom, even as the town's total number of Black residents dropped. The number of Black females eventually caught up with and finally surpassed the number of Black males. By 1850 Portsmouth had 21 Black males and 29 Black females. In 1860 there were 10 males and 19 females.[28]

While most of the Portsmouth census of 1790 is in alphabetical order, there is a string of households at the end of the census that are in random order. Among these are two clusters of free Black households.[29] Other records make it possible to locate a few of these households on the landscape. In Boston a free Black neighborhood was coalescing on that city's still rural Beacon Hill, but it appears that no Black neighborhoods were emerging in Portsmouth. Clustering seems to be an illusion created by segregation on paper.

Portsmouth's newly freed Black people lived in several different types of locations. Single people often took live-in employment in white households, for example a Black man who lived with the Chase family on Court Street.[30] Others opted to live in the traditionally affordable edge of the compact part of town, though elite whites were preempting the approach avenues for their new suburbs. Others lived farther out in rural parts of town.[31] Ona Judge moved to Greenland, a rural area once a part of Portsmouth. Roso lived on Frame Point south of New Castle Avenue, an area scarcely developed until the twentieth century. In 1798 Caesar Whidden lived on land belonging to Clement March on State Street west of Pleasant not far from the old Negro burial ground and almshouse, still an edge area on the brink of suburbanization. Patience Rindge (widow of Romeo) and Matilda Clarkson lived at outlying Sheafe's Pasture.[32]

Others stayed in the compact part of town. The Whipples lived on a High Street site loaned by their former owner, and Sambro Stevens lived on Hunking Lane on Katharine Whipple's land.[33]

After 1821 the intermittent publication of city directories locates Black households more

Coloured Persons.

Ames George, Court street
Ashington ——, Partridge street
Barker William, High street
Barnet Andrew, laborer, Bow street
Barney Dinah, Walden's lane
Briant John, clothes cleaner, Bow st.; h. Daniel st.
Carey Liberty; Anthony street
Carman Robert, mason; Pickering's lane
Cole widow of Edward, Dock lane
Cornelius Elvira; Walden's lane
Danforth Jacob, hostler at Simes' stable, Jaffrey st.
Decutry Benjamin; Daniel street
Fogg John, hair dresser, Congress st.; h. Islington r.
Gerrish Sylvia, Pray's lane
Grant David, Partridge street
Hart Dinah; Bachelor's lane
Jenness Diana, widow of Samuel, Anthony street
Johnson Sylvia, Daniel street
Morris Jacob; Walden's lane
Mulneaux Esther, widow; High street
Muzzy Philip; Holmes' lane
Palmer Isaac, Mechanic street
Patterson Nancy, Water street
Parrish William, South road
Purray St. Patrick, barber, Ark street
Rollings Dinah; Broad street
Sankee Jason; Partridge street
Sharp John; Bow street
Simmons Dolly; Partridge street
Thomas George, Partridge street
Victor Esido, barber, Water st.; house Daniel street
Webb Abraham; Walden's lane
Webb Isaac; Little harbour road
Webb Isaac jr. Islington road
Webb William, Islington road
Wentworth Job Locke; laborer; Mechanic street
Whidden Cæsar, truckman; Daniel street
Whipple Dinah, widow; High street
Whipple Rebecca, widow; High street
Williams John, Dock lane

This page from the *Portsmouth Directory*, 1827, is not a complete listing of Black residents. It reflects heads of household and those who were available to answer questions when the directory agent arrived to collect information. For example, single mariners would disappear under their parents' name or not be listed if away at sea. After 1834 the names of Black residents were no longer listed separately.

precisely. Portsmouth's Black families responded to the reordering of the cityscape in terms of their economic condition; most lived in the decreasingly fashionable and increasingly affordable waterfront area.

Simultaneously, more Black men became mariners or waterfront workers. Portsmouth's waterfront included a seaman's bethel (mission) and many boarding houses catering to mariners,

one of them operated by a Black man named William Webb.[34]

Occupations

Throughout New England Black people took jobs that white people avoided because of the danger, low pay, or degradation. These included

Continuing an early nineteenth-century strategy into the twentieth century, self-employment remained an option for sidestepping the limitations of working for white businessmen who excluded Blacks from access to skilled jobs and opportunities to move up with experience. This shoeshine stand was located on Portsmouth's main business street. William E. Allen was listed as a bootblack in the Portsmouth City Directory for the years 1887–1905. *Historic Photograph Collection, Strawbery Banke Museum.*

a lot of miscellaneous labor, occasionally defined by such terms as "truckman" (moving heavy things with a hand truck). Some worked in urban stables or as farmhands. A fair number went to sea, always dangerous, if considerably better paid than any other available job. Some operated modest businesses as barbers or mending and cleaning clothes. The occasional man who had learned a skilled trade in enslavement might find whites now unwilling to hire him; he likely migrated to larger cities like Boston where, in a growing Black population, he found the likelihood of employment by other Black people. A Black property owner might take in boarders, a valuable service to single Black people such as mariners or workers passing through town briefly.

A few surviving scraps of information reveal how free Black individuals made a living in Portsmouth. Identifiable Black employments at the opening of the second quarter of the nineteenth century fell into three rough categories: menial (laborer, hostler, laundress/cleaner, farmhand); absentee (mariner); and self-employed (barber, hairdresser, truckman, clothing repair,

boardinghouse operator). "Laborers" did unskilled heavy work, probably on docks, in warehouses, on farms, and in gardens, tasks carrying over from the days of slavery. In inland towns, working the land may well have been the major source of work for free Black men.[35] Skilled craftsmen were few or unrecognized. The work of many more was unidentified.[36] Women found work in domestic situations.

Individuals with unspecified occupations probably had no single type of employment but pieced together what they could. The diminution of the local Black population suggests that only the few who could carve out and succeed in a specific employment niche stayed in Portsmouth.

Mariners were no doubt more numerous than recorded in the directory, disappearing under their parents' name if single or overlooked if at sea when the directory agent visited. The high number of mariners in 1839 may indicate either increasing maritime employment or homebound mariners during the economic depression of the late 1830s.

Apparently market conditions forced some Black people to practice segregation; of the several Black mariners listed in the 1834 directory none lived at William Webb's seamen's boarding-house at 14 State Street. Webb's lone Black boarder was a farmhand. Otherwise he took only white mariners.

A rare exception to exclusion from skilled trades was a mason, Robert Carman, who lived on Pickering Street. If he had been trained earlier in life while enslaved, he would have been quite old for the heavy labor of this trade. Masonry was backbreaking work involving moving stone for foundations and hefting hods of brick and mortar up ladders and scaffolds to build houses and chimneys. It is unknown whether he was self-employed or took work delegated to him by crews of white housewrights.

The lives of only a few individuals can be reconstructed. In their experience we'll see several ways of surviving. We'll meet the Whipples, who subsisted on numerous pickup jobs, and Siras Bruce, who found full-time employment at a single long-term job. We'll meet Pomp and Candace Spring, self-employed middle-class home owners, and Dinah Gibson, self-employed but then taken back into the family that had originally enslaved her. We'll learn about a prosperous itinerant entertainer, mariners, and a marginally self-employed woman who nonetheless managed to buy her own home. But we'll begin with those who barely survived at all.

"3 Very Old Negroes Almost Good for Nothing": The Plight of the Elderly in Freedom

Post-Revolutionary manumission rapidly became problematic for the elderly. Separated by slave sales from children who might have sustained them, alienated from former owners, and too infirm to support themselves, many faced an impoverished and dependent freedom.[37]

This situation was not without colonial precedent. In the 1770s one of Portsmouth's several white men named John Wentworth willed an enslaved woman named Esther to his wife for her lifetime use, to be passed on to Mary Appleton after his wife's demise.[38] When Wentworth bequeathed Esther, he didn't bother to mention or provide for three other enslaved people who were listed in his probate inventory as "3 Very old Negroes almost Good for nothing." These three may have included "my Negro man Tom, and my Negro woman Dinah," inherited twenty-six years earlier from an uncle, Ensign (or Colonel) Paul Wentworth of Dover.[39] Wentworth's heirs may have taken care of these old people or freed them to fend for themselves. The inventory taker's dismissive wording represents the prevailing white attitude.

White New Englanders hoped for long service from those whom they purchased as children or youths. They valued them as assets, and heirs were content to inherit young, strong, and healthy adults. The elderly and infirm were viewed as liabilities.

In another colonial-era instance Sarah Langdon arranged for the possible freedom of Nanney, previously mentioned in the passage about slaves engaged in colonial agriculture:

> To all People to whome these presentes shall come Sarah Langdon of Portsmouth in the Prov of New Hampr, Widow, sends Greeting. Know ye that the sd Sarah Langdon In Consideration of great Great Regard she hath for & beareth towardes A Negro Woman Slave for Life called & known by the Name of Nanney belonging unto the sd Sarah doth by these Presents declare & make manifest that in Case the Sd Nanney shall out live & survive the Sd Sarah she the sd Nanney shall be free & no more a Slave. In Testimony whereof the sd Sarah hath hereunto set her Hand & Seal the Fifth Day of August 1763.[40]

Sarah's brother-in-law Joseph gave Nanney as a gift "in consideration of the Love and Good Will" he held toward Sarah, rather than selling Nanney for money. Perhaps Nanney was a favorite of Sarah's, sold within the family by

Sarah's late husband in a moment of financial necessity. Whatever the case, Sarah arranged for the possibility of Nanney's freedom the day before the transfer from Joseph. This, combined with her holding "Great Regard" for Nanney, suggests that eventual freedom was well intended. The above was transcribed into the county deeds; presumably the original document was held by Sarah, to be given to Nanney upon Sarah's death. Nanney could then keep the document as evidence of her free status.

While paper evidence records the legal mechanics of this arrangement, the social mechanisms remain obscure. Did Sarah disclose her intentions to Nanney as an expression of her fondness for her? Would such a disclosure bring them closer together, or would it tempt Nanney to gain her freedom sooner by somehow hastening Sarah's death? In the context of slavery, even good intentions were fraught with moral dilemma. The apparent generosity was rendered superficial by the fact that they purchased and kept Nanney in bondage. How Nanney's story turned out is unknown. If Sarah lived long and then predeceased Nanney, her act of intended kindness may have consigned Nanney to an impoverished old age.

White Alternatives to Liability

Some white owners manumitted elderly enslaved people expressly to escape the expense of caring for them. In the eighteenth century most New England towns paid families to take in the town's poor, usually for a year at a time. Portsmouth had a tax-funded almshouse, a tempting option for owners looking to avoid the cost of maintaining elderly slaves.[41] The problem grew so bad in nineteenth-century Connecticut its legislature passed a statute making former owners responsible for the lifetime care of those whom they freed.

The port's first almshouse was built in 1716 and served forty years. A new one was built in 1756 and remained in use for nearly eighty years.

In 1834 this second almshouse was succeeded by a rural "town farm," a new version of an old function then becoming popular throughout New England.[42] In keeping with the eighteenth-century pattern of clustering undesirable but necessary functions at the edges of the concentrated and wealthy compact part of town, each of Portsmouth's three successive almshouses was at the outward edge of the growing town, though their former locations are now engulfed by the modern city center.

Many residents of Portsmouth's almshouse were elderly, some Black, the latter probably manumitted when no longer productive. The earliest-known Black resident of the almshouse was Quint, who died there in 1789. Increasing numbers of Black paupers followed him. Violet Dearborn Freeman, widow of Newport Stiles Freeman, died there at age seventy-five in 1818. Not all were elderly. Some young Black women lived there with their children. Silvia Gerrish and her three children were baptized at the almshouse, as were Dinah Wallis and her son.[43] Perhaps their husbands remained enslaved and unable to support them, or they had lost their husbands to sale, to death, at sea, or to the endless and peripatetic search for work.[44] Free Black people from other towns searching for work sometimes exhausted their meager resources while in Portsmouth and ended up in the poorhouse. In keeping with the laws of the times, the cost of out-of-towners' care was billed to their hometown's poor-relief budget.[45]

Other elderly freed Black people narrowly escaped the almshouse. Scattered individuals lived marginal existences in wasteland areas on the edge of town. Records are too fragmentary to reveal whether rural clusters of poor Blacks existed in Portsmouth, though accounts of poor whites living on the periphery of town illustrate the old pattern of centralized prosperity and peripheral poverty.[46] This affordable option attracted—or trapped—elderly widows Matilda Clarkson and Patience Rindge, both of whom lived at an outlying site called Sheafe's Pasture in 1821, perhaps sharing a small house.[47]

Pre- or post-Revolutionary abandonment of elderly Blacks under cover of manumission would continue until slavery's extinction. Freed youths faced economic marginalization and the prospect of a precarious old age. Many ended their lives alone. Happily, not all ended their days regarded as "almost good for nothing." Following are some stories of families and individuals who found respect and lived in the bosom of family, some lived on the edge.

Prince, Cuffee, Dinah, and Rebecca Whipple: A Sample Family Living in Freedom

The Black Whipples, some certainly African-born, exemplify free Blacks who made a living by picking up numerous odd jobs and building a reputation of excellence at certain tasks. Somewhat repaid in generosity by those who had enslaved them, they made major contributions to the seaport community. Like many in their circumstances, they stayed in the vicinity they had come to know during the preceding decades. Many of their freeborn children would seek opportunity in new places.

We last met Prince Whipple when he was temporarily allowed the rights of a freeman to marry Dinah Chase on February 22, 1781, and freed three years later in February of 1784.[48] Prince may have remained in general William Whipple's employ and residence for the remaining year of the General's life. Cuffee, or Cuff, was manumitted by Joseph Whipple in 1784. He married Rebecca Daverson on August 24, 1786, a rite performed by the minister of North Church.[49]

After General Whipple's death in the autumn of 1785, his widow Katharine Moffatt Whipple gave the Black Whipples the use of a small corner patch of her garden where it backed onto High Street. Prince and Cuffee procured a small two-story house, probably an old one, and moved it onto the lot. The choice to entwine their lives so closely together tends to support the tradition that they were relations, perhaps brothers or cousins. They lived there with their wives and children for the rest of the men's lives.[50]

Prince Whipple as Caleb Quotem

Prince was described fifty years later, by one who remembered him, as "a large, well proportioned, and fine looking man, and of gentlemanly manners and deportment. He was the Caleb Quotem of the old fashioned semi-monthly assemblies, and at all large weddings and dinners, balls and evening parties. Nothing could go on right without Prince."[51]

Prince's presence was much in demand at the bimonthly assemblies, weddings, dinners, balls, and parties, among both the white and Black populations.[52] Why he was in demand is unclear until he is put in the context of Caleb Quotem, a figure in an eighteenth-century comic opera, *Caleb Quotem and his Wife, or Paint, Poetry and Putty* by Henry Lee. The character was a parody of a jack-of-all-trades.[53] Prince Whipple, then, was remembered as multi-talented, a man of many skills. Apparently he filled many roles at many social functions; he was a man who could do or oversee many things, someone to whom a patron would entrust a special and complex event, perhaps comparable to a modern wedding planner. Maybe Prince was also a musician like Cuffee[54] or a caterer like Dinah Gibson, about whom we'll learn more later.[55]

Prince also worked as a kind of master of ceremonies at festive occasions. Prince is mentioned in reminiscences of semimonthly assemblies. These were formal gatherings with dancing and dessert at a private ballroom in the Assembly House. This large building stood on Vaughan Street and included a candlelit upstairs ballroom with musicians' gallery and gilt carved ornaments, drawing rooms on the ground floor, and a large garden with pavilion. It was built in 1771 by local white entrepreneur Michael

Whidden III[56] and funded by accumulated seaport wealth.

Prince Whipple enjoyed only a few years in freedom; he died in 1797 and was buried at the North Cemetery. ". . . his death was much regretted both by the white and colored inhabitants of the town; by the latter of whom he was always regarded as their prince."[57] Prince's age at death is unknown.[58]

Cuffee Whipple and Black Music Making

Cuffee, or Cuff, Whipple didn't sign the 1779 petition for the abolition of slavery in Portsmouth, but he was eventually freed by his owner, Joseph Whipple.[59] This act was recorded in the Portsmouth town records. "Know all Men by these Presents that I, Joseph Whipple of Portsmouth . . . in Consideration of the Past Services of my Negro Servant Cuff, and for divers good causes me thereunto moving have manumitted, and liberated, and Do by these Presents, Manumit and Set free my said Negro Cuff . . . the 25th day of March A.D. 1784."[60] This was one month after William freed Prince.

Until 1751, March 25 had been observed as New Year's Day in Britain and its empire. Joseph, in his late forties, might still have attached symbolic significance to the date as a day for new beginnings.[61] It was certainly a new beginning for Cuffee. A year later he and Prince moved into their own house, and a couple years later Cuffee married Rebecca Daverson.

Like Prince, Cuffee sometimes worked at the Assembly House ballroom. Cuffee and Prince may have been serving their accustomed roles in early November of 1789 when a festive ball was held there in honor of George Washington's visit to Portsmouth.

Early Victorian antiquarian Charles Brewster later recalled Cuffee in the musician's gallery playing "to the elite of the town on the floor below, as he labored with his violin to keep up the mazy dance! Cuffee was not alone, for sometimes that life of the Assemblies, Col.

Michael Wentworth would stand by his side and as an amateur give his aid."[62]

The description of Colonel Wentworth as an "amateur" carries significant class differentiation. In this one word Wentworth is depicted as a leisured, gentlemanly, dilettante lover of music while Cuffee is portrayed as a laborer, making his living at music. In that post-Revolutionary era to which Brewster's personal memory extended, Cuffee was playing professionally; it was one of the ways he could make a living in freedom.

Other Black men in Portsmouth played the violin for their living. Brewster mentions a Black fiddler in an anecdote about Stavers's tavern (the William Pitt Tavern), where there was a large assembly hall on the third floor. ". . . they accepted an invitation to remain and participate in the dance about to commence above-stairs, for which a colored professor of the violin had been included among the arrangements of the landlord."[63]

Music was a common pastime and livelihood for Black Americans in the eighteenth and nineteenth centuries. It could be perfected after work hours, and its portability enabled ready combination with other employment.

Music was an important feature of the Black American experience in part because of its prominence in West African tradition, where instrumental and vocal music and dance were an integral part of life. As with all immigrants, music and dance came to America as cultural baggage.

West African instruments included three-string fiddles, flutes, banjos, tambourines, and drums. Africans in America continued making some of these instruments (except drums, which whites discouraged)[64] or merged them with European equivalents like the four-string violin.

Among themselves Black Yankees must for a while have played African or African-derived tunes until the memory faded. As in other cities, music surely accompanied Portsmouth's coronation festivities and must have been part of the way they "closed their elections by a jolly time."[65] Likewise, music surely accompanied Black funerals in Portsmouth as it did in other New England cities.[66]

When Portsmouth's white population employed Black musicians for their dances, Cuffee and other Black musicians undoubtedly played dance tunes of Anglo-American origin. The "mazy dance" Brewster remembered was probably the energetic British folk form called contra dancing, rather than the more courtly figures taught in dancing schools. Contra dance music would adapt well to the energetic style of playing for which Black musicians were noted. Whites observed that Black Yankees played music and danced with an unfamiliar intensity. This style was not derived from Anglo-American models; it was typically West African.[67]

The Calvinist Puritan tradition in its first century scorned dance and had restrictive views on music. In various New England towns attempts were made to stop Black music and dance. Diarists complained about it or remarked on its unfamiliar energy. For example William Bentley in nearby Salem, Massachusetts, commented on the Black population doing "the most fatiguing dances" under "the never ceasing sound of the violin" on election day.[68]

But secular music is irresistible and prevailed throughout New England before the end of the eighteenth century. Black musicians were active in many towns. Cuffee Whipple's music making was paralleled by Sampson Moore of Concord, Massachusetts, Caesar and Barzillai (Zelah) Lew in Groton, Connecticut, Cato Barker in Wallingford, Connecticut, and others.[69]

New Hampshire was more fertile ground for music than most of New England. Its Anglican governors and councillors never responded to the Calvinist majority by enacting legislative prohibitions of music, dance, or theater. Such prohibitions were law in the rest of early New England. Under Anglican leadership New Hampshire's oligarchy endorsed social music and dance and provided venues for it. After the Revolution Portsmouth was one of the first places in New England to have a theater. By the time Revolution brought an end to Anglican political dominance the Calvinists were beginning to abandon their strict views on music, dance, and—elsewhere by the 1820s—on theater. New Hampshire's lack of restrictive laws may account for the paucity of historic records. Commonplace rather than scandalous, music and dance provoked no comment. Portsmouth was fertile ground for its Black musicians.

Cuffee Whipple died in 1816, but the tradition of local Black musicians continued well into the nineteenth century. For example one recollection mentions a school play that was accompanied by "Esido-Victor, from Water Street, professor of the tambourine, and another colored gentleman, professor of the violin."[70] The white author's recurrent description of these Black musicians as professors may mean that they were full-time professionals, or taught music, or both. Just as likely, he was attempting to amuse his mostly white readers in coded language. By mocking and rendering illegitimate Black action in a white sphere, he subtly undermined the validity of this and any Black activity, no matter how accomplished.

The popularity of Black musicianship gave rise to a heinous white institution of blackface minstrelsy. This phenomenon appeared as early as the 1840s, flourished in the 1850s, and persisted a century. Coloring their faces with burnt cork, white musicians performed songs that were simultaneously imitative, admiring, and cruel caricatures of Black musical and performance style. White composer Stephen Foster of Pittsburgh, Pennsylvania, wrote vast numbers of songs that circulated under the guise of Black origin.[71] The blackface performance style is clearly racist, with its "Ethiopian" dialogue among stock characters named Interlocutor, Bones, and Tambo.[72]

White audiences—especially in areas with few Black people—probably assumed such shows were an authentic portrayal of Black mannerisms. They no doubt took the dialogues as hilarious examples of supposed Black stupidity. Along with the performers these audiences completely missed the fact that these caricatures captured a real and subtle Black subversion of white domination.

Recent scholarship finds a second source and new layers of meaning, supplemental to racist parody of Black music and mannerisms. The additional source is traditional Euro-American folk street theater. New interpretations include differentiation of white and Black labor, commodification of the marginalized by the empowered, and the mix of allure and guilt in cultural thievery. A recurrent pattern was skewering prevailing white social conventions, politics, elitism, and gender issues. This was purveyed by whites comfortably disguised in blackface, hiding behind both comedy and race.[73]

The simultaneous popularity of itinerant Black and blackface white performers sometimes obscures the historical record in Portsmouth, especially since blackface singers performed under the general title of "Ethiopian serenaders" in both America and England. In 1852, when "Smith's Real Ethiopian African Serenaders" performed in Portsmouth, the word "real" may have distinguished a genuinely Black group of performers from their blackface imitators, or it may have been just another level of self-promotion by white performers.[74]

Whites often called Black musicians minstrels, whence the association of the term with both Black and blackface performers. Confusion of identity again arises in regard to a performance on the morning of July 4, 1853, amid Portsmouth's first Old Home Day, an event called the "Return of the Sons." As crowds gathered in Market Square in excited anticipation of such festivities as militia training drills and a parade, a group of musicians enlivened the scene. "A natural accompaniment to a 'training,' was a band of sable minstrels, whose performances, which created much merriment, concluded with the 'Camptown Races,' in which they distanced all competitors. There was in this exhibition nothing to offend the strictest delicacy, which has not always been the case in these exhibitions in other places."[75] The inclusion of a white-composed song and the

class-conscious commentary suggest these were white minstrels wearing blackface.

Whether or not this impromptu street concert was by Black or blackface performers, the reaction shows how an itinerant way of making a living went through a series of permutations in the white mind. First it settled into an expectation of Black music making and then petrified into a racist stereotype of the "happy" Black person lazily humming, cheerfully singing while at work, or unabashedly playing and dancing. By mocking the supposed crudeness or roughness of Black incursion into the artistic domain of white performance, whites devalued Black culture, confirmed its low status in their minds, and eased their unresolved anxiety about the Black presence in their midst.

The heyday of minstrelsy coincided with literature's strain of genteel racism and abolition, expressions of white uneasiness about race when convictions about the immorality of slavery were growing.

Amateur blackface minstrel shows endured in the New Hampshire seacoast area into the 1960s.

While nineteenth-century Black Americans absorbed and played music from the Anglo-American traditions, and contributed to the energetic music of the Methodist and evangelical denominations, they continued to evolve new musical forms incorporating features of African antecedents. Improved communication, internal migration, electronic broadcasting, and commercial recordings introduced these forms to the nation's white population. White Americans followed these developments through the centuries. Sometimes white attention took the form of admiration and adoption, as when spirituals became popular among white Yankees after the Civil War. From the 1890s forward young white adults enjoyed Black musical forms like ragtime and the fox-trot,[76] sometimes to the discomfiture or even alarm of their parents. In the first half of the twentieth century white New England loaded their gramophones with and tuned their radios to the irresistible sounds of ragtime Dixieland and jazz dance bands. An entire era in American history was named for the jazz culture emanating from New York's Harlem.[77] The Granite State Glee Club introduced jazz to Portsmouth by 1919.

Toward the mid–twentieth century "race music" or rhythm and blues caught the attention of a new generation of white youths, and they appropriated it as rock 'n' roll. In 1955 the police of Bridgeport, Connecticut, canceled a dance that featured Fats Domino, fearing the music would trigger a riot.[78] Parents in some communities made public events of burning rock 'n' roll records. In the 1970s disco music's confluence of Black energy, Afro-Caribbean polyrhythms, Gay theatrics, and overt sensuality triggered a new wave of white parental alarm. Even Portsmouth's dance clubs featured disco through the 1990s. Rap and hip-hop renewed the cycle of parental alarm.

Whether we look at the internationally famed blues singer Taj Mahal from Springfield, Massachusetts, Boston disco singer Donna Summer, local blues legend B. J. Johnson, or the current crop of rap artists, all illustrate how Black American musicians continue to follow in the footsteps of Cuffee Whipple's generation, expressing themselves creatively while making a living by music.

This Granite State Glee Club program proudly announces that it was founded in 1916 and was holding its second annual concert and dance on November 26, 1919. Several songs by the club, a reading, and solo performances preceded an evening of dancing to the music of Curts' Jazz Band of Boston. Smaller informal women's and men's singing groups also met weekly in private homes of those who owned a piano. *Courtesy of Geraldine M. Palmer.*

Dinah Chase Whipple

Dinah was born into slavery and was owned by Reverend Chase of New Castle.[79] During the Revolutionary War Chase moved to adjacent Hampton, New Hampshire, taking Dinah with him. There, at the age of seventeen, Dinah was admitted to the church under the theological tutelage of the Reverend Dr. Thayer. At the age of twenty-one Chase freed her, and she moved to Portsmouth,[80] where she married Prince Whipple. Since Puritan days orthodox Congregational marriages were not performed in houses of worship, and for the first centuries not necessarily by a clergyman. They were performed at home, often at the bride's. But when bride or groom were considered the property of others and lacked a home of their own, we cannot know where the minister of North Church performed their marriage.

Four years after marriage, Prince and Dinah moved into their High Street house with Cuffee and Rebecca. It was probably in this house that Dinah taught young children for the Ladies Charitable African School.[81]

Dinah's school was part of a series of small private schools that variously complimented or competed with the public schools of post-Revolutionary Portsmouth. Public schooling began in Portsmouth after some false starts in the 1690s, remarkably late compared with the rest of New England.[82]

When Dinah operated her school many developments were under way in local education.

Portsmouth was experimenting intermittently with schooling girls, both private and public.[83] In 1790 the port town rebuilt one of its boys' schoolhouses in brick. The town did not institute a district system until 1815, when eight neighborhood schools finally provided regular access to public education to boys and girls alike. In 1809 a private high-school-level academy built a large and handsome new building that survives at the corner of Islington and Middle Streets.[84]

The public schools were funded through town taxes supplemented by a per child or per diem tuition paid by the parents. The parents sent along books from which the children learned reading, writing, ciphering, and—for older Portsmouth boys—Latin. Some private schools duplicated the curriculum of the public schools.

Other "schools," usually operated by itinerants, taught single subjects for a few consecutive days: penmanship, singing, dancing. Another type was the dame school, a private nursery school kept by women at home who taught little more than the alphabet and simple sewing, in some ways comparable to modern infant day care.

These were the options for Portsmouth's late-eighteenth-century Black population. Part of Portsmouth's Black population was literate in earlier decades, even in slavery. Cromwell, for example, ran away from Henry Sherburne Jr. of Portsmouth in 1754. The newspaper notice describing him as a runaway says he "talks good English, can read and write and understands Husbandry work."[85] Another enslaved man, "a little upon the yellow Complexion," who ran away from James Clarkson of Portsmouth in 1772, "speaks good English and reads well."[86]

A highly accomplished literacy is demonstrated in the 1779 petition seeking the abolition of slavery. The petitioners included Dinah's future husband Prince Whipple. The manuscript petition has not been located to see whether or not all wrote their names or some signed with a mark.

How the enslaved acquired literacy is not known. While many slaves were uneducated or

minimally so,[87] there were obvious exceptions. If they were admitted to public schools, their owners must have paid tuition (similar cases are documented in Connecticut).[88] Some may have been instructed by pious owners intent on giving them access to scripture, or for the convenience of having a literate servant.

In the post-Revolutionary era, Portsmouth's Black citizens probably attended public schools, especially once the district system was adopted. Though no accounts for Portsmouth have turned up, accounts and reminiscences from rural New England, 1800–1840, indicate school attendance by Black children, though isolated in segregated seats.[89] By the time the technology and tradition of school class photographs reached Portsmouth in the late nineteenth century, one or two Black students occasionally appear among the white students.[90]

Dinah Whipple herself was literate; a note in her handwriting survives in the North Church records.[91] Her literacy was remarkable when all seacoast females had limited access to formal schooling. Perhaps the college-educated Reverend Chase of New Castle, or more likely his wife, was enlightened enough to educate Dinah along with their daughters.

The records of the Ladies Charitable African Society, which sponsored Dinah's school, have never been located and may not survive, leaving many tantalizing questions. Was it a dame school preparing infants for public school? Was it an alternative to exclusion from public schools? Was it for those who couldn't afford tuition for public school? Was it a girls' school or coeducational?

A reminiscence that mentions small children suggests Dinah's school may have been a dame school. Black literacy suggests access to public schools. Her school's sponsorship suggests it was tuition-free or nearly so, making it accessible even to the poorest of Portsmouth's Black families. Its sponsorship hints that it may have been a girls' school. Its economic function must have been critical, freeing both parents from daytime child care to pursue paying work.

This charitable school was equivalent to

practices in other northern cities. Philadelphia, which lacked New England's early tradition of tax-subsidized schools, relied mostly on churches to operate its schools. That city gained a school for Black people starting in 1758, operated by an Anglican philanthropic society. Quakers and abolition societies in Philadelphia followed the same model through the next seventy years. The Black-founded Bethel Church operated a Sunday school starting in 1785. Black Philadelphians began operating schools in their homes in the early nineteenth century, coincidental with a city ordinance subsidizing poor children in private schools, which in practice excluded Black children, an annoyance repeated in the enforcement of a similar state law of 1818.[92]

As in other northern cities Portsmouth's Black community organized to improve its situation. There were several African societies in Philadelphia, a dozen by the 1830s, when that city's free Black population was among the largest in the country.[93] Boston's African Society was founded in 1796 as a mutual aid and charity society,[94] and probably was the immediate model for Portsmouth's. In addition to its Ladies Charitable African Society Portsmouth had another—probably men's—African society whose president was a baker, Pomp Spring.[95] A few miles away, Exeter's Black population attempted to organize a charitable society in 1817.[96]

The founders of these societies included the last generation imported from Africa. They acted in the spirit of a recollected West African tradition of communal responsibility, where it was understood that helping the individual helped the community.[97]

The local Black societies were probably organized along lines similar to those of white charitable societies. Knowledge of political culture was transmitted and shaped by general conversation, newspapers, and thoughtful listening by Black domestics while preparing and serving refreshments to the white charitable societies that didn't admit Black people to membership. Following the experience of slavery and neglect during the Revolution Black people had plenty of reason to remain attuned to politics.

Women were more aware of political culture than modern people might expect. White women carefully drew up constitutions for their societies just as men did. Black women and men who had hopefully tracked the Revolution's progress and the Constitution's recent ratification probably adopted this same model. In addition to providing mutual help and services, society meetings also provided pleasant socializing. As the annual Negro Coronation passed from the scene, charitable societies likely became the venue for conveying community values and traditions to a new generation.

The details of Dinah's school may never be known. It was still in operation in the 1850s, under the auspices of Dinah's successors in the charitable society.[98] Her school adapted a familiar regional institution to serve the needs of Portsmouth's Black children, equipping them for a better life should the chance come. Prince and Dinah had several children of their own, as did Cuffee and Rebecca; certainly they attended this school.

Dinah was widowed by Prince's death in 1796. Ever afterward she kept Prince's manumission documents as a treasure of immense symbolic and personal value.[99]

Dinah continued to work for decades. Intermittent records indicate the widow augmented her family's income through small tasks. In August 1820 North Church directed its treasurer to pay Amos Tappan in compensation for "cash paid Dinah Whipple $2 and Mrs Barnard $3." She and Mrs. Barnard were working for pay for their church, possibly providing more schooling, needlework, or other labor.[100] Yet Dinah could not entirely support herself. In 1825 North Church assisted the sixty-five-year-old widow and her aged in-law Rebecca with a cash gift.[101]

Dinah was not alone among Black people doing small tasks for money at North Church. In 1828 and 1829 North Church paid a "Black boy for blowing Organ—5."[102] This boy was probably Richard Jennings, who a year later was paid five dollars for a year of pumping the pipe organ bellows. He was probably a member of Samuel and Dinah Jennings' household, a

Black family living on outer Water (now Marcy) Street.[103]

Dinah continued to live in the High Street house as her children grew up, some moved away, and her resident kin died, Cufffee in 1816, Rebecca in 1829. By 1830 the seventy-year-old Dinah was the sole member of her household on High Street.[104] By then the secondhand house on loaned land was "much dilapidated and scarcely tenable, and dangerous to the neighborhood on account of fire."

In 1832, after Madame Whipple's death, her heirs gave Dinah lifetime use of a small house they owned on Pleasant Street and gave her a small annuity. Dinah lived at the new address for fourteen years, sometimes with her grown children Esther Whipple Mullinaux and Elisabeth Whipple Smith.

In her new location Dinah had Black neighbors. In a small and tight-knit community they likely provided some company and support to the aging widow.[105]

In her last years Dinah was probably infirm and unable to do the money-earning tasks by which she had formerly supported herself. She could no longer make ends meet. Winter's demand for fuel was particularly difficult. An undated note written in Dinah's own hand asks North Church for help: "Deacon Tappan will please to let me have one dollar for to get me some wood.—Dinah Whipple."

Inscriptions on the note written by another hand record that on February 1 and again on February 26 North Church gave her one dollar, or a dollar's worth of wood.[106] North Church also gave cash to Dinah and her daughter Esther Mullineax in January 1844 and again to Dinah and Esther in February 1844.

In the end, winter got the best of Dinah; in February 1846 North Church gave a cash gift to Esther and paid $8.62 for Dinah's funeral.[107] Dinah died at age eighty-six.[108] Although no grave marker or documents record her burial place, Esther probably saw to it that Dinah was laid to rest in the North Burial Ground with her late husband Prince.

Dinah's education, extended family, and the kindness of others could not protect her from an impoverished widowhood. Probably only the lifetime loan of a house and her small stipend kept Dinah from the almshouse.

Rebecca Daverson Whipple

In the remarkably well-documented Whipple clan, Rebecca is least understood. She was married to Cuffee on August 24, 1786, by the minister of North Church. She probably worked with Dinah at the tasks of managing a household, raising children, and teaching others' children in the charitable school. Perhaps she accompanied Prince and Cuffee on their social or musical contracts and assisted in the arrangements. She was widowed by Cuffee's death in 1816, remained with Dinah, and died in 1829, three years before Dinah moved to Pleasant Street.[109] Overall, Rebecca remains in the shadows.

The Next Generation

By midcentury the Portsmouth directories list no more Black Whipples except for Esther Whipple Mullinaux, who remained in Portsmouth for the rest of her life. The children of colonial Portsmouth's last enslaved people mostly evaporate from the records. Their parents' lives had bridged the continents, the seas, slavery and freedom; they had constructed new lives, families, and careers in the place of their former enslavement. Their grown children were willing and eager to move on, sometimes in the process abandoning the surnames of those who had enslaved their parents.

Siras Bruce and Flora Stoodley Bruce: New Freedom, Limited Options

Siras and Flora Stoodley Bruce had an employment experience very different from that of the Black Whipples. Siras found a permanent posi-

Siras Bruce [or Cyrus DeBruce, as written by John Langdon] signed with his mark an annual contract to work as "Domestic Servant" for wages of $6 a month, half to be paid in cash and half "in any goods the said Langdon may have at the general cash price." The agreement was dated September 17, 1783, and is one of several similar contracts between the two men during the period. These rare and interesting documents reflect the transition being made by Africans and Black Americans in the region as they went from enslaved to freemen. *New Hampshire Historical Society.*

tion with a single employer, for which he was paid in a combination of cash, goods, and housing, and for which special outfits of clothing were provided. Siras Bruce's birthplace is unknown, but his classical first name indicates he had been enslaved at birth.[110]

By 1783 the last battle of the Revolution was three years past, and the peace treaty with Britain was being negotiated and signed in Paris. In that same year Siras signed a contract with John Langdon. Langdon, senator from and eventually governor of New Hampshire, ultimately disapproved of slavery. Siras agreed with Langdon to "serve him in the capacity of a domestic servant, in any sort of business the said Langdon may require for a term of twelve months in exchange for wages, one half in cash and the remainder in any goods Langdon may have for the general cash price."[111] Siras signed with his mark, an X. He had never been taught how to write.

Siras worked in and around Langdon's house, an old tavern formerly belonging to Sheriff Thomas Packer, where Langdon had lived since his marriage in 1777.[112] Though the initial contract was for one year Siras evidently continued for many years more. By 1785 Langdon had moved into a spectacular new mansion a half block down Pleasant Street from the previous home.

An oral tradition written in the mid–nineteenth century tells of John Langdon's maintaining a Black man, Siras Bruce, in livery, or elegant uniform. "There could scarcely be found in Portsmouth, not excepting the Governor himself, one who dressed more elegantly or exhibited a more gentlemanly appearance. His heavy gold chain and seals, his fine Black or blue broadcloth coat and small clothes, his silk stocking and silver-buckled shoes, his ruffles and carefully plaited linen, are well remembered by many of the present generation."[113]

Bills from 1783 and '84 surviving among Langdon's papers confirm this reminiscence.[114] One bill describes the equivalent of a full dress outfit, well beyond the utilitarian trousers, shirt, kerchief, jacket, and cap usually worn by male laborers. The use of metal buttons (instead of cheaper wood or bone buttons) and details such as silk thread, buckram, and stays (probably to stiffen collars or lapels) verify the recollected elegance.

Another bill implies a complete outfit either of uniform fabric or of coordinated parts. Siras must have been a grand sight to those whom he greeted at Governor Langdon's door. While Langdon intended to aggrandize himself by outfitting Siras in livery, Siras's rather spectacular clothing preserved his memory in his own right.

Siras Gets Married

Perhaps Siras's impressive clothing caught Flora Stoodley's eye too. In the year following his contract with Langdon, Siras married Flora, on May 4, 1785.[115] Flora had been owned by tavern keeper James Stoodley on Daniel Street, where, a decade earlier, she might have glimpsed Paul Revere's arrival. Upon Stoodley's death in 1779 she had been recorded as "a Negro Wench Named Flora—£100" in the probate inventory of Stoodley's estate.[116] Flora's whereabouts in the intervening six years is unknown, as is her status—enslaved or free—when she married Siras.

Their marriage followed a pattern characteristic of eighteenth-century Portsmouth: the partnering of Black people from white families of equal status. Local antiquarians overlooked this pattern when they assumed enslavement was practiced only by the wealthy. Though a generation apart in age, John Langdon and James Stoodley were active patriots in the recent Revolution, prominently established in town, and wealthy. The pattern expresses the aura of white status and its adherence to Black members of the household. It also illustrates how social interaction among whites provided the opportunity of interaction among their enslaved people.

Envisioning Work

The contract with Siras was made on the eve of Langdon's first contract for the construction of a splendid new mansion two lots down Pleasant Street. It was built from 1784 to 1789. Siras was certainly witness to the prolonged construction of the mansion. The "any sort of business the said Langdon may require" of Siras likely included errands, message bearing to construction crews, and miscellaneous tasks peripheral to the building project, in addition to routine tasks back at the old Packer house.

The new, hipped-roof house, enormous for its time, still stands.[117] Two brick outbuildings stand sentry on either side of the front yard, one of them a mercantile office, an arrangement used elsewhere in postcolonial Portsmouth to separate family from business as the elite increasingly specialized and differentiated space and furnishings.[118] The mansion's interior was richly embellished with rococo carving about the mantelpieces, scenic wallpapers, and suites of handsome upholstered chairs.

When the new mansion was finished, Siras and his work moved along with his employer. It was probably here that Siras was remembered as a "waiter" opening the paneled door into the broad hall.

No doubt Siras was present in his handsome clothing when George Washington had tea at Langdon's house on October 31, 1789, and again a few days later when Washington "Dined at Col. Langdon's and drank tea there with a large circle of ladies" on Monday, November 2, 1789.[119] John Langdon had served in the Revolution and been a representative to the Constitutional Convention. As president of the newly formed United States Senate Langdon had informed Washington of his election as first president and swore Washington into office in April of 1789. There were other local connections. William Whipple had attended the Continental Congress that issued the Declaration of Independence, presided over by Washington. In the 1780s Portsmouth native Tobias Lear was serving as Washington's personal secretary and tutor to his children. Many other local men had seen or served with Washington during the Revolution and could provide firsthand accounts. He was a living national hero.

Siras was likely excited and perhaps proud to

Siras Bruce greeted visitors to Governor John Langdon's elegant new mansion on Pleasant Street wearing custom-tailored livery of fine fabrics and accessories. *Photography by Brad Randolph. Portsmouth Black Heritage Trail.*

play a role in Langdon's entertainment of the president. Surely Siras despaired several years later when Washington signed the Fugitive Slave Act of 1793. In 1796, when Ona Marie Judge ran away from enslavement in Washington's household and found her way to Portsmouth, a "Miss Langdon" informed Washington of Ona's presence here. As Washington's agent Burwell Bassett stayed with John Langdon during his hunt for Ona, it is unclear whether Siras, John Langdon, or others alerted her to slip away at night. If Langdon, Siras must have been pleased with his employer's criminal morality.

A Place to Live

Apparently Siras continued working for Langdon for many years. A contract dating to fourteen years after the original contract shows that eventually Siras received part of his pay in housing. Langdon paid a number of his employees in a mix of cash, goods, and housing. Some lived in the mansion's garret; others lived in a brick house built for Langdon in 1795 at the rear of the mansion's grounds on Washington Street, back to back with the mansion.[120]

Siras's residence in a Langdon outbuilding is mentioned in an August 7, 1797, work contract

Langdon made with Charles Prilay. Part of Prilay's pay consisted of the use of "one-half of said Langdon's small house, near the bridge where Cyrus Bruce now lived—free of rent." Prilay and Siras may have lived in the brick house or an adjacent wooden house that stood beside the bridge that carried Washington Street over Canoe Creek at the head of Puddle Dock.[121] Siras probably threaded his way from this house through the adjoining back lot of Langdon's mansion daily as he went to work.

But life did not consist solely of work. Flora was active in Saint John's Episcopal Church, the new name for the old wooden Queen's Chapel. On January 21, 1798, after being instructed and examined by the Reverend Willard, Flora Bruce was baptized.

John Langdon died in 1819. Prior to his death he wrote a will in which, "To my Servants male and female who shall live with me, at the time of my decease I give as follows, viz. a Suit of mourning to each, and a pecuniary reward to each, from Fifty Dollars to two Hundred Dollars or more, at the discretion of my Executors—and to each of the wives of my Men Servants also a Suit of mourning."[122]

Langdon wanted to be buried as spectacularly as he had lived; no second-rate mourning apparel would suffice. He also had become sufficiently attached to his servants to leave them cash gifts. Langdon's daughter, Elizabeth Lang-don Elwyn, was principal heir and executor of the estate. How she interpreted these provisions is unknown. If Siras was still in Langdon's employ (this was thirty-six years after the original contract), he and Flora presumably benefited from his largesse, receiving mourning clothes and a cash gift. Langdon's death might also have propelled them out of job and home.

Pomp and Candace Spring: A Glimpse of Home and Home Life

Among those inventing a new life after slavery we find Pomp and Candace Spring, who operated their own business. They managed to acquire a house and live middle-class lives in the center of town. They were also leaders in the local Black community.

Two deeds, two probate inventories, church records, two obituaries, and a petition to the probate court provide a rare glimpse into their lives and home, just when slavery was disintegrating in New Hampshire. Though the Springs' house doesn't survive, the records reveal much about the setting in which they lived.

Pomp Spring was born circa 1766.[123] His classical Roman name reveals that he was born into slavery and named by his owner. We may reasonably speculate that Pomp was born in or near Portsmouth, because he reached desirable purchase age during the Revolution, when importation of enslaved people was interrupted, and because his mother lived locally, an unlikely preservation of the family unit in the transatlantic slave trade. Pomp's mother, Phyllis, was probably brought from Africa and Pomp born here.[124]

Phyllis and Pomp's former owner, and how and when they became free, is unknown. Options included buying their freedom or being freed through the will of their former owner. Pomp was too young to win freedom for service in the Revolution. If Phyllis was already free, it

is unlikely she would have named her son with one of the pet names favored by white owners.

Pomp may have been enslaved in an agricultural context; his deed of purchase of a house in Church Lane (now Street) describes him as "yeoman," meaning he was a property-owning farmer.[125] Somewhere, somehow, Pomp had owned and tilled land before deciding to move to downtown Portsmouth.

When Pomp was about twenty-seven years old, he married Candace Wentworth on November 28, 1793.[126] The timing of their wedding followed a classic New England pattern. Weddings in the region were often scheduled near Thanksgiving because farmwork was at a lull between the autumn harvest and winter's butchering, threshing, and logging. In this interval food was plentiful, a celebratory mood prevailed, and frozen roads facilitated wedding guests' travel.

Little is known of Candace's background. She had been enslaved by the Somersworth, New Hampshire, branch of the seacoast's many Wentworth families. One of Candace's brothers lived in Berwick with Major Andrew Wentworth at the time of her marriage to Pomp. Perhaps Pomp and his mother were from that area too.

Pomp and Candace took his mother into their household, mentioned in his will as his "aged mother who now resides with us."[127] Elderly whites expected to live with or be cared for by one of their grown children, as they had done for their parents. Scattered slave families had no such hopes. For Phyllis, living with Pomp and Candace was a rare and welcome alternative to being freed, perhaps to live in solo impoverishment and die in the almshouse, a sobering block-and-a-half walk from Pomp and Candace's house. Perhaps Phyllis knew and visited friends at the almshouse.

Other relatives lived in Portsmouth and adjacent Piscataqua-region towns. Pomp's sister and her husband Caesar Whidden lived nearby in Portsmouth. Caesar made his living as a truckman or hauler of goods. He remained close to the family. When the widowed Candace died, brother-in-law Caesar applied to be executor of her estate as her "only relation willing to administer said estate."[128]

Candace had two brothers: Thomas Fyal (or Fial), a laborer in Somersworth, and Scipio Fyal, a laborer in Berwick who lived at Major Andrew Wentworth's.[129]

Other than blood relations, the Springs were at the center of a larger family of local Black people because Pomp was president of the African Society. Like Boston's African Society, founded in 1796 as a mutual aid and charitable society, Portsmouth's African Society was probably a men's group, especially given the presence in Portsmouth of a Ladies African Charitable Society.[130] In addition to general assistance for its members the society may have adopted special projects for community improvement, comparable to the ladies' society's school.

The founders of these societies included the last generation of people from Africa. The society's names show that they still thought of themselves as African. They founded the societies in the spirit of a recollected West African tradition of communal responsibility, where it was understood that helping the individual helped the community.[131] In addition to providing mutual help and services, society meetings also provided pleasant socializing.

Six years after Pomp and Candace's marriage, when Pomp was about thirty-three years old, they bought a house on Church Lane, which ran a short distance from Market Square to Court Street. This narrow lane began below the arched pulpit window of North Church, from which it took its name, and ended only three blocks away opposite the almshouse. The Springs' home stood on the west side of this lane, in the middle of the lane's second block. Though newly purchased, it may have been nearly a century old, as the lane and its lots had been developed starting in 1705.[132] The Springs bought their house from Jacob Waldron, owner of an adjacent lot, for $475.

The year after buying the house, Pomp spent another $300 to increase his house lot by ten feet along its north edge and gain ownership of a small bake house. This year saw Pomp shift from a yeoman to a baker in the county records.[133] The Springs' lot had a frontage of thirty-two feet and extended back from the lane fifty-three feet. The property expansion enabled Pomp to bring his sleigh and handcart to and from the backyard, and firewood could be delivered by cart directly to the backyard. Prior to this purchase the house was probably coterminous with the lot lines, or nearly so, with no more than a narrow footpath along one end connecting the public lane to the backyard. This was a common arrangement in the densely settled compact part of town.[134] A path too narrow for a cart must have required dumping firewood in the lane and carrying it in armloads or wheelbarrow loads to the backyard for storage, a labor-intensive task particularly forbidding in light of the increased wood supply necessary to sustain commercial baking.

Pomp's accumulation of money sufficient for these purchases as a young yeoman is something of a marvel. He may have acquired and sold land elsewhere; perhaps his freedom came with a gift of cash or land. Either way, surely he worked extremely hard to parlay it into such buying power.

Portsmouth, like other late-eighteenth-century cities, was not sorted into districts by function or social rank. Its organization by hierarchy of function and status along highways, streets, and lanes tucked the smallest businesses and homes immediately behind the grandest in a fairly uniform mix across the city. The "highways" of State, Pleasant, Congress, and Fleet bound the Springs' neighborhood, while narrow Church and Porter Lanes bisected it.[135] The Springs' neighbors were the back of North Church across their lane to the east, the Revolutionary-era Major Joseph Bass on their south, Dr. Joshua Bracket on their west, and a scion of the ancient Waldron family on their north, all facing outward on the major highways.

Pomp was a conscientious thirty-eight-year-old. Having accumulated family, home, and business, he wrote a will in January of 1804 to assure care for his mother and wife should he predecease them. He left all to Candace—they had no children—and appointed her executrix of his estate. His will also required Candace to care for his aged mother at the expense of his estate. In his will he instructed Candace to write a will of her own should she outlive him and to provide for continued care of his mother. When the time came, Candace executed the estate. Candace, however, neglected to write a will of her own, whence her brother-in-law's petition to become executor of her estate.[136] Pomp's mother Phyllis outlived both Pomp and Candace.

Pomp's cautionary will writing was in keeping with guidelines of the African Society, which instructed members to provide for their families. Dues insured proper burial of indigent society members, although Pomp's estate paid for his (and later Candace's) burial expenses, including matching gravestones. Pomp's will writing may have been prompted by chronic ill health; he died only three years later, at the unusually young age of forty-one, on July 18, 1807.[137] Whatever his state of health, Pomp was a baker to the end, indicated in a notice a month later calling in any outstanding claims on his estate.

Pomp was sufficiently well known in Portsmouth to merit an obituary in the local paper. "Died . . . On Friday in the 41st year of his age, Mr. Pomp Spring (a man of color). He was President of the African Society in this town, and during a long series of years, by his conduct and manners, obtained not only the esteem of those of his color, but of all the inhabitants of the place. Whilst the people of color and especially the poorer class of them, have abundant cause to regret his death, we have no hesitance to declare that his loss will be felt by all this town."[138]

Candace Spring died only four months after Pomp, on November 14, 1807. She too was well known enough to inspire an obituary in the local paper, if in considerably briefer terms. "Died . . . Mrs. Candace Spring, (a woman of color), relict of the late Mr. Pomp Spring."[139]

A House Tour

Because Pomp and Candace died within four months of one another, the Springs' house was inventoried for the Court of Probate twice in a single year, a step toward settling their estates. Such probate inventories provide a snapshot of house furnishings. Theirs give a rare and detailed glimpse of the daily life of New Hampshire's first generation of free Black people. Though the inventory takers did not go strictly room by room, they were orderly enough to enable an imaginative tour of the Springs' house. We find the Springs living a modest if highly fashion-conscious middle class life.

The Entry. The Spring's front door opened into a vestibule or hall furnished with a pair of fire buckets, a stove, and five jugs.

The "stove" was a foot stove or foot warmer, a small sheet-metal box with a handle. Filled with embers, it served as a heated footstool for use during sedentary tasks on winter evenings, or while traveling in a sleigh, or while sitting in an unheated church.

Fire buckets were deep narrow leather vessels, painted and marked with the owner's initials or name. The law required householders to be equipped with them. When the cry of fire was heard, householders like Pomp and Candace took their buckets and joined a line, or bucket brigade, to pass water to the town's primitive fire engine's tank and back to the source for refills. The painted names and initials helped get buckets back to their owners after the fire. Surely Pomp and Candace grabbed their buckets and ran in December of 1802 when all the buildings on the north side of Market Square, a few hundred feet away, went up in

Pomp Spring, and his widow, Candace Wentworth Spring, died just 4 months apart in 1807. The choice of stylish neoclassical headstones was consistent with their level of affluence and the Black population's knowledge of fashion, as shown in the Spring's final estate inventories. *Photography by Brad Randolph. African American Resource Center.*

flames, which spread around a corner and burned both sides of Market Street. Again the cry of fire went out in December of 1806 when all the buildings along the water side of Bow Street burned, as did Saint John's Church, the old wooden Queen's Chapel. Lesser conflagrations probably drew them to help as well.

The jugs were probably empties waiting for the next visit to the shed or basement to be re-filled from one of their three barrels of cider (which kept company with six bushels of pota-toes) or refilled at a nearby store with molasses, rum, or other imported goods. The jugs repre-sent a routine household chore interrupted by death and frozen in time by the inventory takers' pen.

The Parlor or Sitting Room. Pomp and Can-dace furnished their best room with a dozen Windsor chairs, a four-foot-long cherry table,

another cherry folding table with a protective oilcloth, and a candle stand. The fireplace had brass andirons and flanking hooks for shovel and tongs.

The room's walls were ornamented with a mahogany-framed looking glass highlighted with gilt and with eight pictures in gilt frames. The mirror probably hung in the customary place between two front windows where the Springs could glimpse themselves in a flood of daylight before answering a knock at the door. The eight pictures were probably inexpensive engravings purchased from a local stationer or printer. Biblical scenes, political figures, and lit-erary scenes were the best-sellers of the day.

The parlor windows were curtained, at that date still a rare feature outside the homes of the wealthy. Proximity to the public lane and an ab-sence of interior or exterior shutters may have made curtains desirable for privacy especially to a couple whose minority status might have drawn curious glances.[140]

The Springs kept their best glass, china, and earthenware in a cupboard in this room, and probably their "images" too. These were likely ceramic figurines, popular for table and mantel decoration. Three japanned tea trays and a couple of walnut platters or "waiters" in this room facilitated moving dishes between sitting room and kitchen.

The Springs probably spent many nonbusiness hours in this room. Like most Yankees they ate their noon dinner and evening supper in the sitting room, and the oilcloth was handy to protect their cherry table. The ceramic images added elegance to the bare polished cherry table for the dessert course on important days like Thanksgiving or Coronation Day (if it continued into this period).

Chairs and tables stood in rows against the wall and were pulled forward and rearranged when needed. No doubt the dozen chairs were drawn into a circle for meetings of the African Society. Since Dinah Whipple's house was full of children, perhaps the Ladies African Charitable Society met here too.

This parlor or sitting room was probably to the left of the front vestibule, as Portsmouth tradition typically placed the common sitting room on the south or west side to take advantage of afternoon light. Heated for noon dinner and sunny, the room was ready for Candace and Phyllis to settle down with their foot stoves for sedentary winter afternoons of sewing clothing, sheets, or quilts, or knitting (bedding and a bundle of yarn are listed in the inventories). As twilight settled, the candle stand provided flexible lighting for continued needlework, reading, or bookkeeping. Sparkling brass andirons enlivened the primary source of heat in the room.

The Bedrooms. No clues reveal whether the Spring's house was a one- or two-story house. If it was of the widespread form now called a "cape," with a slope-ceilinged second story tucked under the roof, they must have had a downstairs bedroom to accommodate their high-post birch bed with its "1 suit copper plate bed curtains," a canopy of imported French printed fabric. Whether downstairs or up, their best bedroom was also outfitted with bedding, a half dozen more Windsor chairs, a fashionable "Swell'd front Mahogany Bureau," a looking glass of mahogany and gilt, a "toilet table" or dressing table, and brass andirons. The combined quantity of parlor and bedroom furniture argues for separate rooms. Like the white elite, the Springs had ceased keeping the best bed in the parlor.

Additional bedroom furniture suggests the Springs' house had one or perhaps two more bedrooms. There were two maple bedsteads with bedding, plus extra "beds" or mattresses (perhaps stored in the attic). A pine chest of drawers, trunks of clothing, a small mahogany writing desk, two small looking glasses, eight small pictures, another toilet table, and two old window curtains filled out these bedrooms. Probably one was mother Phyllis's room.

Together the bedrooms had quantities of sheets, blankets, quilts, pillows, bolsters—all necessary when indoor winter temperatures plunged below freezing. Bedroom fireplaces were used only in times of sickness, and then an attendant stayed awake to watch the fire. Perhaps this is how Candace's last nights in November of 1807 were spent.

The Domestic Kitchen. The Springs' kitchen was probably to the right or north of the front entry and was equipped with common iron fireplace tools, three tables, four chairs, knives and forks, two "pigs" (probably piggins, small wooden tubs to hold cooking scraps destined for disposal), and three "washing tubs." The kitchen had four window curtains and a looking glass. These were extremely rare items in regional kitchens. The curtains suggest the kitchen was a front room hard up against Church Lane. The curtains may have provided privacy from curious stares at the Black family during the early darkness of winter afternoons, or perhaps

Phyllis slept here if age made the stairs too great a challenge.

A floor plan consisting of two front rooms—parlor and kitchen—separated by a vestibule and chimney serving the rooms on either side was a common one in modest Portsmouth homes and many survive today. Pomp and Candace may have eaten breakfast in this room, especially in winter when the fire was newly started.

Elsewhere on the Property. When Candace's estate was inventoried in November she had in the house two barrels of cider, six bushels of potatoes, and a barrel of beef. Perhaps these were in the bake house, a shed, or—most likely—in the cellar.

Here and There around the House. In unspecified locations the Springs had six silver teaspoons, a silver watch, four rings, and a pair of earrings (Pomp's, in the African tradition, or Candace's?). Pomp left fifty dollars' worth of wearing apparel, plus three hats, two coats, two muffs, two "tibbets" (tippets or scarves), and an umbrella.

Back of the House. Pomp's "bread cart" and sleigh, harness, and ax were no doubt kept back of the house. Surely uninventoried firewood for heating and baking was also stored in the backyard, perhaps protected by a rough shed.

The Bake House. A small building out back, apparently against the north boundary of their house lot, was equipped with all the Springs' needs for commercial baking. It was outfitted with two scales and a leaden weight, eight barrels of flour, a brass wire sieve, an ax for splitting firewood, an iron rake for pulling embers from the ovens, four peels for sliding bread in and out of the oven, two dozen tin baking sheets, three baskets, and assorted unitemized objects.

Laundry equipment was kept in the bake house, an adjacent shed, or perhaps in an ell. It included a clotheshorse and a folding board,

three cotton sheets, three blankets, and a barrel and a half of soap, probably the gelatinous soft soap so common at the time.

The Springs' accumulation of fashion-conscious objects and sorting of their house into separate entertaining, working, and sleeping areas were modest adaptations of the physical symbolism of inward refinement. Through the entire eighteenth century a concern for refinement had been percolating through Portsmouth society starting with the white elite. It originated in British aristocratic ideals. This meant refinement of the mind through education, of the person through conduct and cleanliness, and of the environment through specialized rooms and utensils, all outwardly expressed through elegant appointments that demonstrated connoisseurship. Among the elite these became tools of social differentiation in a stratified society.[141] The Springs' polished cherry tables, gilt mahogany mirrors, framed pictures, figurines, window curtains, canopied bed, fashionable bureau, and dressing table were all props of refinement.

Some of Portsmouth's Black residents had been privy to close contact with elite life. During enslavement, they were daily exposed to the trappings of refinement. Through their travels as attendants to military officers during the Revolution, or as caterers and musicians at the Assembly House or private parties, they could see these symbols and comprehend the mechanisms of inclusion and exclusion. Black people were better informed about this aspect of white culture than middle-class and poor whites, and were quite capable of adopting the outward style of refinement if they had the inclination and the money. As president of the African Society, Pomp may have felt it particularly appropriate to adopt a style associated with a leadership class.

Style aside, there was work to be done, day in and day out. Pomp, Candace, and Phyllis arose early to fire their oven with wood split and laid the previous evening. Given Pomp's agrarian upbringing and the likelihood of Candace and

Phyllis's past domestic labors, the skill of baking was probably centered in the women. The amount of baking equipment suggests an ambitious scale. Local-grown rye flour and cornmeal (at that time often called "injun") were the regional norm, and wheat flour imported from New York and Philadelphia was available at a price. Grains, spices, and nonperishable foods were available in local shops. The new brick market house in the square and Langdon's market house at the foot of Daniel Street probably specialized in farm produce, as the old Spring Hill market house now specialized in fish.

Goods baked on the two dozen tin sheets were transferred to the three baskets, probably purchased from itinerant rural basket makers,[142] and loaded onto Pomp's handcart or sleigh. We can easily imagine Candace and the aging Phyllis glancing out the kitchen window to see Pomp trudging out the narrow ten-foot passage along the north side of the house into the street. Then they'd turn to negotiating the day's tasks of cleaning up, preparing noon dinner, inventorying and procuring supplies, and planning their afternoon's handwork.

Pomp's bread cart (called a wheelbarrow by Candace's inventory taker) was probably a handcart like those described in a reminiscence of street peddlers gathered near the Spring Hill fish market on Ceres Street circa 1800. "On the other side of the hill was a range of bakers' carts—small vehicles, drawn by hand—bearing the names of Plumber, Clapham, and Barry, kept there with an eye to the country trade."[143] Other vendors sold oysters from temporary trestle tables adjacent to the market.[144] Pomp's "slay" was probably a winter variant of his handcart, enabling him to take his business to the consumer in all seasons.

We can only conjecture about Pomp's marketing methods. Local tradition provided several models. He may have had a regular stand like the oyster vendors. Pomp may have rented space in one of Portsmouth's several market houses. He may have placed himself strategically where people gathered for market days,

court sessions, militia-training days, holiday orations, arrivals of visiting dignitaries, and ship arrivals. Perhaps Pomp followed a regular route, presenting his goods to boardinghouse proprietors, tavern keepers, or merchants or shopkeepers too pressed for time to return home for dinner. He may have swung by construction sites to appeal to hungry workmen during the building boom that swept the city from 1795 to 1805. Maybe he filled large orders of ship's biscuits for chandlers. Certainly the Springs' baked goods appealed to anyone who didn't have time to fire their oven or who wished to avoid baking in hot weather.

Pomp did not own a horse, but he owned a whip and harness. This suggests he hired a horse and perhaps a larger vehicle as needed for hauling large loads of firewood or baking supplies, using his yeoman's skills rather than hiring a teamster. Perhaps the Springs occasionally rented or borrowed a horse to visit Candace's relatives in Somersworth and Berwick.

The Springs lived when the last generation of imported Africans were beginning to die off. Africa by now seemed a remote, mythic or legendary place familiar only through their elders' reminiscences. The Springs and their contemporaries implemented inherited African values in terms of familiar local models. The African Society was an example of this emerging African-American culture.

Pomp and Candace risked self-employment, found a market niche, prospered, and made a comfortable home. The irony of slave-produced items in their house—mahogany, cotton, and no doubt coffee, sugar, molasses, rum, rice, spices, and other goods from the South and the West Indies—was probably obscured by distance from the source.

The Springs did not enjoy the national fame and wealth of ventriloquist Richard Potter, whom we'll meet soon, nor did they live in borrowed space like the Whipples, nor endure the indignities of the almshouse. With real estate and personal goods worth over a thousand dollars, the Springs were secure in Portsmouth's middle class.

Dinah Gibson: Making It on Her Own

Our sampling of those freed from slavery includes Dinah Gibson. Her work experience was, like the Springs', one of culinary self-employment. She enjoyed less success and ended up dependent on the charity of those who had once enslaved her.

Newly freed women usually turned to the domestic tasks acquired in slavery—cooking, laundry, sewing, child rearing and housekeeping—to support themselves. Dinah turned to cooking.

People of European ancestry throughout the Americas noticed Black women's exceptional cooking skills. This was probably because the first generation brought an African sense of seasoning to the bland or salty Anglo-American foodways their mistresses were accustomed to. Indeed, legendary "southern" cooking is Black cooking, and in most of the Americas celebrated regional specialties are usually associated with Africans, Natives, or non-Anglo immigrants. Enslaved women who worked in the mansions of seaport merchants had access to a world of imported delicacies, enabling them to reinvent African culinary traditions, spicing foods with subtlety and complexity not indigenous to Anglo-American foodways.[145] Dinah Gibson, formerly enslaved by the Rice family of Kittery, worked in Portsmouth, making a living from her inherited culinary knowledge.

Dinah's life in Kittery is a reminder that the story of Black people in Kittery is one and the same as their story in Portsmouth, dating back equally far and involving the many people who glided back and forth across the river. Their stories diverge only in that—as Maine was a province of Massachusetts until 1820—slavery's earlier dissolution in Massachusetts meant the same in Maine.

Dinah Gibson catered events at the Assembly House ballroom previously mentioned rela-

tive to Cuffee Whipple. It survived until 1838.[146] During an evening of dancing at the Assembly House,

> about ten o'clock, sandwiches of tongue and ham, with thin biscuit, were handed round on large waiters, in turn with sangaree, lemonade, and chocolate.... At the Washington['s Birthday] Ball a great fruit-cake was placed in a corner of the ball-room, where one of the managers cut.
>
> The family of Mr Whidden prepared the rooms and entertainment for the elegant company. I remember that Dinah (who in the days of slavery was owned by my grandmother, and who assisted the Whiddens in the arrangements) used to tell a great deal about the sandwiches, and how long they boiled the chocolate, which had spice in it.[147]

From time to time Dinah no doubt encountered Cuffee Whipple, who often played violin for balls at the Assembly House.

Dinah was married to John Gibson by the North Church minister on August 20, 1804.[148] Both John and Dinah eluded the compilers of the first city directory in 1821, but she lived on in the area until her death in 1825. Dinah's whereabouts during her married years is unknown.

Dinah found her way into the hearts of others than John Gibson. The Rice children loved her too. She sustained her popularity with them as they grew into adulthood.

> My first recollections of Kittery were associated with Dinah. My Grandfather Rice bought her about 1760 when she was eighteen years old & she remained faithful & devoted to the family until her death in 1825 or 6. My Father was the youngest of my grandmother's twelve children & she [Dinah] was exceedingly fond of him. He always took tea with her on Saturday afternoons & his family often went with him.[149]

The author of this reminiscence, Sarah Parker Rice Goodwin, spent her girlhood, 1805–15, on

Deer Street in Portsmouth. Dinah, by then in her eighties, seems again to have been living on the old Rice property in Kittery. The Rice family's name is memorialized in the name Rice Avenue, which even then traversed the land they owned, running down to the river to a wharf that once served the ferry to Portsmouth. It is unclear whether Dinah and her husband lived there all along in an arrangement like that enjoyed by the Whipples and Bruces, or whether Dinah returned there as a widow.

In this period Portsmouth was enjoying returned prosperity after the economic slump of the Revolution. In spite of the removal of the state government to a series of inland towns, Portsmouth continued to lead fashion in New Hampshire. New meeting halls and ballrooms were built, such as Jefferson Hall over the new brick market house of 1799 and Franklin Hall in the Franklin Hotel on Congress Street in 1819.[150] These were the scenes of many banquets, balls, and festive occasions. While neither the buildings nor receipts for catering survive, the halls were settings where Dinah likely worked.

Dinah Gibson died when she was about eighty-three years of age. Her death in 1825 was recorded in the North Church records with poignant brevity: "Dinah Gibson Found dead on ice near her home, fell in the night, Froze."[151]

Richard Potter: Making an Itinerant Living in Entertainment

Richard Potter provides a startling contrast to others whom we've met in newly acquired freedom. He was a self-employed itinerant, an itinerancy necessary even when success and prosperity provided him a permanent home. He also moved from an urban to a rural setting, the reverse of the norm, to stretch the value of his prosperity.

MR. POTTER, Ventriloquist, Would respectfully inform the Ladies and Gentlemen of Portsmouth and vicinity, that he contemplates

exhibiting his Performance for a few Evenings at the Franklin Hall commencing on Monday, June 21. Tickets had at the Bar. For further particulars see Bills of the day. June 19, 1830.[152]

This newspaper advertisement announced the performance of a Black Yankee who was one of America's earliest and most famous performers, noted as a ventriloquist and magician. Making a living in entertainment would become a staple recourse for Black Americans through the coming centuries.

Richard Potter was born in 1783 or earlier. His mother, named Dinah, had been enslaved by Sir Charles Henry Frankland, colonial-era customs collector of the Port of Boston. Frankland's son Henry Cromwell is believed to be Richard Potter's father, though his paternity has not been established with complete certainty.[153] Frankland was a wealthy man with both a Boston house and a country seat in outlying Hopkinton, Massachusetts. Richard may have been born—and apparently spent most of his childhood—in rural Hopkinton. He possibly spent some time at Frankland's city house in Boston. Apparently Potter was allowed to attend the village school in Hopkinton.

At the age of ten, about 1793—when slavery was gradually disintegrating in Massachusetts—Richard Potter went to England serving as cabin boy to a friend of the Frankland family, Captain Skinner. In Britain the child was left on his own, apparently abandoned. Potter found employment as a servant with a circus and remained with it for several years.

By the time he was fifteen Potter had become a cast member of the circus, when it toured America. Apparently it was a prolonged tour. At age eighteen, around 1801, Potter left the circus to remain in America.

Potter soon took up with a ventriloquist known as "the elder Rennie," with whom he is believed to have traversed much of the United States and the West Indies. Between performing tours with Rennie, Potter worked as a servant in the Boston home of Reverend Daniel Oliver. Oliver's children later recollected being amused by Potter's tricks performed beside the kitchen fireplace. Among the Oliver cousins was Oliver Wendell Holmes, who later mentioned Potter's mother Dinah.

During that period Potter worked briefly in Portsmouth as a servant in the New Hampshire Hotel. That hotel stood at the foot of State Street at the inner end of the 340-foot-long Portsmouth Pier, perhaps the most bustling part of the Portsmouth waterfront at that time. The hotel's clientele was mostly ship's masters (captains) and mates.[154] Potter's time working in Portsmouth was brief, though he would be back.

In 1808, when Richard Potter was about twenty-five years old, he married Sally Harris, a Black woman from Roxbury, Massachusetts. This was a rural town on the southwest approach to Boston that had long been an easily accessible rural retreat for Bostonians and now was rapidly filling with fashionable suburban villas for the wealthy. She may have grown up on a farm in Roxbury or elsewhere and gone to work as a servant in one of its elegant suburban mansions. An agrarian upbringing is implied in Potter's later description of her as "well acquainted with country business."[155] In 1809 they had a son, Henry.[156]

On November 13, 1811, Richard Potter was admitted to the Masons, joining Boston's African Lodge no. 459, America's first Black Masonic lodge (later renamed the Prince Hall Lodge, for one of its founders and first grand master). Potter received his first three degrees two weeks later. In 1827 he would be among the signers of the declaration separating this lodge from its parent lodge in Great Britain.[157]

Also in 1811 the ventriloquist Rennie retired, opening the field to Potter. Potter promptly launched a career of his own. Sally became his performance assistant. They performed frequently in Boston, charging a stiff admission price of twenty-five cents. Secure in his reputation, in 1817, during the depression of 1815–20, Potter raised admission to a dollar, at a time when unskilled laborers earned about fifty cents per day.

Potter sometimes earned enough to worry about his personal safety. While in Mobile, Alabama, he had accumulated $4,800, mostly in coin. For security he left town in the middle of the night, traveling the opposite direction from his next advertised venue.

Though Sally may not have found their performing career particularly congenial, it served them well. In 1814, when Potter was in his thirties, they had both the prosperity and the foresight to provide for a secure old age. "Having a good wife, well acquainted with country business, I concluded, that instead of carrying her about with me as an assistant, it would be better to have a home, which would be to her a congenial occupation, and to me a polar star, towards which I could always set my course. I accordingly took up about two hundred acres of nearly wild land in New Hampshire, and laid out a plan of improvement."[158]

This land was in an undeveloped part of Andover, New Hampshire, northwest of today's state capital of Concord. It was in a landscape that Potter had admired on an earlier trip. He built a house that included in its upper story a large performance room, probably comparable to the ballrooms that filled the upper front of many inns in urban and rural New England. Apparently the Potters operated something of a tavern; in 1824 Potter procured a liquor license from the town authorities.[159] Potter enjoyed his farm and described himself as a "yeoman," a landowning farmer, on legal documents.

Richard continued to tour, sometimes taking Sally along. Their prosperity, travels, and urban connections enabled Sally to wear up-to-date fashions that never failed to impress her rural neighbors. Potter implemented considerable improvements to his land when he was home, and no doubt Sally oversaw their continuing implementation while Richard was away.

Meanwhile remote Andover grew into a town, its change noted by Potter at every return. "Here, as I returned periodically from my excursions, I found a bank established, which gave me a good interest for my deposits. My purchases and my improvements have cost me more than ten thousand dollars."[160]

Most of Potter's performances were in New England.[161] One of Potter's Boston performing venues in the 1830s was the New England Museum, operated by Ethan Allen Greenwood, who was also a portrait painter. Greenwood painted a likeness of "Potter the Ventriloquist," though the whereabouts of this painting is unknown. While earlier portraits of Black people had often been in the context of servants hovering in the background of white people's portraits, finding a Black man as the central subject of a portrait signifies a sea change in status, at least for this one individual.[162]

Potter's reputation and travels spread. He performed in Quebec, Baltimore, Philadelphia, Saint Louis, New Orleans, the West Indies, and Europe. A Victorian-era chronicler of Portsmouth remembered Richard Potter as "the celebrated ventriloquist Potter, whose fame was world-wide in his day."[163] Victorian poet John Saxe mentioned Potter in a poem called "The Great Magician," in which he used magicians in an allegory for falsehood among others.[164]

The best information about his shows is found in advertisements early in his career when the still obscure Potter had to attract spectators with beguiling detail. They provide a glimpse of what his Portsmouth show might have included:

MULTUM IN PARVO!

An Evening's Brush to sweep away Care; or A Medley to please. Mr. Potter, the Ventriloquist, most respectfully informs the ladies and gentlemen, visitants and inhabitants of Saratoga, and its vicinity, that he will exhibit a few evenings at the Large Room in Walton's Row, and hopes, by his exertions to please, to receive the patronage of a generous and enlightened public. His first entertainment will take place on Tuesday Evening, August 12.

Part 1.

—Mr. Potter will bring forward 100 curious but mysterious EXPERIMENTS, with eggs, money, fruit, birds, boxes, cards, &c.—among

which will be presented the COFFER OF MAHOMET; Or . . . a Lady's Glove turned to a live bird! Glass Casket and Mysterious Desk, Pexis Metalica. With several other recreations not mentioned in this bill. To conclude with the TUMOROUS BALLS!!!

Part 2.

—Mr Potter will deliver his DISSERTATION ON NOSES, and personate the different characters of the wearers. This satirically lashes the vices and follies of mankind, and forms a source of rational amusement. Mr. P. will sing a number of Comical Songs adapted to each character.

Part 3.

VENTRILOQUISM. Mr. Potter will display his wonderful but laborious powers of Ventriloquism. Tickets, 25 cents. . . .[165]

Other advertisements mention the "rising cards," "cutting a woman's lace and restoring it," and the "wonderful nefiskus box."[166] Recollections by those who saw Potter mention his stuffing tow (raw flax fibers) down his throat with a sword and pulling forth yards of multicolored ribbon, as well as tricks in which he endured fire without apparent pain.

Exoticism was a part of Potter's act; sometimes he performed in the guise of a turbaned Asian or introduced his wife as a Penobscot Indian. This gave rise to much speculation about his origins, wrongly assigning his birthplace to the West or East Indies.[167]

Richard Potter died on September 20, 1835, at age fifty-two.[168] Sally died a year later on October 24, 1836, at age forty-nine. They were buried in front of their house in Andover, New Hampshire, in a neighborhood still known as Potter Place. His stone is inscribed "In memory of Richard Potter, the Celebrated Ventriloquist."

The prosperous Potters, with their farm and inn, far-flung travels, and enviable city fashions, attained a secure place in their rural town. However there were profoundly tragic elements to their lives. In 1816 their seven-year-old son Henry was killed when run over by a loaded farm cart. Fifteen years later, in 1831, their daughter Jeannette died young. Perhaps overcome by these tragedies and the loneliness engendered by an absent husband, racial marginalization, and rural isolation, Sally and their son Richard Jr. became alcoholics.[169]

Potter's successful career notwithstanding, whites viewed Black accomplishment as an aberration. White antiquarians routinely omit Black people from town historical narratives, dismissing any potential significance in their presence. Whites were secretly ashamed of why Black people were among them. Mid-twentieth-century novelist Grace Metalious evoked this in her 1956 novel *Peyton Place* in part inspired by Potter Place. It tells stories of small-town New Hampshire life, of outwardly proper people made inwardly miserable by shame and the numerous secrets they harbor in their hearts. Framing all this unhappiness is the secret that their pretty town was founded by and named for a Black person.[170] In this detail the novelist successfully captured twentieth-century white ambivalence about race.

Black Mariners of Portsmouth: Life at Sea and at Home

While some free Blacks lingered in domestic employment in specialized self-employment or in itinerancy, most picked up an endless round of arduous and unskilled odd jobs. Another option was work of such danger, violence, or hardship that only desperately unskilled whites and marginalized Blacks would take it. Among this kind of work was life at sea.

The itinerancy of a mariner's job was distinctive in all ways. It was in a single place that was constantly in motion; an engagement lasted not a day or a night but for weeks, months, or years; and it was subject to different laws than obtained on land. But much as itinerants were constantly searching for a new venue for their specific skill, a mariner had to find new work at the end of each voyage.

In a seaport like Portsmouth great numbers of white people were in one way or another connected to maritime work: at sea, on the docks, in shipyards, or laboring in such supply-trade workshops as ropewalks, sail lofts, or chandleries. Others were investors, insurers, exporters, or owners of retail shops and emporiums. Of these pursuits all but unskilled dock work and the sailor's job were off-limits to Black men.

Black mariners had been sailing out of Portsmouth since the colonial period. In 1727 Captain William Bowen of Portsmouth charged £22 for the rental of his brigantine together with his enslaved man by someone who had maritime business in Casco Bay.[171] Cato Wheelwright appears to have been a mariner too, before his purchase by Jeremiah Wheelwright.

In 1752 Nathaniel Warner, captain of the *Princess Dowager* took an enslaved man on a voyage to Saint Christopher (Saint Kitts) in the West Indies. The African may have gone as a personal attendant but as likely served with the crew.[172] This is the same man beaten by British mariner John Stavers, later an innkeeper in Portsmouth.

Portsmouth merchants were not averse to renting others' slaves when in foreign ports. In 1765 Captain John Langdon, when on the West Indian island of Montserrat in the Lesser Antilles aboard the *Damon*, rented slaves from Edward Sankey and others daily for several weeks.[173]

In 1777, early in the Revolution, mariner John Wheelwright (son of the Wheelwrights mentioned earlier as owners of a Black cooper named Nero) captained a privateer. He wrote back to Portsmouth that "I have bought half a Negro but have not Paid for him."[174] In all probability the man Wheelwright purchased was a mariner.

One Revolutionary-era case is remarkable for a master's response to an enslaved man's request to be sent on a privateer. "To be SOLD for a CERTAIN TIME, or Let by the month, A

The ship *Horace* of Portsmouth was built in 1805 by Stephen Paul. This painting by Nicholas Camillieri in 1807 includes among the crew one hatless man who is Black. *Courtesy Portsmouth Athenæum.*

genteel sprightly NEGRO FELLOW, in fine health, about eighteen years of age, He can be recommended for Many good qualities, has served well at sea and land, waits on company well, and is extreme desirous of belonging to a Captain of a privateer, or going in one, as may be agreed. For further particulars enquire of the printer."[175] Perhaps the "extreme desirous" man had arranged with his owner for a share of any profit, raising the hope of buying his freedom. Ordinarily the pay and share of prize money earned by a slave at sea was the property of his owner. Enslaved men were sent to sea from many colonial New England seaports during the war.[176]

Many Black men in Portsmouth "served well at sea." In 1800 a Black Portsmouth sailor named Moses acted valiantly when the French seized his ship off Saint Croix.[177] Maritime experience was a training ground for later employment in freedom. Not enough whites were interested in this extremely dangerous work, so white employers opened the field to Black men. As a result, in the early nineteenth century Black men were enrolled in ships' crews in numbers disproportionate to their part of the general population.

Crews were more noticeably integrated than almost any other occupation. Integration in most areas of employment aroused white animosity and bigotry. But work at sea was frequently tempered by unusual degrees of co-operation, interracial friendship, and tolerance, making it more appealing to Black men than many land-based occupations.[178]

Over the centuries, the physical separateness of life at sea had allowed the evolution of a dual culture mixing the necessities and strictures of sea life with cultural assumptions developed in the many separate home ports of the crew. Egalitarianism characterized seamen's relations to one another.[179] It necessarily encompassed Black crew members where safety and success relied on unified purpose and action. To some degree this egalitarianism evolved in resistance to—or mutual support in the face of—the severe restrictions, codes of conduct, and impersonal harshness of maritime law and tradition.

Where strength, quality of work, and experience were highly valued, white employers overlooked race. For equal work and status, Black men received pay equal to or even in excess of the pay of some white mariners.[180] In a few instances Black men attained the rank of officers, notably on the dangerous, dirty and, unpopular whaling ships and on some coastal schooners.[181]

Equal pay was appealing. In cities like Philadelphia, with large free Black populations, maritime work was the largest single employer of Black males in the early nineteenth century.[182]

Effects of Racism on Maritime Employment

Coastal shipping (as distinct from international trade) was more land-based and was noticeably less open to Black men. In all branches of maritime work Black men were the first to lose ground when the economy slumped.[183] After the Embargo, the War of 1812, and the depression of 1815, Portsmouth's international trade changed. This caused a drop in the number of Portsmouth-based vessels and voyages and a corresponding drop in the number of mariners in town; no doubt it contributed significantly to the precipitous drop in the number of Black mariners in Portsmouth. In larger ports like Providence and Newport overt discrimination surfaced as soon as the Embargo took effect and the scramble for the few available coasting jobs intensified.[184] Discrimination against minorities when jobs are scarce remains a fixture of American culture.

White exclusion of Black men from land-based occupations was sometimes at odds with the tradition of their presence at sea. When in 1798 Secretary of the Navy Benjamin Stoddert barred Black and biracial men from enlisting aboard navy ships, his prohibition was frequently ignored.[185]

Black mariners faced special dangers. In 1822 South Carolina passed a Negro Seamen Act to prevent free Black sailors from moving among the general population or spreading word of the advantages of freedom among the enslaved population. While in the state's ports, free Black mariners were temporarily imprisoned at the expense of the ship captain and released when the ship departed. Seamen in violation of this act could be sold into slavery on the auctioneer's block. Similar laws were soon passed in North Carolina, Georgia, Florida, Alabama, and Louisiana.[186] Black mariners must have been hesitant to ship out on vessels headed to southern ports to pick up rice, tobacco, or cotton for the Piscataqua region's mills at Dover, Newmarket, and Portsmouth.

Mariners' work was not only dangerous; it was extremely difficult and menial. Most Black sailors were not career mariners but went to sea as only one job among a series of base-level positions available to Black men in a white-dominated economy.[187]

By the mid–nineteenth century industrial work became an alternative to maritime work for low-skilled white men. Life at sea slipped to an ever lower level of esteem in the public mind, and—in a time of increasing rhetoric of democracy—even white sailors began to equate mariners' work with southern slavery.[188] Wages decreased and brutality increased.[189]

One might expect white abandonment of harsh life at sea to leave the field entirely open for Black mariners. Instead a new and marginalized white group increasingly took up work as mariners—immigrants.

Simultaneously, responsibility for hiring crews shifted from ship owners or captains to shipping masters. Unlike their somewhat indifferent predecessors the shipping masters, or their crimps, favored white mariners over Black. Blacks at sea were increasingly limited to the menial tasks of cook, steward, and cabin servants, with the perennial status of "boy."

By the 1850s Portsmouth's whites assumed mariners were white and maritime servants were

Black. An 1853 parade in Portsmouth included floats representing the major trades. A float depicting a ship illustrated this outlook: "Ship *George Washington*, Capt. Harrat, passed along the street propelled by three-horse power. The pilot was William Pierce. The ship was fully rigged, twenty-six feet in height, had a crew of ten, a small Black cook was seated on the caboose: two swivels mounted on the bows were frequently discharged, and the whole was an object of much interest."[190] "Caboose" or "cab house" is an old term for a ship's deck-top kitchen.

Because cooks and stewards worked and quartered separately from the rest of the sailors, the traditional integration of crews diminished sharply, and Black mariners were increasingly alone in a white crew.[191] A long history of Black mariners was drifting toward its end, except among that most dangerous of maritime pursuits, whaling. Whaling was not much practiced by Portsmouth vessels. Only a few vessels went out in a brief period, providing scant local opportunity for this line of employment.

By 1862 Black mariners were remembered as a feature of Portsmouth's past. November of that wartime year saw the presence at the Portsmouth Naval Shipyard of an armed ship whose crew included twenty-five Black sailors. The Black mariners' unfamiliar presence when in town on leave drew racist commentary in a local newspaper's letters to the editor. In somewhat condescending defense of the sailors, the newspaper editorially retorted that they were well behaved and that "we remember that when Black sailors were numerous in this port, they behaved as well as the white ones."[192] By 1862 Black mariners were a memory from the past and a novelty to the present.

Black sailors didn't disappear instantly or entirely. Larger ports had larger Black populations and vastly more ships to crew; edging Black sailors out of the field was therefore a slower process in such ports as Boston and New Bedford. Immediately after the Civil War shipowners in the small port of Newburyport, Massachusetts, just south of Portsmouth and of nearly identical size and history, brought up from Boston and New Bedford an all-Black crew for the maiden voyage of their new ship *Montana*, in 1865. The ship's first voyage was to New Orleans via Mobile.[193] With the war over and slavery abolished nationwide, the old southern codes requiring free Black sailors to stay in jail while in ports were no longer a threat. Nonetheless the days of Black mariners were over in small ports and were numbered in larger New England ports.

Though the 1862 newspaper writer remembered when "Black sailors were numerous in this port," individual Black mariners are irregularly recorded in Portsmouth. An abstract of seamen's protection certificates issued by the port's customs officer for part of 1801 provides some information. Though not representing all who sailed from this port, the abstract includes name, age, height, complexion, and place of birth of those who applied for certificates. Of the thirty-six African-American seamen listed, sixteen, about half, were born in Piscataqua towns.[194] Only three were born in inland New Hampshire. Because mariners could apply for these papers in any port, we find seventeen were born in other ports ranging from Portland, Maine, to Virginia. While all these Black mariners were between fourteen and thirty-eight years old, their average age was twenty-three; the average age of those from the Piscataqua was just shy of nineteen. Five of these mariners carried names indicative of birth in enslavement (London, Prince, Duce, Scipio, and Jolly). The rest bore Christian names (and one was named Liberty), suggesting they had been born in freedom or had chosen new names upon manumission. There is no discernible age differentiation in naming patterns.[195]

In 1821, the year Portsmouth's first directory was compiled, the port had at least twenty-eight Black households.[196] Yet no Black people are listed as employed in the trades of mariner, caulker, shipmaster, ship carpenter, stevedore (a dock worker), rigger, boatbuilder, sail maker, line manufacturer, or rope maker, nor in support trades such as mathematical (including navigational) instrument maker. Nor are they found listed among those several blacksmiths and barrel makers whose shops were on wharves. The absence of Black mariners in a period "when Black sailors were numerous in this port" is probably because they were away at sea or did not have the status of head of household, making them invisible to the compilers of the directory.

In 1834 seven Black mariners were among Portsmouth's population,[197] and nine in 1839. The latter are not the same men who were recorded in 1834, probably because of constant departures on prolonged voyages and only brief stints at home. Curiously William Webb, a Black proprietor of a seamen's boardinghouse on State Street, had no Black mariners among his boarders, although a Black farmhand named Charles Nerrett boarded with him. When crimps came around seeking crew members, Webb likely spread word of the employment opportunity to any Black mariners he knew of.[198]

Most of Portsmouth's nineteenth-century Black residents lived within a couple of blocks of the river, where housing was increasingly affordable and where informal waterfront work was available.[199] Like most households in town, those headed by Black persons consisted of both related and unrelated people. A mariner's return to shore ended egalitarian camaraderie, returning him to the more overtly racist and exclusionary mainland culture and the company of loved ones, family, and old friends.

Mariners were fairly well-paid compared with the pay available to land-based Black workers. Sailors often received their pay in a lump sum at the end of a voyage. Like few land-bound Black people, mariners could accumulate the wherewithal to purchase a modest home, raise a family, start a business, or fund migration to a more promising place. Black mariners who were heads of Portsmouth households had probably saved a nest egg, acquired a home and family, and then, to support them, continued with the relatively well-paid mariners' work.

Compared with white mariners, Black sailors were more rooted in their home ports, continued going to sea longer, and as a result were more likely to be married.[200] White mariners tended to find land-based employment upon marriage; their sailing days were an employment phase rather than a career.

Like all mariners in their home port, Black mariners had a special esteem among family and friends. They could tell tales of faraway places, exotic cultures, foreign spectacles, thrilling moments of danger, proud victories of will against captains, or boastful narratives of fistfights with other sailors.[201] They could also report on Black life in other places, a topic surely of immediate interest at home.

Work at sea yielded unexpected opportunity. One Black Portsmouth native, whose name is unknown, went to sea around the year 1800 as a steward under Captain Charles Coffin carrying cargo to Russia for Thomas Sheafe. At Saint Petersburg the steward went to see a military display of troops before the emperor. The czar was fascinated by the Black man's unfamiliar appearance and hired him as a butler. A few years later he returned to Portsmouth to take his wife and children to live with him in Saint Petersburg. He made a stunning appearance in Portsmouth's streets dressed in imperial livery with gold lace and silk stockings.

Another Black mariner of Portsmouth who found unexpected opportunity at sea was John Francis. He was serving on a Portsmouth ship when it was seized in the War of 1812. He hid fifteen thousand dollars of the cargo owners' gold coin in a grease tub. He continued serving on the ship under its captors, and when released asked for the tub of grease in payment, thus saving the cargo owner's investment. In thanks for preserving and returning their gold, John and Nathaniel Haven built a house for Francis on Union Street.[202]

By 1851 the number of Black mariners in Portsmouth was declining, along with the number of Black households. The local decline in numbers of Black mariners paralleled similar developments throughout the eastern seaboard as they were gradually displaced from a traditional field of employment by competition from marginalized immigrants and increasingly rigid and racist hiring practices in assembling crews.[203] An important and historical employment had ceased.

Esther Whipple Mullinaux: Kinship and Cluster Diffusion

Esther Whipple Mullinaux followed her parents' pattern of piecing together what work she could. Self-employed like caterer Dinah Gibson and others, Mullinaux was a laundress. Often at the edge of poverty, she ultimately managed to buy a house of her own. Esther bought a house on Walden Lane in September 1851 and continued there until her death in 1868.[204] Her story provides an interesting narrative of how one resident came to live in a back-channel neighborhood typical of the places where Black families clustered.

Mid-nineteenth-century Portsmouth had no discrete Black neighborhoods. But kinship, employment, and affordable housing sometimes brought Black households into close proximity. This clustered diffusion is the closest Portsmouth has ever had to Black neighborhoods.

Such a loose cluster was discernible within sight of the river in the old downtown area on Bow, Daniel, and State Streets. Two modest clusters took shape on the west side of Portsmouth in neighborhoods that were being built over hitherto rural areas in the wedges between approach highways. One of these clustered on Union (then called Anthony) Street near its intersection with Middle Street. Another cluster was also visible at the south edge of town along a shallow back channel behind Pierce Island. Together they provide an interesting case study of the movement of Black people through such neighborhoods.

An old seventeenth-century highway called Water Street (now Marcy Street) ran along the river, connecting the downtown waterfront with the site of the earliest church and continuing to a causeway connecting to Portsmouth's earliest settlement center on Great Island. Where this highway emerged from the eighteenth century's compact part of town, a series of short and extremely narrow dead-end lanes developed, connecting Water Street to the back channel. Today they remain crowded with the small early- and mid-nineteenth-century homes of middling artisans and others who could not afford houses on the more prominent streets. Among them were the homes of Black families who attained the means to own property—on Walden, Holmes, Partridge, and Pray Lanes.

In the years from 1821 to 1839 the number of Black families in the neighborhood rose to eight, then eleven, then dropped to six and then two. At the end both these households lived on Walden Lane. This trend paralleled the general decline in the numbers of Black families in Portsmouth.[204] In many instances these apparently modest numbers represent whole households. For example, in 1830 Andrew Barnet headed a household of seventeen people.[205]

The absence of classical names among the Black residents of this waterfront neighborhood indicates they were freeborn. Their surnames were mostly new to Portsmouth, and a steady turnover suggests a coming and going in search of work. Short-term residents were probably renters rather than owners.

By 1851 there were only two Black heads of household in the area, and they had removed from Walden Lane, which had briefly been home to three Black families.[206] Late in this year a third new Black household appeared in the neighborhood when Esther Whipple Mullinaux, a matronly widow, moved into her new home on Walden.

Esther was the daughter of Prince and Dinah Whipple. She had started life with them and her Uncle Cuffee and Aunt Rebecca and various siblings and cousins in their house on High Street at the end of Madame Whipple's garden. Like her mother, Esther was an active member of North Church, and she had stayed with her mother much of the time through Dinah's widowhood and the infirmity of her last years.

In April of 1801 Esther married William

Esther Mullinaux bought a house on Walden Lane in 1851 where she lived for 17 years until her death. Several Black families lived on the street during that time. This view is from Marcy Street, c. 1995. *Photography by Tulani Freeman. Portsmouth Black Heritage Trail.*

Mullinaux.[208] What became of William is unknown. Perhaps he was a mariner so long gone to sea he was presumed lost. Maybe he abandoned her. Around 1815 Esther married again.

In 1817 the church learned that Esther had been still lawfully married to William when she remarried. They admonished her and transcribed into the church record book her confession of "shame & confusion of face." In this confession she expressed her "lamentation" for her "dreadful wickedness" and implored "a merciful God" to "wash me thoroughly from mine iniquity" and asked "the Brethren & Sisters of this Chh." to look toward her with a forgiving spirit. Her confession was read aloud before the assembled church on "Lord's day, Decr 6, 1817."[209] Several of New England's Protestant denominations used such public confessions to resolve conflicts and curtail behavior unacceptable to them. The church record gives no detail on the resolution of this double marriage. Her continuing use of her first husband's name hints that the second marriage may have been considered null.

By 1827 Esther was a widow. Perhaps she had

at last heard definitive word of William's fate. At this time Esther lived on High Street, the street of her childhood residence, but in a separate household from her widowed mother Dinah. In 1830 Dinah constituted a household of one person, while Esther's household included seven people. These were a boy and a girl under age ten, a male and two females ages twenty-four to thirty-six, a male over fifty-five, and a female over thirty-six.[210]

A considerable number of Black Mullinaux can be extracted from local church records, probably mostly Esther's household. These include William Prince, Anna, Elizabeth, Richard, and Horace William. Apparently William Prince was named for his father William and his maternal grandfather Prince. A Nan Mullinaux mentioned in 1779 was likely Esther's husband's mother or sister.[211]

Add Esther's siblings and other Whipple relatives, and it becomes apparent that Esther was part of a sizable clan in Portsmouth. Historical records often mention an individual only once with no corroborating information. This case shows how an apparently solitary individ-

Esther Whipple Mullinaux was the daughter of Prince and Dinah Whipple, a wife and mother, and worked as a laundress. She and her entire family attended North Church. When Mullinaux died in 1868 she was buried in North Cemetery near her father (her mother's unmarked grave probably is there too) and a daughter who had predeceased her. *Courtesy of North Chruch. African American Resource Center.*

ual like the widowed Esther, or her widowed mother Dinah Chase Whipple, did not necessarily lack an extensive kinship network.

In the 1830s Esther moved with her widowed mother Dinah to Pleasant Street[212] and by the 1840s shared in her mother's poverty. North Church gave cash gifts to Esther in the winters of 1844 and 1846, as well as paying for her mother's burial.[213]

Sometime after Dinah's death in 1846 Esther lived for a time on Water Street. In 1851 Esther was making a living as a laundress.[214] She was evidently working hard and saving money. In September of 1851 Esther attended a real estate auction and for two hundred dollars—well

below actual value—bought a little house on Walden Lane where she lived the rest of her life.[215] Her house was on the north side of the street. There are only a few feet between Walden Lane and the next lane north of it; the houses on that side of the street are narrow and abut both streets.

Esther probably continued as laundress and may have done other tasks nineteenth-century women were trained in and often turned to when widowed: taking in paying boarders, sewing, and housekeeping.

Esther remained active in her church. In her will she left everything to North Church, stipulating that it be applied to foreign and home missionary work. Clearly she wished to extend to others the benefits of her religion. Esther was likely particularly interested in the home mission projects of funding schools and other services for newly freed Black Americans in the rural South, sponsored by Portsmouth's North and South Churches alike.[216] When Esther died in 1868 she was buried in North Burial Ground near her parents Prince and Dinah and a daughter who had predeceased her.

By the 1860s the probate process no longer required an item by item inventory of personal goods. Esther's probate inventory simply lists cash on hand ($11.20) and a lump sum value for the real estate. Her house was appraised at $300, well above what she had paid for it. In an era when real estate usually declined in value, it is impressive that she had acquired it for so low a price that even with depreciation it turned a profit.[217] Better yet, the executor of Esther's estate was able to realize the appraised value and sold it for $300. A large-scale local landlord, Leonard Cotton, owner of forty properties in Portsmouth, purchased it.[218]

Esther appears to have represented the end of an early-nineteenth-century clustering of Black families on these adjacent waterfront lanes. While declining numbers meant such clusters would no longer be a part of the Portsmouth scene, Black individuals and families continued in town, sprinkled throughout the South, North, and West Ends through the remainder of the nineteenth and the entire twentieth century.

Esther Mullinaux, Dinah Gibson, the Whipples, Siras and Flora Stoodley Bruce, Pomp and Candace Spring, Richard Potter, and the various Black sailors who shipped out of Portsmouth provide sketches of the general experience of the first generation of free Black Yankees making livings and homes in Portsmouth. Their varied careers, migrations, and the occasional modest prosperity that enabled some to purchase homes show persistence and tenacity in a difficult and often hostile world. All the while these early Americans chipped away at white resistance to their citizenship and dignified employment. They worked unceasingly against distant slavery. Soon, the issue of slavery would convulse the nation.

CHAPTER 4

Abolition

❧⟡❧

Esther Whipple Mullinaux was excited in spite of the chilly spring drizzle. That morning the news had spread through Portsmouth like wildfire: General Lee had surrendered and the terrible war was ending in the Union's favor. The Emancipation Proclamation could now be enforced throughout the South! She was free, of course, always had been. The proclamation hadn't been unalloyed good news, since it didn't apply to slaves in the North. But freeing who-knows-how-many slaves in the South would be a great victory for justice.

The day's news had sent an exhilarating jolt through her and everyone she met, Black and white. It made the hike across town with the heavy basket of laundry a little easier. The surrender was all anyone was talking about. She could hear snippets of conversation among shopkeepers checking out rumors at one another's doors, people craving verification and detail.

Esther paused at the street corner, adjusted her wrap against the penetrating mist drifting in off the river, hefted the heavy basket to her other hip, and rounded the corner. What she saw made her stop in her tracks.

A block ahead of her hundreds of people clogged Daniel Street. No, not hundreds—there seemed to be thousands of people. Cautiously she moved closer. They were making quite a racket, with numerous shouts of individuals rising angrily above the general murmur. As she got closer she could see by the tilt of the mass of umbrellas at the periphery that they were facing upward toward a building on the north side of the street.

She glanced upward just in time to see the striped and starry flag of the Union poking out of a window. Shouts to wave it were followed by a wobbling back and forth of the wet wool banner. Esther paused. Though curious and excited, she was elderly, heavily laden, and didn't want to get mixed up in a dispute among angry white folks. It didn't matter what they were angry at.

Then there was a shift in the crowd's focus, a new commotion of some sort. The flag was pulled in, and a few moments later all the upstairs windows were thrown open. Furniture, wooden cases, sheaves of paper cascaded from the windows and crashed into the street below to roars of approval. Esther revised her route in a hurry and scuttled away from the riot. This had to be about the war and the news. But whatever it was about, those white folks were a little late in getting angry.

Slavery precipitated a divisive war among whites in the 1860s that would have repercussions for a century more. Sometimes the Civil War is described as a war over territorial settlement policy, states' rights, or divergent economies. Because each of these contributing causes was defined by slavery, the war was, in the end, all about slavery.

The impulse to abolish slavery began with and was led by Black Americans throughout the process, a fact so fundamental that its displacement from history by narratives of white abolitionists is astounding. White abolitionists were genuinely impassioned and immensely influential, but they operated in a context of gradually learning from, and eventual friendship with, inspiring Black leaders.

White antislavery sentiment gradually evolved through several phases of argument about how to end the institution. Though the white citizens of New Hampshire were especially slow to join the antislavery cause, the state and Portsmouth eventually saw the founding of several antislavery societies. The Black and white antislavery orators who held forth in this small city provide a case study for tracing the articulation of abolition in New England.

Slavery's domination of mid-nineteenth-century American political debate had important precedents. For generations the enslaved resisted slavery by ignoring or deliberately misinterpreting work orders, by liberating themselves, by moral persuasion, by petitions for abolition and other legal challenges. Some whites saw the evils of the institution even before it was ingrained in the New England economy and occasionally tried to prevent its entrenchment. In 1643 the New England Confederation assisted runaway servants, including slaves. In 1652 the Rhode Island government, perceiving slaves as comparable to indentured servants, re-

quired that slaves be freed after ten years of work. The colony of West New Jersey prohibited slavery in 1676.[1] Unenforced and ineffective, these early efforts failed to prevent the establishment of slavery.

Legal antecedents for abolishing slavery began in eighteenth-century Europe. When Britain's Chief Justice Lord William Murray found in 1772 that slavery could not exist there without specific legislation to permit it, the importation of slaves to Britain dropped sharply, and by attrition slavery nearly disappeared there over the course of a generation. This set the stage for British disapproval of slavery throughout its empire. But abolition did not come quickly or easily.

British reformers founded Sierra Leone in 1787 as a colony for freed slaves. In commemoration of this original purpose, its capital was named Freetown.

That same year a Cambridge University student named Thomas Clarkson realized the necessity of stopping the slave trade as a preliminary step in eradicating slavery. In 1787 he organized the Society for the Abolition of the Slave Trade. The society's membership included former slaves such as Olaudah Equiano and even former slave traders, and set about convincing members of Parliament to present their cause.[2] Twenty years of argument eventually swayed Parliament. In 1807 it passed a bill making participation in the slave trade illegal for any English vessel.

Decades of continuous work culminated in abolition throughout the empire. The effort was advanced when Member of Parliament William Wilberforce and Thomas Buxton founded an antislavery society in London in 1823 to enlist more people to spread the word of the evils of slavery and build further pressure on Parliament. International events swayed public opinion. In Jamaica Samuel Sharp led a rebellion of slaves in 1831. A coincidental drop in sugar prices led to public indifference to the plantation owners' dependence on slave labor. News of Sharp's execution and the flogging of other slaves involved in the rebellion shocked the British conscience.[3] Public outcry encouraged Parliament to pass a bill abolishing slavery throughout the empire, effective August 1, 1834, though it took nearly twenty years to accomplish its goal.[4] Through this British legislation America's northern neighbor Canada was freed of legally established slavery beginning in the 1830s. In the eighteenth century as many as six thousand Africans had been held in slavery in the province of Quebec, a number augmented in the late 1770s and early '80s when some Loyalists fleeing the American Revolution took their slaves to Canada with them.[5] The same legislation would end slavery in Britain's sugar islands in the West Indies, in British Honduras (Belize), and British Guiana (Guyana).

Meanwhile, in the New World slavery had already ended in the French colony of Saint-Domingue (Haiti).[6] This began in 1791 as a slave revolt that attained freedom for all the country's slaves by 1794. Saint-Domingue's population included over 450,000 slaves, over 25,000 free people of mixed race, and about 30,000 French planters.[7] While this slave-led revolution alarmed slave owners everywhere, the United States eventually recognized Haiti's independence and the authority of General Toussaint L'Ouverture as commander in chief. When President Jefferson took office in 1801 he recalled Edward Stevens from his post as consul to Saint-Domingue and appointed in his place Portsmouth native Tobias Lear, former personal secretary to George Washington. General L'Ouverture was taken aback that Lear arrived with a commission but no letter from the American president to the Haitian leader. He was reconciled when he understood this detail was not an insult on account of his color but an expression of the difference in status between a consul and an ambassador.[8] Although the French did their best to suppress Haitian independence, they failed. In 1848 France abolished slavery in its colonies.[9]

Mexico, as New Spain, had imported about 200,000 African slaves over a period of three centuries, but the institution was abolished by the leaders of newly independent Mexico in 1829.[10] Thus by the mid–nineteenth century the United States was surrounded by free nations.

Slavery and the Constitution

British progress toward ending slavery in its dominions, beginning as it did on the eve of American independence and culminating in later decades, had no legal impact in the United States. It provided only a moral model to Americans that the task could be done.

Whites were heavily invested in slavery. Southerners were unwilling to face the costs of hiring wage laborers. Northerners were major consumers of slave-produced goods, and they shipped quantities of manufactures to slave states and other slave nations. Emerging racism made most white Americans unwilling to increase a free Black population.

In the late 1780s an intended revision of the Articles of Confederation produced instead an all-new Constitution. The white men who framed the Constitution negotiated over the institution of slavery. Many considered it heinous, yet virtually all believed it economically critical. In the interest of producing a document likely to be ratified by a majority of states, the convention members wrote into the new Constitution two political compromises at the expense of the enslaved.

First, they allowed the importation of enslaved people from foreign sources for the next twenty years, after which it was to stop.[11] Though they couldn't see twenty years into the future, the framers' intentions would, by chance, end slave importation at nearly the same time Britain would outlaw the carrying of slaves by British vessels in 1807. When the constitutional deadline arrived in 1808, Congress and President Jefferson confirmed and bolstered it by signing the Slave Trade Act forbidding Americans from participating in the foreign slave trade.[12] Importation dropped off sharply, though the act was ill enforced and a diminished trade continued illegally on the sly.

Second, slavery was written into the formula for proportional representation in Congress. The framers agreed that the decennial census would count three-fifths of enslaved people toward each state's total population.[13] Because the material property of northern farmers and merchants was not counted toward their states' congressional apportionment, this compromise significantly tilted the balance of power in Congress in favor of states with large slave populations.

Abolition

The American abolitionist movement that had begun with on enslaved petitioners in the 1770s was continued by their free successors in the post-Revolutionary North. They found white allies in the Society of Friends (Quakers), who forbade slave ownership among their members. Quakers became open advocates of abolition.

Any forward motion in the political sphere depended on convincing voters. Due to the gradual abolition laws, northern slavery diminished to the brink of extinction by the 1820s. White northerners who cared could comfortably assume, without feeling economically threatened, that slavery elsewhere wasn't a good thing, even if they had no strong or defined ideas of what to do about it. A few white Yankees very gradually came to believe that slavery elsewhere in the nation was an evil.

Varied proposals for ending slavery emerged. While Black Americans knew the moral answer lay in abolishing the institution, enfranchised whites dissected the issue in political terms, encumbered it with their ambivalence about race, and ended up confused about its resolution. As the Constitution reserved to the states all powers it did not assign to the federal government, including the power to make decisions about slavery, it appeared improbable that southern states, whose economies were dependent on the institution, would abolish slavery by legislation.

Over the decades several approaches to the task were proposed. One was gradual discontinuance of slavery, as already in progress in several northern states, called gradualism. A second tactic was prevention of the spread of slavery into the western territories. Another approach advocated overriding the Constitution by immediately abolishing slavery nationwide through federal legislation, an approach called immediatism or, most commonly, abolitionism. Some proposed sending Black Americans to Africa on the British model, called colonization.

The notion of colonization was acceptable to both northern and southern whites in that it both freed and removed Black Americans, thus satisfying both antislavery and racist impulses. Even those who accepted slavery but not the presence of free Blacks welcomed the idea. Colonization could accomplish all this behind a mask of morality.

A colonization society was founded in 1816 to assist free Black Americans who might be willing to emigrate to Africa. Robert Finley, a white Presbyterian minister from New Jersey, proposed it. At his best Finley believed free Black people in America would be held back from realizing their full potential because white Americans would not accept and integrate them into general society. In Africa they would have a fair chance and could also spread Christianity. Finley hoped this project would encourage a gradual end to slavery in America. At his worst, Finley believed that the Black presence in America was unfavorable to American industry and morals and that their removal would spare America from interracial marriage and supporting Black paupers.

Finley won the support of influential people in Washington, D.C., and together they convened an organizational meeting and founded the American Society for Colonizing Free People of Color in the United States. Eventually branches were formed throughout the country, and the society operated till after the Civil War. (A local chapter was founded in Portsmouth in 1833.)[14] Working in cooperation with the United States government, in 1817 the society established the colony of Liberia, naming its capital Monrovia after President Monroe. A few prominent Black Americans were proponents, and an estimated twelve thousand Black Americans opted to emigrate to Africa under the society's auspices (another three thousand free Black people emigrated to other countries through other agencies). The imposition by whites of a Black American governing class over Liberia's native populace engendered resentments that reverberate to the present day. Most Black Americans disapproved of the notion of exile and vigorously opposed colonization schemes.[15]

Whites found preventing the extension of slavery into the western territories less appealing than colonization and responded to the issue along regional lines. The small numbers of white antislavery northerners liked the idea. Southerners saw that new states carved out of the territories would be free states, inevitably tipping the balance in Congress against the South and possibly paving the way for national abolition. The idea of preventing slavery's expansion gave its name to the Free-Soil Party and the policy was later adopted by the new Republican Party.

The very idea of immediate abolition by federal legislation had an enormously inflammatory impact on national politics. Ending slavery by overriding the Constitution was unpopular among white people everywhere. Nonetheless, a very few whites began to advocate the idea in the 1820s, and a few more accepted this approach in the 1830s. Abolitionists attempted to sidestep the constitutional argument by arguing that the Declaration of Independence implied—and the Constitution's 1808 deadline for importation of enslaved people proved—the Founding Fathers' intentions to abolish slavery. They said that taken together the internal evidence of these documents legitimized overriding the Constitution's Tenth Amendment provision that "powers not delegated to the Unites States by the Constitution nor prohibited by it to the States are reserved to the States respectively, or to the people." But most white people—even most antislavery whites—found the idea of immediate abolition incendiary.

There were gender issues at play too. White males typically assumed slavery was an aspect of business, finance, trade, and the economy. As a topic for debate, men felt slavery fell squarely in the male domain. Women and abolitionists viewed slavery as a moral evil, an outlook that brought the debate within what was called the woman's sphere. Many female antislavery societies were founded in the 1830s and '40s, including in Portsmouth. Among whites women became major advocates of abolition. In an era when the sexes and races often moved in separate spheres, these societies were at first segregated by gender and race.

Antislavery and abolition groups found a variety of ways of promulgating their message. They published their ideas in letters to newspaper editors and in special-audience newspapers such as the antislavery periodical *The Liberator*.[16] They even published antislavery songbooks for use at their rallies. Oratory provided another way of spreading the message, whether tactically chosen as an Independence Day topic, argued before a lyceum society's membership,[17] or, occasionally, preached from the pulpit.

Abolition and Religion

Conservative whites gradually shaped an antiabolition argument around the disruption abolition would wreak. Northern church memberships divided on the slavery issue, and some pulpits were closed to abolitionist orators. Antiabolitionists feared war and argued that such a conflict over slavery would be a greater moral evil than slavery itself. Clergy tended to harbor this sentiment.

By the late 1830s frustrated abolitionists publicly declared that the silence of clergy and church members made them partners in the sin of slavery. Clergy and abolitionists became polarized antagonists. Many abolitionists, whose stance was inspired by their religious beliefs, felt driven away from their churches.

In New England, meetinghouses were the usual venue for all oratory, sacred and secular alike, as well as for town meetings. In this same period many towns were for the first time building town halls; churches increasingly controlled meetinghouses, and the buildings were beginning to be viewed as sacred space unsuited to secular activity like political debate. Churches sometimes refused to lend their meetinghouses to abolitionist guest orators. In 1841 abolitionist Stephen S. Foster—not to be confused with the songwriter—was ejected from both North and South Churches in Concord, New Hampshire, when he attempted to make an antislavery appeal.[18]

A century earlier New England's predominant Congregational Church had diverged into theologically conservative and liberal "new light" branches. In Portsmouth North Church represented the traditional "old light" conservative branch of Congregationalism. In the early nineteenth century many liberal congregations declared themselves Unitarian and were not long in joining the Quakers in advocating abolition. Portsmouth's liberal South Church, by this time housed in a new stone meetinghouse a block away from North Church, identified itself as Unitarian, and of the two was the earlier to provide a home for abolitionists.

Larger religious denominations debated slavery at their national conferences. The national organizations of the Presbyterian, Methodist, and Baptist Churches ultimately split along regional lines over slavery. They were not reunited until the mid–twentieth century.

Antislavery Organization in New Hampshire and Portsmouth

New Hampshire's white population was notoriously slow to adopt abolition. By 1837 there were eight hundred antislavery societies in the North,[19] of which relatively few were in New Hampshire. Without the invitation and support of local societies, traveling orators found it difficult to get a venue.

In 1841 white abolitionist William Lloyd Garrison exhorted another white abolitionist, Parker Pillsbury: "Do not despair of New-Hampshire! It is true her religion turns out to be devoid of humanity, and her republicanism is of a spurious quality. It is true, a very large majority of her inhabitants seem to be deaf to the cries of a bleeding humanity, and to glory in their opposition to the sacred cause of emancipation. Still, renew the injunction, do not despair of New Hampshire!"[20]

In 1844 Black orator Frederick Douglass and his associates had a hard time finding a place to speak in Concord, New Hampshire, eventually arranging to speak in the courthouse.[21]

By 1839 Portsmouth had two antislavery societies. The men's was headed by the Reverend David Millard of the Chestnut Street Baptist Church and—in a symbolic gesture—held its annual meeting on the Fourth of July. William Ladd, a relation of the Ladds who occupied the old Whipple mansion (where Prince Whipple and Windsor Moffatt once lived), was an active abolitionist in northern New England.[22] The Portsmouth Female Anti-Slavery Society met annually in August. As throughout small-town New England these societies' directors and most or all of their membership were white.[23] Under their auspices many of the leading American abolitionists gave public orations in Portsmouth, several prominent Black abolitionists among them.

The stationery of the Anti-Slavery Societies used a widely circulated image of a kneeling nude Black man in chains encircled by the text "Am I not a Man and a Brother?"[24] This image was borrowed from the British society for the end of the slave trade founded in 1787. The nude figure follows neoclassical conventions of the day and nobly implies that freedom is natural. The gesture is one of supplication for emancipation. However, other signals are present in this symbol. The nudity equally hints at paganism and savagery, a conventional iconography found in artistic personification of the continents. The posture converts supplication to gratitude for the white people's good deed of ending an evil they had invented in the first place. Unintentionally, the white-designed seal conveyed assumptions of Black inferiority and white superiority even as it intended to help.[25]

The Legislative Backdrop

The ideals of Black and white abolitionists were likely to be realized only through legislation, a process controlled by landed white males. For seventy years slavery shaped national debate and legislation. In the interest of legislative progress it was critical that Black abolitionists keep the debate alive and enlist enfranchised whites to articulate the cause with them.

In the 1810s President Monroe presided over a brief Era of Good Feelings, when senators from free and slave states were equal in number. In 1820 this balance was threatened when Missouri prepared to enter the Union allowing slavery. Crisis was averted when the province of Maine separated from Massachusetts to enter the Union as a free state, a balancing act called the Missouri Compromise. This same compromise also prohibited slavery in territories (and future states) north of the 36° 30′ latitude, giving hope to the antislavery dream of free states someday outnumbering slave states in Congress.

During congressional debate over the compromise New Hampshire's senator, David Lawrence Morril, opposed a legislative detail that would forbid people of mixed race from entering or becoming citizens of Missouri. He cited the career of the recently deceased Wentworth Cheswell (son of housewright Hopestill Cheswell) as a model of patriotism and public service. Were this worthy citizen alive, Morril argued, he would be forbidden from entering Missouri.[26]

Southern whites grew uneasy as gradual emancipation increased the numbers of free Blacks in the North and antislavery ideas and arguments multiplied. In 1822 South Carolina passed the aforementioned Negro Seamen Act, and it was soon replicated in five other southern coastal states.[27]

Other informal and legislated expressions of southern anxiety in the 1830s included offers of cash rewards for the murder of selected abolitionists and outlawing circulation of abolition publications.[28]

Abolitionists—especially women, who were disfranchised—exercised their constitutional right of petition. In 1836 the southern majority in the House of Representatives pushed through a gag resolution that tabled discussion of any and all antislavery petitions. Technically this resolution didn't abridge the constitutional right of petition, but it meant certain petitioners' texts could never be heard or debated. This resolution remained in effect until 1844.[29]

As early as 1844 a national-level antislavery political party, the Liberty Party, was organized and fielded James G. Birney of Kentucky as its presidential candidate. The other candidates that year were representatives of the Whig and Democratic parties.

Meanwhile, westward migration was not directed solely to the vast territories of the Louisiana Purchase. Many southerners emigrated directly westward to settle in northern provinces of Mexico. In the 1840s some of these American expatriates declared independence from Mexico as the Republic of Texas, triggering a war of independence between them and Mexico. Amid vitriolic debate that included anti-Catholic subtexts the United States entered the war on behalf of Texas, was victorious, and annexed Texas plus the entire northern half of Mexico.[30] Annexation intensified debate on whether or not slavery would be extended into new states. In 1845 Texas entered the Union as a slave state. The settlement of California five years later during the gold rush of 1849 raised the possibility of yet another slave state. Whites squabbled over how to proceed.

In 1850 Henry Clay engineered another congressional compromise. It had three features, all related to slavery. California was admitted to the Union as a free state. The territories of New Mexico and Arizona were organized with legislative language that neither admitted nor forbade slavery. A new Fugitive Slave Law was enacted by Congress to facilitate the return of runaways to their owners, and President Millard Fillmore signed it into law.[31]

The new act superseded the Fugitive Slave Act of George Washington's day. It dealt severely with captured runaways, with anyone who assisted them, and with any official who failed to prosecute both. It signaled the arrival of an especially dangerous time for Black people everywhere. Southern slaves who contemplated escaping to free northern states knew this destination could no longer provide adequate protection. The situation was dire for free Black Yankees too, because they could not find defense from false kidnapping; town officers were now obligated to uphold the new act even against their will. A handbill printed in an array of typefaces to emphasize the urgency of its message was issued in Boston, warning

> Caution!! Colored people, of Boston, one and all, you are hereby respectfully cautioned and advised, to avoid conversing with the watchmen and police officers of Boston for since the recent order of the mayor & aldermen, they are empowered to act as kidnappers and slave catchers and they have already been actually employed in kidnapping, catching, and keeping slaves. Therefore, if you value your liberty, and the welfare of the fugitives among you, shun them in every possible manner, as so many hounds on the track of the most unfortunate of your race. Keep a sharp look out for kidnappers, and have top eye open.[32]

Such fears ran through the Black population of Portsmouth and every northern seaport. New Hampshire native son Franklin Pierce supported the new act as a congressman, and later,

as president, he continued its severe enforcement. He virtually federalized the Boston police force in order to uphold it. Sympathy for escapees increased among the white public. Riots broke out on Boston's waterfront when a captured runaway was loaded onto a southbound ship.

Now that even the large free Black neighborhoods of Philadelphia, New York, or Boston were insufficient cover for fugitives, escapees from southern slavery needed to leave the country altogether for genuine safety. Deep secrecy was needed to protect them in their flight. A network of allied people breaking the law in the service of moral justice came to be known as the Underground Railroad. They left virtually no paper trail for historians; oral tradition leaves an approximate record showing that escapees flowed in a steady stream to Canada, especially through Ohio and western New York but also passing through New England seaports. Known routes included Boston and Portland, to Portsmouth's south and north.[33] While no evidence of Portsmouth's role in the Underground Railroad has come to light, the presence of active local abolitionist societies leaves no reason to doubt that Portsmouth played a role too.

Four years later, in 1854, Congress passed the Kansas-Nebraska Act, and President Franklin Pierce signed it. This act annulled the provisions of the Missouri Compromise of 1820 by repealing the prohibition of slavery north of the 36° 30′ line. It admitted Kansas and Nebraska as territories, stipulating that residents of the territories would make their own decisions about slavery as they entered the Union. In signing the act Pierce, a Democrat, adhered to the sanctity of states' rights and personal property rights. He was also interested in organizing western lands into territories preparatory to constructing a Chicago-to-California railroad through Nebraska Territory.[34] Tensions ran high. Kansas became a bloody battlefield between settlers from diverse regions with divergent views.

Not long after, the nephew of Senator Butler of South Carolina beat to unconsciousness abolitionist Senator Charles Sumner of Massachusetts in the United States Senate chamber. In this atmosphere the Free-Soil Party was formed to oppose the extension of slavery into the territories as they became states.

In the fractious politics of the 1850s the old Whig Party disintegrated. In the Old Northwest (today's upper midwestern states) people who had become alienated from many parties— Free-Soilers, Whigs, dissident Democrats, idealistic immigrants, anti-immigrants—allied on a single shared belief in preventing the spread of slavery into new states. They emerged as a mostly northern party called the Republicans. While divided on every other aspect of dealing with slavery, their agreement on that one policy of preventing the introduction of slavery into new states propelled them into the forefront of national politics, an unusually rapid rise among the many proliferating political parties of the era. Nonetheless, in the 1856 election, with the anti-Catholic third party "know-nothing" candidate drawing one-sixth of the nation's popular votes, the Republicans lost to the Democrats, placing Democrat James Buchanan in the White House.

Two days after Buchanan took office in March of 1857, the Supreme Court annulled the Kansas-Nebraska Act through its *Dred Scott v. Sanford* decision. Their decision said that although Congress was authorized to administer territories, it must do so in a way that provided equal privileges to those entering a territory. Thus, prohibiting slavery in the territories would deny slave owners from equal enjoyment of their property. The decision also stated that Black people whose ancestors had arrived in enslavement were not and could not be citizens of the United States, even if individual states gave Black residents rights equivalent to those of free white people in their state. This decision inflamed abolitionists and split the Democratic Party along regional lines.

In 1858 Minnesota entered the Union as a free state, throwing the balance in the Senate to the free North's favor. Several decades earlier

the South's population and economic productivity had fallen behind that of the North. Now its political clout was beginning to drop sharply.

The next year, in 1859, John Brown led a group of abolitionists who seized a federal arsenal at Harper's Ferry, Virginia (now West Virginia), hoping to inspire an uprising of the enslaved and the overthrow of southern state governments. The effort failed, and Brown was tried and executed. Both major parties disowned his action. Fear, paranoia, and witch-hunts for sympathizers swept the South.

Through this period many northern states displaced the gradual emancipation legislation of the post-Revolutionary era with outright abolition: Rhode Island in 1843, Connecticut in 1848, and New Hampshire in 1857.[35] This legislation was of no practical consequence to Black people in those states, because virtually all of them were already free. But it bore immense symbolic significance to Black and white abolitionists alike, showing legislative weight was moving in their direction. It was also a step toward white people's someday denying the historical presence of slavery in New England.[36]

Portsmouth's Continued Participation in Slavery

Through all these developments New England's inhabitants continued to support slavery by supporting the slave economy. They did this by importing vast quantities of slave-produced goods and raw materials from distant sources and by shipping manufactures to slave states and nations. New England's ships carried this trade, and occasionally illegally carried slaves too.

Consumer Goods

The abundant flow of slave-produced goods entered New England mostly through its seaports. These were relayed to the inland market via the new share-held bridges and turnpikes, canals, and railroads in which maritime fortunes had been invested to link old ports with the hinterland. The flood of goods moving on salt water—outbound or inbound, international or coastal—was reported to customs officers. Portsmouth customhouses surviving from 1817 and 1857 attest to the scale of this activity.[37]

Ready-to-consume slave-produced imports included Virginia tobacco, Carolina and Louisiana rice, West Indian sugar, molasses, rum, chocolate, coffee, citrus, tamarinds, and some spices. Raw material imports included indigo from the Carolinas, cotton from Georgia, Alabama, and Mississippi (and later from Texas), and mahogany, rosewood, ebony, and palm leaves from the West Indies and Central America.

White Yankees manufactured and distributed finished goods made from slave-produced raw materials, notably cotton cloth and palm hats. They cultivated southern markets for fine manufactures for white enjoyment and low-grade cloth, hats, and shoes for slaves.

New Englanders of all economic classes were to some degree consumers of slave-produced imports. Portsmouth's biggest consumers were the wealthy, who entertained and dressed lavishly and filled their mansions with luxurious furniture, favoring mahogany from the mid–eighteenth century onward and, by the 1840s, sometimes turning to rosewood and ebony too.

The elite gathered in their new suburban mansions the material goods of a second consumer revolution that eclipsed the materialism of their wealthy colonial antecedents. This consumerism contributed to the increase of slave economies in faraway locations.

Portsmouth's mansions too were monuments to these developments. Cabinetmaker Robert Harrold and immigrant cabinetmakers from London had richly furnished the city's colonial mansions. Now native sons Langley Boardman, and the team of Judkins and Senter satisfied a new generation's demand for fashionable furniture. All worked in mahogany harvested by slave labor in Central America and the West Indies.[38] Cabinetmaker Langley Board-

man's mansion, built 1803–6, has a mahogany front door. The door's inset oval borders of whalebone remind the thoughtful passerby of the maritime source of this money and of the Black presence in the especially dangerous work of whaling.

Among the row of mansions on Middle Street, that built by merchant importer and proto-industrialist James Rundlett is particularly impressive. Like the others, it was lavishly furnished with mahogany. Here as in the other mansions the family's cotton clothing and consumption of tropical delicacies were also dependent on distant slavery.[39]

Among the mansions that once lined Islington Street stood one acquired by Ichabod Goodwin. His story illustrates an internal conflict emerging between economy, religion, and politics. Goodwin rose from cabin boy to captain, became a land-based shipowner and merchant, invested in industry, and entered political office. A major stockholder in the Portsmouth Steam Factory on Hanover Street, Goodwin eventually became its president. His investments in the Eastern Railroad followed a similar course. Cotton came to the factory via his ships and railroad.

The Portsmouth Steam Factory's production gives a sense of how New England's textile industry drove the expansion of slavery in the American South. In 1845–46 the founders sold shares to raise $200,000 to initiate the factory, drawing many local investors into a slave-supported manufacture. They built a six-story building. A year's operation by its four hundred employees required over 127 tons of raw cotton to supply its 21,250 spindles and 420 looms. These machines churned out 2,500,000 yards of fine cotton cloth a year.[40] This factory was a modest version of hundreds like it proliferating in New England and Great Britain. With such a demand for raw cotton the institution of slavery burgeoned in the South.

In a local microcosm of the contradictions that riddled the region, Goodwin's prosperity was in conflict with his religious affiliation and

CLIPPER SHIP "NIGHTINGALE"

The clipper *Nightingale* was among the most luxurious and fastest ships of its time. It was built in Eliot, Maine, and launched in 1851. Later, the *Nightingale* was refitted and known for its efficiency in the Afro-Brazilian slave trade. This lithograph by Currier shows the gracefully designed clipper off New York's Battery. *Courtesy Portsmouth Athenæum.*

politics. He belonged to the Unitarian Church, a prominent advocate of abolition. In the 1850s Goodwin joined the newly emerging Republican Party, which was gathering around opposition to the extension of slavery into territories and new states. Preventing the extension of slavery into the territories was consonant with his religion and was no immediate threat to his source of raw cotton. But in 1859 and 1860 Goodwin served as New Hampshire's first Republican governor, just as the Civil War erupted. The outbreak of war interrupted the cotton trade. As the war progressed, rhetoric shifted from preserving the Union to abolishing slavery, potentially overturning the economy that produced cotton. He entertained Franklin Pierce

at his Portsmouth home. Goodwin left no diary to reveal if and how he perceived the conflicting relationships of his shipping, household furnishings, industrial investments, religion, political social obligations, and antislavery politics.[41]

Continued Slave Trading

While the legal internal slave trade continued, participation in international slave trading—made illegal by the Jefferson-era Slave Trade Act—also persisted. The act was strengthened in 1820 when Congress passed an act for punishing violations and authorized the president—Monroe by that date—to apply navy ships to its enforcement. The navy found enforcement so problematic that in 1843 it created a permanent African Squadron to patrol African slave harbors. In the next eighteen years the squadron captured more than one hundred illegal slaving ships. A famous Piscataqua-built vessel participated in this illegal international trade.

As in so many small New England ports where international trade diminished after the War of 1812, Portsmouth shipwrights continued to supply vessels to buyers in the region's larger ports, drawing home some of the world economy's wealth. In fact Portsmouth's greatest shipbuilding era came after its international trade tapered off. One of the great ships of the era, the *Nightingale*, was built in Portsmouth Harbor in Eliot, Maine. Local people still find romantic allure in its dedication to Jenny Lind, its luxurious fittings (it was expected to carry passengers to the World Exposition in London), and its remarkable speed. They quietly ignore its role in the international slave trade.

The *Nightingale* was a model of the newly emerging form of ships called clippers, used mostly on international trade routes during a brief period when speed was more important than capacity. Upon completion in 1851 the *Nightingale* was sold in Boston and, because of excitement about discovery of gold in Australia, immediately entered the Australian trade, then the Asian and European. In numerous voyages in the Pacific, Indian, and Atlantic Oceans it proved to be one of the fastest ships in the world.

The *Nightingale* was sold at Salem in 1860 and immediately sent to Rio de Janeiro where it was sold again, apparently to American owners. They illegally applied it to the Afro-Brazilian slave trade, flying the United States flag indicative of its ownership and registration. Captain Francis Bowen, who bore the unsavory sobriquet "Prince of Slavers," commanded it. Though capable of eluding British antislavery patrols in the West Indies, the vessel's famous fleetness did not save it. On April 21,1861, while engaged in slaving off Kabenda, Congo, a boarding party from the USS *Saratoga*, of the navy's African Squadron, found a cargo of 971 captives. Seized by the United States government, 160 of them died en route to release in Liberia. The commander of the *Saratoga*, Lieutenant Guthrie, himself a slave owner, allowed Bowen to escape.[42]

In short, even at the height of the abolition movement white Yankees remained entwined in slavery in every way shy of outright ownership. Swaying public opinion by oratory was a mighty task, and brilliant talent rose to the cause.

Frederick Douglass, Charles Lenox Remond, William Wells Brown: Black Abolitionist Orators and the Civil War Years in Portsmouth

The civil War was not a war to address a Black problem but a war to resolve a white failure. It was against the tense backdrop of political quarreling and looming, then actual war that abolitionist orators toured the North, holding forth in country towns, county seats, and coastal cities.

The political influence of white abolitionists was extremely important to the cause. They shared a moral conviction of the wickedness of slavery but held varied degrees of confidence in the Black capacity for improvement and citizenship. Today their stories are so well known that abolition is told as a story of white people successfully fighting injustice. Just as a collective amnesia overlooks or denies the existence of slavery in colonial New England,[43] the modern telling of abolition omits Black men and women who originated and led the movement and were widely published.

In Portsmouth many abolitionists, white and Black, spoke at a new public lecture hall on Chestnut Street called the Temple.[44] Some were guests of antislavery societies or the Free-Soil Party; others came on their own or were invited by the Lyceum, a self-improvement society.[45]

Portsmouth's earliest known oratory on slavery was ensnared in religious issues. In July of 1841—the same year Douglass was nearly frustrated in his attempts to find a speaking venue in Concord—Abby Kelly gave a series of five lectures in Portsmouth.[46] Abby Kelly was a white Quaker woman from Worcester County, Massachusetts, who was raised in a religious tradition that believed both sexes and all races were equal. In their religious meetings all could speak; Kelly's public oratory was within her religious tradition. This outlook was in fundamental conflict with mainstream Protestant thinking, which held it was unseemly for a woman to address a mixed audience of men and women, an outlook routinely reinforced by biblical citations. The larger culture considered slavery a topic suited only to the men's sphere of political and economic concerns. The moral points made by women orators were often lost on an audience distracted by these other issues.

At this point overt antipathy to abolition erupted in Portsmouth's North Church. The reverend Edwin Holt alienated abolitionist parishioners by his combined antiabolitionist views and his autocratic temper. He suspended some young men from membership and excommunicated others for speaking out against slavery. In November of 1842 the Reverend Rufus W. Clark of Washington, D.C., succeeded Holt. Reversing his predecessor's stance, Clark alarmed antiabolitionist church members. In one of his sermons he questioned biblical interpretations that seemed to justify slavery. Growing tensions were relieved when Clark accepted a call from a Boston-area church, and North Church had a third chance to fill its pulpit.[47] Clearly, local religion was far from allying itself with the antislavery cause.

Frederick Douglass's First Visit to Portsmouth

From September 15 to 30, 1844, Frederick Douglass, Abby Kelley, Stephen S. Foster, Parker Pillsbury, and J. M. Spear toured New Hampshire and Maine under the auspices of the American Anti-Slavery Society.[48] They found New Hampshire less receptive to their message than Massachusetts and encountered resistance to borrowing or renting halls for their public orations. Two months later, during December 21–22, 1844, Frederick Douglass (1818–95) visited Portsmouth's Female Anti-Slavery Society, though it is unclear whether this visit was part of this New Hampshire/Maine tour or part of a new round of touring.[49]

Though Douglass was a feisty orator, the newspapers seem not to have announced his presence. He probably did not give a public oration but a more intimate presentation to the society's membership. Such voluntary societies usually met in a society member's parlor. A look at Douglass's early career suggests the content of his conversation.

Douglass had spent his early life enslaved in Maryland. In 1838 he escaped, and he eventually settled in New Bedford, Massachusetts. In 1841, after making some unplanned remarks about his life experiences to an antislavery society meeting, Douglass was asked to become a regular speaker for this group. Its white founders awoke to the fact that someone speaking from firsthand experience would bring authority and the message would command greater respect among hesitant whites.

Douglass began his oratorical career with simple accounts of his enslaved life, sometimes finding startling metaphors to convey his point. He began a lecture in January of 1842 with: "I appear before the immense assembly this evening as a thief and a robber. . . . I stole this head, these limbs, this body from my master, and ran off with them."[50] When Douglass spoke in Concord, New Hampshire, in 1844 he explained that he was not a fugitive from slavery—but a fugitive slave. So long as he remained in the United States he would be a slave living a fugitive life; to get away from slavery he must leave his own country.

Douglass rhetorically asked his audience why he must walk in their midst both a fugitive and a slave. He must have startled them when he answered that it was because of their religion, which sanctified the system of slavery. After recounting his life in slavery he continued in what one witness described as a "volcanic out-break" presaging a "storm of insurrections" by the enslaved "roused up like the Numidian lion," which would one day strike "terror to the hearts of the dismayed and despairing mastery."[51]

This presentation in Concord was given the same year as Douglass's visit to the Portsmouth Female Anti-Slavery Society. His remarks to them were probably very similar.

Douglass's visit was followed by increasingly overt white antislavery activity, intensified by the draconian Fugitive Slave Act of 1850. This was met by promotion of antislavery candidates for public office and a string of white antislavery orators.

In September of 1852 local members of the Free-Soil Party hung a banner across Market Street near Bow Street bearing the names of "Hale and Julian."[52] John P. Hale was a founder of the party and its presidential candidate in 1852.[53] The banner probably promoted the party's rally at the Temple the following month.

In October of 1852 a rally at the Temple of the "Free Democracy" or Free-Soil Party included an oration by Horace Mann.[54] Mann was a Massachusetts state legislator best remembered as leader of a school reform movement initiated there in the late 1830s. To that important task Mann added abolitionism.

In February of 1853 abolitionists Parker Pills-bury and Stephen S. Foster commenced a series of lectures at the Temple beginning Wednesday evening, February 23.[55] Though audiences were large, not all white listeners were convinced. Most listened respectfully as they tried to balance their economic, political, and moral assumptions, but not everyone remained tacit. The last lecture became "almost a riot" thanks to disruption by drunkards in the back of the hall. The speaker made the mistake of haranguing them and lost the audience's sympathy when he implicated Portsmouth resident, and United States Supreme Court Justice, the late Levi Woodbury, as a bad influence.[56]

In April of 1853 Miss Sallie Holley gave antislavery lectures at the Temple on a series of Sunday evenings. White audiences continued to be distracted by the question of the propriety of women orators. Rather than evaluating her message, the newspaper wasted space on the novelty and style of a female orator: "Miss Holley is decidedly the best lady orator we have heard. She speaks without notes, and with readiness and fluency—and save a little too much of a whining accent, is a very pleasing speaker. She is perfectly ladylike in her deportment—modest and unassuming, yet dignified and self possessed; thoroughly understanding her subject and fearlessly proclaiming what she believes to be truth."[57]

On three consecutive evenings in early summer of 1853 Mr. G. W. F. Mellen of Boston delivered three lectures at the Temple. His topics were the "Causes of Color" in the different races, the financial bearings of slavery on the commercial, manufacturing, and industrial interest of the country, and what constitutes a free American citizen. Fees were fifty cents for the course, twenty-five cents for single lectures.[58] In Mellen's topics we can see a convergence of the Lyceum movement's interest in the findings of rational science, the era's characteristic application of science to racial differentiation, and the politicized questions of race, economy, and politics.

In 1854 the Whig Party disintegrated, and the Republican Party was formed. Also in 1854 Congress passed and President Pierce signed the Kansas-Nebraska Act annulling the aspect of the Missouri Compromise of 1820 that prohibited slavery above the 36° 30′ line.

Charles Lenox Remond

In February of 1854 Black abolitionist Charles Lenox Remond (1810–1873), a native of Salem, Massachusetts, spoke at the Temple in Portsmouth. He came to Portsmouth with an amazing international career already behind him. He had started as an agent of the American Anti-Slavery Society, founded at a convention of regional abolitionists in December of 1833 at Philadelphia.

Remond was active and important in the American immediatist movement throughout its vigorous and ultimately triumphant life. He was also instrumental in introducing white abolitionists to the practical idea of employing free Black people in jobs other than those that were menial or degrading. White abolitionists hadn't made the connection between economic security and the enjoyment of freedom. Remond spoke on the subject before an antislavery society in Rhode Island in November of 1837, and they subsequently voted to help Black people get jobs as clerks. Notwithstanding his efforts to convince white abolitionists to employ Blacks in dignified jobs, after the Civil War the only work Remond would find was as a lowly street light inspector for the city of Boston, though he was eventually hired as a clerk in the city's customhouse.[59]

In the summer of 1838 Remond toured Maine. Soon after, two branches of the national antislavery society were organized in that state.[60] Also in 1838 Remond spoke before the Massachusetts legislature, arguing that since Black men could vote in that state, they should have all other rights of citizenship. While Massachusetts never repealed the right of Black men to vote, its residents and legislators had found a variety of race-based methods of exclusion. Remond beseeched the legislature to integrate public transportation (railroads and steamboats).[61]

Remond became president of the Essex County (Massachusetts) Anti-Slavery Society, an office he filled for six years.[62] This was characteristic of the 1840s, when Black and white abolitionists realized that unified action through integrated groups was crucial to attaining their goal in a hostile nation.

Remond chastised those Black businessmen who shied away from publicly advocating abolition for fear of alienating customers. He urged involvement among uninterested Black youths who had never experienced slavery.[63]

Like all Black abolitionist orators, Remond

was subject to abuse. While on a lecture tour in Bucks and Montgomery Counties in Pennsylvania he wrote a friend that mobs or rumors of mobs were always to be expected.[64]

In 1840 Remond was one of the American Anti-Slavery Society's four delegates to the World Anti-Slavery Convention in London. His costs were paid by donations from the Bangor Female Anti-Slavery Society, the Portland Sewing Circle, and the Newport Young Ladies' Juvenile Anti-Slavery Society. He went to the convention in the company of delegates William Lloyd Garrison, Nathaniel P. Rogers, and Lucretia Mott. When they found that the convention refused to seat women as delegates, all three men left their seats to sit in the observers' gallery with Mott. The lessons of inequality were sinking deeper and finding broader application. Lady Byron, duchess of Sutherland, joined the Americans and conversed with Remond about this topic of world importance.

Remond remained in Britain for nineteen months, orating for many consecutive nights on abolition, colonization, racial prejudice, and temperance. While in Britain he met the Irish patriot Daniel O'Connell, who had urged British abolitionists to follow their successful accomplishments of 1834 with work on behalf of American abolition.

When Remond returned to America he brought with him an address urging Irish Americans to unite in the abolitionist effort. It was signed by sixty thousand Irishmen, Daniel O'Connell's name among them.[65] The outlook among Irish who had come to America didn't follow the expected course. "Native" Protestants viewed the Irish—and all non-Protestant immigrants—as non-Christian and treated them as non-white. Irish immigrants were the target of brutal nativist violence, their houses stoned, their Boston convent torched. Socially and economically marginalized, the Irish struggle for limited bottom-rung jobs put them in direct competition with Black Yankees. They adopted native-style racism, not incidentally a step toward alliance with the dominant class in a process some modern historians view as "becoming white."[66] In the Civil War the Irish couldn't afford to buy their way out of the draft as could wealthier whites. Expected to sacrifice their lives in the cause of freeing more Blacks with whom they would then compete for jobs, resentments grew greater. A street fight in Portsmouth between a small gang of Irish immigrants and several Black men walking to their boat at the foot of Daniel Street in 1864 was a typical expression of these complex resentments.[67]

Through the 1840s Remond argued for the enfranchisement of Black Americans, who were forbidden from voting even in many of the states that no longer had slavery. Remond, along with many others, concentrated on the Pennsylvania legislature, a state with a very large free Black population that had disfranchised its Black voters in 1838.[68]

In 1849 Remond was one of an impressive roster who spoke at the Shiloh Presbyterian Church in New York in refutation of a remark made in Britain by a member of the American Colonization Society that American Negroes were generally in favor of the goals of colonization. Most were not, which was made abundantly clear at this conference. It had been noted that Black people in some American cities publicly celebrated the abolition of slavery in the French West Indies, but nowhere were such celebrations noted when the news of Liberia's independence was heard.[69]

In response to the new Fugitive Slave Act of 1850 the white abolitionists of Boston held a huge rally at Faneuil Hall assuring their Black brethren of their support in preventing the enforcement of this heinous act. Among the leading white abolitionists on the platform was Black abolitionist Charles Lenox Remond.[70]

Four years after this, in February of 1854, with these remarkable experiences behind him, the forty-four-year-old Charles Lenox Remond spoke at the Temple in Portsmouth. "On Monday evening, at the Temple, a respectable and numerous audience listened to an Address on American Slavery, delivered by Mr. Remond, a colored man of Salem, Mass. The address was a very eloquent, spirited, and in some parts indignant exhibition of some plain and undeniable features of an odious system. He dwelt not at all on horrible details, but attacked the system itself, as upheld by prejudice and fashion, cowardice and avarice. His lecture was favorably received and frequently applauded."[71]

In mid-October of 1855, a year after his oration in Portsmouth, Remond was a delegate to the Colored National Convention in Philadelphia.[72] In May 1857, two months after the Supreme Court issued its Dred Scott decision, at New York's Shiloh Church Remond and Frederick Douglass debated whether or not the Constitution was fundamentally proslavery. Remond argued that the Constitution was a proslavery document, a stance that was leading some abolitionists to abstain from participation in what they felt was a contaminated political process.[73]

Remond's February 1854 appearance in Portsmouth was one of three closely spaced antislavery orations. That same month Reverend A. T. Foss of Manchester, New Hampshire, lectured on American slavery at the Temple.[74] "Mr Foss delivered an able lecture at the Temple on Sunday evening, on the religious aspects of slavery; and on Monday evening he spoke in a condemnatory strain of the Nebraska Bill, now pending in congress."[75] That the speaker was from Manchester shows how antislavery views were finally taking hold even in stubborn New Hampshire.

A month later, on Thursday evening, March 30, 1854, William Lloyd Garrison spoke at the Temple on individual responsibility in reference to slavery.[76] Garrison was the most prominent white abolitionist orator, as well as publisher of the antislavery newspaper *The Liberator*. He delivered passionate appeals deeply rooted in religion and morality. Southerners offered cash rewards for his assassination,[77] and distribution of his newspaper was illegal in much of the South. Even in Boston a riot broke out in the streets around his office, leading to his arrest. The Portsmouth paper described his lecture as including "many unpalatable truths."[78]

Three years after this cluster of lectures the Supreme Court's Dred Scott decision of 1857 annulled the Kansas-Nebraska Act and declared Americans of African descent not to be United States citizens. Also in 1857 New Hampshire formally abolished slavery, a symbolic rather than instrumental gesture, since the last slave listed in New Hampshire had been in the U.S. census of 1840.[79] The following year, 1858, Minnesota entered the Union as a free state, and the year after that, 1859, John Brown raided the federal arsenal at Harper's Ferry. Tensions over regional economies, states' rights, and the status of territories and new states all revolved around slavery, and had reached their apogee of divisiveness.

As the 1860 election approached, the nationwide Democratic Party split along regional lines over slavery policy and nominated two separate candidates. This split guaranteed both candidates' losing the election to Republican candidate Abraham Lincoln.

Lincoln wished to limit slavery to the South, where he hoped it would die of attrition as it had in the North. Because the Republican Party was a fragile alliance of dissimilar interests, the party would not adopt the abolitionist's ideal of ending slavery by immediate legislation.

Demonizing rhetoric characterized the regions' descriptions of one another's citizens. In the supercharged atmosphere, southerners would not tolerate the Republicans' proposed exclusion of slavery from the territories, because as new states were added they would likely tilt the balance in Congress ever more against the South.

Lincoln had no vigorous interest in abolishing slavery, and he suspected he could not gain white support for a war to abolish slavery. He argued instead, when the war did come, that it was to preserve the Union. From this stance he forbade enlistment of Black soldiers into the army through the early part of the Civil War.[80]

Lincoln was elected in the fall of 1860, and several states of the Deep South seceded. As war approached, the question arose of the proper role for Black Americans. Many who served in the Revolution had been rewarded with continued enslavement. Why should Blacks participate in a white man's war now? Other Blacks saw the imminent war as another tool of abolition worth joining. Among whites the Quakers, whose members had introduced abolitionism to whites, were in a dilemma because of the pacifism required by their faith. The deep religious roots of non-Quakers like Garrison had led them to pacifist conclusions at an early date. Charles Remond had begun to break from his pacifism as early as the 1840s.[81] In 1852 he had been among the petitioners asking Massachusetts to admit Black men to the militia (rejected by the governor as late as 1859). Whites no longer remembered the nationwide Black service in the Revolution, when Massachusetts fielded an entire Black regiment, the Bucks of America.[82]

When Lincoln took office in March of 1861 he made it clear in his inaugural address that he did not intend to end slavery where it existed, nor repeal the Fugitive Slave Law. These remarks deeply disappointed the enslaved, free Blacks, and all abolitionists. Yet these same conciliatory remarks failed to ease the minds of southerners. Additional states seceded and quickly declared themselves a new nation, the Confederate States of America. When the Confederacy asked the "foreign" Union troops to evacuate Fort Sumter its commander refused, and Confederate forces fired on the fort. War had begun.[83]

Frederick Douglass Returns to Portsmouth

On March 15, 1862, Frederick Douglass returned to Portsmouth; this time he spoke at the Temple. Experience had made Douglass more comfortable with public speaking since his last visit to

Portsmouth eighteen years earlier. In the intervening years he had expanded his topics. He demanded the abolition of slavery in the District of Columbia (the slave trade was stopped there in 1850). Douglass criticized Congress's new Fugitive Slave Act of 1850, scorned the annexation of Texas as a slave state, and condemned the extension of slavery into the territories allowed by the Supreme Court's Dred Scott decision of 1857.[84] In 1847 he had become president of the New England Anti-Slavery Society.[85]

In public oratory Black abolitionists were more subject to abuse than white abolitionists. After an 1847 rally in Harrisburg, Pennsylvania, at which white abolitionist orator William Lloyd Garrison was respectfully heard, Frederick Douglass was interrupted by catcalls and firecrackers and targeted with rotten eggs and brickbats. Douglass tartly observed that a hated opinion is not always in sight whereas a hated color is.[86]

By his 1862 visit to Portsmouth Douglass was well known, and no place smaller than the Temple could have accommodated his audience. The Civil War was in progress; white northerners were almost wholly antislavery and many ready to accept abolition. If the Union prevailed slavery would almost certainly be eradicated (the Emancipation Proclamation was issued six months after Douglass's second visit to Portsmouth). Douglass looked ahead; his topic was "The Black Man's Future in the Southern States."[87]

Douglass's oration (and an oration by William Wells Brown six months later, on the heels of the preliminary release of the Emancipation Proclamation text) touched a raw nerve among Portsmouth racists, triggering a series of cantankerous letters to the editor of the *Portsmouth Chronicle* under the pseudonym Uncle Toby. The letter writer predicted Black Americans would find free life little better than enslaved life and arrogantly suggested enslavement in America was surely better than life in Africa.

Like many white northerners, the prospect of equal status for Black Americans made that anonymous author bristle. The newspaper responded with unwittingly condescending editorial refutations. Its editors pointed out the dignified behavior and respectable conduct of a crew of freed Black men then stationed at the Navy Yard and cited the contributions made to Portsmouth by an earlier generation of free Black mariners.[88] These exchanges signaled the problems that already existed for Black Yankees in the free North and would continue once the whole nation was free of slavery. While most northern whites were antislavery, virtually none were in any way pro-Black.

In September 1862, following the not-unalloyed Union victory in the horrifically bloody Battle of Antietam, President Lincoln released a preliminary version of his Emancipation Proclamation. It would declare freedom for all slaves in states that were in rebellion and not yet in Union hands and admit them to Union military service. While it was meant to demoralize the South, it was also calculated to avoid upsetting northern and border-state slave owners who still perceived the war in terms of preserving the Union. It would leave about a million people enslaved, all in the Union or recently conquered parts of the Confederacy.[89]

Reactions were varied. Some criticized the regional limitations. Frederick Douglass thought the proclamation would be a "moral bombshell" to the Confederacy. But he, along with many Black Americans and abolitionists, feared Lincoln would succumb to influence of northern conservatives and fail to carry through with the promise of abolition. But on January 1, 1863, Lincoln issued the final version of the Emancipation Proclamation, effective immediately. Its effectiveness, of course, depended entirely on Union advancement and ultimate victory.

The army responded by officially accepting Black soldiers, and Black northerners willingly enlisted. The now famous Massachusetts Fifty-fourth Colored Regiment was formed. Similar regiments were mustered elsewhere, and by spring the War Department established a Bureau of Colored Troops.[90] This sequence—abolition only in enemy territory but not in the Union, separate Black regiments and bureau—illustrates persistent white ambivalence about the capacities of an "inferior" race and the suitability of Blacks for citizenship.

In less than two years, white war rhetoric had tilted from preserving the Union toward abolishing slavery. Slavery had been abolished in much of the South, and Black soldiers were proving their abilities and dedication.

William Wells Brown

William Wells Brown (c. 1814–84) spoke at the Temple on Sunday, October 12, 1862. He was formerly held as a slave in Kentucky, where he had only one name, William. When he escaped, a Quaker named Wells Brown helped him in his flight. When William reached freedom he adopted Brown's name to honor him and later dedicated his first book to him. William became a speaker for antislavery societies, mostly in New York and Massachusetts.

William Wells Brown came to Portsmouth with a brilliant career behind him. He belonged to that first generation of abolitionists to articulate immediatism and to describe slavery as a sin of grave danger to the nation. This platform was first defined at the first national antislavery conference in Philadelphia in 1833. The attendees' rhetoric was electrifying, condemning all who compromised with slavery as participants in sin. They condemned clergy who failed to take moral leadership.[91] In 1850 William Lloyd Garrison described William Wells Brown, Frederick Douglass, and Henry Bibb—all formerly enslaved—as the best abolitionist orators.[92]

Brown was also known for fine writing, among the first of America's many accomplished Black authors. He wrote drama, novels, and travel literature. His autobiography went through four editions in only two years. True narratives of enslaved life and escape were gaining popularity in the North.

In addition, Brown compiled *The Anti-Slavery Harp*, a collection of forty-six antislavery texts to be sung to familiar tunes.[93] Antislavery songs from this and similar sources were common features of antislavery evangellical meetings, which followed the format of evangellical worship services, including prayer, exhortation, and oratory.

In the spring of 1842 Brown founded and served as president of the 215-member Union Total Abstinence Society in Buffalo, New York.[94] The movement to temper alcohol consumption arose in response to the highest levels of alcoholism in American history; total abstinence represented a new goal that emerged in the 1840s.[95] During the years he lived in Buffalo, Brown made his home a stop on the Underground Railroad; in a single seven-month period in 1842 he spirited into Canada sixty-nine people who had escaped enslavement.[96]

William Wells Brown believed that peace was as important as liberation. At a convention of Black freemen in Buffalo in August of 1843 the twenty-seven-year-old Reverend Henry Highland Garnet announced in an oration, metaphorically addressed to the enslaved, that there was little hope of achieving freedom without bloodshed. He urged the enslaved to arise and strike a blow. Neither Brown nor Frederick Douglass could agree with him. They preferred to pursue abolition through persistent but nonviolent moral persuasion.[97]

In July of 1849 Brown went to Paris to represent the American Peace Society at the International Peace Society convention.[98] After "speaking admirably" he attended a reception sponsored by the French foreign minister Alexis de Tocqueville. The founder of the American Peace Society, William Ladd, had Portsmouth connections, so it was perhaps inevitable that Brown would one day come to Portsmouth; perhaps he had been there prior to his 1862 visit.

Brown lingered on in Europe. In 1850 his oratory was much admired in England. At Bristol four hundred people showed up at a tea party held in his honor.[99] In 1851 he toured the midlands with William and Ellen Craft. To escape enslavement they had taken a bold and risky move. Ellen disguised herself as a slave-owning white man (enabled by a light complexion) traveling with his enslaved man. This group spoke to enormous crowds, sometimes accommodating thousands and turning hundreds away for lack of room.[100]

In August of 1851 Brown was in London as chairman of a public meeting of Black American performers, convened to celebrate the end of slavery in the British West Indies and condemn continued slavery in the United States. Among his audience were the literary giants Thomas B. Macaulay and Alfred Tennyson.[101] Brown went on to tour numerous towns in Great Britain.

After five years in Europe, William Wells Brown returned to the United States. He arrived amid the rising sectional tensions and increasingly shrill abolition debate. He continued orating through the Civil War.

On Sunday, October 12, 1862, William Wells Brown spoke in Portsmouth at the Temple. This closely followed President Lincoln's September release of the Emancipation Proclamation, which would take effect the following first of January. Brown chose as his topic "The Effects of Emancipation on the Blacks of the South and the white Laborers of the North."[102] It was a germane topic; white northern laborers processed slave-produced cotton and palm, and manufactured cloth, hats, and shoes for the South's enslaved people. Unskilled white laborers were traditionally hostile to free Black Americans because they were competing for the same jobs. Brown's text does not survive, but a string of barbed letters to the *Portsmouth Chronicle* ensued.

Like many nineteenth-century reformers, Brown became involved in several causes: abolition, temperance, and peace. Adherents of all these causes introduced moral arguments to spheres traditionally considered social, political, or economic. Men and women advocates of all these reform efforts articulated their arguments in evangelical language and style. Historians refer to the interlocking membership and leadership among reform movements and societies as the Evangelical United Front. William Wells Brown was very much a part of this front when he addressed Portsmouth on the meaning of the imminent Emancipation Proclamation.

Riot in 1863

In the Civil War white America paid deeply for its history of enslaving Black people, as civil disorder, bitterness, and bloodshed were brought upon the nation. The early 1860s were troubled times in Portsmouth as elsewhere.

The public expected the war to end perhaps three months after it began. It lasted four years. Like most places in the Union, Portsmouth at first responded with spirited volunteer enlistment. As the war dragged on and the rhetoric shifted from saving the Union to abolishing slavery, enlistment throughout the North diminished. Diaries and letters of New England soldiers make it clear that most would not have gone to fight if they had thought it was to free the slaves—they went to save the Union. Congress had to institute a military draft to prosecute the war.

When Congress passed the Draft Act of 1863 Portsmouth citizens scheduled a public assembly to discuss it at the Temple on Thursday evening, July 16, 1863. Then news of the bloody battle at Gettysburg a few days earlier arrived in Portsmouth. Sensing growing tension, city authorities revoked license for the assembly.

Nonetheless, on the appointed evening two hundred frustrated people gathered in Portsmouth's downtown. Unsure what to do, they moved aimlessly through the streets. Eventually

Billy Seabrook (*far right*) poses with the Third New Hampshire Regiment Band at Hilton Head Island, South Carolina, during the Civil War. Young Billy was not a band musician but a former slave who had been hired as a servant and to carry the drum. Daniel Eldredge wrote about Seabrook in his book *The Third New Hampshire and All About It. Photography by Henry P. Moore. New Hampshire Historical Society.*

they followed the model of their ancestors of 1774 and marched to Fort Constitution but were turned back by a full garrison. They returned to town, scattered, and intermittently reassembled through the evening and night.

The event culminated at 1:00 A.M. in an armed melee with police. Mayor Jonathan Dearborn summoned marines from the Navy Yard to break up the riot. The crowd scattered, leaving several wounded but none dead. Subsequently Sampson Russell, Richard Walden, Augustus Walden, and Richard Smart were arrested and charged with inciting the riot.[103]

Tension rose when the draft commenced, with the wealthy able to pay substitutes to go in their place. When the following year a ship at the Navy Yard introduced yellow fever, a frustrated public scapegoated the yard and charged the Portsmouth Board of Health with an inadequate response.[104] In July a calamitous fire burned much of the east side of Penhallow Street from Daniel to Bow Streets.[105]

As these events and the war dragged on, the local public grew increasingly demoralized. Yet when individuals questioned the conduct of the war, the loss of life it entailed, or in any way seemed not entirely supportive, they were branded unpatriotic southern sympathizers. Some zealous Portsmouth patriots annotated their copies of the city directory noting "copperhead" in the margins.[106] Among the most prominent to be so branded was Joshua Foster, editor of the *States and Union* newspaper. He was a states' rights Democrat and opposed both the war and the way it was conducted. He expressed his opinions in his newspaper, which carried on an editorial sparring match with the pro-Union *Morning Chronicle*. The war's last bit of news triggered another riot.

Riot in 1865

On April 10, 1865, news of General Lee's surrender the previous day reached Portsmouth. An elated crowd of two thousand gathered in the spring drizzle in the downtown streets. Some in the crowd, feeling that their pro-Union views were now vindicated in victory, wished to press the point with the *States and Union* newspaper.

They assembled in front of the newspaper offices, which were in upstairs rooms on the northeast corner of Daniel and Penhallow Streets, next to the pre-Revolutionary relic, Stoodley's Tavern.

> . . . a large and excited crowd soon gathered about the establishment, some clamoring for the proprietor, others crying "clean out the office," and yet others to "hang him," "string him up," and other like threatening language. . . . The crowd, frenzied with the excitement of the day, would listen to nothing but the promise of the appearance of Foster, the editor, to throw out *with his own hands* the ensign of Freedom [the American flag].
>
> At last, this individual, pale with fear or rage, and well nigh overcome by the sight of about two thousand determined men, appeared at the window of his counting room, and with apparent reluctance put out his flag, giving it a slight toss with his hand; which not satisfying the majority of the crowd, they instantly demanded from him a speech. . . .
>
> But from some cause he immediately disappeared (it is said through a back door, taking his books), which was the signal for a change of programme with the excited multitude.
>
> In less time than we are occupied in writing this, the office was completely ridded of type, presses, press boards, ink, paper, and everything connected with a printing estab-

lishment, —all thrown out of the windows into the street below. The Mayor appearing shortly after, and reading the riot act, the crowd dispersed.[107]

In the following weeks, Lee's symbolic surrender was followed by the surrender of the Confederate Armies. The war had ended.[108]

Seven years later Joshua Foster moved to Dover and founded a new newspaper, which evolved into today's local newspaper *Foster's Daily Democrat*.[109]

The war had cost the lives of 617,000 people, approximately equal to the number who have died in all the nation's other wars combined.[110] Ongoing debates about divergent economies, states' rights, preserving the Union, and slavery notwithstanding, all these were defined by slavery, and the war would not have occurred had slavery never been introduced to the country.

When the war ended it was politically and rhetorically awkward, perhaps impossible, for northern whites not to abolish slavery at home. Near the end of the Civil War, in January, 1865, Congress had promulgated the Thirteenth Amendment to the Constitution, abolishing slavery throughout the United States, and it was ratified by early December.

But five days after Foster's riot, Portsmouth was again paralyzed. Solemn crowds assembled in Market Square for several days, and on Wednesday, April 19, three thousand people filled the square to mourn the murder of President Abraham Lincoln.[111]

"Most of the Colored People of the City, Both Old and Young": Celebrating Emancipation

For all the tragedy brought upon whites by their institution of slavery, the long-term horror of slavery had been endured by Black Americans. In political and legal terms, the Civil War and emancipation seemed to propel the Black experience in new directions.

Many early annual celebrations of the Emancipation Proclamation, funded by a grant from a Unitarian minister, Rev. Daniel Austin, were held in South Ward Hall. This city-owned building on Marcy Street was also the first home of People's Baptist Church, the only Black church in New Hampshire until the mid-twentieth century. The congregation met here from the early 1890s until 1915, when they moved into their own church on Pearl Street. *Portsmouth Black Heritage Trail.*

the Underground Railroad were ended. The insult of institutionalized exclusion from voting and citizenship was over. A bloody and divisive war had ended. Black people in America were now to be free.

Though many civil rights limitations and battles lay ahead, emancipation was an ideal worthy of celebration. In the enthusiastic afterglow of the Thirteenth, Fourteenth, and Fifteenth Amendments formal celebrations became a part of the Portsmouth scene.

These were set in motion by a bequest from the Reverend Daniel Austin. A Unitarian minister variously of Portsmouth and Kittery, Austin left a bequest in 1878 of five hundred dollars to the City of Portsmouth for the "colored" population to hold perpetual celebrations of Lincoln's signing of the Emancipation Proclamation.[112]

Four years after Austin's death, late in 1881, the invested bequest generated an annual income of forty dollars, sufficient to implement Austin's intentions. The first celebration was scheduled for January 1, 1882, the seventeenth anniversary of the proclamation. At the celebration an association was formed called the Austin-Lincoln Emancipation Association. "The colored citizens are to celebrate the day by a grand ball and collation at the South Wardroom," the local newspapers reported.[113]

In June of 1865 the Fourteenth Amendment was added to the Constitution, granting citizenship to all people born or naturalized in the United States. This overrode the Supreme Court's Dred Scott decision. Three and a half years later, in February 1869, the Fifteenth Amendment was added to the Constitution. No American could be denied the right to vote on the basis of race.

The fear of kidnapping and sale into southern slavery created by the Fugitive Slave Acts of 1789 and 1850 was ended. The southern port laws regarding Black mariners were unactionable. The rancorous debate over slavery in new states and the illegal harboring of runaways in

The celebration of the anniversary of the adoption of the Emancipation Proclamation by the colored citizens of this city, provided for by the will of Rev. Daniel Austin, took place at the South Ward-room last evening as previously announced. The room was decorated with the American flag. Most of the colored people of the city, both old and young, were present, and they kept up the festivities until three o'clock this morning. The exercises were commenced at about eight o'clock by the reading of that portion of the Austin will which described the gift of that gentleman, and the Emancipation Proclamation by Miss Katie Brown. Mr. Peter Williams acted as chairman of the evening, and introduced as speakers, Col. Wm H. Sise, Col. D. J. Vaughan, Michael E. Long, City Marshal Entwistle, George E. Bogdon, Alderman Siater, representatives of the press and others, all of whom made brief but very appropriate remarks. Alderman Siater rendered a poem in such a manner as to bring down the house. An oyster supper, prepared by Frank Rice, supplemented with a large quantity of pastry, was served during the evening. After the literary exercises, Turner's band furnished the music for the grand march, and the supper was served at midnight. The hall was well filled with invited guests, there being over a hundred white people present.[114]

Celebrations on this model—with oratory, a festive collation, and invited white dignitaries—continued for nearly a century. For the first several decades they were held in the South Ward Hall, built in 1866 to accommodate functions of one of Portsmouth's three voting districts.

Through the years Americans took note of abolition elsewhere. Slavery had already ended in Haiti and in the British and French West Indies. Abolition continued in the remaining colonies and nations of the West Indies and in Central and South America. In the midst of the American Civil War in 1863 the Dutch abolished it. It was abolished in Puerto Rico in 1873 and in Cuba in 1880.[115] Slavery in the Western Hemisphere finally ended twenty-three years after abolition in the United States when in 1888 Brazil abolished the institution.

Through the decades the Emancipation Day program was expanded and moved to varied sites[116] (for example, 1932 was one of several years it was held at People's Baptist Church), but the format stayed roughly the same except for the schedule inversion of serving refreshments before oratory and song. The Gettysburg Address was also added to the program.

A special symbol of self-determination occurred in 1958 when the newly founded local branch of the National Association for the Advancement of Colored People (NAACP) received its charter at the Emancipation Day celebration. Associating emancipation and the NAACP was a reminder that the goals of equal protection and opportunity were unrealized.

Following a typical mid-twentieth-century New England practice meant to inculcate a sense of citizenship, a local high school student, Valerie Cunningham, was invited that year to read the Emancipation Proclamation. She went on to become the principal collector and custodian of the three-century history of Portsmouth's Black residents.[117]

By the 1960s revenue from Austin's gift could no longer fund a celebration on this scale. It was discontinued.[118] The annual celebrations had seemed increasingly outdated, patronizing, a bit hollow. Whites across the nation had spent the century following the Civil War blocking Black access to full citizenship. Black Americans were amid a climactic struggle for full civil rights.

While campaigning for and celebrating abolition, Black Americans had pursued their daily lives. They served their country in peace and war, and while seeking legal improvement through legislation, they improved their communities and daily lives through mutual association.

CHAPTER 5

Community

❧❦❧

That late summer night in 1927 Reverend Custis watched the sky from his home behind People's Baptist Church. Looking southward he saw Portsmouth's sky light up with fireworks. He worried about the safety of his congregation, here, tonight, as he did about Black people every day and everywhere in the country.

Life for Black Americans was turning out differently from what anyone might have expected sixty years earlier amid the emancipation jubilation. The modern nation seemed like a new version of the old one. Recent cityward migration in search of work had brought a lot of change for Black Americans like those who comprised his flock, while white Americans clashed over change and wars, or indulged in a headlong pursuit of wealth and partying. Certainly they weren't interested in hearing dissenting voices.

Tonight's display was the culmination of a weekend of festive activities: a clambake, baseball games, visits to local churches, an open-air service, an evening lecture, and now these fireworks. All were heavily attended. Custis sighed.

If tonight were the Fourth of July this show would be a splendid sight. But this was the celebration of a different vision for America. The festivities were a presentation of the Knights of the Ku Klux Klan.

In the seventy-plus years between the Civil War and World War II Black Americans nurtured community, founded institutions, and produced perhaps the most original, creative, and influential culture of any in the nation's history. They did this amid a context of segregation, internal migration, and white infighting.

In white minds, north, south, east, and west, Black Americans remained a slave class, a status forced on them in the South and West by the unsavory economics of sharecropping and obstacles to exercising citizenship such as landownership, literacy requirements, and complex registration procedures for voting. In many states, but particularly in the old Confederacy, segregation was legislated or de jure by the notorious "Jim Crow" laws. Lacking legislated segregation, it was nonetheless de facto in the North.

Regionalism in Black Communities

Centuries of limited mobility and segregation had made African-American cultures distinctly regional. The South and North had large urban Black communities. While the South had significant small-town and rural Black communities. In the North most of the small-town and rural racial communities were not defined by geography. In small places like Portsmouth, with insufficient numbers of Black residents to constitute a discernible neighborhood, institutions would cultivate, express, and convey community as neighborhoods did elsewhere.

The old and large free Black neighborhoods of mid-Atlantic cities led the way in founding institutions. In a response to local exclusionary laws, every type of institution was founded, often large in membership and existing in multiple variants. This was especially conspicuous in Philadelphia.

Migration and Its Effects

Twentieth-century technologies and markets increasingly fractured and mixed these traditional cultures. Hope for employment in the industrial North or on the West Coast drew all types of Americans away from agricultural work. Among Black Americans this city-bound migration was mostly from the rural South to the urban North or West, from field-hand work and sharecropping to booming cities.

A powerful impetus to Black migration was a plunge in cotton prices in 1920. This coincided with a revival of the Ku Klux Klan and its terrorist tactics, active nationwide but especially virulent in the rural South. The Great Depression of the 1930s was a further spur. Those who headed north or west found few jobs; they were at the bottom of the hiring ladder.

World War II brought a tremendous demand for industrial labor, a further motive for migration. The movement of military personnel

Frances Tilley Satchell (1910–92) was from one of twentieth-century Portsmouth's oldest Black families. They were founding members of People's Baptist Church and its successor church, New Hope Baptist. She earned a reputation for her phenomenal ability to memorize poetry as a young child and for her total recall after many decades. One of her great joys was being allowed to groom and braid the tails of her father's prized team of horses. *Photography by Kelvin Edwards. African American Resource Center.*

combined with the search for wartime work created the largest internal migration in American history. Half a million of these migrants were southern Blacks.

In 1944, in the midst of the war, International Harvester Company perfected a cotton-harvesting machine, putting vast numbers of sharecroppers out of work. Many southern rural Black farmworkers followed relatives who had preceded them to cities. After the war most people stayed in the new places where they had found work.[1] All this movement, both Black and white, obscured the historical presence of

---

TILLEY'S EXPRESS
Light and Heavy Teaming

Furniture Moving   Piano Moving
152 Dennett Street, Portsmouth, N. H.
Telephone 315-4

Clarence W. Tilley operated a hauling business from his home. His horses were well known around town for their beauty. He and his team would also pull floats in city parades, and work for the fire department, and the Navy Yard. *Portsmouth City Directory, 1910.*

Blacks in New England, facilitating collective forgetfulness about the region's Black past.

Some migrants started moving earlier, and not all ended up in big cities. For example, when Frances Tilley Satchell's grandmother was released from slavery, she came North as a baby-sitter for a white family and eventually ended up in Portsmouth. Her son was a teamster. As his daughter Frances remembered him, probably in the 1920s and '30s:

> My father was in his own moving business. He moved with horses not a truck. We didn't have trucks in his days. He'd go from here to New-buryport and different places, even to Boston. He used to take his team, get up two and three o'clock in the morning and get my brothers up and they'd go off on a moving spree. He would move anything. He also worked on the Navy Yard, moving stuff for the government. He had four horses. They were a team of horses. We had the stables right in back of the house. I used to comb their tails and braid them. My father would shine—his harnesses would shine like new money! We had the most beautiful horses in town! They were in parades and everything. Those horses would eat if he didn't have a job and nothing came in. He'd say to my mother, "I'm sorry, Kate, but the horses have

got to eat." So she'd have to go out doing housework and make it for us while he made it for the horses.[2]

In the following pages we'll meet others who made a new home in Portsmouth: Rosary Broxay of Florida, Louis Gregory of North Carolina, Thomas Cobbs of Florida, George Straughn of Virginia, and James Slaughter of Virginia.

National migration introduced to one another hitherto insular Black cultures. The interaction generated great ferment in politics, social organization, religion, music, literature, and the arts. This Black renaissance was centered in the urban neighborhoods of the North's largest cities, especially Saint Louis, Chicago (particularly favored destinations for those from the Mississippi Delta), Detroit, Philadelphia, Cleveland, Los Angeles, and New York. There was corresponding spillover into smaller cities and towns within the economic sphere of each of these major cities and ultimately it trickled out to the Black populations of even small cities like Portsmouth. Black cultural creativity was so marked in 1920s New York that the national phenomenon is still referred to as the Harlem Renaissance.

Migration and Black cultural ferment occurred amid white infighting that today might be dubbed "culture wars." Whites agreed on little but racial segregation, authorized by Supreme Court decisions in the 1880s and 1890s. In 1883 the Supreme Court interpreted the Fourteenth Amendment (preventing abridgment of citizenship) to restrict only the acts of governments, not the acts of individuals. In 1896 the Supreme Court's decision in *Plessy v. Ferguson*—involving segregation on public railroads in Louisiana—approved the "separate but equal" policies that gave legal legitimacy to America's segregated public and private facilities into the mid–twentieth century.[3]

Other than nearly unanimous and unquestioning acceptance of these Supreme Court decisions, white Americans rejoiced or bickered over almost everything else. The opening decades of the twentieth century were characterized by rapid and electrifying changes: in fashion and art; female suffrage (effective in 1920); the heedless pursuit of money; rancorous debates over religion and morality; and American engagement in wars in Cuba, Puerto Rico, and the Philippines.[4] World War I traumatized many Americans; victory notwithstanding they continued to quarrel over isolationism.

Anglo-Protestant Americans grew uneasy about losing their grip on national and local affairs as millions of immigrants arrived from non-Protestant and non-European nations. Retrenchment was manifest in the Anglo-Protestant seizure of American history as a tool to resist change. Their teaching claimed to reassert old values, but these were the values of a conservative Protestant and now shrinking portion of the white population that had never in the nation's history been embraced by all.

With the Supreme Court's permission the government and public cast a blind eye on resurgent racism directed toward Black, Jewish, and Hispanic Americans. The Roaring 'Twenties included the anticommunist Red Scare, anti-immigrant fervor, crackdowns on homosexuals, and Klan lynchings. In the Great Depression and Dust Bowl of the 1930s few white people would be distracted by pleas for tolerance in the hardscrabble fight for survival. The 1920s and '30s were perhaps the most fractious and contradiction-fraught era in the nation's history.

In a single day in 1941 the nation was converted to stunning unity when Pearl Harbor was bombed. During World War II even white divisiveness and debate were pushed into obscurity by a common purpose.

From 1865 to 1946 every Black individual's experience differed, and even within a single localized population communities were numerous and overlapping. They often were organized into institutions around such shared concerns as spiritual solace, recreation, benevolence, education, and public service. It is these that we explore in this chapter.

People's Baptist Church: Spiritual Life, Religious Community

Black churches sometimes emerged in all-Black neighborhoods but as often were founded for deliberate separation from predominantly white congregations. In the latter cases there was a palpable need to escape white systematic hostility and marginalization. The old hierarchical seating practices of the seventeenth and eighteenth centuries, and annual pew auctions of the nineteenth century, were followed by free seating with segregated pews in the back. Separate Black churches sidestepped such offense.

Black churches also supplied a need for community and solidarity. Through much of the nineteenth century New England's Black population experimented with the alternatives of fighting for equal inclusion in white-controlled institutions like public schools or the peaceful enjoyment of community in parallel Black institutions. Each had benefits and drawbacks.

Denominational Appeal

In the colonial period the enslaved population frequently heard the Christian religion used by established churches as a tool to reinforce Blacks' subservient status. The enslaved were given minimal access to literacy and scripture. The Methodist and Baptist denominations—viewed by the legally established churches as illegitimate or as outcasts—conveyed their message in a style that appealed to the hearer's heart through vigorous preaching and a call for personal commitment. This made these denominations widely accessible at the outset, even to people of limited literacy. These denominations grew rapidly among white and Black populations before the Civil War and remain the South's largest churches. The style of these denominations was also more consonant with the traditional participatory style of religion in western Africa. They won early converts in America's Black population, were quicker to recognize independent Black churches, and never lost their lead in serving the needs of Black Americans.

Black Americans did of course belong to other denominations. In cities with large Black populations they sometimes founded churches of other denominations, if denominational polity allowed. The small Black population of lesser towns usually precluded or delayed this. Individuals attended churches whose theology spoke to their hearts and whose communities tolerated or welcomed them.

Some Black Americans, against great odds, became prominent in predominantly white denominations. An example is the Most Reverend James A. Healy, bishop from 1875 to 1900 of the Roman Catholic Diocese of Portland, Maine. This diocese encompassed all of Maine and New Hampshire. In his pastoral visits he no doubt came to Portsmouth's Immaculate Conception church.[5]

Antecedent Black Churches

The earliest-known Black church in what is now the United States was founded in the early 1770s by enslaved people at Silver Bluff, South Carolina, led by David George. He and other founders of this Baptist church subsequently founded Black churches in Jamaica, Savannah, Canada, and Sierra Leone. The Savannah church has endured to the present.[6]

At Philadelphia a Black congregation opened the Bethel Methodist Church in 1794, which by 1810 had reached four hundred members. By 1815 its membership was greater than the city's white Methodist population.[7] It is informally known as the Mother Bethel.

In the same year and city the nation's first Black Episcopal church was formed, Saint Thomas.[8] The sermon of Samuel Magaw, the guest preacher at the opening service, illustrates the source of the desire to separate into an all-Black parish. Magaw, a white Episcopal minister, with traditional paternalism emphasized gratitude and humility. Obviously somewhat irked by

this, a month later Absalom Jones issued a responsive statement. In it he declared that it was the founders' intention to "throw off that servile fear, that the habit of oppression and bondage trained us up in" and "to establish some orderly, Christian-like government" and to "avoid all appearance of evil by self-conceitedness, or an intent to promote or establish any new human device among us," in a church that would "be governed by us and our successors for ever."[9]

The founding of independent Black churches moved steadily northward through big cities. A Black congregation opened the Zion Methodist Church in New York City in 1799.[10]

Boston's African Meetinghouse off Joy Street on the west side of Beacon Hill was founded in 1805. Its founding minister was Thomas Paul of Exeter, New Hampshire, not far from Portsmouth. His parents Caesar Gilman Paul and Love Rollings (or Rawlings) lived briefly in Portsmouth in 1771 and subsequently in Stratham, just outside Portsmouth.[11] In 1828 the Abyssinian Religious Society of Portland, Maine, built a meetinghouse.[12]

Portsmouth's Black citizens had been members of local churches since the 1700s, but there is no evidence of their attempting to establish a church of their own until the last quarter of the nineteenth century.

A first, if not lasting, attempt was made in 1873. Under the leadership of Edmund Kelly a group of Portsmouth's Black citizens gathered for worship in the Baptist tradition at the South Ward Room. The gathering flourished briefly. Then Kelly was "unavoidably called away" to Massachusetts. The group continued under the guidance of Elder John Tate. When Tate died a short time later services ceased.

Not long after, Kelly returned to Portsmouth. While in Massachusetts he had visited and assisted churches he had earlier helped organize in Lawrence, Haverhill, and West Newton. In 1879 Kelly reconvened Portsmouth's fledgling church. Meetings for worship resumed, now in the home of Mr. R. Braxton, probably Robert Braxton, a local laborer.

The meetings brought new attendees, many

James F. Slaughter managed the Seaman's Home for the Seaman's Aid Society, then was sexton of a North Church chapel. He was considered the founder of People's Baptist Church, where he served as deacon for the rest of his life. *Portsmouth City Directory, 1892.*

Seaman's Home and Coffee House,
104 MARKET STREET, PORTSMOUTH, N. H.

Breakfast from 6 to 8 A. M.   Dinner from 12 to 2 P. M.   Supper from 5 to 7 P. M.   Lunch served at the Counter all Hours of the day. Reading Room free, with interesting Books and Papers.

J. F. SLAUGHTER, Manager.

inquiries, and a new convert, with baptisms planned for the near future.[13] Nothing further is heard of this gathering. Its membership may have been absorbed into a Bible study class that was organized a decade later.

Beginnings and Leaders of People's Baptist Church

A third and this time lasting effort began in 1889. In that year James F. Slaughter moved to Portsmouth and began conducting Bible study classes in his home at the corner of Bridge and Hanover Streets at 3:00 on Sunday afternoons. Attendance grew rapidly; they moved to the South Ward Room in 1890, the same building in which Edmund Kelly's group had convened eighteen years earlier and where the Emancipation Proclamation had been celebrated annually for eight years. They held Sunday school at 3:00 P.M. and preaching at 8:00. They called themselves the People's Mission. The seventeen members of this nondenominational group consisted of twelve Baptists, four Methodists, and one Episcopalian.[14]

Three years later, in 1892, the People's Mission voted to reorganize. Twelve members pledged to reorganize as the People's Baptist Church. The other five remained affiliated with them and continued to work in the church. This church would have a distinguished seventy-year history.

Portsmouth's People's Mission was founded in the years between the Supreme Court's narrow interpretation of the Fourteenth Amendment (1883) and their *Plessy v. Ferguson* decision (1896).

At the start the church was affiliated with the Middle Street Baptist Church, though meeting separately.[15] The pastor and moderator of People's Baptist Church was the Reverend James Randolph. James Slaughter continued as deacon, and James Handsend served as clerk.

James Slaughter is considered the founder of People's Baptist Church. For the rest of his life he served as a deacon and for many of those years as treasurer too. He had come to Portsmouth around 1890 from Virginia, where he was born in Danville. For a time he was a deacon at Boston's Joy Street Baptist Church (now the African Meetinghouse Museum).[16]

During his first decade in Portsmouth Slaughter was in charge of the seamen's home operated on Market Street by the Seamen's Aid Society. After this Slaughter worked for the remaining twenty years of his life as the sexton of a chapel operated by North Church. He married a New Hampshire woman, Miss Ossie Turnson of Rumney.

James Slaughter was remembered as living by the Golden Rule, and he won the esteem of the whole community. When he died in January of 1921, his loss was regretted by all who knew him. Portsmouth's Mayor Hartford and many businessmen attended his funeral. The ministers of People's Church and North Church jointly officiated at his funeral.[17]

George Straughn was a longtime member of People's Baptist Church. He came to Portsmouth from Petersburg, Virginia, where he was born in 1857. He was very active in the commu-

Built in 1857 by Free Will Baptists, and enlarged with a new facade in 1868, the Pearl Street Church was sold to New Hampshire's only African-American congregation in 1915. The church continued to serve the Black community of the greater seacoast area for three generations. It is on the New Hampshire and National Registers of historic places. It is a designated site on the Portsmouth Black Heritage Trail. *Courtesy Portsmouth Athenæum.*

nity in a variety of ways. In addition to serving as deacon of the church, he was treasurer of the People's Mutual Benefit Society and a member of the Granite State Social Club. He and his wife adopted and raised two daughters. He worked for the Jackson Express Company, then for Boardman and Norton Apothecary, and lastly at the Navy Yard. He was described as "well-known by his kind and pleasant disposition" and "quick to make friends with those he came in contact with."[18]

By 1908 the People's Baptist Church had proven its stability and was formally set apart from the Middle Street Baptist Church as a fully independent congregation. Their next goal was to acquire a permanent home.

In the next several years, under the focused leadership of Reverend John L. Davis, church members raised a fund of $2,000 for the acquisition of a suitable building. In 1915 People's Baptist Church used $1,200 of this fund to purchase an old church building at 45 Pearl Street. The church had been built in 1857 by the Free Will Baptists and expanded in 1868.[19] With some modest alterations it was ready for use, and it would continue as the home of the People's Baptist Church for the remaining fifty years of the church's existence.

Reverend Davis conducted the first service in this new home on June 6, 1915. At this service Mrs. Cynthia Hall, one of five nonmember affiliates from back in the mission days, became a member and was baptized, fulfilling her promise to join the church when they had acquired their own building. The congregation later procured an adjacent house at 40 Parker Street for a parsonage.

Several Sunday service bulletins survive, recording the order of service with its hymns, invocation, responsive reading, anthem, scripture text, and sermon title. They also identify the scriptural texts on which Sunday school classes were based. Some of these Sunday bulletins end with the admonition "*Come* to worship, *Leave* to serve."

In September of 1943 People's Baptist Church celebrated its fiftieth anniversary with a special service. Pastor Charles R. McCreary conducted this festive service. Present as guest speaker was E. D. McCreary Jr., pastor of Saint John's Baptist Church in Woburn, Massachusetts. Reverend C. Raymond Chappell, state secretary of the United Baptist Convention, delivered the sermon. Howard [probably Haywood] Burton delivered a narrative history. Much festive music rounded out the service.

Other Sunday bulletins tell of pulpit exchanges with neighboring churches; for example, on February 8, 1953, "Race Relations Sunday," People's Baptist Church welcomed as a guest preacher Reverend Raymond Smith of their old affiliate, the Middle Street Baptist Church.

This photograph shows the Pearl Street Church sanctuary (c.1900) as it was before the People's Baptist congregation installed a mahogany pulpit, electric lighting, and an extant pressed tin ceiling. When sold in 1984, the building was converted to apartments and an upscale restaurant. With the sanctuary room still intact, it now serves as a function hall and wedding chapel. *Courtesy Portsmouth Athenæum.*

Many happy memories of religious faith, close community, and hard work linger around the Pearl Street Church and its parsonage. In the 1940s Sophie Scott and a committee wrote a report about the activities of the church. These included care of the sick, charitable work, fundraising dinners, chicken suppers, and an account of one elderly church member's memories of slavery eighty years before. Those who worked so hard at these activities were sometimes honored with a gift of the decorative flowers used at Sunday services. Recipients of the flowers and why they were being recognized were announced in the Sunday bulletin.

Records of its vigorous Sunday school and ladies' sewing circle augment knowledge of these activities. Sunday service programs record guest choirs, honors for special guests or members, and the names of guest preachers.

Guest preachers and presenters included pastors from other churches, guest speakers from the local Baha'i assembly, and occasional seminarians for whom the experience was important training. Among the latter was, on the afternoon of October 26, 1952, a graduate student from Boston University who would subsequently emerge as one of the leading voices of the civil rights movement, the young Reverend Martin Luther King Jr.[20]

King had already established a reputation as a powerful speaker when he delivered the keynote address at a national Baptist convention. At People's Baptist Church King's sermon was titled "Going Forward by Going Backward." Fifty years later Viola Wilson reminisced about speaking with the young seminarian that day. "I never shall forget the words he said to me. I said 'Are you going to stay in Boston?' He said 'No, I've got a mountain to climb.'" The guest choir from Malden, Massachusetts, included soloist Coretta Scott, a student at Boston's New England Conservatory of Music and King's future wife. This service was in observance of People's Baptist Church's fifty-ninth anniversary.[21]

Alternatives

In the early and mid–twentieth century some of Portsmouth's Black residents belonged to other churches, where they were conspicuous by their small numbers relative to the predominantly white congregations. Sophie Scott, for example, was a member of Christ Episcopal Church (then located on Lovell Street), where she took care of their communion linens, and at the same time she was a dedicated worker for People's Baptist Church. Her simultaneous activity at the

Scripture Reading	Luke 2:41-52
Anniversary Prayer	Rev. Arthur L. Whittaker
*Hymn — 274 "I Am Coming to the Cross"	
Sermon: "Going Forward by Going Backward"	Rev. Martin L. King
Solo — "City Called Heaven"	Johnson
MISS CORETTA SCOTT	

Young Reverend Martin Luther King Jr. was building a reputation as a dynamic speaker even while still a graduate student at Boston University, when he was invited to be the guest preacher at People's Baptist Church for its 59th anniversary in 1952. Note that the program also lists the soloist with the visiting choir: Miss Coretta Scott. King and Scott had met previously and would marry the following April. Many distinguished visitors were attracted to the Pearl Street Church over the years, as it and Green Memorial AME Zion Church in Portland, Maine, were the only two Black churches in northern New England until the latter half of the twentieth century. *African American Resource Center.*

People's Baptist Church illustrates its extensive role in the life of the small city's Black community.

Portsmouth also had a small number of African Methodist Episcopal Zionists who established a church. Their original gathering date is unknown, but they probably met for worship in members' homes. Some might also have attended People's Baptist Church, a common practice where Black communities were small. After World War II, in July 1946, they bought for $4,500 an old church building on Hanover Street.[22] It is unclear whether they acquired the building because of, or in hope of, growth, and it is unknown whether they ever held services in their house of worship. The building remained in their possession, gradually fell into disrepair, and in the mid 1960s was swept away with the rest of the North End by Portsmouth's urban renewal authority.[23]

Transformation

The 1960s brought changes to all of American society. Fewer black people would tolerate either the subtle or overt expressions of racism that had for so long been taken for granted by whites.

In 1965 Malcolm X, who had risen to national prominence as an outspoken advocate of Black self-determination, was assassinated. Martin Luther King Jr. led a fifty-mile march from Selma to Montgomery, Alabama, in nonviolent protest of that state's stubborn denial of voting rights to Black people. Riots erupted in Black neighborhoods of Omaha, Nebraska, and Los Angeles.

In 1966 Edward W. Brooke of Massachusetts became the first Black person elected to the United States Senate. Constance Baker Motley became the first Black federal judge. States from coast to coast added names to the list of "first black elected to. . . ." The Black Panther Party was born in Oakland, California. James Meredith, the first Black student to be admitted to the University of Mississippi, started a "one-man pilgrimage against fear" down U.S. Highway 51 and was shot in the back; hundreds of others took up his walk and were dispersed by tear gas, but persisted. Meredith recovered. That summer, racial uprisings occurred in Chicago, New York, Cleveland, and Grenada, Mis-

Deacon Haywood Burton is second from the right in the back row of this candid photo taken at the Pearl Street Church, probably after a Sunday morning service. Burton was a founding member of People's Baptist Church. Standing to Burton's left is Deacon Leslie Ramsay and to his right Ramsay's wife Gustavia, who was the church organist and choir director. Three Ramsay children are in the picture along with the young Beatrice Satchell, second from left, in a beret. In later years, "Bea" Satchell Goodwin was a founding member of New Hope Baptist Church, which would continue the legacy of a Black spiritual center in this church until 1984. Standing next to Bea are two tiny Pettiford sisters with their mother. Sandra Pettiford, barely visible, would become one of the founders of the Portsmouth Black Heritage Trail, and this church is one of its sites.
Photograph courtesy of Geraldine M. Palmer.

sissippi. The Black Power movement swept across America, arising from impatience with the slow progress of the United States to fulfill its promises of equal opportunity and protection under the law.

But different people had different opinions about how to proceed. Reverend King denounced the war in Vietnam on March 4, 1967, urging Blacks and whites not to fight but to register as conscientious objectors. Two weeks later the National Association for the Advancement of Colored People (NAACP) voted against King's position on the war. That summer, racial violence tore through Boston (9 people injured), Buffalo (14 people shot), Newark (1,500 injured and 26 dead), Detroit (2,000 injured and 43 dead). In the years to come, images of the two

slain civil rights leaders, Malcolm X and Martin Luther King Jr., would be juxtaposed to symbolize the polarization within the unifying framework of a deep yearning for justice.[24]

Things were changing in Portsmouth, New Hampshire, too. Among African-Americans the struggle for civil rights dominated conversation and often influenced the seemingly simple choices they made in the course of daily routines. When Black people dressed for work, school, or to party they increasingly chose hair and clothing styles to make a political statement.

The tone of Sunday morning services at People's Baptist Church was different. Its reserved Yankee style was giving way to a more expressive character commonly associated with southern Black churches. Meanwhile many church members were actively involved in both the NAACP and the interdenominational Seacoast Council on Race and Religion (SCORR) to address local civil rights issues. The NAACP approached problems from the legal angle while SCORR focused more on moral suasion. Whether they were engaging in test cases for access to housing and public accommodations, or facilitating race relations workshops, the participants would include some Black people from People's Baptist Church. Whatever transpired in one of these institutions spilled over to the others.

In this national and local context People's Baptist Church underwent a transformation. How it began may not ever be fully understood; the process was as complex as it was painful— and perhaps inevitable. The Reverend Raymond Hailes was the pastor in 1967, but change had started before he arrived. The small congregation was having ever more frequent and heated debates over the style and substance of what individuals expected from their church community. Finally came the ultimate question of whether continuing a Black church was relevant in this time of struggle for equal civil rights and integration.

The congregation separated into two distinct entities. The birth of New Hope Baptist Church was recorded on April 7, 1967, in Newington, New Hampshire, a town at Portsmouth's north border. Services were held in Newington's old town hall. The principal participants were Willie M. Matt and Lige A. Williams, both of Kittery, Maine, Frances Tilley Satchell of Portsmouth, and Bette L. Jarmon and Joseph Shaw, both of Pease Air Force Base. They signed their names as charter members to the articles of agreement of the new church. New Hope was incorporated two years later, on April 14, 1969.[25]

Meanwhile, the dwindling membership of People's Baptist Church agreed to disperse. On February 8, 1968, they voted to transfer their building to the United Baptist Convention of New Hampshire.[26] About a year and a half later, in the autumn of 1969, New Hope Baptist Church procured the use of the old Pearl Street building, moved in, and later acquired title to the building.

New Hope's membership increased, and although still a small group, they had a clear vision of a new house of worship. They purchased an outlying sixteen-acre parcel of land with a house that they used as a parsonage, had architectural plans prepared, and sold the old church in 1984. In the interim, they met for worship where they had started, at the unheated town hall in Newington, then moved services to Little Harbor School in Portsmouth, and then the city granted permission for church members to gather for worship in their parsonage.

Within three years, on October 11, 1987, the small congregation held their first Sunday morning worship service in their newly constructed church on Peverly Hill Road. To the amazement of all, except the members themselves, they paid off their mortgage in just eleven years and symbolically burned the papers in a public celebration. Since its beginning, eleven ministers and spiritual leaders have served New Hope Baptist Church.[27]

New Hope Baptist Church has continued its legacy as a spiritual beacon for the Black community of the seacoast. The influence of and high regard for this small New Hampshire church extends to all of New England.

Deacon Haywood Burton: Community Leader

Haywood Burton was a leader in turn-of-the-century Portsmouth's Black community. He belonged to the founding generation of People's Baptist Church and was the church's treasurer on the first slate of officers in 1893. In his later years Burton was superintendent of the Sunday school. As a deacon, he continued as a church leader through his whole life.

In 1896, shortly after People's Baptist Church was founded, Haywood Burton was recorded as a coachman for Dr. John W. Parsons. Parsons was a physician and surgeon who owned an old-fashioned merchant's mansion that stood on a block-long downtown lot.[28] While working for Dr. Parsons, Burton boarded on the waterfront at George H. Straughn's, another leading figure in People's Baptist Church.[29] By the 1920s Burton had acquired a house on Union Street, a significant purchase on his modest pay. He lived there until his death in the early 1950s.[30]

The advent of the automobile obviated Dr. Parsons's need for a coachman. Burton found work as a janitor at the hospital, a job in which he continued for the remainder of his working years. The hospital was housed in a brick structure built in 1895.[31] Burton supplemented his income by opening a restaurant. After a short time he closed the restaurant in favor of catering, which he continued into the 1940s, pursuing a local Black tradition dating at least to the early 1800s.[32]

While Burton continued as a deacon at People's Baptist Church, he was also treasurer of the Portsmouth Baha'i Assembly.

Evidence that Haywood Burton was recognized and respected as a responsible citizen was his appointment as a justice of the peace. This role enabled him to perform marriages and conduct other minor legal functions not yet redistributed to other specialty courts. He was also appointed a notary public.

These appointments raise interesting questions. Were they modest admission of Portsmouth's Black population to the prerogatives of local white society? Were they a tool to isolate the Black population by enabling it to provide these functions internally? Did they come at the insistence of a highly motivated man who had already proven himself to be a community leader? Did recently arrived Black lawyer and fellow Baha'i Louis Gregory help negotiate the appointments? In any scenario, Burton had to have won some degree of respect from those

empowered to bestow these offices. In addition to his church leadership, these offices made Burton a valuable resource to Portsmouth's Black citizens in a time of de facto segregation.

George M. King, Ralph Reed, Albert Auylor: Social Clubs and Political Action

In the early twentieth century the local newspapers carried various notices of Black social clubs. Among them were Our Boys' Comfort Club (later the Lincoln American Community Club), the Black Pythians, and the Portsmouth Colored Citizens League.

While these three were new in the 1920s they had been preceded by other Black social clubs. The published order of parade for Portsmouth's Independence Day parade in 1910 included a float from the "Colored Fraternities."[33]

These clubs were expressions of the late-nineteenth-century fashion of forming societies around particular activities or common interests. Some were direct responses to exclusion from white clubs or services; others simply provided comfort in a segregated world. Several of them met in upstairs rooms on the southeast corner of Market Square.

Our Boys' Comfort/Lincoln American Community Club

Our Boys' Comfort Club was organized early in February of 1919 "for the purpose of entertaining colored enlisted men attached to the receiving ship at the navy yard and others in the service."[34] For Black sailors from remote parts of the United States, a long-term stay in Portsmouth harbor during ship repairs could be a lonely if not an uncomfortable experience. Yankee racism was expressed differently from racism elsewhere. Rather than the harsh but clear Jim Crow laws of the South, northern whites had unlegislated racist customs that they expected

Foresters of America

COURT ROCKINGHAM NO 6, Patrick L Lonergan, rec sec, 287 Dennett; meet 1st and 3d Thurs at 11 Daniels

Fraternal Order of Eagles

MERCEDES AERIE NO 682; meet 4th Thurs at 43 High

Grand Army of the Republic

STORER POST NO 1, Wm H Lovell, adj; meet 1st and 3d Wed afternoons at Memorial Hall, 11 Daniels

Improved Order of Red Men

MASSASOIT TRIBE NO 16, Leslie H Gardner, sachem; Chauncy B Hoyt, K of W, 47 Market; Charles W Hanscom, chief rec; meets 2d and 4th Mon at 73 Congress

Independent Order of Odd Fellows

Odd Fellows Hall, 48 Congress

CANTON SENTER NO 12 P M, John H Yeaton, clk, 377 Richards av; meet 2 Tues

NEW HAMPSHIRE LODGE NO 17, Fred Irving, N G; Stanton M Trueman, sec, 768 Middle rd; meet every Wed at Franklin blk

OSGOOD LODGE NO 48, Charles H Kehoe, rec sec, 788 Islington; meet every Thurs

STRAWBERRY BANK ENCAMPMENT NO 5, John H Yeaton, treas, 377 Richards av; meet 2d and 4th Mon

REBEKAH LODGES I O O F

FANNIE A GARDNER NO 82, Mrs Ida A Urch, rec sec, 393 Newcastle av; meet 1st and 3d Mon

UNION NO 3, Mrs M Alice Hilton, fin sec, 3 Congress; meet 1st and 3d Tues

Independent Workers Circle

Reuben Task, sec; meets 2d and 4th Sun at 43 High

K K K K

PORTSMOUTH CLAN NO 1, 73 Congress

Knights of Columbus

PORTSMOUTH COUNCIL NO 140, George S Pridham, fin sec, 15 Hawthorn; James A Fullam, treas; meet 1st and 3d Tues 133 Islington

Knights of Pythias

LUCULLUS CO NO 8, U R K P, Harry H Woods, capt; Fred Horner, 1st lieut; Max Gelman, 2d lieut; Morris Weston, treas; 48 Columbia; meet 1st and 3d Thurs at 73 Congress

DAMON LODGE NO 9, Frederick E Harmon, K of R and S; Harry H Foote, M of E, 387 Richards av; meet every Tues at 73 Congress

S W STARK LODGE NO 28, Alexander Richardson, K of R and S; Haywood B Burton, M of E, 179 Union; meet 2d Wed at 11 Daniels

Loyal Order of Moose

PORTSMOUTH LODGE NO 444, Herman C Moore, Maplewood av cor Northwest; meet 2d and 4 Thurs at 111 Daniels

New England Order of Protection

KEARSARGE LODGE NO 268, Cora E Cooke, sec; Charles W Greene, fin sec; Harry H Foote, treas, 358 Pleasant; meet 2d and 4th Fri at 11 Daniels

Order of DeMolay

PORTSMOUTH COUNCIL, Norman Lomus, scribe; Wm Varrell, treas; meet 1st and 3d Thurs at 27 Congress

Patrons of Husbandry

STRAWBERRY BANK GRANGE NO 251, Mrs Nellie B Pettigrew, sec, 19 Pearl; Fred Oldfield, treas; meet 2d and 4th Thurs at 73 Congress

Pythian Sisters

CRYSTAL TEMPLE NO 36, Lillian F Hall, fin sec and treas; meet 2d and 4th Wed at 73 Congress

HARMONY COURT NO 474, Mrs Martha W Countee, fin sec; Mrs Annie Taylor, treas; meet 2d Tues at 11 Daniels

Royal Arcanum

ALPHA COUNCIL NO 83, H A Brown, sec; James O Pettigrew, collr, 9 Market; meet 1st and 3d Mon at 73 Congress

Sons of American Revolution

PAUL JONES CLUB, George A Wood, sec, New Hampshire Bank bldg

Sons of Veterans U S A

CAPT THOMAS ASTON HARRIS CAMP NO 3, Charles W Greene, comdr; George E Howe, sec; meet 1st and 3d Mon at 11 Daniels

Sons of Veterans Auxiliary U S A

9, Hazel Tuttle, pres; Nellie Howe, sec; meet 1st and CAPT THOMAS ASTON HARRIS AUXILIARY NO 3d Tues at 11 Daniels

United Order of Independent Odd Ladies

STAR LODGE NO 2, Mrs Florence Wood, rec sec; Susie Delano; meet 2d and 4th Mon at Sons of Veterans Hall, 11 Daniels

United Spanish War Veterans

CAMP SCHLEY NO 4, John Woodward, comdr; Patrick J Browne, adjt; James P Kelley, quartermaster, 98 Bridge; meets 1st and 3d Wed at 43 High

Woman's Relief Corps

STORER RELIEF CORPS NO 6, Mrs Nellie M Moody (Kittery), sec; Edith M Paul, treas; meet 1st and 3d Wed at 11 Daniels

Black people to know and respect. As a result southern Black sailors could be reluctant to interact personally with white Yankees.

The absence of discrete Black neighborhoods in either Portsmouth or Kittery made social contacts with local Black residents difficult. The Black populations of Maine and New Hampshire at the time were approximately 1 percent of the total populations. Though the greatest percentage of New Hampshire's Black people were concentrated in Portsmouth, their real numbers were few, and their population was diffused. Our Boys' Comfort Club provided a pleasant setting for welcome social contacts in the Portsmouth-Kittery area.

Two weeks after its formation was announced the club was ready to host its first social gathering, an informal Lincoln Day observance in rooms above Grace's drugstore in Market Square.[35] Simultaneous whist, checkers, and dominoes games were played, while others danced. These pastimes were followed with hot coffee, ham sandwiches, and ice cream. George M. King, a self-employed local popcorn vendor in Market Square, was secretary of the Comfort Club. He announced receipt of a gift

Opposite: Some fraternal organizations of the day are listed on this sample page from the *Portsmouth City Directory* of 1926. Here are listed the Knights of Pythias Lodge No. 28 and their counterpart, the Pythian Sisters Court No. 474. Since there are no apparent clues about race, the reader would have to know the identities of people mentioned, and know that such organizations were not integrated at this time, to realize that these two Pythian groups were Black. On the other hand, it is doubtful that any Native people were members of the Improved Order of Red Men, Massasoit Tribe No. 16. Meeting at the same location, just two blocks away from the Black Pythians on the main business street, was Portsmouth Clan No. 1 of the KKKK, or Knights of the Ku Klux Klan. Names of their officers were not revealed.

of one hundred dollars to continue the good work. Club officers were appointed, a committee formed, and plans begun for another social evening.

Many visiting sailors and local people alike remarked that this was the most enjoyable day they had had in Portsmouth, even those who had lived in town nearly a decade. The club was off to a good start.

By autumn, the Comfort Club had changed its name to the Lincoln American Community Club. Among the activities it provided were a "community sing" on Sunday, September 28, at its gathering place on Market Square. This sing-along was offered in affiliation with the War Camp Community Services. The singing was followed by a social hour with refreshments. The club's advertisement for the day indicated that all "respectable persons" were welcome and that "Colored enlisted men, Phillipinoe [sic], Porto [sic] Ricans, and other darker racial groups of the service are especially solicited to join with us in making these meetings a success. All civilian Colored people 15 years of age and older are urgently requested to be present."[36]

In the intervening months since organization, the club had received assistance from others in town. The local War Camp Community secretary, Dr. Hanscom, had arranged for an appropriation for "Colored work in this community," which was conveyed to the club.

While the club was geared to welcoming Black enlisted men, women were an important part of making it work. Miss Maude Smith was "Girl Organizer," probably appointed at the February meeting or shortly afterward. In September she was succeeded by Miss F. Roe, who was present to get acquainted with the enlistees. The race of these women is not stated. They may have been part of the local Black community or white women representing the War Camp Community Services, the parent organization of the Comfort Club.

The duration of the club is unknown, but by

Mrs. Martha W. Countee, seated front row center in light dress and dark hat, was said to have been the last person around Portsmouth who had experienced "slavery times" in the South. She was involved in church activities and a member of the Granite State Glee Club, gathered here with their families for a clambake. The Black community of the seacoast area was experiencing the "Negro renaissance" that was sweeping the nation during the 1920s. Several groups formed after World War I, such as one to provide services for the recent influx of military men, another to motivate wider participation in the political process, and others, like the glee club, that provided creative expression and entertainment. *Photograph courtesy of Geraldine M. Palmer.*

autumn it was anticipating the "most successful season's work in its career." It may have declined and disbanded as the military was scaled back after World War I. It was still around in March of 1920 sharing its club room with the Black Pythians.

The Knights of Pythias

A lodge of the Knights of Pythias was organized by local Black men in February of 1920 and named the S. W. Starks Lodge No. 28.[37] The Pythians advocated a code of personal kindness and service to all.

This lodge was preceded by a white lodge of Pythians founded in 1871, the Damon Lodge,

which by 1881 numbered 135 members. Like most nineteenth-century men's lodges, it had its own meeting room, Pythian Hall, at 13 Pleasant Street.

The Pythian fraternity was founded in Washington, D.C., in 1864 by Justus H. Rathbone with the primary object of promoting friendship among men and relieving suffering, to allay the hatreds and division at play during the Civil War. The Pythians' founding principles were friendship, charity, and benevolence, each lodge adopting some particularly worthy principle as a further objective.

Though the club was organized with chivalric titles borrowed from medieval Europe, its name was ancient Greek in origin. Names from classical antiquity had been popular for men's clubs since the late eighteenth century, when the first American college fraternities were organized with Greek initials.

The Pythians took their name from the story of two friends in the Pythagorean Brotherhood, Damian and Pythias. Damian found himself captive and condemned by the king of Syracuse. Pythias presented himself as a hostage while Damian was given temporary liberty to bid farewell to his wife and child. Such was their loyalty that each would die for the other. People with a classical education had long known this story. It received a wider audience through a very successful play by John Banim, an Irish dramatist and poet, first produced in 1821.

The story inspired Rathbone to found the Order of the Knights of Pythias. When advised of the group's organization Abraham Lincoln approved of its principles and encouraged them to apply to Congress for a charter.[38]

Significant among the values promoted by the Pythians was tolerance. Even so, its lodges were sorted by race. Founding a Black lodge was an option not offered by all fraternities then. Lodge-based chivalrous conduct was one of many strategies adopted by Black Americans to promote and celebrate their dignity and identity.

Portsmouth's Black Pythians had several principal officers. George M. King, secretary of Our Boys' Comfort Club, was also chancellor commander for the Pythians. He and his wife Gertrude lived on Manning Street next door to the Black Pythians' "Sir Knight" Ralph Reed and his wife Mary.[39] Sir Albert Auylor was prelate or chaplain, a recurrent office in men's fraternal organizations. The Portsmouth Pythians had a female counterpart in the Pythian Sisters Harmony Court No. 474.[40]

The stated goals of the Pythians were to promote friendship, charity, benevolence, and tolerance, which in some ways were parallel to the work for legal protection being advanced at the same time by the NAACP. In towns where both societies existed (not yet the case in Portsmouth) there was overlapping member-ship. Such was the case with Sir Butler R. Wilson, grand attorney of the Pythians' Grand Lodge of Massachusetts, who visited the Portsmouth lodge.

Butler Wilson was a practicing attorney, a member of the American Bar Association and very active with the NAACP.[41] He was the guest speaker at a March 29, 1920, meeting of Portsmouth's Black Pythians. This meeting began with a procession from the Lincoln American Community Club's Market Square club room to the People's Baptist Church. There, Wilson described his work with the NAACP, which for a decade had been taking cases to the Supreme Court and was at the time pressuring Congress to making lynching a federal crime. Wilson's address skillfully wove in the Pythian duties of community responsibility with Black civil rights.[42]

Federalizing lynching law was an urgent issue. The summer of 1919 was called "the red summer" because of the blood that flowed in race riots and lynchings, violence that continued through the 1920s. New Black social and political action groups were formed across the nation in response to these developments. Sometimes they created entirely new organizations, like the Universal Negro Improvement Association (UNIA), founded by Marcus Garvey and still functioning today in the United States and other countries. Others turned to existing formats for the convenience of connection to a national organization because of such organizations' defined and sympathetic ideals and for the implicit (if unrealized) fraternity with white lodges.

The craze for fraternities among whites derived from a chivalric revival that originated in early-nineteenth-century Britain. By the turn of the twentieth century it pervaded American male culture and reached its final flowering in World War I.[43] The Black Pythians' name, presence, goals, and officers' titles were derived from this cultural tradition, but beyond this chivalric revival, these lodges addressed urgent contemporary social and political needs.

Clarence W. Cunningham (b. 1913) became one of a group of 9 Black Freemasons who formed the Octagon Club, probably in the late 1930s. While members were affiliated with the Prince Hall Masons of Boston, the local club gave the men an opportunity to have monthly meetings without traveling to Massachusetts. The Octagon Club disbanded after several members moved out of the area. In later years, a Black Brotherhood of Freemasonry established the Triple 8 Travelers Lodge #32 in Portsmouth. Cunningham migrated from North Carolina to Portsmouth in 1936 at the invitation of two sisters who had arrived several years earlier. Like him, a majority of African-Americans moving into the area prior to World War II came from North Carolina and Virginia, following the course of available railroad transport. *Photography by Kelvin Edwards. African American Resource Center.*

The Colored Citizens League

In November of 1922 some Black residents of Portsmouth convened to organize a citizens' league. For some time there had been discussion about bringing the city's Black people together for "harmonious activity" and unified action.[44]

People's Baptist Church, in keeping with its community role, provided a site for an organizational meeting, with Reverend George R. Riley taking part.

The Colored Citizens League adopted the task of encouraging Portsmouth's Black citizens to participate in the political process by registering and voting. At the time of the most recent state election 140 were registered. The league hoped to drive the number up to 200 in time for the city's December election. The organizers' aim was to cooperate as the election approached. Presumably this meant working within the political system to identify and support sympathetic candidates who might represent Black needs, or at least not ignore them.

This goal was not new. The Black civil rights movement had revived after the Civil War when many states evaded the Constitution's Fifteenth Amendment of 1870[45] by instituting complex qualification laws designed to exclude Black voters. Political empowerment and social advances gained during the decade of Reconstruction were reversed. The goal of the new Black groups was to regain that power and kill Jim Crow.

During the First World War Black Americans had to some degree suspended their civil rights advocacy in the interest of supporting the patriotic cause, once again hoping that patriotic and honorable military service would lead to full citizenship. The 400,000 Black men who served in World War I returned to the same segregated life they had left. Now they were ready to fight for their rights as citizens. The need for a political advocacy group was significant in Portsmouth as everywhere.

The Black Masons

Black Masons were meeting in Portsmouth by the 1940s. Its name was the Octagon Club in reference to one of the geometric figures of symbolic significance to the Masons.

Portsmouth had white Masonic lodges from an early date. Saint John's Lodge was founded in 1736, and the Dewitt Clinton Commandery of the Knights Templar was founded in 1826. By 1881 these had been joined by eight more lodges, councils, chapters, and associations related to Freemasonry.[46]

The Octagon Club was a twentieth-century expression of a tradition of Black Masonic lodges that began during the Revolutionary era. The first Black chapter of the Freemasons in America was founded at Boston in 1778 or '79. It operated without a charter until a grand lodge in England issued it a charter in 1784, though the charter did not reach its Boston lodge until 1787. Under its new charter the lodge was called African Lodge No. 459. In 1827 this lodge became independent of the chartering lodge in England. It was subsequently renamed in honor of a founding leader, Prince Hall.[47]

Portsmouth's Octagon Club had nine members. George Francis Bowles, a draftsman at the Navy Yard, was a founding member. He used his rather remarkable graphic skills to render a record of these founding members in pale blue and gold amid the symbols of Freemasonry. The members of the Octagon Club met in one another's houses for several years. Later another group formed, chartered as the Triple 8 Traveler's Lodge #32, which continues into the twenty-first century.

The Klan in Portsmouth

The Pythians, Masons, and other groups whose names and officers' titles evoked the days of knights in shining armor were almost entirely meant for pleasant social interaction, mutual support, and community service, albeit segregated. But one group used the vocabulary of chivalry toward very different ends: the Knights of the Ku Klux Klan.

White Yankees tend to think of the Klan as a southern phenomenon, but lodges were founded in South and North alike. The peak of the Klan's seacoast activity is illustrated in a chilling 1926 advertisement in the local newspaper:

KKKK
Rye, N. H., Monday, June 21, 7:30 P.M.
Go to Lang's Corner, turn to left, go straight ahead until you meet Klansmen in robes.
FIERY CROSS[48]

The Klan had first emerged in response to changes that followed the Civil War. A victorious Union Congress set about "reconstructing" the South in a new image. It imposed military occupation on the South, and laws were instituted protecting Black southerners and propelling them into participation in the political process, including officeholding. Three new constitutional amendments were passed. Amendment Thirteen (1865) abolished slavery. Amendment Fourteen (1868) guaranteed all citizens "equal protection under the law," revised apportionment of state representatives based on numbers of males over age twenty-one allowed to vote (thus punishing states who kept Black citizens from voting), forbade Rebels from holding federal office, and required states to void debts incurred during rebellion. Amendment Fifteen (1870) guaranteed the right to vote to all American adult males without regarding race or previous condition of servitude.

The early Klan sought to resist and reverse these gains. Their methods were intimidation, terror, and murder. Congress countered with the Force Acts of 1870 and 1871. These set stiff penalties for interference with access to voting and permitted use of federal troops against terrorists. Outwardly, the South obeyed, even as the Klan worked against Reconstruction.

The end of Reconstruction was signaled by the Supreme Court's 1873 ruling that the Fourteenth Amendment protected only federal rights derived from federal citizenship, and that other rights—including most civil rights—were in the domain of the states. In 1877 the Union Army withdrew from the South. Between 1890 and 1905 the South passed state laws that screened their Black citizens out of the voting process and implemented a series of segregationist Jim Crow laws. The Supreme Court's

The Knights of the Ku Klux Klan had an office on Portsmouth's Congress Street during the 1920s, when Klan activity was visible nationwide. Newspaper ads announced special events and welcomed new members. This float was in the Portsmouth tercentenary parade of 1923. *Courtesy of Whalley Museum and Library.*

Plessy v. Ferguson decision legalized segregation. The accomplishments of Reconstruction vanished. Its mission realized, the Klan faded.[49]

In the 1920s the Klan reappeared—this time nationwide—when some Protestant white Americans were increasingly fearful of change in the nation and world. Some felt economically threatened by the millions of immigrants who over the previous eighty years had come to America from non-Anglo and non-Protestant sources. Others feared what they perceived as a rising tide of secularism as early Victorian scientific theories of evolution began to gain acceptance. Communism, articulated in the 1840s, made its first political gains in the Russian Revolution of 1917, an experiment that at first fascinated some Americans as a possible route to unrealized equality but alarmed others as potentially destructive of the principles of a republic.

Insecurity and hatred combined. In the 1920s Congress sharply curtailed immigration through carefully constructed acts that allowed continued immigration from the Protestant north of Europe. Religious fundamentalism was born, accompanied by rancorous debate over who would define, articulate, and own religion. Some Americans joined a eugenics movement, complete with pseudoscientific theories of race hierarchy. Groups like the American Legion debated both foreign foes and imagined internal foes as the first Red Scare swept the nation. In this context the Ku Klux Klan was revived.

The revived Klan's white hoods enabled members to articulate their fears and hatred anonymously. Adapting to the new times, the Klan expanded its targets to encompass immigrants, Catholics, Jews, and northward-bound Blacks.[50]

The Klan used religion to validate its outlook, including visits to churches and worship services as features of its public rallies. This implied that a moral nation was a segregated white Protestant nation, a point driven home by the crosses on their robes and the burning crosses of their rallies and on the lawns of those whom they wished to intimidate. The Klan perpetuated and grotesquely expanded a white American habit of equating patriotism and Protestantism.

Since its revival in the 1920s, the Klan has lingered through the decades even in the North. The Klan held rallies in northeastern Connecticut and in Rumford, Maine, in the 1980s, and a very small group existed briefly adjacent to Portsmouth in Exeter, New Hampshire, in the early 1990s.

Announcements of Klan activities in the Portsmouth area was first reported in local newspapers in 1924. On May 5, the *Portsmouth Herald* noted that a cross had been burned at the Atlantic Heights neighborhood on Sunday night, apparently an act of intimidation. An investigation was in progress; names of participants were being sought toward arrest.

In November, 1925 the Klan ran an advertisement in the *Herald* cleverly designed to look like a news article. It consisted of a photo of nine hooded and robed Klansmen with a headline above: "First Photographs Ever Made Public of the Officers of Portsmouth Klavern, No. 2, Realm of New Hampshire, The Knights of the Ku Klux Klan." A caption below the photo read: "The above Klansmen are the officers entrusted with local Klan affairs, recently appointed and elected to offices of honor by all local members. MEMBERS ONLY know who they are." This was followed by the boldface invitation "Why Not You" and small-print directions for application. Recognizing the format's duplicitous character, the editors of the *Herald* placed above it the heading "advertisement advertisement advertisement."[51]

On Memorial Day of 1926 a statewide Klan gathering, called a field day, convened with parade and speakers in nearby North Hampton. Scheduling the event on Memorial Day subtly grouped the Confederacy's fallen with those who had died in other wars. Several thousand people attended.[52]

Two weeks later the advertisement emphasizing a burning cross on the summer solstice cited above made its first appearance. Clearly the burning crosses thrilled and fascinated Klan members as much as they frightened their victims. The nature of the Klan's self-perception was evident in an advertisement they ran a month later in July. It announced a public "Konclave" at their usual open-air meeting place on Wallis Road in the town of Rye, abutting Portsmouth to the south, for "all Who Want to Learn the Truth About the Klan." There were to be refreshments and a "BIG FIERY CROSS," and "All Americans Are Invited." Nativist xenophobia and a supposedly traditional Protestantism were equated with the truth.[53]

Such rallies were held throughout New Hampshire and New England in the mid-1920s. In August of 1926 several hundred Klan members wearing their white robes passed through Portsmouth on their way from Rhode Island and Connecticut to a Klan gathering in Portland, Maine.[54]

The Klan's nativist quality was evident the following year when Portsmouth resident Charles H. Partridge petitioned the Portsmouth City Council in March for a Klan parade permit for Independence Day of 1927.[55] The Klan wished to associate itself with the very founding moment of the nation, implying its goals fulfilled the Founding Fathers' intentions. Linking political or social goals with Independence Day was a long-established practice. William Lloyd Garrison, for example, had delivered an antislavery oration at Boston's Park Street Church on Independence Day 1829. Rarely had such a link been so scurrilous as that proposed now.

Much of the white population seems to have viewed the Klan's presence and public activities with indifference, but obviously some were ambivalent. What would normally have been only a few minutes of discussion in the Portsmouth City Council chamber regarding an application for a parade permit turned into a debate of over an hour's duration. Still, when the council voted, only one councilman objected. All the rest voted to approve the permit.[56]

Someone must have vehemently objected. Four days later the city council convened a special meeting to reconsider their vote.[57] They rescinded the vote, requiring that their original vote be "removed from the records."[58] Their motive in purging the record may have been a healthy dose of shame or anxiety about reelection.

In mid-July 1927 Partridge was again before the council seeking permits for a parade, a field day, and a fireworks display. The council first denied all, then approved the permits for the field day and fireworks.[59]

The regionwide Klan field day was held on

Labor Day weekend at Bracket Field off South Street and was heavily attended by overnight campers. It featured a clambake and baseball games, a Sunday morning "church visitation," a Sunday afternoon open-air service, an evening lecture, and "an excellent display of fireworks which were witnessed by a large crowd." The city marshal thwarted an attempted unpermitted parade when he said arrests would begin as soon as the lineup reached the public street.[60] It must have been a weekend of combined curiosity and apprehension for Portsmouth's Black, Roman Catholic, and Jewish residents.[61] The Klan's choice of this holiday weekend implied that these groups had played no role in building America.

Klansmen in the area were by no means limited to Portsmouth and Rye. There was also a Klavern not far away in rural Rochester, New Hampshire.[62] Local Klan activities tapered off after their brief heyday in the mid-1920s, though one might expect the Great Depression to have heightened this particular expression of racial and ethnic resentments. Perhaps local activity diminished because of the departure from Portsmouth of the Klan's primary local agent and organizer, Charles Partridge.

Some local Jews and at least one fair-skinned Black man quietly attended local Klan rallies to monitor the group's activities and rhetoric. In so small a city they couldn't hope for anonymity. There are no known cases of direct physical violence wrought by the Klan against local people. Perhaps the monitors' greeting of neighbors they encountered at the rally reversed the sense of exposure.

Louis George Gregory and Louisa Matthews Gregory: Spiritual Leaders for Racial Unity

In the 1920s a Black lawyer, Louis George Gregory, lived in Portsmouth and then lived across the river in Eliot, Maine. He was one of a string of highly educated graduates of segregated southern institutions who made a home in Portsmouth. More important, he was a member of the Baha'i faith and dedicated his career not to the practice of law but to promoting his faith and advocating understanding between the races, an important tenant of that faith. Gregory was educated and licensed as a lawyer in Washington, D.C.

Born in 1874, Gregory was descended from an enslaved grandmother and white grandfather. He grew up in South Carolina, where he attended Charleston's first integrated school, then went to Avery Institute, a private secondary school there. He went to college at Fisk, a Black university in Nashville. He received a law degree in 1902 from Howard University Law School in Washington, D.C. The South's large Black population and the region's segregation of practicing professionals supported Black legal services.[63] Gregory found employment in the Treasury Department in Washington.

As a youth Gregory had been encouraged by his grandmother to appreciate both his Black and his white heritages, while his freeborn stepfather George Gregory helped him attain a distinguished education. Gregory's liberal outlook and liberal education were important resources amidst American apartheid. He grew up during post-Reconstruction retrenchment and was a young adult when in 1896 the Supreme Court gutted the American dream for Blacks through its *Plessy v. Ferguson* decision.

Gregory's intelligence and vision brought him to the attention of W. E. B. DuBois, whose Niagara Movement of 1905–6 brought together Black intellectuals to promote justice and civil rights and gave rise in 1910 to the NAACP. DuBois thought Gregory a potential leader.

At the Treasury Department Gregory occasionally discussed Black activism for social reform with his colleagues. One of them, Joseph Hannen, invited him to a group meeting of the Baha'i faith to discuss racial unity. Gregory was impressed. The faith teaches that all people

worship the same God, that they are equal before God, and that racial distinctions are human
inventions. These precepts were consonant with
Gregory's concerns. He came to the conviction
that progress in politics and society must be
spiritually based. He studied the Baha'i faith
and joined it in 1909. Gregory corresponded
with the faith's leader, 'Abdu'l-Bahá in Haifa
(then part of Egypt), gaining further insight
and inspiration.

Soon Gregory began traveling widely as a
lecturer, sharing his faith's message. He was well
received at many of the South's Black colleges;
Booker T. Washington twice invited him to
speak at Tuskegee Institute in Alabama. Under Gregory's influence America's first Black
Rhodes Scholar, Alain Leroy Locke, a professor
of philosophy at Howard University, joined the
Baha'i faith. Gregory's travels were always arduous, sometimes dangerous, and even illegal
because of regional laws forbidding interracial
assemblies.

In 1911 Gregory traveled to Egypt. There he
met a Baha'i named Louisa Matthew, a white
woman from Great Britain. They shared many
convictions of faith and interracial harmony.
'Abdu'l-Bahá encouraged them to marry in the
United States, despite prevailing attitudes and
laws. They married in 1912.[64]

A New Home

The Gregorys' interracial marriage challenged
convention throughout the United States. In
many states their marriage was forbidden by law
and therefore not recognized. The Gregorys
looked northward to states where their marriage
would be legally recognized, if disapproved by
most whites. They resided in Massachusetts
before moving to Portsmouth, then finally
moved to Eliot, Maine—across the river from
Portsmouth—where they could be near the
Green Acres Baha'i Center.[65] Though Gregory
was admitted to the New Hampshire Bar, he

appears never to have formally practiced law
there. Rather he was listed as a "lecturer" in the
city directories. Louis and Louisa continued
their speaking tours, necessitating periodic separation from each other. When the Gregorys
retired, they remained in Eliot.

On July 30, 1951, Gregory died at the age of
seventy-seven, after nearly fifty years dedicated
to improving community life by promoting a
spiritual basis for racial understanding and
equality.[66] DuBois' evaluation that Louis Gregory would make a difference had been prescient.

Elizabeth Virgil: Quiet Pioneer, Witness to a Changing World

For Elizabeth Virgil community revolved around
music and education. In a pattern that became
recurrent in the small-town North, she had to
take her credentials south; they might have been
earned in New England, but they could not be
applied there to practical purpose.

In 1910 as a seven-year-old girl she moved to
Portsmouth with her family. Years later she remembered walking with her sister from the railroad station near Deer Street to stay at the
home of one of her mother's friends on Marcy
Street along the waterfront. Like other Black
residents, she would encounter Portsmouth's un-
spoken racist customs. But she grew up to pioneer beyond the limits they attempted to impose.

Elizabeth and her sister Henrietta had come
with their mother Alberta Curry Virgil from
Plymouth, Massachusetts, where Elizabeth was
born in 1903. Their father Wilcox, originally
from the West Indies, returned to Virginia,
where he had met and married Alberta.

After their initial brief stay with friends the
Virgil family moved to an apartment on Bow
Street. This was the first of many moves in a
small area of downtown, presumably in search
of a home that was more convenient or in better condition for the money. In their first six
years they moved every two years,[67] and in 1916

Elizabeth Ann Virgil (1903–91) graduated from Portsmouth High School and in 1926 was the first Black graduate from the University of New Hampshire. After teaching in Maryland, Virginia, and North Carolina, she returned to Portsmouth to care for her ailing mother. She was active in area choirs and especially proud of her lifelong volunteer service with the Red Cross. *Photo by Jane Fithian. African American Resource Center.*

the children and their mother moved to an apartment where they stayed for six years.[68] In 1926 Elizabeth was grown and venturing out on her own. With a reconfigured household her mother and Henrietta moved again, this time just down the street.[69]

Girlhood impressions made lasting memories. When in her eighties, Virgil could recall their first home on Washington Street, a six-family tenement owned by landlord Benjamin "Benny" Webster. Webster was a quirky survivor from the nineteenth century, still wearing a swallow-tailed coat. Grown-ups considered him stingy, but Elizabeth recalled him generously giving baskets of fruit to her and her sister, who

were grateful for his visits when their mother was at work.

A Pioneer Student, and Employment

In 1926, just when the local KKK reached its peak, Virgil broke new ground when she became the first Black person to graduate with a bachelor's degree from the University of New Hampshire. Her degree was in home economics.

Virgil wished to teach. White social convention prevented Black teachers from being hired in New Hampshire. So Elizabeth took a series of positions in the South's segregated school system, where Black teachers were in demand. First she taught at the Virginia Normal and Industrial Institute in Petersburg, Virginia. Later she taught at the Bowie Normal School in Bowie, Maryland. Normal schools were state-operated teacher-training schools, and in the South they were segregated by race. At the Maryland school she trained graduates of rural schools to become teachers. Lastly Elizabeth went to teach seventh graders in Smithfield, North Carolina. She then took advanced courses at Columbia Teachers College in New York and with unbounded energy and goodwill she found time to direct a church choir and a girls' singing group in her spare time.

All this while Virgil came home to Portsmouth for summers and holidays when she could. Eventually, when she knew that her mother's health was failing, she gave up teaching and returned to New Hampshire to care for her.[70]

Her education and experience notwithstanding, Virgil found that teaching in New Hampshire remained inaccessible to those of her race. After working at odd jobs in a doctor's office, demonstrating gas appliances, and as a domestic worker, she was hired as a clerk-typist in the Programming Department of the Portsmouth Naval Shipyard. Still later she took a job as secretary in the Soil Conservation Department of the University of New Hampshire, where she worked for twenty-two years. She retired in 1973.

Making a Home, Pursuing Interests

Upon her return to Portsmouth Elizabeth Virgil at first lived with her mother, then with her sister, Mrs. Henrietta Virgil Williams.[71] By 1952 the house was in Elizabeth's name. This deed transfer follows a recurrent pattern among many people of all races and ethnic backgrounds in Portsmouth's old waterfront neighborhoods. Such transactions sometimes secured a property for heirs or survivors but seem also to have functioned as collateral for loans to people who could not get loans through banks.

By 1957 Elizabeth had purchased her own house. This was her first Portsmouth residence away from the waterfront, about ten blocks from her sister's home. It was in a part of the West End near the railroad and factories that border the tracks. The factories and railroad, which had stimulated the neighborhood's emergence, were now in decline, taking the neighborhood into affordability. Elizabeth Virgil lived there for the remainder of her long life.[72]

Known as "Miss Virgil" to all, she was a woman of many interests and talents. She especially enjoyed music. She played organ and piano at local weddings. Though her West End home was only a couple of blocks from People's Baptist Church, she sang in several church and community choirs, including North Congregational Church choir, the York, Maine, Congregational Church choir, and the Rockingham Choral Group. This participation in the community of musicians was augmented by volunteering for the Red Cross, which she had first begun when she was a high school student in Portsmouth and continued until the last years of her life. Though no longer a classroom teacher she remained dedicated to education. At the University of New Hampshire she established the Alberta Curry Virgil Scholarship in memory of her mother and served on the University President's Council.[73]

Like most of Portsmouth's Black citizens Elizabeth Virgil spent her lifetime sidestepping the limitations of racism or combating in her own way its subtle or overtly hateful aspects. However, when she reminisced she preferred to talk about goodness in people. To do otherwise would, perhaps, have been too painful.

Miss Virgil's 1973 retirement from the University of New Hampshire occurred when the Black civil rights movement had made significant legal headway and was beginning to be internalized by whites. It coincided with the revived quest for women's rights, nearly dormant since suffrage was attained in 1920.

National legislation and regional culture had changed sufficiently for white people to recognize what Black people and women had known all along; individuals like Elizabeth Virgil were bold pioneers. Nearly twenty years later, in 1991, when she was eighty-seven, Miss Virgil was honored at the university's alumni center for the barriers she had overcome and the trail she had blazed as the first Black woman to graduate from that institution. In recognition of these accomplishments Elizabeth Virgil's portrait (which includes her beloved piano) now greets students in the university's Dimond Library. She died a few months later.[74]

Another Who Went South

Whites' reluctance to hire Black professionals was a common obstacle to employment in New England in the first half of the twentieth century. Like Elizabeth Virgil, George M. King went south. He has been mentioned earlier as a community organizer in Portsmouth. He graduated from Dartmouth in 1907 with dreams of starting his own business. For a while he sold popcorn in Market Square, preferring to be self-employed rather than do menial work for a white employer. Ultimately he went south, where he pursued a career in Black educational institutions, while his wife Gertrude and their children remained in their home on Manning Street. This divided life was an alternative to menial employment in New England. Improbably, dignified work was made possible by the segregated institutions of the Jim Crow South, but it brought with it the indignity of seasonal and prolonged separation from family.

Owen Finnigan Cooper, Eugene Reid, John Ramsay, Emerson Reed, Doris Moore, Anna Jones: World War II and Patriotic Service

World War II changed many American assumptions and customs. It set in motion tremendous change that continued into the next century. Many wartime factors helped initiate change. These included, during the war itself, the reorganization of the labor force and the internal migration of 9 million Americans. This migration exposed Americans to people from other regions with differing customs. Other features of the war years were overseas duty, temporary civil rights violations in the name of national security, the near exclusion of some laborers from the workforce, and widespread turmoil. Black Americans were unwilling to relive the World War I experience of patriotic service followed by racist exclusion. They became more vocal in demands for equal civil rights. The methods of civil rights advocacy developed during and after the war and their accomplishments remain a part of American social and political culture to the present.

Groups most subject to prewar racial and ethnic discrimination were Americans of African, Japanese, Hispanic, and Native ancestry. During the Great Depression these minorities had been at the bottom of the hiring list, usually below white women. When prosperity returned with high wartime employment, the white majority continued to limit these Americans to second-class status.

During World War II discrimination found new expressions and caused new tensions. Some minorities were singled out for special mistreatment. Japanese-Americans on the West Coast were declared a national security risk, deprived of their jobs and property, and sent to deten-

tion camps in the Great Plains states. Some conscientious objectors were, in effect, interned in work camps. One such camp was located in New Hampshire.

Black Americans, the Military, and Wartime Employment

America's wartime population was 10 percent Black (13 million), yet Blacks comprised 16 percent of the armed forces.[75] They were excluded from the air force, marines, and Coast Guard, and admitted in only limited numbers in the army and navy, where they were banned from becoming officers. Most Black men in these two branches were assigned menial tasks in segregated units. Black men preferred to avoid the army's segregated units. Oral history reports that Portsmouth's Black men favored the navy as more advanced.[76] Perhaps this was a faint echo of the early nineteenth century's camaraderie and rough equality at sea.

No branches of the military accepted the enlistment of Black women. But women could serve in auxiliary groups; local Black women like Anna Jones and Doris Moore served in segregated units of the Women's Army Auxiliary Corps (WAACs).[77]

Late in the War Black Americans were allowed fuller military participation and continued to serve heroically, though still in segregated units with white officers. Black men were occasionally allowed to become military policemen. They constituted the famed 369th Air Squadron based at Tuskegee Institute in Alabama and participated in the invasion of Sicily. To get these assignments they were trained at camps mostly located in the South. When off base, Black recruits endured the insults and harassment of the surrounding civilian population and its officials. In Beaumont, Texas, and Little Rock, Arkansas, Black men were arrested and shot for sitting in the wrong section of buses.[78]

The industrial expansion in support of the

war vastly increased employment opportunities. Yet the half million rural Black Americans who made wartime migrations to northern industrial cities found employers reluctant to hire them. Trade unions excluded them. African-Americans were excluded even from industries with government war contracts.

During World War I Black Americans had temporarily halted their appeal for civil rights to avoid competing with the war effort, a cooperation that had been unrecognized, unappreciated, unrewarded.

Determined not to be ignored again Black Americans took an unprecedented step. Under the leadership of A. Philip Randolph of the Brotherhood of Sleeping Car Porters a civil rights march on Washington was planned in 1941 to protest the unofficial exclusion of Black Americans from employment in war-related industries. Attendance was expected to reach 100,000. A panicking President Roosevelt bargained for its cancellation by issuing Executive Order 8802. This banned racial discrimination in industries with government war contracts and in the federal government itself (though this was not widely heeded), and established the Fair Employment Practice Committee to investigate abuses.[79] The marchers did not convene.

Some white officials recognized the detrimental effects of racism. Arthur Upham Pope, chairman of the Committee for National Morale, wrote in 1942:

> We say glibly that in the United States of America all men are free and equal, but do we treat them as if they were? Far from it. There is religious and racial prejudice everywhere in the land, and if there is a greater obstacle anywhere to the attainment of the team-work we must have, no one knows what it is. . . . We expect the Negroes to serve in our fighting forces—and we see to it that they do serve—but we don't expect them to serve as equals. The less said about our treatment of them as citizens, the better.[80]

Pope recognized the problem but didn't know what to do about it, so he recommended that it be ignored in the interest of "public morale," meaning white morale.

In spite of modest forward steps, equal civil rights were neither uniformly available nor uniformly violated. German-Americans, for example, were never interned, although some of them had participated in prewar pro-Nazi demonstrations. Nor were Japanese-Americans in Hawaii interned. Discrimination and segregation were irregularly applied, often according to darkness of color, and generally taken for granted or ignored by white Americans.

Second-class citizenship took new forms during the war. Black Americans were excluded from the emergency housing built to accommodate the great migration of workers to war-related industries. This was the case in Portsmouth, where Blacks were prohibited from home ownership in the new emergency wartime housing built at Pannaway Manor[81] and the rental units at Wentworth Acres (now Osprey Landing and Spinnaker Point).[82]

At the national level race and ethnic riots erupted when white racism collided with the pent-up anger of the marginalized. In New York, riots in August 1943 killed 5 people, injured 367, and caused millions of dollars of damage. In Los Angeles in the summer of 1943 25 Black and 9 white people were killed, over 700 injured, and several million dollars of damage was reported. Also in Los Angeles anti-Hispanic riots, referred to as "the zoot-suit riots," erupted during the war. There were violent riots in Detroit, in Mobile, and in Beaumont, Texas, as well.[83]

Wartime Work in Portsmouth

During World War II some Blacks expressed concerns about sacrificing for another war without access to full citizenship, yet Black Americans generally were ready and willing to serve in the war effort, as shown by their enlistment beyond their proportion of the nation's population. Others took advantage of new job opportunities in industries with government contracts or directly in federal facilities like the Portsmouth Naval Shipyard. The shipyard's employee roster ballooned during the war, with shifts operating twenty-four hours a day. This yard had produced both submarines and surface ships during the First World War. During the second war its specialty became submarine design and manufacture, with the yard turning out a submarine every week during one year.[84]

Among local people who took wartime work in the shipyard were Rosary Cooper and Thomas Cobbs. Rosary had come to the area from her native Florida as a children's nurse, then took a job as a crane operator at the yard. Thomas Cobbs took a job there as an electrician.

Because of the way Navy Yard employment records were kept, no statistical information is available about Black employment at the Navy Yard during World War II.[85] But interviews give a glimpse into its workings. Hazel Sinclair later recalled how "I got a job on the Navy Yard. They were taking women on during the war and several of us Black women went to the yard to work. I got in the woodworking shop. I was a woodworker's helper. They didn't let women work on the machines. You just stood there and a man was behind the machine and you were in front of it, and as the lumber came through you would take it and put it on a little cart, pile it up on the cart. I was there two years and four months."[86]

Other Black residents of Portsmouth served in the armed forces, taking them far from home. They included Owen Finnigan Cooper, Eugene Reid, John Ramsay, Emerson Reed, Doris Moore, and Anna Jones. Doris Moore later recalled her service in a segregated unit. She

was in the first WAC unit to go overseas. We were the 688th Central Postal Battalion. All Black women. We went over on a French passenger ship. It was huge. They also had the soldiers and the Red Cross nurses on there. We landed in Glasgow, Scotland, and came on

down to Birmingham, England. When we got there, all the English chicks had the Black men! Later, I had a boyfriend. I guess it was who comes first. It was no problem. About two years later, we went across the English Channel and were stationed in France. We had a ball! I had a chance to go to Switzerland and we went to Paris and the Left Bank. I was in Paris on VE Day.[87]

Though they served in several branches of the armed forces, Black men knew that the best conditions for Black servicemen in previous wars had been in the navy. This would change only after the war.[88]

Black Americans from other parts of the country sometimes passed through the Portsmouth area as part of ship crews, or served at Forts Foster, Stark, Dearborn, and Camp Langdon, all hastily built to protect the Navy Yard.

Anna Jones was the first Black woman from New Hampshire to join the armed forces. She graduated from high school in Seneca Falls, New York, in 1940. Her father had moved ahead to Portsmouth to work as a refrigeration specialist at the shipyard. Soon the rest of the family came to Portsmouth. A year later Anna moved to Washington, D.C., and shortly after joined the Women's Auxiliary Army Corps. She was a technician fifth grade working in commissary managing inventory and distributing supplies to soldiers. After two years she left the corps (just when its name was shortened WAC) for what was described as "war appointment" work at the Portsmouth Naval Shipyard. She started as a messenger but then worked in the drafting room copying blueprints. She was in training to be a draftsman when the war ended and women were expected to vacate jobs to free them for returning veterans. She took work at the Liberty Bridge Steam Laundry on Marcy Street,[89] where she remembers shaking out sheets and pressing sailors' white uniforms. Then she took work at Halprin's Cleaners on Daniel Street. Nonetheless, Anna Jones remained interested in art and graphic design, and continued doing artwork into the 1990s. Her sister recalls how Anna used her artistic talents to special patriotic purpose, designing a war poster.[90]

The Home Front Battlefield

All civilians had a part in what the United States government dubbed the "Home Front Battlefield," necessarily adapting to wartime rationing. The government's War Production Board used posters to promulgate patriotism, remind Americans of their duties, and show them how to do their share. Posters urged merchants to adhere to wartime price ceilings, explained to shoppers why rationing was necessary, promoted vegetable gardening and home canning, illustrated balanced diets, and promulgated security-inspiring slogans like "loose lips sink ships." They urged people to mail overseas packages early, promoted saving, encouraged contribution of cooking fat to the government for the manufacture of explosives. Posters promoted purchase of war bonds to fund the war effort, encouraged enlistment of the able-bodied, and publicized many other war-related causes. Collectively the posters encouraged Americans to endure and triumph over the countless little irritations and big worries brought by the war. The posters were stylized, using only a few words in block letters and simple bold images that were attention getting and immediately comprehensible.

Regardless of their disproportionate numbers in the armed forces, few Black Americans were portrayed in war posters. Joe Louis, a much admired boxer, lent his celebrity status to the war effort by appearing on a poster. In 1943 a poster was released that showed "ex-private Obie Bartlett," who had lost an arm in the bombing of Pearl Harbor yet went on to work as a welder in a wartime shipyard. An inscription on the poster quotes him: "Sometimes I feel my job here is as important as the one I had to leave." Another 1943 poster depicted Dorei Miller. He was stationed aboard the USS *West Virginia* as a mess attendant when it was bombed in Pearl Harbor. He carried the wounded and dying skipper to safety, then returned to operate a machine gun against dive-bombers, though he had never been trained for this. The poster depicts him wearing the Navy Cross he received for bravery in May 1942. Later he died in the sinking of the USS *Liscombe Bay*.[91]

Many ordinary people went beyond the forced participation in rationing to volunteer for scrap metal drives, plant victory gardens to sustain nutrition and a healthy population during food shortages, or provide recreation for off-duty servicemen and -women.

The latter need was met by Portsmouth churches and the local United Service Organization (USO). Their combined efforts provided dances most nights during the war years. The USO had two halls and a club in the downtown area,[92] and offered regularly scheduled segregated "colored night" dances.

For Black soldiers and sailors from other parts of the country a serviceman's usual homesickness was compounded by New England's unfamiliar ways and, when stationed at the Portsmouth Navy Yard, by the area's lack of a discrete Black neighborhood with its own businesses and institutions. Local Black families welcomed these soldiers. They attended USO socials and invited servicemen to People's Baptist Church. Servicemen and -women whose leave schedule allowed off-base church attendance received further invitations to Sunday dinner in church members' homes and were introduced to others in the community. Every effort was made to ease the unfamiliarity of the region and the usual discomforts and loneliness of the soldier's life away from home.[93]

Rosary Broxay Cooper: Migration, Career Options, Patriotic Service

Rosary Broxay Cooper's life incorporates many aspects of both women's experience and the Black experience in twentieth-century America. Born in 1913 to a Baptist minister, she grew up in Florida, which during her girlhood was growing as a tourist destination.[94] For some Black Floridians this meant a shift from agricultural labor to service jobs, a modest improvement. Black communities near tourist destinations grew as demand for service workers increased. Rosary's father was a Baptist minister to the Black population of such a community, Winter Haven. That town is adjacent to Eatonville, one the of oldest Black towns in America.[95]

Rosary attended Crooms Academy there, then attended Florida Agricultural and Mechanical College. After one year she transferred to Florida Normal School, from which she graduated with certification as a children's nurse. These schools were all-Black institutions, as required by Florida's Jim Crow laws.

Rosary was sixteen when the Great Depression began. During this severe decade-long slump 25.2 percent of the American workforce was unemployed. Because employers hired white males over any other group, employment was critically difficult for racial and ethnic minorities and worse for their women.

In spite of the Depression Rosary found work caring for children of the Merrill family, prosperous owners of resort hotels in Florida, Arizona, and Ogunquit, Maine, a coastal resort about fifteen miles northeast of Portsmouth.

In 1938 Rosary married a Portsmouth man, Owen Finnigan Cooper. She lived with Cooper's mother and sister Jane.[96]

Wartime Work

When World War II broke out a year after Rosary's marriage, unemployment in the United States dropped to 1.2 percent.[97] The combined military demand for young men and industrial demand for laborers opened to women employment fields never before available to them. Male laborers objected to women's presence, but government propaganda encouraged acceptance of women as a patriotic duty. Women in industry acquired the collective nickname of "Rosie the Riveter," inspiring posters, newsreels, songs,

and even a romantic comedy film around the phrase. Like most war posters, these media usually omitted Black people.

Portsmouth played its part as several small manufacturers converted to making materials for the war effort. The Portsmouth Naval Shipyard's employment surged from slightly over 1,600 in 1933 to almost 22,000 by 1944.

Roosevelt's executive order was widely ignored or sidestepped, but it had some effect. Between 1940 and 1945 employment of Black people in industry rose from 0.5 million to 1.5 million, and another 200,000 found employment in the federal civil service. The number of Black women working as servants dropped from 72 percent to 38 percent as nearly 300,000 of them found jobs in manufacturing. Black membership in labor unions doubled to 1.25 million by the end of the war, and the numbers of skilled Black workers almost tripled thanks to wartime on-the-job training. Monthly wages for Black Americans quadrupled.[98]

In this changed environment Rosary, like many other Black women, left domestic service and found work at the Portsmouth Naval Shipyard. She later reminisced:

> When I first went to the shipyard, I was a file clerk. And then they were training the women on the cranes . . . you had to climb all those catwalks. . . . I'm not going to say I wasn't afraid, I was. But I wasn't going to give [the men] the benefit of the doubt of knowing it. They had the wall cranes but they didn't pay as much money as the twenty-tons, so that's what I wanted. You . . . had three months to qualify and . . . six months to make your first rating. So I kept going up until I got to be a first mate's crane operator on the twenty-ton crane. That's the one that lays the keels for the submarines, the cradle, and the engines, torpedo tubes, anything like that. I worked on those 110 feet in the air. So I did that during wartime.[99]

There, as in most industries, men objected to women's presence. The man of French-Canadian ancestry who was assigned to train Rosary spoke little English and was pleased to find that the college-educated Rosary spoke French. The two of them got along well, and Rosary's training was a success.

Operating a twenty-ton crane was a challenge. The crane operator's perch was very high, and Rosary found the first climb harrowing. Once seated she learned the operator couldn't see the work in progress far below. She had to follow the hand signals of a rigger on the ground, manipulating the levers and cables carefully so the heavy submarine components were lifted into place accurately and safely. It was a job of considerable responsibility, a tangible contribution to the war effort, and it certainly paid much better than child care.

While Rosary operated this crane, her husband Finnigan was in the army. He became a master sergeant in the 509th Quartermaster Division, assigned to Europe. Toward the end of the war, when white infantrymen were in short supply, the army finally allowed Black platoons in combat. Of the Black soldiers already in Europe 4,500 volunteered for these platoons.[100] The Tuskegee airmen made significant contributions. Skilled Blacks were organized into specialty groups like the 387th Engineering Battalion, which kept the Allies moving northward up the Italian Peninsula, building Bailey bridges and other facilities where the retreating Fascists had destroyed them, as in Florence.[101]

When the war ended, young veterans surged back into the American workforce. Amid a pervasive rhetoric of patriotism urging women to leave their wartime jobs to make way for returning war heroes, government facilities like the Navy Yard could only reduce employment rather than revert to peacetime manufactures. For Rosary and Finnigan, as for many Black Americans, peace meant sudden unemployment.

For virtually all Americans the combination of employment, rationing, and service abroad had provided little opportunity to spend new earnings, enabling many to save for the first time in years. With their combined savings Finnigan and Rosary bought an eighteenth-

In a wing of her family's home on Washington Street, Rosary Cooper (1913–97) operated her beauty salon. She also took in boarders, including many military people. She was a volunteer on behalf of the New Hampshire Soldiers' Home and a fundraiser for the VFW's home for widows and children of veterans, and she initiated a scholarship fund for children of veterans. However, many people remember this woman as "Rosary the Crane Operator" for her contribution to the war effort, laying submarine keels at Portsmouth Naval Shipyard during World War II. *Photography by Kelvin Edwards. African American Resource Center.*

century house in the waterfront neighborhood known as Puddle Dock.[102] A hundred and fifty years of suburbanization in Portsmouth and a shift of commerce away from the waterfront had left waterfront neighborhoods in Portsmouth as affordable havens. This one was under a pall of iron dust from towering scrap metal piles, representing the self-employment of another marginalized group, eastern European Jews who had immigrated at the turn of the century and settled in this neighborhood.

Rosary saw a market niche in segregated

hairdressing. She went to beautician school in Boston for certification, procured a New Hampshire beautician's license, and around 1949 set up shop in their new house. Rosary was the only Black hairdresser in Portsmouth at a time when local white beauticians and barbers would not serve Black customers.[103]

Her husband found employment as a messenger at city hall.[104] He worked there the rest of his short life.

In Portsmouth's segregated housing the Coopers found another economic opportunity. They rented rooms in their sixteen-room house to Black boarders. Rosary's home employment made her available to look after her landlady responsibilities.

People's Baptist Church had a tradition of honoring a distinguished member each Sunday by presenting them the flowers. Rosary was honored on Sunday, February 1, 1953. The bulletin announced: "The flowers of the week go to Mrs. Rosary Cooper. Mrs. Cooper is the daughter of a Baptist minister, and the wife of Mr. Owen Cooper, who was raised within our church. Mrs. Cooper is making a distinctive contribution to our community as our only beautician. May God bless you Mrs. Cooper for the part that you have played, and still are playing in the enrichment of the community life of Portsmouth."[105]

In 1964 Rosary was widowed by Finnigan's early death. Continuing the patriotic service she and her husband had given their country, she joined the Ladies Auxiliary of Portsmouth's Veterans of Foreign Wars, where she filled the office of president. Later she became state chairman of the Ladies Auxiliary of the VFW. While chair of the VFW Auxiliary she presided over its Voice of Democracy competition for high school students. Mrs. Cooper also established a scholarship fund for high school students and raised funds for it.

Well into the 1990s Mrs. Cooper coordinated fund-raising and volunteer services for the Veterans Administration hospital in Tilton, New Hampshire, and for the New Hampshire Soldiers' Home. She led efforts to raise funds to buy televisions, clothing, books and magazines to make the home a more comfortable place for aging veterans. As recently as 1991, at the age of seventy-eight, during the interview at her house through which this information was gathered, Mrs. Cooper busily crocheted a lap rug for the Soldiers' Home, unwilling to be idle when she could be helping others who had helped their nation. Mrs. Cooper died on January 3, 1997.

Americans who had been systematically excluded from the mainstream of American life before the war made modest gains during the war when they proved their abilities in the armed forces and in industry. They also glimpsed the promise and possibilities of American life.[106] Some white Americans grasped the hypocrisy of fighting Nazi oppression of minorities abroad while practicing it at home. To these few, Blacks' and other minorities' participation in the war demonstrated the contributions they might make if fully admitted to the mainstream of American life.

A prelude of the possibility of attaining equal civil rights came shortly after the war, in the form of an incumbent presidential candidate's vote-winning gesture. Truman, who had completed Roosevelt's last term in office and planned to run for office again, was faced with a divided Democratic Party. He needed Black votes to win a close presidential contest. Under pressure from Black leaders and to gain these votes he issued Executive Order 9981 on July 26, 1948, requiring equal treatment and opportunity in the armed forces regardless of race. With the help of Black voters Truman was reelected.

The air force, independent of the army since the previous year, was already successfully experimenting with integration. The rest of the armed forces vehemently objected that it would destroy morale, order, discipline, and effectiveness.[107] They managed to slow integration to a near standstill for nearly ten years. Objections and stall tactics notwithstanding, integration of the armed forces was accelerated by the Korean

War when exclusion would have impeded the war's rapid developments and its need for manpower and cannon fodder. Through the 1950s and '60s racial integration of the armed forces was gradually accepted and implemented, though officers were long underrepresented.[108] Seeing the competence of Black servicemen and no disruptions in the armed forces, white civilians hesitantly began hiring Black employees in the 1960s. This was less in response to recent military example than to pressure and legislation stemming from civil rights efforts initiated and led by Black people. The institutions into which Black communities had been gathering for two centuries would provide critical organization, communication, and leadership for the battle that lay ahead.

CHAPTER 6

Civil Rights

◈⟡◈

$\mathcal{E}$merson Reed straightened his tie and swallowed hard. Jane Reed made a last fleeting glance at her elegant dress and put her arm in her husband's. They approached the sprawling gingerbread piazzas of the grand Victorian resort hotel, steeled their nerves, and proceeded. It was too late to turn back.

They could hear their own footsteps on the path as they approached the wide porches draped in red, white, and blue. They tried not to feel the burning stares of white couples—the men in jackets and ties like Mr. Reed, and the women improbably fur-clad on this warm summer night—dining on the veranda. They proceeded up the steps, crossed the wide porches, and entered the opulent old-fashioned lobby of the Wentworth-by-the-Sea Hotel. At the doors of the dining room on this sold-out gala evening they paused and told the maître d' they had dinner reservations.

"I'm sorry, we don't seat colored people here."

Mr. Reed had hoped against hope he wouldn't hear this expected reply. "Nor Jews, nor Greeks," Reed thought to himself. He repeated that they had reservations, not in their names, but in

the names of their friends, Hugh and Jean Potter. The bright young professor and Mrs. Potter were probably already seated and expecting them. When the waiter stiffened and hesitated, Reed pressed on with a reminder of the new Civil Rights Act. The maître d' excused himself and went into the dining room in search of the Potters. He returned with only Professor Potter.

The Reeds and Potter drew themselves to their full height—all of them were tall—drew lungfuls of air, nerving themselves to press on. The owner appeared and the three men went together into his office, leaving Mrs. Reed by herself on the broad carpets of the lobby, enduring the curious stares of guests descending from their rooms or arriving from the veranda for their festive Independence Day dinners.

White Americans are profoundly uncomfortable with equality. Those who are fully or even narrowly empowered view the extension of equality to others as somehow eroding their own rights. This American discomfort has been visible time and again, from the anti-Catholic and antisuffrage movements of the nineteenth century to today's anti-Gay and anti-Latino tactics. The Reeds and Potters were testing the Civil Rights Act of 1964, signed into law forty-eight hours earlier. But civil rights laws would not of themselves bring equal civil rights; there had already been three prior laws with that name. Power and culture allowed whites to resist change. This was especially true if no one challenged the norm in support of the unfamiliar new laws. Many, perhaps most, whites wondered why things couldn't go on as usual.

During the two decades since 1945, the United States government transferred the expectation of public unity it had vigorously cultivated during World War II to the fight against communism. Centralized national decision making on the Depression-era and wartime models continued. White Americans adopted these as the new status quo. National dialogue among diverse voices was suppressed or ignored for twenty years. As the very existence of diversity was denied, a false illusion of a monolithic national culture and opinion took hold.[1] Whites lived in the pleasant glow of an imagined consensus. They were confident in the belief that the nation was great and would only get better. Yet many Americans were having a separate and unequal experience.

Statistics, at first glance, seem encouraging. From the Great Depression to the mid-1960s Black employment doubled, and the number of Black families living in poverty decreased 3 percent. These developments seem consonant with the general prosperity enjoyed in postwar America.

The rising tide of prosperity did not raise all boats equally. Improved conditions were startlingly disproportionate. While Black poverty dropped 3 percent, white poverty fell 27 percent as white unemployment diminished sharply. During this same period infant mortality among nonwhites grew from 70 percent to 90 percent greater than among whites.

These and other startling statistics were announced by President Johnson's administration. Whites were reluctantly awakening to the obvious: something was very wrong. These were the effects of generations of exclusion, aggravated by ongoing resistance to the century-old guarantees of the Thirteenth, Fourteenth, and Fifteenth Amendments to the Constitution, as well as by the de facto apartheid enabled by the Supreme Court.

Johnson's announcements were particularly significant because of radical changes in the interpretation of constitutional law as applied to issues of race over the previous several years. Most white Americans resisted these changes too, whether actively or passively.

Legislation and Responses

In 1954 and 1955 the Supreme Court made decisions in two phases regarding the case of *Brown v. Board of Education,* which reversed sixty years of Court-approved segregation in schools. The justices' decision annulled their predecessors' 1896 *Plessy v. Ferguson* decision, which had allowed separate but ostensibly equal facilities for different races. The Court now unanimously found that separate was inherently unequal.[2] In 1955 the Court ordered integration of public accommodations.

The Black citizens of Montgomery, Alabama, immediately demanded integration of the public buses. In a sign of things to come, the transportation authorities would neither comply with nor enforce the reinterpreted law. Black people then organized a boycott of the buses. This was a considerable hardship because most depended on public transportation to jobs downtown or, in the case of domestics, to white neighborhoods far from the Black neighborhoods. They persisted through this hardship for an entire year. Heavily dependent on Black fares, the bus company suffered considerable financial losses and finally capitulated. Soon similarly effective protests against Jim Crow laws took hold. Black students in Greensboro, North Carolina, for example, staged a "sit in" at a segregated lunch counter, winning its integration and establishing a model for future non-violent protesters.

Whites were particularly resistant to school integration. They couldn't effectively teach their children racism if, through constant personal contact, their children discovered that Black kids were just like them. Whites found many ways to circumvent the integration of public schools. These included setting up publicly funded "private" schools, pressuring local school boards to delay integration, threatening Black students with violence should they attempt to attend a white public school, and in some instances closing rather than integrating public schools.

President Eisenhower, who had no particular stand on race issues, civil rights, or segregation, found himself an advocate through a very public battle of wills. Orval Faubus, governor of Arkansas, so opposed integration of schools that in 1957 he used the National Guard to prevent it. Eisenhower sent in federal troops to enforce it.

Television, a recent technology, gave national exposure to these civil rights actions. Segregation and violence were no longer remote abstractions. Television made them real and offensive to many white people.

Congress began to respond to pressure from Black and white Americans for civil rights guarantees. In 1957, two years after the Court's order for integration of public accommodations, Congress passed a federal Civil Rights Act. It established a permanent commission on civil rights to investigate discrimination and disfranchisement. This was followed by the Voter Rights Act of 1960. It allowed court-appointed officials to protect the voting rights of Black Americans. While Eisenhower signed these into law, he did nothing to promote them. The Voter Rights Act was designed to endure twenty-five years, then expire.

Some whites symbolized their resistance to court decisions and congressional acts in overt, if legal, ways. In 1956 Georgia discontinued its old state flag and adopted the Confederate battle flag in its place. In 1962 South Carolina moved its flag, also incorporating the Confederate battle flag, to the top of its statehouse.[3]

In 1962 President John Kennedy and Attorney General Robert F. Kennedy repeated Eisenhower's model when they sent several hundred federal marshals and federal prison guards plus 16,000 federal troops to uphold a federal court order admitting a Black student, twenty-eight-year-old Air Force veteran James Meredith, to the University of Mississippi. This pitted traditionally states-rights oriented Democratic local governments against a Democratic national government, and presaged a realignment of the major national parties and electorate by region at the end of the decade.

The Supreme Court handed down additional decisions favorable to the progress of civil rights as activists pressed cases. Through its 1962 decision in *Baker v. Carr* the Court guaranteed a one-person one-vote enfranchisement and banned land qualifications for voting. Though most New England states had abolished landownership requirements as early as the 1820s and '30s, property qualifications had remained entrenched in other regions. The *Baker v. Carr* decision shifted the weight of American ballots from rural to urban areas for the first time in the nation's history.

The Supreme Court struck down state laws banning interracial marriage. It upheld federal laws permitting federal registrars to enroll qualified voters when state or local registrars refused. A Supreme Court decision in 1968 gave equal access to housing for people of all races, surpassing and superseding a recently passed congressional act on the same issue.

When the constitutionality of new civil rights laws was challenged, the Supreme Court reviewed and upheld them. It also handed down a number of decisions that were not argued in the context of race but that nonetheless dismantled long-standing legal methods of disfranchising or intimidating nonwhite Americans.

In its 1963 *Gideon v. Wainwright* decision the Supreme Court ordered states to provide legal counsel for indigents accused of felonies. Two Supreme Court decisions in 1964 and 1966 limited police interrogation to a context of understanding one's legal rights (*Escobedo v. Illinois* and *Miranda v. Arizona*). While these rulings did not specifically address race, they proved to be critical protections for the poor. Often cut off from the advantages of education, wealth, and high-quality lawyers, poor people of ethnic or racial minorities were especially vulnerable to confusion and missteps during police booking and interrogation, and to victimization by lower courts that had a record of being more lenient toward whites.

In 1963 a march in Washington, D.C., was organized to advocate equal civil rights. It drew about 250,000 peaceful and orderly people. Heavily attended by both Blacks and whites, it showed Congress that equal opportunity was not the preoccupation solely of a marginalized minority but was something Congress dared not ignore. Kennedy presented Congress with drafts of bills to establish voting rights, to ban discrimination in federally funded projects, and to forbid discrimination in public accommodations. After Kennedy's assassination President Johnson advocated these as a memorial to the slain president, nursed them through Congress, and signed them in 1964.

Protests over racial discrimination in Birmingham, Alabama, in 1963 were repressed with electric cattle prods, high-pressure fire hoses, and police dogs. News of this retaliatory violence by civil authorities triggered public debate that led to a new federal Civil Rights Act in 1964. Its prominent features included enforcing the constitutional right to vote; conferring jurisdiction on federal district courts to provide injunctive relief against discrimination in public accommodations; authorizing the attorney general to institute suits to protect constitutional rights in public facilities and public education; extending the Commission on Civil Rights; preventing discrimination in federally assisted programs; and establishing a Commission on Equal Employment Opportunity. By this act discrimi-

nation or segregation was not allowed in voting, accommodation, education, or employment on grounds of race, color, religion, sex, or national origin.[4]

Also in 1964 the Twenty-fourth Amendment to the Constitution banned poll taxes. This brought increased access to the polls for all poor Americans but was especially significant to Black Americans.

In 1965 Congress passed another federal Voting Rights Act. It suspended literacy tests. It enabled the attorney general to bring suits to end poll taxes where local authorities tried to continue them. It authorized federal officials to register voters in areas where fewer than half the population voted.

These developments were continuations of Kennedy's civil rights policies. They were also part of President Johnson's War on Poverty and his vision of the Great Society. Out of this came the 1964 Economic Opportunity Act (which created the Head Start preschool program among other features), the Job Corps, and VISTA (a domestic program modeled after Kennedy's Peace Corps).[5] Most Supreme Court decisions and congressional legislation on race and rights known to Americans today were in place by 1968.

The next president, Richard Nixon, had grown up in an earlier era of institutionalized racism. When Nixon ran for reelection in 1972 the South at last abandoned the Democratic Party, to which it had clung since the Civil War, though it had been an increasingly uncomfortable fit. Nixon's reelection completed the philosophical reversal of the Republican Party's nineteenth-century origins. Henceforth it would focus on protecting states' rights from federal influence and exhibit little discernible interest in advancing equal civil rights.

Nixon appointed conservative justices to vacancies in federal courts, and as some of them percolated up into the Supreme Court it became less sympathetic in its interpretations of civil rights cases. This left Justice Thurgood Marshall increasingly as a dissenting voice in the Court. As a lawyer he had brought thirty-two cases before the Supreme Court—including *Brown v. Board of Education*—and won twenty-nine of them. In 1961 Kennedy appointed him judge for the United States Court of Appeals, where he wrote 112 opinions, none of which was overturned on appeal. In 1965 President Lyndon B. Johnson appointed Marshall solicitor general of the United States, essentially the nation's chief counsel. Two years later Johnson nominated Marshall to fill a vacancy on the Supreme Court. Marshall was the first Black man to serve as solicitor general and to serve as a Supreme Court justice. But Marshall entered the Court as successive appointments grew ever more conservative. He won a reputation as the "great dissenter."[6]

By the 1970s legislative action on Black civil rights goals had ground to a halt. Since the late 1960s the Vietnam War had dominated public interest, political discourse, and judicial review. Following the war's end the attention of white civil rights allies drifted off to preoccupation with other issues such as natural conservation and pollution control, while for others an exhausted inertia or preoccupation with money making took hold.

The legislative accomplishments of the civil rights movement and compliance with them didn't happen by themselves. Nor were they the result of spontaneously awakened virtue among white legislators. They came about in response to advocacy from many hardworking people and organizations. Among them were the legal defense arm of the NAACP, the Urban League, and the Reverend Dr. Martin Luther King Jr.'s morally based model of nonviolent protest.

Less spectacular than actions in Montgomery and Birmingham, perhaps, but no less important, were countless local actions that urged legislation and nudged local compliance with the law. In the following pages we'll learn how Emerson and Jane Reed, Thomas Cobbs, and dozens of others, both Black and white, worked in Portsmouth to bring this small New England city into step with the law. But first we'll look at a local case illustrative of shifting attitudes in the local scene.

Lost Boundaries, Broken Barriers

When a local white filmmaker chose a topic about racism and then butted heads with a hotelier over his still legal segregationist practices, he signaled that some of the white public was ready for significant changes.

During and after World War II Louis de Rochemont of adjacent Newington, New Hampshire, made documentary newsreels under the title *The March of Time*. In 1949 he made a film drama inspired by a seacoast story about Black life in a segregated and racist white nation. The film was *Lost Boundaries,* and its subject was—to white audiences—controversial.

His story line was suggested by the life of a real person, a Black physician of light complexion named Dr. Albert C. Johnston. Johnston graduated from Rush Medical College in Chicago. When it was time for Johnston's internship, he was turned away at the nearby Chicago Presbyterian Hospital, while Rush Medical College advised him that an internship at one of the South's Negro hospitals was unacceptable to fulfill his course of studies.

Johnston applied to many hospitals. General Hospital in Portland, Maine, didn't inquire about race, and Johnston didn't tell; he was accepted and interned there. As he completed his internship Johnston was informed of the death of a small-town general practitioner in Gorham, New Hampshire. Johnston took over his practice. Later he practiced in Keene, where he moved his wife Thyra Baumann Johnston and their children Albert Jr., Donald, Anne, and Paul. In 1947 Johnston's story was published in a book called *Lost Boundaries* by William L. White.[7]

Inspired by . . .

In Hollywood tradition de Rochemont restructured the outline of Johnston's story into a narrative he thought dramatically compelling. The resulting film was only loosely based on the outline of Johnston's life, a case of "inspired by," rather than a factual narrative.

The film tells the story of a light-colored graduate of a Black medical college and his wife who experience double racism. Too light to be accepted in any of the South's Black hospitals the doctor takes temporary work with a physician in a small New Hampshire town. Intending only a short stay the couple don't reveal their race. When the rural physician dies, their stay stretches to many years. When the doctor is called for duty in World War II his is revealed, shocking the local community.

While bearing little resemblance to the facts of Johnston's life, the film made legitimate points about difficult decision making amid complex circumstances. In treating racial issues with thoughtfulness and sensitivity de Rochemont crossed a boundary that circumscribed white assumptions and expectations.

Racism plagued de Rochemont's filming efforts. He had difficulty filling the lead roles, partly because white actors thought their careers would be ruined if they played a Black role. He eventually found willing actors for the main characters (of Mediterranean ancestry) and brought his cast and crew to the New Hampshire seacoast to begin filming, circa 1948. He assembled extras from the local white and Black population.

Louis de Rochemont arranged to use Portsmouth's Rockingham Hotel as his center of operations. James Barker Smith owned it. In keeping with de facto practices the hotel didn't admit Black patrons; it was what was called a "restricted" enterprise. Black cast members needing to meet with the director, attend meetings, or have meals were not welcome. The director held to his convictions. He told the proprietor that if all his cast and crew were not admitted, all would go elsewhere. The prospect of losing this client's business broke the restriction, and the Rockingham was made available to white and Black cast members alike for the duration of the filming. A significant local barrier was broken before any law required it.

Filming required many extras, Black and white, adults and children. They were paid five dollars for each day of work, pay enough for one extra, Jane Faust, to buy that special pair of black patent leather shoes for her little daughter.[8]

Place-names and people's names were fictionalized, and multiple buildings and sets were merged to evoke a semifictional New England setting, all in keeping with the moviemaking conventions of the times. The minister of Saint John's Episcopal Church made his church interior available and was delighted to fulfill his love of acting by playing the role of a Congregational minister. Views of Saint John's were combined with shots of other churches to represent a rural Congregational church. The Reverend John Papandrew of South Church, sometime guest preacher at People's Baptist Church, also participated.[9]

Lost Boundaries was released in 1949. White theater proprietors thought it was too controversial to play in their movie houses. Exposing the subject matter of "passing" made it a curiosity in Black movie houses. Some Black Americans viewed passing for white as inexcusably offensive; others were indulgently tolerant of those who escaped the harsh limitations of racism by passing.

Louis de Rochemont's film is a parable about the damaging effects of segregation and the enlightening effects of compassion. Among whites this was uncharted territory for the times. In the midst of the summer of filming, in 1948, President Truman issued his executive order for integration of the armed forces. The Supreme Court had not yet reversed *Plessy v. Ferguson* ("separate but equal"), so segregation remained the norm in America.

In such a national culture one film director and his diverse cast of professional and local talent broke down one barrier in one town, making a local hotel and its restaurant accessible to all. They moved one local businessman a step toward a new understanding.

Integration of public accommodations in America could not be effected when segregation was condoned by the Supreme Court and codified in regional practice or law. Even when national laws changed shortly after this inci-

Successor to Queen's Chapel and familiar to "Venus, a Black" in 1807,
St. John's made a splendid backdrop for one of the closing scenes in the
1949 film *Lost Boundaries*. Rev. Robert Dunn, a white Episcopal priest
who was an amateur actor, was thrilled to be given a part in a Hollywood
movie. In this character role, he stood at the pulpit as he admonished his
flock for their reactions to an African-American family among them
who had been passing for white. Years after that movie and Father Dunn
were gone, in the 1960s, the church's congregation would struggle with
its own real-life racial issues as the creation of the Seacoast Council on
Religion and Race challenged some members' capacity for change. *Courtesy
of Whalley Museum and Library.*

dent, local pressure would be necessary for compliance. In subsequent years many businesses
had to be pressured to comply with changed
law. This included Smith too, who did not respond to changed law by opening to Blacks his
other hotel, the Wentworth-by-the-Sea, until
pressed to do so. Eventually Smith complied.
The Rockingham Hotel became one of the meeting places of the local chapter of the NAACP.

Thomas Cobbs: Making a Living, Making a Difference

Thomas Cobbs came from Florida to Ports-
mouth during World War II to work in the
Portsmouth Naval Shipyard as an electrician.
His wife Gretchen continued as principal of a
Black school in Florida, summering first in

Portsmouth, then in their home in nearby York,
Maine, until retirement.

When the war ended, Cobbs stayed in Portsmouth. He used his electrician's skills to open
an electrical repair shop on Washington Street,
where his business remained through the 1940s.
In the 1950s he bought a house on Deer Street
to which he moved both residence and business.
He expanded his specialty to include repair and
sale of radios and the newly popular television.
He operated his business under the name "Cobb's
Radio and Television Sales and Service."[10] In
the 1960s or '70s, about the time urban renewal
obliterated their Deer Street neighborhood, he
and Gretchen retired and moved to York, Maine
where they had bought a house.

Cobbs found in Portsmouth much of what
he found everywhere in the United States.
Most white-owned hotels, restaurants, barber-

shops, and other public accommodations excluded Black Americans. The doctrine of separate but equal hadn't given rise to separate Black facilities and services, because there were insufficient numbers of Black residents in Portsmouth to sustain them. White owners simply excluded Black customers.

Decisions made in Washington, D.C., would overcome local white resistance in New Hampshire only through local pressure for compliance and enforcement. As a step toward this, in 1958 Cobbs worked with Black and enlightened white citizens of Portsmouth and environs to found a local chapter of the NAACP.

The NAACP originated in 1910 in a coalition of Black and white progressives called the Niagara Movement, led by W. E. B. DuBois. Ultimately, many chapters of the NAACP were founded throughout the nation. Now it was the seacoast's turn. The seacoast's chapter received its charter on January 1, 1958, at Portsmouth's Emancipation Day celebration.

In 1965, as president of the local NAACP chapter, Thomas Cobbs described the goal of the association. "When you join the NAACP you pledge yourself to work with others toward our Association's ultimate goal, which is to establish equal rights for Americans of all races and creeds in respect to security of the person's voting, education, employment, treatment in the courts, and public housing accommodations."

Cobbs sensed that direct personal involvement was critical, especially if a small-town organization was to accomplish its goals. "The difference between a branch spirit that drags along and a spirit that lifts heart and soul and mind is YOU. The difference between a branch that stands strong and vigorous in the community and exerts a vital influence and one that is neither strong nor influential is YOU."[11]

Cobbs knew that in so small a local branch individual actions counted heavily toward success. The local chapter followed the prescriptions of the national organization. In addition to an executive committee, the board and membership organized the thirteen recommended committees: Church Work; Community Coordination; Education; Freedom Fund; Labor and Industry; Legal Redress; Membership; Political Action; Press and Publicity; Veterans; Speakers Bureau; Youth Work; and Housing. With a small membership not all committee chairs could be filled at all times. Their number and range suggest the ambition and vision of the movement. Such committees stretched far beyond the usual offices typical of New England voluntary associations. Whites who valued the goals of the NAACP joined it too and served on its local board.

Under Cobbs's leadership the NAACP formulated effective tactics to pressure local institutions into compliance with law. Committed individuals implemented them.

A Sample Action

The Civil Rights Act of 1964 required public accommodation without regard to race. By spring of 1964 it had passed the House but had been languishing in the Senate for months. When the Senate finally passed it, President Johnson immediately signed the act into law on July 2, 1964. The local NAACP board and its Legal Redress Committee, of which Emerson Reed was chair, organized a series of tests, planning them even before the act was signed into law. Black and white members would test local places of public accommodation. Some participants would be placed as apparently passive bystanders, should they need to testify at public hearings.

The Wentworth-by-the-Sea Hotel is in New Castle, a town on an island in the mouth of the Piscataqua River and once a part of Portsmouth. The historic institution, then owned by James Barker Smith—also owner of the Rockingham Hotel—adhered to his policy of neither serving nor employing Black people. Nor were known Jews, Greeks, or other minorities welcome as guests.[12] The planning to test Smith's accommodation to the new law covered every detail down to the most proper attire for the participants. Emerson and Jane Reed teamed

Emerson K. Reed (b. 1921) was born in Portsmouth to a family with deep roots in the area, including an ancestor from southern Maine who served in the Revolutionary War. Reed graduated from Portsmouth High School, served in the U.S. Navy during World War II, and retired from the Portsmouth Naval Shipyard where he was the first Black worker to make general foreman. He served on the Equal Employment Opportunities Committee at the shipyard. During the 1960s he was president of the local branch of the NAACP and, later, its legal redress officer, and a member of the U.S. Civil Rights Commission's Advisory Committee on Civil Rights in New Hampshire. *Photography by Kelvin Edwards. African American Resource Center.*

up with white University of New Hampshire professor Hugh Potter and his wife Jean. The white Unitarian minister and his wife, John and Betty Papandrew, would serve as witnesses.

The Potters, young midwesterners new to the area and living in New Castle at this time, made a reservation for dinner for four at 7:00 in the hotel dining room and prepaid. By careful plan, Professor and Mrs. Potter arrived first, he with receipt of prepayment in his pocket as potential evidence of denial of service. The Potters

were momentarily caught off guard when upon their arrival Smith—greeting everyone in his proud role as host of this festive Independence Day evening—invited them to enjoy the fine weather by dining on the porch. It was critical to the test that they all be seated in the dining room. Mrs. Potter thought fast and said that as she'd just had her hair set she preferred to be seated in the dining room, and so they were shown in and seated there. Papandrew had stationed himself in the lobby.

The Reeds then arrived to join the Potters. Emerson Reed later recalled with astonishment that in spite of the July weather some of the women were wearing their fur coats for the gala occasion. "A nice shining day. We're just a couple of American Yankees going in the Wentworth Hotel," Reed recalled. "We walked in the reception area . . . and we politely told them we had reservations for dinner in the dining room with Mr. and Mrs. Potter; we were there for dinner." Evidently a staff member other than Smith intercepted them. "We were held up a while. Finally, they didn't know what to do with us now, they had a problem. They had a problem and we had a problem. So they escorted us . . . right into the kitchen, to a table piled with dishes this high, pushed the dishes over to let us sit down." Jane and Emerson recalled how they refused to sit down, as they had reservation for the dining room. "I remember saying to myself 'I don't care what you say. I'm going to the dining room. You can stop me if you want to, but I have reservations and I'm going."

Potter, meanwhile, was summoned from the dining room. Mrs. Potter stayed in her seat lest they lose their table there. Reed's reminiscence continues: "Well now, here comes Mr. Smith. His office was on the right side of the lobby. . . . At this time Hugh Potter's coming out of the dining room so he and I meet and all three of us go into . . . the office.'"

Reverend Papandrew watched and noted all this as he pretended to read the newspaper in the lobby and browse in the adjacent gift shop.

Mrs. Reed sat in the lobby while the men argued in the office.

Reed recalled Smith's reaction to his situation: "I remember the first thing he said was 'Why are you coming over here?' I said 'We made reservations.'" Somehow Smith brought up that he had been in the armed forces, where he "was in charge of Blacks and I don't like Blacks. You're not coming in this dining room. . . . I do not care whether it's public accommodations, I gave you a place in that kitchen." Reed replied "I do not care what you say, I'm going in that dining room, even if they arrest me. I am going in that dining room." Reed argued the legality of the issue while Potter argued the morality. The argument was heated and loud. "We were back and forth. Everybody was listening, even out in the hall. Everybody could hear. We were carried away. . . . I said 'I'll bring so many Blacks back here that you'll wish you had of let us in,'" Reed recalled.

Mrs. Potter, meanwhile, held her ground at the dining room table. She resisted staff pleas to wait in the lobby, fearing that if she let the table go they'd have conceded the battle. But when a third and high-ranking employee asked her she began to fear the others were being arrested, in which case they'd need her help in a different kind of way. She left the table for the lobby, only to end up seated there with Jane Reed wondering what the outcome of the men's debate would be.

In the office Smith charged Potter with not saying his companions were Black when making the reservation. "No, nor did I tell you I'm Scotch-Irish," Potter replied, indicating the irrelevance of race and heritage under the new law. Smith feared offending his southern clientele, some of whom stayed the entire season for many consecutive summers. "I'll lose thousands and thousands [of dollars] a day for letting you in," Reed recalls him saying. Of course those guests, like Smith, were now obliged to accommodate themselves to justice. Smith at one point asked Potter why he didn't go back to Africa with all the Blacks. Reed sensed that

Smith knew if he made a scene it would end up in the newspapers, that he couldn't fight it, and that this or further confrontation would be a "wonderful situation" for the advancement of civil rights. The turning point came when Professor Potter produced the receipt for the prepaid dinner as legal evidence of denial of the Civil Rights Act requiring public accommodation.

The Potters *and* the Reeds were seated in the dining room around 9:00 P.M., two hours after their original reservation. At this point the only available table for four was very prominently situated near the door and beside a desert buffet. Guests had been encouraged to see, admire, and help themselves to sweets at the buffet, which included an American flag composed of after-dinner mints. In this location their presence couldn't be overlooked by any of the other diners. The women confided to one another that their stomachs were so knotted by tension that they couldn't eat. Mr. Reed, however, informed his companions that he would eat every morsel on his plate in honor of his late father, who through his whole life had been denied such accommodation.

The following week a different foursome from the NAACP, including a Black officer from Pease Air Force Base, repeated the whole process at the Wentworth and were seated without delay. Eventually the Wentworth-by-the-Sea employed Black people too.

Numerous comparable actions were set in motion all over the seacoast testing for illegal discrimination in employment, housing, and public services. At local barbershops, for example, arriving Black customers were often told a shop was just closing and couldn't take any more patrons, no matter what the time of day. The civil rights tactic adopted was carefully timed consecutive arrivals of a white, then a Black man whose business would be turned away, then a white customer to whom the shop would suddenly be open again. Professor Potter again participated in one of these actions and bore witness against exclusionary proprietors before the visiting circuit Federal Civil Rights Commission. A white chaplain tested a different barber-shop almost every week and quipped—once it was over—that he didn't think he could bear another haircut and shave.[13]

Other efforts concentrated on overturning discriminatory policies that persisted in war-time housing projects, critical as the demand for housing increased with the opening of Pease Air Force Base. New air force families increased the need for jobs too.

Court decisions and legislation did not bring change; they enabled it. Local people brought change by countless small-scale challenges of entrenched tradition. Everywhere and always tense, such methods were profoundly dangerous in some parts of the country where activists were sometimes attacked, even killed. These actions required immense commitment and bravery.

Further Afield

Thomas Cobbs was also on the board of directors of the New England regional chapter of the NAACP and attended its meetings in Providence, Rhode Island and Pittsfield, Massachusetts in 1965. At such a meeting the Portsmouth directors learned about the programs of the Economic Opportunities Act—one of President Johnson's Great Society reforms—and about the need to encourage local agencies to apply for them.[14]

Black Americans had successfully pressured Congress to pass an act guaranteeing access to voting. This act overrode state laws expressly designed to exclude Black Americans from participating in political discourse. The Deep South, particularly Alabama and Mississippi, had the most restrictive laws. As federal reforms were mandated, southern registrars of voters found ways to exclude Blacks. One effective method was keeping Black people uninformed of the basic requirements anyone must go through to register to vote.

Emboldened by the recent success of the Montgomery bus boycott, and by the show-downs between Eisenhower and Orval Fauvus and between Kennedy and the University of Mississippi over school integration, the national NAACP pursued adherence to the new voting access laws. It organized a massive voter registration drive. This Mississippi Freedom Movement called for three hundred volunteers to help Black voters in the South get through the complex registration process.

Tom Cobbs volunteered although in his sixties and with poor eyesight. He invited members of both the local NAACP and the Seacoast Council on Race and Religion (SCORR), of which he was also a member, to join him. Knowing the dangers of the project he jested about its risks with his remark, "We guarantee you won't get thrown in jail, but if you do, we'll get you out."[15] A local newsletter reports:

> Tom's journey took him to Jackson, Clarksdale, Thunica, Greeneville, Indianola, and Greenwood. All in all, Tom, himself, personally helped 100–125 voters register, despite many obstacles. Not the least of these obstacles were the requirements for registering. At one time, Mississippi voters had to read and write, interpret a section of the Constitution, and deliver up an essay on citizenship. Gov. Paul Johnson, to soften criticism, simplified the procedure, but there are still plenty of tricks the registrars can use. For example, immediately after registering, the voter must ask if he is registered. If he fails to do this, his registration is void. Names of those who pay their poll taxes are posted publicly. This gives the employers of Negroes who register a chance to fire them. This in an economy where a Negro who chops cotton gets only 30 cents an hour and men can earn as little as $2.85 for a ten hour day. But Tom came back full of optimism. There were incidents such as the policeman who ceased his harassment of CR [civil rights] workers as soon as he learned they were members of the NAACP. And people *were* registered—10 an hour for five days a week.[16]

Later, the local NAACP contributed to the purchase of school buses to bring Black Mississippians to the polls on voting day. For the first time since the brief era of Reconstruction, widespread access to the political process was available to Black southerners.

Local planning meetings supported this distant work. Originally the Portsmouth chapter of the NAACP met in the homes of its members, including the Cobbs residence. As the local ci-vil rights movement gained momentum it gained members. By the mid- and late '60s meetings had outgrown private homes. The Seacoast Chapter of the NAACP moved to the Rockingham Hotel, where larger meeting rooms were available.

With legislative enactments increasingly enforced, new enactments slowed to a halt, and with a strong Black leadership and membership, white members of the local NAACP receded from participation.

Dozens of local people, Black and white, had worked toward equal civil rights. In addition to Thomas Cobbs, the Reeds, the Potters, and Reverend Papandrew of South Church, they included Juanita Byrd (Bell), Clarence and Augusta Cunningham, Thomas and Dudley Dudley, Eric and Helen Ebbeson, Kenneth Harris, Beatrice (Tilley) Hart, Barney and Betty Hill, Dallas and Mary Narcisse, Randy and Valerie (Cunningham) Randolph, Ruth Price Silva, Clayton and Hazel Sinclair, Lieutenant Colonel (Ret.) Charles Vaughn, and many others. Great strides were made in the twenty-five years following World War II.

Legislating Destruction: Government Policy and the Black Experience

Simultaneously with civil rights legislation other federal legislation was passed that had catastrophically detrimental effects on Black Americans. Perhaps few foresaw it.

After World War II the Veterans Administration made low-interest loans available for college tuition and home buying. Armed with a college education, a steady job, a car, and a mortgage loan, young veterans followed the inherited common wisdom that houses declined in value as they aged. Making the best of their opportunity young couples, mostly white, bought in the new—and often racially restricted—suburbs.

The VA loans produced the side effect of draining city centers of young white residents. Those who remained behind in the city centers were often poor, elderly, or Black. White-collar offices continued to flourish downtown; investors built new office towers. But small downtown businesses began to founder as the downtown's resident middle class diminished. They closed or moved to the suburbs.

In addition to these social and economic changes, city centers underwent massive physical change that in turn brought further social change. Cities had suffered decades of physical decay due to deferred maintenance during the Great Depression, wartime rationing of supplies; and wartime redirection of labor. This was especially true of housing. Much was judged substandard and unhealthy. Black neighborhoods in large cities were already deteriorating under the presence of additional forces. White absentee landlords were indifferent to maintaining income-producing properties they had inherited at little or no cost. City services were minimal. White flight to the suburbs took prosperity with it and generated indifference to the schools, infrastructure, and collapsing job market left behind. Bankers continued a practice dating to the northward migration of southern Blacks, "redlining" Black neighborhoods where issuing a mortgage seemed a bad financial risk. White realtors wouldn't handle homes in Black neighborhoods, and they steered middle-class Black house hunters away from homes in white neighborhoods.

The federal government responded to urban deterioration with the Federal Housing Act of 1954, its authority later absorbed into the federal department of Housing and Urban Development (HUD). It made federal loans available to municipalities for replacement of substandard housing, ideally with new housing.

Meanwhile, city streets could not accommodate the ballooning volume of commuter automobiles. A federal interstate highway system was initiated by the Federal Highway Act of 1956. White bureaucrats, many of them suburban residents, proved more concerned with traffic flow than with the social fabric of city centers.

Through the housing and highway acts urban renewal was born. It usually began with eminent domain seizures and demolition on a massive scale to create empty parcels for a fresh start.

Advance rumor or news of approaching eminent domain takings caused owners of threatened buildings to cease maintenance. Property sale values dropped. Businesses moved, often taking jobs beyond the reach of public transportation. As properties were seized the displaced population was scattered and the familiar environment reduced to rubble. The slashing angles of highways, new arteries, and massive off-ramps isolated surviving neighborhood fragments. Good for cars, these renewed cities proved untenable for people.[17]

New high-rise low-income housing projects proved socially unworkable. The urban renewal projects of small cites often replaced housing with businesses and parking lots, or found themselves stuck with vacant lots for fifty years for lack of investors. Time would prove this form of urban renewal disastrous in every way, though sometimes yielding economic benefit to a few investors.

A major feature of Black life in midcentury America was displacement by urban renewal, compounding the effects of long-term poverty. The social mechanisms that regulated quotidian community life were dismantled. Isolated, neglected, and unloved, urban areas became unsafe as desperation and anger simmered.[18]

New England cities were no exception to these developments. Boston swept away its West End with a promise of low- or mixed-income housing but instead put up luxury high-rise apartment buildings. Scollay Square was replaced with a sterile paved government office plaza. The elevated Fitzgerald Expressway, Interstate 93, divided the downtown. Hartford eradicated acres of buildings between its old State House and the river, and built an elevated plaza that was quickly identified as a national model of failed planning. Interstates 91 and 84 quartered the city and separated it from the river that had given it birth.

Portsmouth too joined the demolition derby. In the 1950s the city prepared to demolish the waterfront neighborhood called Puddle Dock, a close-knit area comprised of Anglo, ethnic, and a few Black families. Fifty years later its evicted residents remain justifiably bitter about the dispersal of their community. Failing to draw any investors, this seizure was sold cheap to preservationists who restored its surviving fragments as Strawbery Banke Museum.[19] The city leaders failed to learn any economic or social lessons about the limitations of urban renewal, nor did they grasp the potential virtue of historic preservation. They proceeded to tear down Portsmouth's historic North End, dispersing its ethnic population and alienating preservationists.[20] New arteries were slashed through the North End, reusing old street names, and over the next fifty years a few warehouse-style buildings and a hotel were built, with most of the acreage put into parking lots. Around 1970 the city abandoned unimplemented plans to demolish Portsmouth's South End, which subsequently underwent gradual gentrification.

The nationwide abandonment, destruction, and segmentation of cities, combined with ongoing white resistance to new civil rights legislation, caused long-simmering tensions to escalate. Peaceful sit-ins, stand-ins, and pray-ins filled jails with wave after wave of Black Americans. When urban conditions became intolerable, riots erupted. Over a three-year period in the 1960s they broke out in the Black districts of Los Angeles, Newark, Omaha, Cleveland, Louisville, Detroit, Washington, New York, and other cities. Unlike the similar uprisings during World War II, these riots were televised, promulgating images that shocked complacent white Americans. Any pretense that America had no race problems crumbled.[21]

Further Developments on the National Level

Attentive people knew unenforced legal reforms were useless to the deeply impoverished. In 1968 a vast march on Washington, D.C.—partly inspired by the 1941 and 1963 civil rights marches—called the Poor People's March emphasized these shortcomings.

In the late 1960s, with civil rights legislation and court decisions slowing to a halt and inner city conditions at their worst state in memory, the Black Power movement emerged. Stokely Carmichael, head of the Student Nonviolent Coordinating Committee, first articulated the phrase around 1966. It was a call for Black Americans to find strength in unity, heritage, and community, to define their own goals and organizations, and to reject racist institutions and values.[22] The Black Power movement discomfited whites because it didn't ask for equality; it assumed equality.

Soon the Black Panther Party emerged. It was a small but articulate and influential group founded in Oakland, California, by Huey Newton and Bobby Seale. The Panthers articulated the rage of Black urban youths trapped by poverty in dysfunctional cities and captured the imagination of many who didn't join their ranks. They advocated Black pride and solidarity, self-determination, and the right to employment, decent housing, and education. They urged separation from the decadence and snares of white society and politics, which seemed to them tools of white supremacy. The revolutionary garb of their founders frightened many whites; Panthers were harassed by local, state,

and federal authorities and were generally misunderstood and misrepresented.[23]

Meanwhile Black men and women served in increasingly integrated armed forces in the midst of the Vietnam War. Many served willingly and valiantly. Others were unwilling draftees for a war whose purpose and legitimacy were widely and publicly debated. They could not afford the postponements and exemptions available to some college students, nor could they get the safer assignments available through advanced education. Black veterans began trickling back from jungle warfare with no tolerance for resuming the role of second-class citizen. The new Black Power and Black Panther rhetoric was consonant with their mood. This outlook astonished most whites and was abrasive to racists.

These shifts coincided with urban riots and the assassinations of Martin Luther King Jr. and Robert F. Kennedy. Presently President Nixon expanded the Vietnam War into Cambodia without congressional authorization or knowledge. Large-scale public antiwar protests convened in Washington, D.C., at the United Nations, and elsewhere. National Guardsmen shot and killed several students during an antiwar demonstration at Kent State University in Ohio. Police murdered two Black students at Jackson State College in Mississippi. The American public was repeatedly shocked.

While most Black Americans understood the frustrations in which protest and violence originated, thoughtful whites searched for an understanding of the sources. Following riots in 1967 President Johnson appointed the Kerner Commission to investigate civil disorder. Their report squarely blamed riots among Black urbanites on the institutions and conditions created by a racist white society. The unpopularity of the way Johnson conducted the Vietnam War led him to withdraw from running for office again, and Nixon was elected.

In this national context Portsmouth's churches vowed not to repeat the mistakes of the 1830s,

This view up Chapel Street from Daniel Street shows St. John's parish house and the church. The Seacoast Council on Religion and Race met regularly at the parish house during the 1960s. SCORR brought Black and white people together from churches around the seacoast area to struggle with questions of race. *Photography by Brad Randolph. Portsmouth Black Heritage Trail.*

when their forebears were complacent or hostile to the abolition of slavery.

Working Together, Seeking Understanding: The Seacoast Council on Race and Religion

In 1963–64 a group of local citizens, white and Black, gathered to explore the proper role of religion in the American dialogue on civil rights. They were ordinary people who had been watching extraordinary developments.

They gathered slowly and cautiously. In November of 1963 a small number met at Saint John's Episcopal Church for a study group on race and religion. It was—in the group's own words—a manifestation of a church at long last seeking to involve itself and its members with the controversial issue of race relations. A year later the group had grown to include people of diverse races, denominations, and towns. They learned much through discussion.

In September of 1964 they issued a letter to members and prospective members inviting participation in a more formalized group. Evaluating their first year of conversations about estrangement of Black and white people, they reported their initial findings:

> We have looked, discovered, and faced the fact that this is a deeply complex disease of society—that it definitely is a religious issue— but that the Religious Community has been most reluctant to take the lead in dealing with it. We have concluded that the approach of a religious oriented group must *not* be that of merely treating the symptoms—*not* in trying to achieve a superficial surface healing (polite acceptance) that can let deep-seated infections go on undermining the health of both races; not in "sweeping it under the rug" and pretending it's not really our problem. Neither must our approach be that of making self-righteous pious pronouncements about what others *ought* to be doing.[24]

They understood that a group of individuals constitutes a group of outlooks, not a single outlook. They decided on a threefold plan of action:

1) To explore areas of local inequality and injustice in the matter of Civil Rights and to recommend and assign possible remedial action;
2) To plan for continuing support, training, and education of ourselves and
3) To provide opportunity for new groups to explore the problems, and to express their understandings and convictions, to raise whatever questions and concerns they might have.[25]

Gathered at the Portsmouth Naval Shipyard in May 1965 to discuss employment opportunities for African-Americans (*left to right*) are Kenneth Richardson, member, Equal Employment Opportunities (EEO) Committee at the shipyard; Joseph Derwiecki, EEO chairman; Barney Hill, legal redress officer, Portsmouth NAACP; Captain William Hushing, shipyard commander; Helen Ebbeson, acting chair of the Seacoast Council on Religion and Race (SCORR); Thomas Cobbs, president, Portsmouth NAACP; Dudley Dudley, executive secretary, SCORR.

SCORR Archives, courtesy of Augusta R. Cunningham.

The group planned to cooperate with the National Council of Churches and the local Ministerial Association, and perhaps offer training sessions for social action committees. At this point the participants adopted the name Seacoast Council on Race and Religion (SCORR).

They invited an expanded range of people to a reorganizational meeting, with the Reverend Parkman Howe of East Concord as guest speaker. He had just returned from the Delta region of Mississippi, where he had been registering Black voters and conducting "freedom schools."[26]

SCORR went into action quickly and persisted at an intensely productive level for several years. Members mailed notices to New Hampshire churches encouraging attendance at Martin Luther King's upcoming rally in Boston in April of 1965 and sought funds to support his work. They set up a bureau of twenty speakers available to local adult and youth groups. They worked with the City Missionary Society to host nine children from Roxbury and Dorch-

ester. They sent local representatives to conferences on racism. SCORR members raised money to help the NAACP send a local representative to help with the voter registration drive in Mississippi. Members collected trading stamps toward the purchase of buses to take newly registered Black voters to the polls in Mississippi. SCORR members introduced the (Quaker) American Friends Service Committee's curriculum "The Green Circle" to local schools. They canvassed the local community on the status of civil rights. They set up liaisons with other New Hampshire civil rights advocacy groups. They accompanied NAACP members to the Portsmouth Naval Shipyard to meet with the yard's Equal Employment Opportunity Committee. SCORR members met with seacoast chapters of the League of Women Voters. They sponsored a youth skit as part of the local annual Emancipation Celebration. They wrote letters to the editor and editorials condemning a continuing Newmarket tradition of blackface minstrel shows. SCORR members trained sixty University of New Hampshire senior students to tutor in area schools. They collected money and supplies for the 1968 Poor People's March on Washington.[27]

SCORR left no record of the findings of its canvass on the status of civil rights in the local community. Other records reveal problems at federal and state levels and in public and private activity. The federal exclusion of Blacks from wartime emergency housing in Portsmouth turns out to have included twenty-year deed covenants explicitly forbidding resale to Black buyers after the war.[28] At the state level Governor John King had to be pressured to establish a state Commission on Civil Rights, and when he did he failed to include any Black people among the commissioners he appointed. SCORR united with the local NAACP to write a letter of protest to the governor. Some offenses were not codified in law, nor did white people grasp the nature of the offense, as when minstrel shows perpetuated cruel stereotypes. Other offensive behaviors were more private though not so subtle, as when many white people would not welcome their friends into their home for a visit if they arrived accompanied by Black visitors.[29] In addition to these were the aforementioned refusals among local businesses to accommodate Black people. It was time to effect the removal of "Negro" labels from local church pews.

SCORR also brought the remote southern experience to Portsmouth's doorstep at its second anniversary meeting. The guest speaker was Father John Swanson, who reminisced about a young Episcopal seminarian, Jonathan Daniels of New Hampshire, who had recently been murdered in Alabama while there promoting civil rights. Swanson read aloud from Daniels's writings. Whether originating in the Black community or from integrated efforts, the involvement of churches and appeal to religion provided both leadership and moral argument for equal rights.

SCORR enabled its members to understand one another during fundamental intellectual shifts that eluded many whites. They had to keep pace with rapid developments, as when the civil rights movement elided into the Black Power movement. Entrenched in fundamentally racist habits of thought, even liberal white Americans were confused by the Black Power movement's rhetoric. They found it shrill, combative, and threatening. Overt racists willingly blamed Blacks for race riots and their own poverty. SCORR provided a safe setting for dialogue through which people could understand what was going on, and find the words to convey it to friends and acquaintances.

SCORR also initiated high-profile demonstrations to highlight entrenched inequity in America, as when it responded to news that some Black military personnel from the West Coast were imprisoned at the Marine Retraining Command at the Portsmouth Naval Shipyard. Following several years of race riots and at the height of the Vietnam War William Harvey and George Daniels, both twenty-year-old Black marines, had been overheard during their free time one afternoon and evening in July 1968 at Camp Pendleton, California. They had discussed the Vietnam War as a "white man's war" that no Black man could conscionably support while Blacks at home suffered injustice. A court-martial found them—after an eighteen-minute hearing—guilty of violating Article 34 of the Universal Code of Military Justice. They were dishonorably discharged, forfeited all allowances, and were sentenced to six (Harvey) and ten (Daniel) years imprisonment. They did not have the right to discuss unpopular political ideas. Interpreting conversation about equality and injustices as "an intent to interfere with, impair, or influence the loyalty, morale and discipline" of other members of the Marine Corps struck many Americans as based solely in racism and fear, not in national security needs.[30] Churches prayed for the prisoners' well-being. Articles about their case appeared in religious magazines. Clergy issued letters about their plight to their flocks. White military opinion was little changed since the armed forces first resisted President Truman's 1948 executive order to integrate the military.

SCORR organized a public demonstration. A group with placards marched from Portsmouth across the bridge to picket at the Navy Yard gate, then returned to Jones Park at the Kittery end of the bridge for further demonstration in that high-traffic area. Their intent was to focus press attention, stir public thought, and bring shame on the racist military authorities for misuse of power. Their transit of the World War I Memorial Bridge and gathering in John Paul Jones Park linked the message of equal civil rights with American Independence and centuries of patriotic military service. Military people assigned to the Navy Yard or Pease Air Base who wished to participate in this demonstration were faced with the possibility that their involvement—or even their spouses'— might lead to discipline or imprisonment. They had to weigh the risk of participation carefully.[31] Even the simplest efforts to awaken white understanding of the scale of inequity in this country involved wrenching personal and career decisions.

By July of 1967 SCORR members were becoming conscious of the historic times in which they lived and their role in them. They began to think of preserving documents. In their newsletter they put out a call for back issues of the newsletter and for news clippings that mentioned their work.[32]

Religion, Ecumenism, and Civil Rights

Officials of various local religious denominations had been on courteous terms since the 1870s. The 1960s were an era of considerable ferment in national-level ecumenical dialogue among denominations. Locally, ecumenism and civil rights issues began to overlap. Several denominations were represented in SCORR's membership. The Roman Catholic Diocese of New Hampshire added to its adult education series four sessions on the problem of racism. When the series ended, three hundred of its participants met with SCORR and NAACP members.[33]

On Wednesday evening, March 1, 1967, a Lenten evensong service at Saint John's Episcopal Church was conducted jointly by Franciscan Roman Catholic father Neal O'Connell, the Black Bostonian activist Reverend Virgil A. Wood, and host rector Charles Hodgins. Black and white, Catholic and Protestant residents of Portsmouth and adjacent communities attended the service. In his sermon, Wood summed up their motive and goals. "When the hand of hatred is let loose, we are unable to protect our loved ones from the very venom of hate. In this country—in the world—there must be a new thrust of good will—a politics of partnership between the persons who need help and the rest of us who can put tools into those needy hands in order to enable them to help themselves."[34]

Affirming the point of the Poor People's March on Washington that equal civil rights could not be realized without a fair chance at making a living, SCORR collected funds and supplies to support the march.[35]

By the time federal civil rights legislation and court decisions wound down around 1970, major gains had been made at the national and local level. SCORR disbanded in 1972.

The seemingly sudden steps toward equality after generations of Black exclusion inspired a succession of similar civil rights efforts by and for other groups or minorities through the last three decades of the twentieth century. The suppressed story of abuse of Native Americans was made public and brought modest gains to them. Equal civil rights acts were advocated by and eventually legislated on behalf of the handicapped, veterans, and the elderly. Protections for women lurched forward when southern congressmen attempted to defeat proposed race-based legislation by amending women's rights to it; instead, the two passed together. Courts eventually mandated modest reparation settlements for Japanese-Americans who had been interned and whose property had been seized during World War II. A few states passed legislation guaranteeing equal civil rights for Gay Americans, though when proposed at the federal level the idea caused panic and retrenchment. Whatever any group's experience when pursuing equal civil rights, its practice is inevitably modeled on the methods tested and proven by the Black civil rights movement.

CHAPTER 7

Living with Diversity

◀❦❧▶

"Well, baby, we finally done it," she typed at six in the morning. "The vote was 212–148, at 12:00 high noon. Such joy you have seldom seen. Involuntary gasps, grins, heads shaking off the disbelief that it had finally come after two decades of struggle, elderly shoulders quaking, grown men crying, women-hands trembling wringing damp tissues, little kids looking around in happy wonderment. The proceedings had droned on unexpectedly for 1½ hours (we thought this happened only at hearings, not for the actual vote) while key proponents spoke once more about how much the world needs the nonviolent guidance given us by MLK and the opposition desperately attempted to launch a final attack, poorly informed and sadly/comically misguided, on our symbol of compassion, justice and hope that was to prevail, finally on this day, over us all. Governor Shaheen later came outside to address the impromptu rally on the State House steps and rejoiced with us. She will sign the bill and it shall be effective in the year 2000. So it was and so it will be. I was relieved to witness this event in my lifetime. I called Kirby to tell her that is one

burden I will not pass on to her and her brother, Brad. She's happy, too. And proud of all of us who [are] in the struggle. Next is to plan a community celebration ... I'll keep you posted." Valerie Cunningham moved the mouse and clicked on "send."[1]

Americans know that the notion of a monolithic culture, promulgated through the Cold War, is both false and unsustainable. Few would deny the extensive variations of experience and outlook stemming from region, creed, ethnicity, gender, affective orientation, age, veteran status, and race. Through the last quarter of the twentieth century Americans have, in a demonstration of diversity itself, made a complex show of acknowledging, celebrating, and denying the presence and significance of diversity. While most of what makes people similar to or different from one another is not apparent to the casual observer by visual clues, race always is. Science increasingly views race as merely visual. But this visual otherness of race has given it a profoundly defining role in American history.

By the mid-1970s, for the first time since a

Dutch merchant offered Africans for sale in Jamestown in 1619, most *legal* obstacles to Black participation in public political life in the United States were essentially removed. White resistance tended to become subtler, though not always. Exemplary of the presence of resistance and the role of persistence was the twenty-year battle for adoption of a Martin Luther King Day in New Hampshire, an accomplishment celebrated in the correspondence above.

Some people in every generation learn racism anew, so every generation must deal with this inheritance. A survey of the country since 1970 reveals a mix of accomplishment and change, stasis and resistance.

The nation's white population has begun to adjust to the legal implications of civil rights laws. Much as whites in the armed forces learned the advantages of integration once they got used to it, employers, landlords, businesses, and neighbors reluctantly began to learn how to live with equal civil rights. From the late 1960s through the '80s segregation gradually diminished in the public sphere.

While unprecedented numbers of Black Americans entered the middle class, numerous factors cause American poverty to be conspicuously race related. While younger white Americans have generally ceased perceiving Black Americans as a servant class, they continue to merge poverty and color so completely that they overlook both white poverty and Black prosperity.

In 1972 Congress extended the protections of the Civil Rights Act of 1964 to areas such as access to credit and access to education. Today employers may not legally discriminate on the grounds of race, color, religion, sex, national origin, age, or disability.[2] Black people have entered all fields and attained executive-level corporate jobs, though not in numbers proportionate to the total Black population, and professional-level employment often carries an air of tokenism.

Integration was further supported by federal mandates for at least minimal inclusion of mi-

nority individuals or minority-owned businesses in projects with federal funding. Many states followed with their own legislation.

Because urban neighborhoods continue to be sharply defined by race, school districts continue to be too. Where integration could not be attained through adjustments in district lines, courts ordered the transport of students to other districts, though South Boston whites clamor against this busing even after twenty-five years.

Historically white colleges were integrated too. Nonetheless, at the opening of the twenty-first century race-based incidents between students periodically flare up at many colleges.

Cities have for the first time hired considerable numbers of Black and female police officers, firefighters, and other municipal employees, though not without resistance by white employees. The Metropolitan Boston Transit Authority continues to be plagued by internal racial friction.

Through the remainder of the twentieth century Black Americans were elected to public office in small numbers, though many of America's major cities have put Black mayors in office. New England cities such as Boston are notable exceptions to this significant pattern.

Public Celebrations of Identity

The Black Pride movement of the 1970s inspired a parallel ethnic pride movement among other populations. Typically expressed through ethnic fairs, the phenomenon continues in the Lowell Folk Festival, Caribbean festivals in Cambridge and Boston, and Portsmouth's Grecian Festival, a fund-raiser of its Orthodox Church. This model succeeded in part because of the superficial ease of enjoying one another's music, foodways, and colorful holidays while letting more complex issues lie dormant.

A new generation, seeking more depth than the festival mode could offer, went on to collect, record, preserve, and share their cultures' traditions. As ethnic clubs closed they organized archives, collections, oral history projects, and tours, a development as pronounced in Black communities as in ethnic communities. Unlike most other minorities the Black stories sprawl across many centuries. Nor is the Black narrative parallel to the traditional ethnic narrative, which begins with leaving hardship in a distant home for a new land of hope.

African-American culture for the most part lacked the calendar of religious and patriotic festivals of other ethnic groups. In 1966, during the civil rights movement, Maulana Karenga, professor and chair of the Department of Black Studies at California State University, Long Beach, created an Afro-American holiday called Kwanzaa. He did this with the intention of building community, enriching Black consciousness, and reaffirming the value of cultural grounding for life and struggle. Reaching past a history that too often begins with a narrative of slavery, Kwanzaa re-creates and expands upon ancient African ingathering traditions in a new American context. Kwanzaa builds its traditions around seven principles derived from various African cultures, especially the Swahili, favored because of the breadth of the language and culture across a large portion of Africa. These communitarian values are unity, collective work and responsibility, cooperative economics, purpose, creativity, and faith. Kwanzaa was developed as a cultural, not religious, holiday accessible to all people of African descent.[3]

Lately "June 'teenth" or "Juneteenth" observances have spread across the country. This is the Texas equivalent of Portsmouth's old Emancipation Celebration, its distinctive name derived from the delayed news of emancipation reaching that state after the Civil War. It shares a season with the extinct and forgotten coronations. In partial similarity to them, it is sometimes a day of celebration and of relaying heritage and values. With congregants of diverse geographical origin, Portsmouth's New Hope Baptist Church began sponsoring Juneteenth activities by the late 1990s.

Commercial Images of Identity

Meanwhile movies, television, and advertising—indices of the American self-image—began to include Black people, though often portrayed in expansions of white stereotypes: the strong-willed mama, the powerful crime fighter, the drug runner. They were glamorized, violent, oversexed, or shallow, factors that won the genre the pejorative epithet of blaxploitation films. Hollywood's apparent enthusiasm for Black characters in the early 1970s notwithstanding, it was responding to Black audiences as an economic resource more than to the Black experience as a source of humanistic themes.[4]

Television tested Black protagonists as it did female and Gay characters, first with a serious drama or two, then fielding comic characters, and then occasionally tackling balanced portrayals. The splintering of television from three major networks to dozens has sometimes improved underrepresentation, if for an ever narrower audience. White viewers rarely watch Black Entertainment Television (BET), and there is only one Black news outlet in northern New England.

Print advertising, in its efforts to attract all buyers, is slightly better balanced. This development is made possible in part by the proliferation of special-audience periodicals supported by narrowly targeted advertising.

Beginning in the 1990s images of Black Americans appeared on United States postage stamps. Characteristic of white perceptions, these stamps are set apart in a Black Heritage series, while white subjects are not segregated into a white heritage series. For whites, heritage is implicitly white unless otherwise stated; acknowledging Black affairs remains a self-conscious gesture.

Urban Developments

City neighborhoods nationwide for the most part failed to recover from the devastation wrought by urban renewal and the interstate highway system. In some cities poor neighborhoods dropped to catastrophically low points, a problem compounded when entire cities declared bankruptcy. The ever innovative urban drug market became a new economy of its own, a source of funds for survival as for weapons. Drugs themselves became a vehicle for the arrival and spread of AIDS as governments equally hostile to Gays, Blacks, and Latinos suppressed health education efforts. Drug lords and youthful gangs emerged to fill the void left by imploded community and indifferent government, a dangerous environment for poor Black families who can't afford to live elsewhere.

Problems for America's urban poor were compounded by the new urbanism beginning circa 1980, when gentrification of old neighborhoods displaced and outpriced the urban poor and middle class. In 2002 an estimated three-quarters of America's white families owned their own homes while fewer than half of all Black and Hispanic families did.[5]

Beginning in the 1980s and '90s a few cities began to replace desolate high-rise low-income housing with more human-scaled housing. Boston did this at the inconveniently remote Columbia Point as well as building Tent City and other human-scaled affordable housing in the historically Black but much gentrified South End. Battles continue in Boston over the development of parts of Roxbury and the substitution of buses for the old subway line that once served the district.

Urban poverty continued to be race defined. As Latin peoples augmented the poor urban population, activists gathered under a broader umbrella of People of Color to advocate solutions to displacement, marginalization, and poverty.

Nationwide, even as part of the white population continued to be vexed by its own ineptitude, indifference, and violence in matters of race, admittance of Black Americans into the mainstream grew apace. By way of a sample, a single section of a single issue of the *Boston Sun-* *day Globe* in June of 2002 carried three stories related to Black affairs.[6]

White Reactions

The ongoing Black effort to sustain legislation for equal civil rights was met with varied white reactions. These included support, bewilderment, and resistance into the opening of the twenty-first century.

Ongoing white support sometimes came in the form of overtly organized action and speech. More typically, whites viewed Black civil rights status with increasing indifference. This and the silence of potential white allies were problematic as reactionaries became more vocal and active. Conservative presidents appointed more conservative justices to the Supreme Court, and in 1991 Thurgood Marshall retired.

By 2000, civil rights accomplishments seemed always to have been in place. Anyone under forty did not have personal memory of or direct experience with even the notion of struggling to attain or sustain civil rights. In the popular revivalism of the late twentieth century the 1950s, '60s, and '70s were portrayed, respectively, as quaintly tranquil, picturesquely rebellious, and goofy. Young adults—and certainly not the spate of nostalgic television sitcoms set in these decades—didn't identify these years as the same ones in which the approaching end of American apartheid included turning fire hoses, dogs, and the National Guard against civil rights protesters, decades of rioting, assassinations, and the division of families and nation by an unfocused war. Whites didn't necessarily become enemies of civil rights, but in taking them for granted they became indifferent. Most whites gave lip service to equal civil rights but didn't go out of their way to protect them. They meanwhile tacitly let others' racist—or classist, homophobic, anti-Semitic, or sexist—remarks go unchallenged.

The shift from action to speech was so complete that debate itself came to center around speech. To inhibit social action conservatives hurled charges of "political correctness" toward inclusive language or behavior. This shift emerged in academia, where many practiced and encouraged courteous speech. The charge of political correctness signaled and obfuscated retrenchment in those who used the term. Political correctness wasn't about speech or politics, of course, but about worthy outcomes. In the 1990s those who wanted the freedom to be bigots coined the phrase to put others on the defensive, to distract from the real issues.

Violence continued to mar the early 1990s. Several rural Black churches in the South were burned. Through the 1990s whites first became aware of the race-based "profiling" by police departments that Blacks had been enduring for decades: police checks of Blacks because they were in the "wrong" neighborhood, the "wrong" car, or matched only the race (and not necessarily any other features) of a suspect. It exemplified a white proclivity to associate Blacks with crime.

More sinister was the impulse of white officers to shoot at Black crime suspects more quickly than at white suspects. Several New York City officers slaughtered a Black man in the confines of an apartment house vestibule as he reached for his wallet to present the identification they had requested. The officers were found innocent of murder, successfully arguing they had taken appropriate self-defensive action in the line of duty. In Cincinnati riots erupted in 2001 in response to the fifteenth killing of a Black man by police since 1995, a period in which no white suspects had been killed in similar circumstances.

Beginning in the mid 1990s white resistance was organized in a new way. Race-based affirmative action provisions of California and Texas law were repealed in public referenda, leading to enforcement of equal opportunity legislation in narrow and literal ways. In 2003 a test case involving admissions to the University of Michi-

gan was bought to the United States Supreme Court by white students claiming that the affirmative action system as applied there was unconstitutional. When Texan president George W. Bush filed a friend of the court brief on their behalf it became clear that the decision could impact wide areas of American life including hiring. Hundreds of briefs—submitted even by the military—with many thousands of signatures were filed on behalf of affirmative action.[7] On paper the anti–affirmative action legislation reads as fair and unbiased in matters of race. Advocates describe themselves and their goals with such terms as "color-blind" and promoting "racial harmony." Their true motives become clear when they describe race-based quota systems as "racial preference" systems, and say they seek to "block the expansion of racial preferences and to prevent their use in employment, education, and voting," and when they complain of "reverse discrimination" against whites in favor of nonwhites.[8] The repeal of quotas was clearly motivated by racism and resentment. Similar referenda or statutes were floated in several other states by the opening of the twenty-first century and were introduced to the New Hampshire legislature in February of 2003. Clearly, race remains a lightning rod in America.

Portsmouth since 1970

New Hampshire in general, and Portsmouth in particular, has in many ways followed the patterns of the rest of the nation, if in some ways it diverged. From 1970 to 2000 the southern part of the state saw the last of its historic textile industry drain away and an influx of population and wealth from its wealthier neighbor to the south. Southern New Hampshire became a kind of oversize commuter suburb for Massachusetts thanks to three interstate highways. Conservative wealthy and blue-collar workers alike were drawn to New Hampshire by its lack

In 1984 James Micelli transformed the sanctuary of the Pearl Street Church into an elegant upscale dining room that he called "72 Restaurant" (derived from its previous address on Islington Street, by which it was known). Although radical changes were made to some interior spaces, Micelli carefully preserved the architectural features that characterize the building as a church. Under the later ownership of Rev. Margaret Britton and a new name, the Pearl of Portsmouth provides a charming setting for nondenominational weddings and a variety of community functions and celebrations. *Photography by James Micelli. Portsmouth Black Heritage Trail.*

of both income and sales taxes and by its libertarian streak. In spite of fees and complexities that drive some businesses away, the state attracts many new businesses. Large portions of the state are rural, dotted with small industrial towns that have long since lost their economic mainspring. A vast array of lakes, national and state forests, and mountain ski areas provide seasonal tourist income to rural New Hampshire. But the small towns generally suffer from moribund economies in spite of numerous small businesses.

The state's population has diversified at glacial speed. The city of Manchester has the largest Black population in the state in real numbers.

Portsmouth holds its traditional place of having the largest proportion of Black people.

Through this period New Hampshire's white population wasn't lacking politicized community causes. The civil rights movement had proven that grass-roots efforts could accomplish seemingly impossible tasks. Coastal New Hampshire's somewhat liberal population mounted and sustained organized resistance to two proposals championed by conservatives for their potential economic benefit. Their resistance—mostly led by the Clamshell Alliance—to a nuclear power plant at Seabrook delayed construction for a decade, though it finally opened in 1990. Another effort successfully blocked construction of an off-shore oil port at the Isles of Shoals and a pipeline to a refinery in Durham, seat of the University of New Hampshire's main campus.[9] Several of the white players in the local Black civil rights movement were vigorously involved in these two campaigns.

In the years from 1970 to 2000 the City of Portsmouth underwent considerable physical and social transformation. These were not a continuation of the ravages of urban renewal but rather were brought about by a local expression of the new urbanism. In the 1970s artists and performers found the town's gritty waterfront affordable for studios, galleries, residences, and theater space. Improbably high-end Gay-owned restaurants followed them. A community block grant funded a pedestrian-friendly reconfiguration of the town square, a project tartly referred to by some old-timers as the Reforestation of Market Square. All these brought a prosperous clientele.

Private citizens adopted the preservation that the city fathers and mothers had failed to grasp in the 1960s and '70s, leading to partial restoration of the surviving South End and some of the commercial center. Preservationists successfully pressured the city to enact a historic district, innovative in acknowledging all historic periods and styles rather than gerrymandering its borders to encompass only the usual canon of colonial mansions. An aggressive self-appointed watchdog group, the Portsmouth Advocates, monitors the city Historic District Commission for laxness or missteps.

Trendy coffeehouses and ethnic or gourmet restaurants sprang up throughout the downtown. Concurrent with this was the revival of the city's Victorian-era opera house as the Music Hall, a not-for-profit presenting agency. Boutiques, computer software companies, and two national-chain clothiers filled storefronts that had been vacant in the depression of 1990. A not-for-profit group celebrated the renaissance of the city with a "First Night" New Year's Eve festival and a June event called Market Square

Day, annual events that drew tens of thousands of people.

Tourism, mostly based in the enjoyment of the arts, history, and the marine environment, grew considerably. Interstate 95 skirted downtown rather than bisecting it, removing through traffic while providing ready access for visitors. Though tourism makes a significant contribution, particularly to the downtown economy, it does not dominate Portsmouth's economy or character. The center has become economically healthy even as other New England towns find their centers vacant. Even so, strip development has mushroomed on Portsmouth's periphery, as around most towns.

The social cost of such success stories is typical. The city's nighttime population doubles by day. Old-timers view the flourishing downtown as having nothing of interest or use to them, and are not sure who are tourists and who are new residents. Newcomers value the place for what it has become. Housing and rental prices have skyrocketed. The artists who led the way have moved to adjacent towns in search of affordable rent. Low-income housing built in an inconveniently remote marshy outland during or just after World War II on Gosling Road is now engulfed by noisy and congested strip development.

The city lost a fifth of its population when the Cold War ended and Pease Air Force Base was closed.[10] This also impacted the Portsmouth Naval Shipyard in Kittery. The acronym "Rif" (Reduction in Force) entered the local vocabulary in the 1990s as several thousand workers were laid off or encouraged to take early retirement.

Fishing, though not a Black institution locally (as it is in southeastern New England, where Cape Verdeans are prominent in the fleet), has been a defining institution of Portsmouth for three and a half centuries. In the last decades of the twentieth century the Gulf of Maine—that portion of the North Atlantic stretching from Cape Cod to Nova Scotia—

was fished nearly to biological sterility. Federally mandated fishing restrictions brought the local fishing industry to its knees. The fishermen's cooperative pier closed briefly in spring of 2002. Decreased fishing left the river as a recreational resource, though it continues to be an occasional shipping lane.

Through these developments, Portsmouth's Black communities have been present, active, and increasingly diversified.

Black Experience in Late-Twentieth-Century Portsmouth

The integration of the workplace has been nearly invisible to whites because of the comparatively small numbers of Black people in an overwhelmingly white area. But it has nonetheless occurred. Portsmouth's Black residents have found work in all areas of employment, including as engineers at the Navy Yard, schoolteachers, guidance counselors, on the school board, as health providers, in public safety, as clergy, insurance agents, pharmacists, mortgage officers, as hairdressers, and in private enterprise including owning their own businesses.

Integration of schools in Portsmouth was a fact of local life from the nineteenth century. Seating was likely segregated at an early date, but if so the practice disappeared before living memory. Schools employed Black teachers and administrators by the last quarter of the twentieth century.

Although George King graduated from Dartmouth in 1907 and Elizabeth Virgil from the University of New Hampshire in the 1920s, in the 1980s and 1990s the university's admissions department noticed that Black students in other parts of New England shied away from its tables at high school college fairs. This was not because of doubt about the university's reputation in academic or racial matters but because of the state's reputation as unwelcoming, even hostile, to Black people. This reputation stems in part from the overwhelming whiteness of the state's

population and in part from its long refusal to adopt Martin Luther King Day.[11]

Portsmouth participates vicariously in a larger world of Black experience through performance art. The local Public Broadcasting Service airs locally produced Black history interviews and occasionally broadcasts *Lost Boundaries* with supplemental interviews of members of the Johnston family, whose story inspired it. The Music Hall built in 1877 on the site of the Temple, where prominent Black abolitionists once orated[12] offers programs that encompass the Black presence in the arts. In the last decade of the twentieth century it presented Black-themed films ranging from *Amistad* to *Mississippi Masala* and live performances by the Alvin Ailey Dance Company, Urban Bush Women, Rennie Harris's Puremovement rap retelling of Romeo and Juliet, the Preservation Hall Jazz Band, Buckwheat Zydeco, Queen Ida, Beausoleil, and Tito Puente, always to packed houses.

New Hope Baptist Church, the predominant Black church in the seacoast area today, flourishes on outlying Peverly Hill Road. Meanwhile a less well known church in the evangelical and fundamentalist tradition was founded in the 1980s. It provides a spiritual home for both Black and white adherents. Emmanuel Church of Christ gathers on Bartlett Street under the pastorate of a white clergyman, Reverend Heard. The area's predominantly white churches all have Black members too. The presence of the Emmanuel and New Hope churches represents a range of spiritual styles as the local Black population continues to diversify.

Revival of Portsmouth's NAACP

As the Seacoast chapter of the National Association for the Advancement of Colored People attained local compliance with federal legislation, an exhuasted leadership tapered off, let activity go dormant, and its charter lapsed. Civil rights actions of national scope continued to be prosecuted by the national NAACP with regional support and encouragement. In 1979 the national NAACP initiated the first bill for a state to allow voter registration at high schools, an example followed in twenty-four states. In 1981 it led the campaign to extend the Voting Rights Act for another twenty-five years. That same year the national organization worked with major corporations to establish the Fair Share Program, which by 1992 had seventy partners. The following year the NAACP helped register more than 850,000 voters and worked with the Supreme Court to prevent President Reagan from giving tax breaks to Bob Jones University, where racial segregation was still practiced. By 1985 the organization expanded its scope to encompass international issues, leading a massive anti-apartheid rally in New York City. In 1987 the NAACP began a protracted campaign to defeat the nomination of Robert Bork to the Supreme Court, culminating in the presence of over 100,000 people at a protest march in 1989 that also protested new Court decisions that were beginning to reverse civil rights gains. In 1991 the NAACP led a campaign to defeat former Klan leader David Duke's bid to re-present Louisiana in the United States Senate. Its efforts brought out 76 percent of that state's Black voters. Responding to increasing anti–affirmative action legislation, the NAACP launched an Economic Reciprocity Program in 1997. That same year it started an antiviolence program aimed at youths. In 2000 the national organization negotiated agreements with television networks to increase minority visibility on the screen. That same year saw the largest Black voter turnout for a national election in twenty years.[13] At that same time, the NAACP mobilized the largest march South Carolina had seen since the civil rights era when it brought 50,000 people together to protest the continued use of the Confederate battle flag as the state flag and its continued display over the statehouse. The NAACP spearheaded a movement that led to the compromise of the flag's removal from the statehouse roof to the lawn, where it flies beside a memorial to Confederate soldiers.[14]

A new Portsmouth NAACP chapter was chartered in April 1974 under the leadership of Nathaniel Holloway. Since then the local chapter has focused on education and been engaged in mediating racial conflicts in area school systems, employment issues, prisoner rights, and advocating adoption of a state Martin Luther King Day. At the opening of the twenty-first century it was involved in community dialogues with area police departments. Presidents of the local chapter of the NAACP since its re-chartering have included Holloway, Algene Bailey, Sheila Reed Finlay, and Charlotte Wood.

Social, Fraternal, and Action Groups

In the absence of a defined Black neighborhood where friendships originate in chance encounters, a number of local Black people deliberately got together to socialize in the 1970s and '80s. These gatherings turned into permanent groups that persisted into the twenty-first century.

The Black Masonic presence continues. The Triple 8 Masonic Lodge is the twenty-first-century successor to the early-twentieth-century Octagon Club.

In 1974 several local Black women got together to socialize. After a few meetings they formalized their purpose and incorporated as a not-for-profit. They named their group Kwanza for the seven virtues of the African-American Kwanzaa holiday, which at that date was little known in this region.[15] They extended their activity beyond socializing to providing recognition and scholarships for African-American students as their primary mission, and funding cultural projects in the seacoast region as a secondary purpose. Kwanza limits its membership to twenty and fluctuates from about eight to eighteen women. Since its founding they have raised $65,000 through private donations, mostly for scholarships. They have also funded a children's art exhibition at a local shopping mall for Black History Month, brought the Library of Congress's resident poet Robert Hayden and

Black poet Dolores Kendrick to Portsmouth for readings, and Smithsonian historian Rex Ellis to offer presentations in local schools and for the public.[16]

The Seacoast Men's Friendship Group was initiated by Algene Bailey and others. The purpose of its monthly breakfast meetings is to provide an opportunity for social gatherings without the stress of the members' other civic commitments. The highlight of its social calendar is the annual formal dinner-dance that attracts people from a wide area. Though overtly social, the group has undertaken such service activities as donating to Kwanza's scholarship fund and collecting clothes and necessities for visitors from Rwanda.

Preserving Stories—an Oral History Project

Motivated by fear of losing the stories of an elderly generation who had been in the area since before World War II, Valerie Cunningham set about interviewing them. She didn't intend to write definitive biographies but to gather memories. She also wanted to save this generation from the anonymity she saw in past generations for lack of individuals' pictures. She enlisted the help of Kelvin Edwards, an engineer at the naval shipyard and an accomplished amateur photographer. Over the course of a year they recorded both the recollections and visages of fourteen people.[17] Others were fascinated by their project, and an exhibit seemed a practical way to share what they had gathered. They created a portable and poignant exhibit of framed photo-portraits with interview excerpts. It has been displayed from time to time in Portsmouth venues ranging from the Children's Museum to bank lobbies.

The African American Resource Center

After Cunningham prepared a scholarly synopsis of her early research for publication in 1989 by the New Hampshire Historical Society, she continued to amass considerable historical research, contemporary interviews, and a library of classic and recent works in Black history. As the subject gained acceptance in school curricula and television newsmagazines, all inquiries seemed to lead to Cunningham. She organized her research into the African American Resource Center and rented a mailbox to cope with the increasing flow of inquiries. A quiet visionary, she has participated in organizing one Black history or cultural project after another from the 1980s into the twenty-first century.

The Portsmouth Blues Festival

In spite of rock 'n' roll's appropriation of rhythm and blues, rock is so deeply absorbed into popular mass culture that no contemporary white audiences think of it as Black music, and rarely does anyone pause to reflect on its Black roots. The blues, however, remains vividly identified with Black experience and culture.

In January of 1985 Valerie Cunningham assisted local white blues performer T. J. Wheeler in organizing an interracial group of blues fans to present a blues festival. With intrepid optimism they called it the first annual festival, and since then it has continued without interruption to become New England's oldest blues festival. A newspaper's misprint of the word "band" gave the group its name, Blues Bank Collective. With its subtle allusion to the city's original name of Strawberry Bank it proved a happy misprint, giving rise to cheerfully tongue-in-cheek slogans like "Blues you can bank on." The poster for the first year announced star performer and local legend B. J. Johnson.

The organization developed a sophisticated mission statement that brought an instrumental perception to the art form. Its mission is to "further awareness of Blues music and its African American heritage; to show the historic context out of which the Blues grew; to use the music as a means of positive social change. Wherever we can, the Blues Bank Collective

This 2002 poster advertises the 17th Annual Portsmouth Blues Festival, featuring Taj Mahal and Maria Muldaur. Proceeds from the festivals support a range of educational and charitable activities throughout the year. *Ligature Designs. Linda Garrett, artist. Blues Bank Collective.*

works to eliminate all forms of racism, intolerance and prejudice."

Each year's festival has explored the depth and breadth of the blues tradition, the "roots and branches" as one year's poster metaphorically proclaimed. At concerts southern rural sounds alternate with northern urban expressions. The fluid interplay of blues with gospel and jazz is featured. Some years the sounds of the African Diaspora trace the spread of African influence through Arab, South American, and Afro-Caribbean musical traditions. The festival has presented such performers as Bobby "Blue" Bland, Koko Taylor, Pinetop Perkins, Mose Allison, and Taj Mahal as well as the finest in regional blues talent. Having outgrown its original dockside location, the festival has convened on the grounds of Strawbery Banke Museum for several years.

The festival is an annual fund-raiser for a larger range of programs. A youth education program called Hope, Heroes & the Blues was created and led by T. J. Wheeler. Through music and biographical narrative it presents blues musicians as heroes who overcame racism and poverty to lay the foundations of contemporary American popular music. It is an antiracism and antidrug program presented in the context of the roots of contemporary music. The program has reached over 165,000 schoolchildren nationwide and abroad.

Not content with these accomplishments, the "Bankers" also sponsor the annual Seacoast Black Heritage Festival, supporting dozens of public programs in many genres. Climaxing in February, Black History Month, the festival's programs spill over into the rest of the calendar year. Improbable in so notoriously white a

Roots and Branches is one of several original designs created by Portsmouth artist Richard Haynes for the annual Seacoast Black Heritage Festival poster, celebrating Black History Month. The festival has been sponsored by the Blues Bank Collective since 1984 as a collaborative effort with community organizations and churches. Its goal is to raise awareness that "Black history is for all people all the time." Roots and Branches, *by Richard Haynes, Jr., Haynes Images. Private collection.*

region, Portsmouth's Blues Bank Collective, with its festival and programs, has endured to be one of the nation's oldest blues education organizations.[18]

The Martin Luther King Holiday in New Hampshire

Martin Luther King Jr.'s birthday was proposed as a federal holiday on April 8, 1968, four days after he was murdered. Nine months later 1,200 autoworkers in North Tarrytown, New York, took the day off as an unauthorized holiday, for which action 60 employees were suspended. In 1970 petitions carrying 6 million signatures were submitted to Congress (via representatives John Conyers, D-Mich. and Shirley Chisholm, D-N.Y.), and that same year California made it a school holiday. Through the decade sixteen more states adopted the day. It took thirteen years of legislative study, debate, and equivocation for his birthday—or rather the third Monday in January—to be declared a federal holi-

day. This happened in November of 1983 when Congress passed the declaration and President Reagan signed it into law, effective in 1986.[19]

New Hampshire took its own tortuous route to proclaiming an official state Martin Luther King holiday. The state seemed to revisit the 1840s, when white abolitionist William Lloyd Garrison exhorted New Hampshire abolitionist Parker Pillsbury "Do not despair of New-Hampshire!" in utterly despairing times.[20]

In 1979 state senator Jim Splaine of Portsmouth proposed a Martin Luther King holiday for New Hampshire. Given the small number of states that had the holiday at that date (seventeen), it is not surprising that his bill did not pass in famously contrarian New Hampshire. As numerous other states and then the federal government adopted the holiday, New Hampshire rejected proposals in 1981, 1985, 1987, and 1989. In the Portsmouth area, Black and white people organized the Seacoast Martin Luther King, Jr., Coalition to build public support for adopting the day as a state holiday. Under the leadership of Nathaniel Holloway, for fifteen years on MLK Day they convened much publicized and well-attended breakfasts. These featured prominent speakers in support of the cause, as well as using the occasion to present prizewinning youth essays on subjects of race relations, to showcase local performers, and to acknowledge people who had advanced the cause of race relations. On Martin Luther King Day of 1990 the seacoast's tiny Klan group wore their white robes and hoods in Portsmouth's Market Square.[21]

In 1991 New Hampshire, by now stung with charges of institutionalized racism, reluctantly passed a compromise bill approving a Civil Rights Day holiday. This holiday was almost scheduled in April to replace the state's Fast Day, much as Massachusetts had replaced its Fast Day with Patriot's Day in the nineteenth century. But in the end New Hampshire's Civil Rights Day was scheduled for the third Monday in January, coinciding with the federal Martin Luther King Day. Why Civil Rights Day rather than Martin Luther King Day? Conservative legislators argued that no holidays commemorated single individuals other than Washington and Lincoln. Based on these models, they argued, it was more appropriate to dedicate a holiday to the principles of civil rights for all rather than to a single advocate for civil rights. This argument was widely viewed as a thin cover for racism because in nobly dedicating the day to civil rights for all, it overtly avoided dedicating the day to a Black man, though he symbolizes the civil rights movement.

In 1992 Arizona, by then the only other holdout, adopted a combined "Martin Luther King, Jr.–Civil Rights Day." This left New Hampshire as the only state without a Martin Luther King holiday.[22]

In 1993 a new governor, Steve Merrill, attempted a compromise when he declared New Hampshire's day to be Martin Luther King Jr. Civil Rights Day and urged the legislature to make this change permanent, but the latter proposal was defeated in the state House of Representatives. This sequence was repeated in 1994, '95, and '96, each time the day being temporarily renamed by governor's decree. In 1994 and '95 the legislature again refused to consider, or rejected, bills proposing a permanent name change. No such bill was submitted in '96.

The third Monday in January of 1996 proved embarrassing for New Hampshire at the national level. While throughout the state privately organized Martin Luther King Day programs were convened, a white supremacist group based in Mississippi held a rally at the New Hampshire State House in Concord, endorsing New Hampshire's stance against adopting the name Martin Luther King Day.

Governor Jeanne Shaheen took office in January of 1997 and immediately repeated the model of her predecessor in proclaiming a Martin Luther King Jr. Civil Rights Day. Her proclamation linked his spirit to the state motto, "Live free or die." The following month identical bills were put before both houses of the legislature proposing a name change. Proponents attempted many tactics to pass it. One approach proposed expanding the holiday name to encompass that of Jonathan Daniels, the white New Hampshire seminarian slain in Alabama while doing civil rights work in the late 1960s. Another proposed an amendment inviting the New England Patriots football team to move to New Hampshire, referential to a powerful sports boycott that had prompted adoption of the holiday in Arizona. In spite of these efforts the name change was rejected. Legislative rules don't allow resubmitting defeated bills within a two-year session, so further action had to wait. The 1998 elections changed the legislative mix slightly, preparing the way for resubmission of bills in 1999.

By this time wildly disparate groups found themselves allied on this issue. The alliances were as improbable as those that came together to form the Republican Party in the 1850s. The AFL-CIO and the New Hampshire Business and Industry Association both supported the name change. The Christian Coalition and the Citizens Alliance for Gay and Lesbian Rights both supported it though they otherwise spent the 1990s going at one another's throats over a Gay civil rights bill (passed in 1997).[23] Rival former senators Gordon Humphrey and Susan McLane alike found themselves advocates of the name change.

Public marches and rallies at the State House, some organized by high school students, called attention to the issue. Petition drives, religious services, letters to local newspapers, and contacts with elected officials lent their support. Finally, in 1999 the New Hampshire legislature adopted the name change, and in January of 2000 New Hampshire observed its first official Martin Luther King Day.[24]

New Hampshire brought considerable shame on itself by being the last in the nation to adopt the King holiday. This is ironic status for a state that claims to be the birthplace of Lincoln's party, a state that finds irrational grounds for pride in the trivial accomplishment of announcing the nation's first municipal election results when two tiny rural villages vote at midnight in a quadrennial publicity stunt. The convoluted tale of resistance in its massive and all-white legislature[25] illustrates the continuing ambivalence about race in white New Hampshire.

While virtually all whites willingly give lip service to the notion of equal civil rights for Black Americans, there is a simmering undercurrent of white resentment toward Black gains, in New Hampshire as throughout the nation.

The Klan—Again

Two people dressed in Klan robes and hoods walked about in Portsmouth's Market Square on Martin Luther King Day in 1990.[26] This action was partly in resistance to the day's observance under any name and partly the outgrowth of a spat between the nearby town of Exeter and a dismissed employee. The disgruntled employee had recently founded a branch of the Klan knowing it would draw attention to him and, he hoped, to his complaint against the town. He further embarrassed his town's select-

men by applying for a license for a Klan rally in Exeter. In light of a parallel case near Chicago ten years earlier, they reluctantly issued the permit.[27] The merchants and residents of the town agreed on a color chosen to indicate their rejection of what the Klan stands for, and the day of the march found the town festooned with like-colored balloons and ribbons.

White racists had learned to articulate their resentments only in the privacy of their own homes or small private gatherings. In the late 1980s white youths, unaware that their elders' public silence was a recently learned behavior, began openly repeating what they had learned at home. Emboldened by their children's example, white adults soon followed suit. Retrenchment reemerged on the public stage and was expressed in a variety of ways. Burning of rural Black churches swept the South. The anti–"racial preference" movement emerged among white conservatives in this context. In New Hampshire, suffering a severe economic depression in the early 1990s, retrenchment was articulated in donut-shop conversational references to French Canadians as nonwhite, in the toppling of statuary at a Portsmouth Roman Catholic churchyard, the painting of swastikas on gravestones, and race-based scuffles at regional schools and colleges. Anti–Gay rights rhetoric in adjacent Maine declared that people had already given up enough and weren't giving up any more. "People," of course, assumed straight white people, a hint of the underlying resentment of Black civil rights gains. The perception persists that new equality for others is somehow a loss of status for one's self.

The Diversity Committee

In resistance to this resistance, a rather remarkable group convened in Portsmouth. Starting under the auspices of the Greater Piscataqua Community Foundation a Diversity Committee convened for informal conversations around a dining table. The members discussed current

This site marker is on the wall of the Music Hall, site of an earlier building where William Wells Brown, Charles Lenox Remond, Frederick Douglass, and other abolitionist speakers appeared. Black abolitionists were the driving force through 90 years that culminated in the Thirteenth Amendment to the U.S. Constitution, which ended slavery in 1865. This cast bronze marker shows the logo and basic design of all markers along the Portsmouth Black Heritage Trail.

Portsmouth Black Heritage Trail.

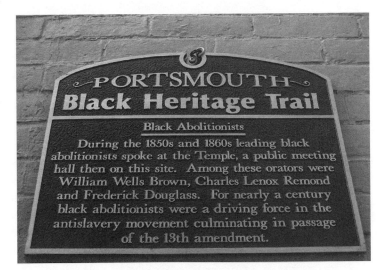

events, how to prevent or discourage this sort of action locally, and how to address the loss of diversity brought by the closing of Pease Air Force Base. The committee rapidly grew to include clergy, teachers, historians, activists, theater directors, performers, bankers, retirees, housewives, students, and others. Wide-ranging conversation about increasingly overt intolerance nationwide led the group to focus on race relations. Education became its main tool.

A wide array of activities emerged. Students at Portsmouth High School and at Marshwood Regional High School across the river in Eliot, Maine, spent eighteen months, including their summer break, preparing an elaborate and sophisticated full-day curriculum on diversity and tolerance. Forty guest presenters addressed topics ranging from race to sexual orientation to the Nazi holocaust. Through the Diversity Committee the Seacoast Repertory Theater, a semi-professional community theater on Portsmouth's Bow Street, staged an entire year of plays and musicals every one of which revolved around themes of diversity, tolerance, and intolerance. The town's largest history museum, Strawbery Banke Museum, dedicated one of its annual community forums to diversity. Guest presenters and workshops linked national and local issues of race, gender, sexual orientation, ethnicity, etcetera. The Community Foundation

worked with the Music Hall to identify and present a number of internationally renowned Black performers who have since become a mainstay of programming there. A performance by a group from the Sea Islands of South Carolina raised funds to help continue these programs.

The Black Heritage Trail

As in so many places in New England, Portsmouth's Black history has gone public. Portsmouth's version originated in 1994 as an outgrowth of the Diversity Committee, with initial sponsorship from the Community Foundation and Strawbery Banke Museum.

New England's Black heritage projects take varied form. These include trails, public programs, exhibits, museums, and archives. Boston's Black Heritage Trail is devoted to the nineteenth-century African-American community that was centered in Beacon Hill, with emphasis on the Black abolitionist movement. The Connecticut Freedom Trail was authorized in 1995 by the state's General Assembly and evolved into a driving tour in pamphlet and webpage form. It links sites associated with the movement from slavery to freedom in an arc stylistically equivalent to the didactic white Pilgrim-to-Revolution narrative. Research, public programming, or ex-

New Hope Baptist Church has continued its legacy as a spiritual beacon for the Black community of the seacoast. The influence of and high regard for this small New Hampshire church extend throughout New England. This was the birthplace of the Portsmouth Black Heritage Trail and is one of its sites.

Photography by Brad Randolph. Portsmouth Black Heritage Trail.

hibits are pursued at the Rhode Island Black Heritage Society in Providence; at the Prudence Crandall House, the Harriet Beecher Stowe Center, Yale's Lehrman Center and the *Amistad* project, all in Connecticut; at Harvard's W. E. B. DuBois Institute and at Old Sturbridge Village in Massachusetts; and at the Maine Historical Society in Portland. African Meetinghouse museums operate in Boston, Nantucket, and Portland. Black history archives have been established at Bowdoin College in Maine and at the Old Stone House Museum in Brownington, Vermont.

Unlike the celebratory tradition of white history narratives that for generations evaded addressing conflict, resistance, or tragedy, Black history necessarily encompasses these along with stories of resourcefulness and triumph. Formerly accustomed to learning New England history in terms of white Protestant homogeneity, white and Black Yankees alike are now less likely to overlook the region's historical Black presence.[28]

Portsmouth adopted the trail model and, parallel to developments in the city's numerous history museums, uses a multicentury organization without emphasis on any one period. With a committee of volunteers the trail's founders developed guided tours, a tour brochure, and a reference manual for guides, with copies placed in the city's schools, libraries, and historic house museums. Subsequently, the trail committee and its volunteers formalized their identity into a not-for-profit corporation, the Portsmouth Black Heritage Trail, Inc., conducting guided tours and undertaking special projects such as working with the University of New Hampshire to present a classical music concert of Black composers. They have made information available to several Portsmouth-based websites. Most stunning, especially in a seaport town famous for the mansions of white colonial merchants, is the group's funding and installation of bronze Black history historical markers throughout the downtown.

The Black Heritage Trail was well received by the proprietors of the historic houses, who shared relevant research findings and trained their docents to encompass Black history in regular house tours. During this period the Macphaedris-Warner House was undergoing reinterpretation, using each room to focus on a different era in the house's history. The two-century narrative concludes with a visit to the kitchen as it was first restored in the 1930s to provide a window into the colonial-revival mentality. In consultation with the trail's founders the house museum's proprietors decided to reintroduce the mannequin of a Black figure kneeling at the fireplace as if cooking, as a starting place for discussions of changing interpretation of race in local history.

Ongoing in Portsmouth

Elsewhere in town, Reverend Margaret Britton, a spiritual leader of the Unity Church and a woman with strong interests in world and community peace, has been drawn into Portsmouth's Black history story. Britton operates a stained glass studio and function hall in an old house of worship. She named it the Pearl of Portsmouth for its address on Pearl Street and was later fascinated to learn the building had once been home to People's Baptist Church and New Hope Baptist Church. Britton has joined with the Black Heritage Trail, Inc., to convey a preservation easement on the historic features of the building and seek funding for its preservation, even as it continues to house her business and serve the spiritual community. She, the Trail, and local preservationists began this long and technical process in the winter of 2001–2, had the first of a series of attention-drawing and fund-raising programs in July of 2002, and in 2003 dismantled the steeple for repair.

In the early 1990s members of Kwanza noticed that Afrocentric organizations in Portsmouth met in borrowed spaces and kept minutes and other records in their officers' homes. Kwanza initiated conversation for an alliance, and late in 2001 negotiated a home for these groups in Portsmouth's community center. It became available in 2002 as a meeting place for the partici-pating organizations. This allowed the creation of a reference library, program space, exhibits, a projected computer lab, and other services still in process of invention. Participating groups include, in addition to Kwanza, the New Hope Baptist Church, the local chapter of the NAACP, the Seacoast Men's Friendship Group, Triple 8 Masonic Lodge, Portsmouth Black Heritage Trail, Inc., the Blues Bank Collective, Inc., the African American Resource Center, and the Seacoast Martin Luther King, Jr., Coalition. Collectively, the site is known as the Seacoast African American Cultural Center.

The meaning of the most recent developments in Black history in Portsmouth remains to be seen. Unlike a novel, the story does not climax or conclude. A living narrative of a local population, the story of Africans and their descendants in Portsmouth continues.

The expansion of the traditional narrative to encompass their stories transforms our understanding of the past. We can only hope to be alert in the future to the implications of the unfolding tale. As from the city's beginning, Portsmouth's Black residents continue to be a fundamental part of the city's social capital. In the stories of ordinary Black people in this small seaport we find that Black history is American history; Black history is everyone's history.

Coffins under the Street
An Afterword

◗§◖

Career historians and antiquarians alike are sometimes caught short by the question, Why bother studying history? The question can be especially startling when one's study focuses on a proportionately tiny minority in an overwhelmingly homogenous region. The relevance of history, of course, is to help us identify how we got where we are today, and also to inform us in making decisions about the future. The past daily intrudes into the present.

On the morning of Tuesday, October 7, 2003, during construction for a Portsmouth water and sewer project, workers unearthed a coffin under Chestnut Street a few feet from its intersection with Court Street. The backhoe operator pulled back promptly. The consulting archaeologists for the construction project were alerted. The coffins were at the eastern edge of what Portsmouth's colonial-era whites called the "Negro Burial Ground."

Given the heightened public awareness and the relatively diminutive size of this old town by the sea, word spread quickly. Through most of that day and the following several days of exca-

vation, a cross-section of Portsmouth was on hand to watch the archaeologists.

Within minutes of the discovery members of the city's Black community were on hand, as well as board members of the Portsmouth Black Heritage Trail and staff from the city's numerous historical institutions. Teachers walked their students over from the nearby middle school. Office workers and passersby stopped to contemplate the history they had unknowingly traversed for years. Newspaper reporters and television crews assembled. They shared their memories of incidents at the intersection and postulated on the past, present, and future meaning of this discovery. Some professed their ignorance of the ancient burial ground—though it is described in the text of a bronze marker a few yards away—and expressed many thoughtful questions.

The city manager, the director of public works, and other officials were on hand. The pastor of Portsmouth's New Hope Baptist Church stood watch. He offered a prayer as the first remains were lifted into a hearse, the services of which were donated, for the short journey to temporary storage at Strawbery Banke Museum. A silent vigil was held at the site that Saturday evening.

Over several days, in a pit enlarged slightly by archaeologists, eight burials were unearthed and the corners of five additional interments were identified. In stratification garbled by more than two centuries of construction for water, sewer, and gas lines, the shapes of coffins were clearly discernable. They were of the old-fashioned, shouldered, hexagonal profile. Some interments were stacked in tiers. All had collapsed under the weight of the earth above and were sodden from water that gathers in an almost imperceptible hollow at this intersection.

This revelation of surviving burials in Portsmouth came three days after the re-interment, with considerable solemnity, of 419 exhumations from New York City's colonial-era burial ground for Africans. It also came in the midst of typesetting this book, illustrating the timeliness of this publication. History is always with us. Research continues, sometimes not as we would schedule it.

As a society we are made of our collective stories. These interacting histories—not only of our multiracial and multiethnic community, but also of our diverse religions, our nearly four-hundred-year-old street pattern, our local political system, our town's filiopietism, and even our two-hundred-year-old public utilities—will all play out in the coming months and years in ways that cannot now be predicted. There are many questions already, but there has not been time to resolve them or to anticipate the many more that will arise.

Some questions will be about the past. When were the streets that so neatly bound the burial ground on the map of 1705 actually constructed? Why did this burial ground hemorrhage out into the street? Was it because the boundaries and streets existed only on paper whereas informal footpaths or cart tracks actually traversed the field or pine barren? Did such tracks even approximate the map? Or had the mapped grid as published in the 1850s been

drawn to conform to actual development after 1705? Did a shallow ridge of bedrock that made heavy going for the modern construction crew also frustrate the gravediggers, driving them to seek more amenable soil a few paces beyond a recognized burial ground boundary? Did interments that penetrated rock represent the intent to keep certain individuals together regardless of inconvenience and extra labor?

How did eighteenth-century whites and displaced Blacks perceive and name this site? Did the Portsmouth Black community, which named its charitable societies the African Society and the Ladies African Charitable Society, in fact think and speak of this as the African burial ground? Did they accommodate to the white usage of "Negro" to describe this place? Did usage vary depending on who was within earshot? Is it now appropriate to discontinue the archaic usage of "Negro" in favor of "African Burial Ground"?

What is the significance of burials stacked one above another? Does this practice indicate familial relationships, an ethnic mortuary custom, a forced efficiency as space was running out, a preference for the in-town end of the burial ground, or some other consideration unknown to us?

It remains to be seen whether, following analysis, the Portsmouth finds will be similar to what has turned up in other African burial grounds in America. Will evidence appear in Portsmouth of the traditional West African use of shells, broken crockery, or white stones to identify and separate the place of the dead from the world of the living?

Does the placement of coffins with the feet to the east indicate retention of an African burial practice or a willing absorption of Christian folk tradition? Does it represent the acquiescence of the enslaved to yet another practice imposed by the dominant culture?

Will artifacts that represent discrete Africanisms, as have been found in other burial sites in America, turn up at these burials in Portsmouth? Some of those other grounds have yielded keepsakes—for instance, cowrie shells—

that, though valued as a medium of exchange in Africa, were also powerful emotional links to a remote homeland and families, symbolic of sustained memory and hope, and subtly emblematic of resistance to enslavement. Other burials have produced inorganic remnants from the clothing of the deceased, like buttons and shroud pins. What will the ground in Portsmouth produce?

Other questions are about the present. How do we as a community feel about disturbing the dead? Does an earnest desire for scholarly inquiry make these remains less sacrosanct than other burials? Certainly this question creates an uneasy parallel to historic white indifference to Black life and death, which once allowed real estate development over a burial ground.

If forensic analysis can provide cultural and biohistorical information on such subjects as ancestry, diet, and health, in addition to identifying age and gender, is this sufficient reason to further disturb the exhumations by separating soil from bones, and bones from artifacts? We face unsettling questions about the propriety of recovering or even disturbing these material remnants of disrupted lives.

Other questions will concern the future. At the moment, a few days after the discovery, intentions are to leave interred under the street several burials that were identified but not exhumed. But does new awareness of these old interments allow a return to business-as-usual on this city street? Does it invite blocking the street and creating a memorial? What additional questions and ideas will emerge?

A burial ground that likely was in use as early as 1705—perhaps earlier—and was not discontin-ued until the end of the eighteenth century spans an era of considerable transformation. African captives became the forebears of generations born into slavery in America. Their forced labor made immense contributions to the development of the modern West. A few individuals, as we have seen, recovered their freedom by the time this burial ground was discontinued. How will these various experiences be recognized?

Some arrived from Africa with animist religious beliefs, some likely with Islamic traditions. By the end of the eighteenth century many were practicing Christians. The nuances of what could or should be commemorated, and how it might be done, are numerous. Their identities will, in all likelihood, remain unknown to us. According to what tradition should the anonymous dead be reburied? Indeed, where will they be buried? Who is authorized or should be empowered to make such decisions?

Suddenly it becomes clear to all that the effects of centuries of slavery, segregation, and racism press upon us still. History begs the question of what the right decision is, even as divergent answers confirm the historic diversity of our community. This archaeological finding is a metaphor for a buried history. We hope that, just as this book brings long-lost stories to the surface, this subterranean discovery will be thoughtfully memorialized in a way that will keep these stories in sight.

Earlier in this book we remarked that the past isn't what it used to be. Expanding the traditional narrative to encompass the story of Africans in our community has transformed history. Now we find that an expanded knowledge of history must transform us.

APPENDIX: PLACES ASSOCIATED WITH NARRATIVES IN THIS BOOK

◆§ ?◆

Readers who visit Portsmouth may wish to visit sites associated with the people mentioned in this book. Some of the sites survive, and of these, several are open to the public. The following list of sites parallels the chapter and section sequence of the book, and notes whether or not the sites are open to the public.

Chapter 1. The Seaport

The Portsmouth Public Library stands on the south side of Islington Street at its convergence with Middle and Congress Streets and Maplewood Avenue. It is housed in a federal-era brick building originally built as an academy, remodeled and expanded for library purposes. At the opening of the twentieth-first century, construction of a new library elsewhere seemed likely. (Open Mondays through Saturdays.)

Strawbery Banke Museum is comprised of a ten-acre fragment of a downtown residential district that abuts the federal-era commercial district and the waterfront. Its main entrance faces the waterfront. (Open seasonally.)

Pease Air Force Base was closed in the 1990s, and its site is now developed as an office park named Pease International Trade Port. Its immense landing strip serves a small municipal airport and serves the local branch of the Air National Guard. Most of the base housing was demolished in the 1990s. A portion of the base facing westward onto Great Bay has been set aside for a nature preserve. A bicycle path connects the site to downtown.

Chapter 2. Colonists

Portsmouth and the Slave Trade

The wharves where slaves disembarked do not survive. Nothing of the utilitarian eighteenth-century waterfront survives. Of the three wharves at Portsmouth's waterfront Prescott Park, the right-hand one approximates the site of the colonial-era Long Wharf. The adjacent Sheafe Warehouse of circa 1705 is the sole surviving eighteenth-century waterfront warehouse. It was moved a few hundred feet from nearby Mechanic Street. No sales of enslaved people are known to have taken place in the Sheafe Warehouse, but it enables the modern visitor to envision something of the waterfront that greeted arriving Africans. (Park open year-round during daylight hours. Sheafe Warehouse open intermittently in summer.)

Sale of Enslaved People

The Stoodley's Tavern site on Daniel Street has been occupied by the McIntyre Federal Building since the 1960s. The tavern was saved from demolition by Strawbery Banke Museum, which moved it to Hancock Street, opposite the museum's main grounds. Much altered through the centuries, its exterior was partly restored in the 1990s and its interior adapted for museum education purposes. (Open for programs and by appointment.)

White Fears, Regulation, and Legislation

During most of the colonial period New Hampshire's General Assembly met in Portsmouth taverns.

Packer's Tavern was the most favored meeting place of the government in the first half of the eighteenth century. It stood at the northeast corner of Pleasant and Court Streets. The building was destroyed in the fire of 1813 and soon replaced by the brick Ann Treadwell mansion that stands there still (private business).[1]

Horney's Tavern was the preferred meeting place in the 1750s. It stood two blocks from Packer's Tavern on the northwest corner of Court and Atkinson Streets. It was demolished circa 1914 and is now the site of Aldrich Park. (Park open in daylight hours.)

The Capitol or State House served the colony's government from 1762 until the Revolution, when the legislature moved inland for safety from invasion and never returned. It was freestanding in the center of Market Square. Removed in the 1830s, surviving fragments of the frame are preserved in storage by the state's Division of Historic Resources.

One Negro Man £200, One Ditto Woman £50: Location, Labor, Value

Sherburne House is part of Strawbery Banke Museum. It stands on its original site on Puddle Lane at the corner of Horse Lane. (Open seasonally.)

Skilled Craftspeople

ADAM, MERCER, AND BESS MARSHALL

The Marshall house and pottery workshop stood on Jefferson Street at the corner of Horse Lane, now within the grounds of Strawbery Banke Museum. The back part of the property at the foot of the slope, where a kiln is conjectured to have stood, was sold off and built over in the early nineteenth century. The Marshall house was demolished in the mid–twentieth century. Museum archaeologists have located the house site; it is outlined in stone. (Open seasonally.)

NERO, CATO, AND JANE WHEELWRIGHT

The Wheelwright house stood on Jefferson Street, now within the grounds of Strawbery Banke Museum. Documentary research, architectural analysis, and archaeological inquiry suggest that Wheelwright's son John removed and replaced his parents' house, probably in the 1780s. (Replacement open seasonally.)

A TAILOR

The Ham-Brown house stands on Washington Street at the corner of Jefferson Street and is owned by Strawbery Banke Museum. Currently known as Conant House, after a later owner, it houses the museum's café. (Open seasonally.)

HOPESTILL CHESWELL

The Bell Tavern was demolished in the nineteenth century and a commercial block in Victorian style built in its place.

The Reverend Samuel Langdon house survives. In 1952, when threatened with demolition, it was moved to Old Sturbridge Village museum in Massachusetts. At Sturbridge it houses administrative offices. (Open by appointment.)

The Gregory Purcell house still stands on State Street at Middle. It houses the Portsmouth Historical Society and is often called by the name of a famous boarder during Sarah Purcell's widowhood, John Paul Jones. (Open seasonally.)

PRIMUS FOWLE

The Fowle house and shop stood on Pleasant Street at the corner of Howard Street. It survived long enough to be photographed. It was replaced in the second half of the nineteenth century by a mansard-roofed brick house that still stands. (Private residence.)

Fortune and James: Invisibility

The first Earl of Halifax Tavern stood on what is today State Street. Oral tradition holds that it occupied a site that is now the sole vacant lot in the block between Penhallow Street and Chapel Street. Stavers moved his business in 1766. The neighborhood of the first tavern was consumed in the great fire of 1813.

The second Earl of Halifax Tavern, renamed by Stavers *The William Pitt Tavern,* still stands on Court Street, at the corner of Atkinson Street. It is part of Strawbery Banke Museum. In the 1980s it was heavily restored to its appearance in the 1760s–70s. (Open seasonally.)

The Samuel Penhallow House, where James Stavers's thievery was first reported, is described below under "Free Black People in an Era of Slavery."

Hannah, Pomp, Nanne, Violet, Scipio: Agricultural Work

The Langdon slave burial ground is off Lafayette Road, behind the rectory of Christ Church, Episcopal. (Open for viewing from its perimeter during daylight hours.)

Quamino, Prince, Nero, a Negro Girl, Cato, Peter, John Jack, and Phyllis: The Role of Slavery among the White Colonial Elite

The Macpheadris house stands on Daniel Street at the corner of Chapel Street, where it is known as the Warner House for its later owners. Since the 1930s the house has been a historic-house museum. (Open seasonally.)

Venus: Decoding Clues

Saint John's Church stands on the brow of the hill on Chapel Street. Its wooden predecessor burned in 1806. This brick replacement was built circa 1807. (Open for worship services and often on weekdays.)

North Church People: Status and Religion

North Church stood on Market Square in the center of downtown Portsmouth from 1711 until its demolition and replacement in the 1850s by the present brick building. The people described in this section—and in the abolition section—met in the earlier wooden building. (Present building open for worship services on Sunday mornings.)

Nero Brewster, Willie Clarkson, Jock Odiorne, Pharaoh Shores: Black Coronations, Internal Status, and Social Control

Portsmouth Plains is west of downtown in an outlying portion of Portsmouth where Middle Road becomes Greenland Road at its intersection with Islington Street (which did not extend this far in the days of the coronations). Coronation processions are presumed to have gone to the plains via Middle Street to Middle Road to Greenland Road. Visitors will find this area unusually flat even for this coastal plain. (Park and ball field open in daylight hours.)

The town pump was one of several public pumps in old Portsmouth. The central pump stood on today's Pleasant Street near the east front doors of the old colonial-era wooden North Church. Neither pump nor church survives today.

The Unnamed, Unrecorded Dead: Health, Medicine, Death, Burial

The Negro Burying Ground was bounded on its east by Chestnut Street, on its north by State Street, on its south by Court Street. Its western boundary is unknown. By 1813 it had been discontinued and built over. Nineteenth-century houses occupy the site today.

The haunted house stood on the north side of lower State Street where the street begins to slope down toward the riverbank. The area was swept away in the fire of 1813, rebuilt, and again stripped circa 1923 to accommodate the approach ramps of Memorial Bridge. Nothing in the visible environs dates from the period of this anecdote.

The Cotton and Hunking Families: Family, Women, Marriage

South Church occupied a seventeenth-century meetinghouse that stood in the angle formed by the divergence of Marcy Street and South Street on a knoll overlooking the South Mill Pond at the time of the people described in this passage. North Church had separated and moved to Market Square in 1711. South Church relocated in 1737, and the previous building was demolished and its site eventually built over with a dwelling house (now a private residence). In the 1820s South Church moved yet again, this time to a stone meetinghouse on State Street where its congregation evolved into a Unitarian church. From the stone building they advocated abolition and supported schools for newly freed southern Blacks after the Civil War. (Open for worship on Sunday mornings.)

Revolutionary Petitioners: Politics and Freedom

The Moffatt-Ladd House stands on Market Street on an urban lot that stretches from the river, across the street, and through a city block. The house is owned and preserved by a chapter of the Colonial Dames. (Open seasonally.)

Prince Whipple: Revolution and Freedom

Prince Whipple's grave is in the North Burial Ground. This burial ground is on the west side of Maplewood Avenue where it crosses the railroad tracks. Prince's grave (and that of his daughter Esther Mullinaux and one of her daughters, and probably that of Prince's wife Dinah) is toward the southwest corner of the burial ground. Pomp and Candace Spring are buried nearby. (Open during daylight hours.)

Free Black People in an Era of Slavery

The Samuel Penhallow house originally stood on Court Street at the southeast corner of its intersection with Pleasant Street. In the 1860s it was moved to Washington Street, where it survives as part of Strawbery Banke Museum. Its saltbox shape is not original. (Awaiting restoration.)

Chapter 3. Early Americans

"3 Very Old Negroes Almost Good for Nothing": The Plight of the Elderly in Freedom

The second almshouse stood on Court Street (1756–1834) about where Central Fire Station now stands. All traces of it have long since vanished. Intensive twentieth-century redevelopment in the neighborhood leaves little to evoke the setting of the almshouse, other than the 1820s South Church and two or three adjacent houses all constructed toward the end of this almshouse's existence.

Prince, Cuffee, Dinah, and Rebecca Whipple: A Sample Family Living in Freedom

The Black Whipples' house, reputedly an old house moved by Prince and Cuffee to High Street, was replaced after the widowed Dinah moved in the 1830s. The newer and unrelated house, though likely similar in scale to the Whipples' house, is not their house. (Private residence.)

Siras Bruce and Flora Stoodley Bruce: New Freedom, Limited Options

Siras Bruce lived with Langdon in the old Packer's Tavern building that stood on Pleasant Street on the northeast corner of its intersection with Court Street. It burned in the fire of 1813.

In 1785 Siras Bruce probably lived in Langdon's new mansion. The house survives today (143 Pleasant Street) with some alterations. The house, outbuildings, and grounds are preserved by the Society for the Preservation of New England Antiquities as a historic-house museum. (Open seasonally.)

By 1797 Siras lived in a brick house built in 1795 on Washington Street behind the mansion. Neither this brick house nor its wooden neighbor, also owned by Langdon, survives. The site is now a woodland garden attached to the mansion. The low brick wall among the trees is believed to be a fragment of the brick house in which Siras (and presumably Flora) lived. (Open

seasonally during daylight hours via the garden of the Pleasant Street Langdon Mansion.)

Pomp and Candace Spring: A Glimpse of Home and Home Life

The Springs' house stood on the west side of Church Street, between Porter and State Streets. Nineteenth- and twentieth-century rebuilding leaves no recognizable features of their neighborhood other than the street pattern.

Dinah Gibson: Making It on Her Own

The Rice home in which Dinah Gibson lived in Kittery, Maine, doesn't survive, though many other and later Rice family properties do. The house was on Rice Avenue, probably the street on which Dinah fell and froze to death in 1825. Faint evidence of an old ferry landing survives at the foot of Rice Avenue, just visible at low tide, and it is the most tangible surviving evidence of the neighborhood in Dinah's day.

Richard Potter: Making an Itinerant Living in Entertainment

Franklin Hall, where Potter performed in 1830, stood on Congress Street at the northwest corner of the intersection of Fleet Street. In the late nineteenth century it was demolished and replaced by a large commercial block that derives its name, the Franklin Block, from its predecessor.

The New Hampshire Hotel, where Potter worked briefly sometime between 1801 and 1808, stood at the foot of State Street. The hotel and pier associated with it were destroyed in the fire of 1813; the environment was again altered when Memorial Bridge was built in 1923 and yet again when Prescott Park was developed in the mid–twentieth century.

Black Mariners of Portsmouth: Life at Sea and at Home

The waterfront in the days of Portsmouth's Black mariners had three sections. Their character changed from downstream to upstream with the topography of the riverbank.

The Water Street waterfront (now Marcy Street) was shallow, lowbanked, and close to high tide level. Its numerous long piers extended out into the river. These were buried during the construction of Prescott Park in the mid–twentieth century. The adjacent neighborhoods of Strawbery Banke Museum and the South End retain much of the look and flavor of the era of Black mariners. (The park is open in daylight hours.)

The central waterfront hugged the base of the hill crowned by Saint John's Church. The precipitous slope, deep water, and fierce current required that piers hug the bank, running parallel with the stream. Today's wooden decks loosely suggest this historic layout, though the surrounding industrial buildings are from later centuries. (The private decks are open in summer daylight hours.)

The Bow Street and Ceres Street waterfront remains much as it was in the heyday of Portsmouth's Black mariners in the early nineteenth century. The rows of tall brick buildings were warehouses and counting rooms. The enormous overhead pulleys that survive in some of these buildings were probably familiar to Black stevedores working this waterfront. (Bow and Ceres Streets are public ways.)

Esther Whipple Mullinaux: Kinship and Cluster Diffusion

Esther Mullinaux's house may be one of the small old houses still standing on the north (left) side of Walden Lane. The vernacular construction of these houses provides no use-ful clues to whether they are from her period or after. This and several adjacent dead-end streets preserve the scale, density, and atmosphere of the neighborhood in Esther's time. (Private residence.)

Chapter 4. Abolition

Portsmouth's Continued Participation in Slavery

The Old Custom House still stands on Penhallow Street on the southeast corner of its intersection with Daniel Street. This red brick building with a row of fan windows across its second floor was built shortly after the fire of 1813. It was purchased in 1817 by the United States Custom Service, which used its upper floors until the 1850s. Previous customs collectors had worked out of their own homes. This building's overall exterior appearance is little changed from when it was new. (Commercial shops open for business on ground floor; private residences on upper floors.)

A New Custom House made of granite still stands on Pleasant Street on the northwest corner of its intersection with State Street. It was built from 1857–60 based on designs by government architect Ammi Burnham Young. It housed several United States government functions: post office (first floor), customs offices (second floor), federal district court (third floor). The exterior survives intact. Few interior details survived extensive renovations in the late twentieth century. (Private offices.)

A row of federal-era mansions representative of the major consumers of slave-produced goods in the early nineteenth century survives on Middle Street, extending from Haymarket Square (the junction of Court and Middle Streets) to Highland Street.

The Langley Boardman House at 152 Middle Street has a mahogany front door with inset ovals of whalebone or baleen, reminding the viewer of tropical slavery and Black Yankee participation in the exceptionally danger- ous work of New England whaling. (Private residence.)

The Rundlett-May House, 346 Middle Street, preserved by the Society for the Preservation of New England Antiquities, exhibits an enormous quantity of Portsmouth-made neoclassical ma- hogany furniture. (Open to the public seasonally.)

The Ichabod Goodwin House originally stood on Islington Street at the corner of Cornwall Street opposite Goodwin Park. To save it from demolition it was acquired by Strawbery Banke Museum and moved to Hancock Street on the museum grounds. It has been restored to its mid-nineteenth-century appearance. (Open to the public seasonally.)

The Portsmouth Steam Factory survives, in part, at 361 Hanover Street. Its several upper stories were removed after severe damage by fire. Only the ground floor survives. (Private professional offices.)

Frederick Douglass, Charles Lenox Remond, William Wells Brown: Black Abolitionist Orators and the Civil War Years in Portsmouth

The Temple, where Smith's Real Ethiopian African Serenaders performed in 1852, stood on Chestnut Street at the northwest corner of Por- ter Street. It was later destroyed by fire, and in 1876 the Music Hall was built on its site. The site of the Temple, then of the Music Hall, was originally retained by the town for a prison when the glebe lands were divided in 1715. In 1803–4 a Baptist meetinghouse was built on the site. In 1844 a group of businessmen acquired, enlarged, and totally rebuilt the old church into a hall for worship, lectures, and concerts, and named it the Temple in allusion to its previous life. It was in this building that many abolition- ists spoke. The Temple burned in 1876. In 1877

the Music Hall was built on its site. Its pro- grams shifted gradually from concerts to vaude- ville to silent films. Remodeled in 1947 as the Civic Theater, it was a movie theater until 1984. Restoration and renovation with a new program began in the late 1980s.[2] The hall re- mains standing today. (Open for concerts and films, including good representation of African- American culture.)

The States and Union Newspaper office no longer stands. It was housed in the upper story of a commercial building that stood on the northeast corner of the intersection of Daniel and Penhallow Streets. Its site (and many adja- cent building sites) is now occupied by a 1960s- era federal government office building. Foster's newspaper continues as *Foster's Daily Democrat.* Based in the town of Dover, New Hampshire, it also has offices in Portsmouth.

"Most of the Colored People of the City, Both Old and Young": Celebrating Emancipation

The South Ward Hall, built in 1866 as a ward voting hall, still stands at 280 Marcy Street. It now houses the Children's Museum of Ports- mouth. With its large second-floor hall and first- floor schoolrooms the building became the meeting place of many kinds of community groups.[3] (Museum, open to the public daily.)

Chapter 5. Community

People's Baptist Church: Spiritual Life, Religious Community

The South Ward Hall is described immedi- ately above in relation to Emancipation Day celebrations.

People's Baptist Church survives at 45 Pearl Street, at the corner of Hanover Street. Its lower floor is used for apartments, and its upper sanctuary is used as a place of worship and function hall. A preservation easement on the sanctuary room and exterior was negotiated early in the twenty-first century. (Open for Sunday services, public programs, and private rentals.)

The minister's house stands around the corner behind the church at 40 Parker Street. (Private residence.)

Deacon Haywood Burton: Community Leader

Haywood Burton's house still stands at 179 Union Street. (Private residence.)

The hospital building where Burton worked as a janitor still stands, much expanded, on Junkins Avenue. Since the last quarter of the twentieth century it has been owned by the City of Portsmouth, which uses the complex's later buildings for a city hall and police station. (The old wing is closed, vacant, awaiting renovation.)

George M. King, Ralph Reed, Albert Auylor: Social Clubs and Political Action

The 14–16 Market Square building survives on Market Square at the corner of Daniel and Pleasant Streets. The ground floor, long a drugstore and stationer, houses a café at the turn of the twenty-first century. Two stairwells access the upper floors, one between the two shop fronts facing the square, the other on the Daniel Street side. (The upper floors house a variety of small businesses.)

Louis George Gregory and Louisa Matthews Gregory: Spiritual Leaders for Racial Unity

The Gregory's house still stands at 47 South Street. (Private residence.)

Elizabeth Virgil: Quiet Pioneer, Witness to a Changing World

Elizabeth Virgil's last residence still stands at 50 Brewster Street, opposite the end of Hanover Street. It is a private residence. Her earlier residences on Washington and Liberty Streets for the most part no longer stand. The house on Hunking Street likely still stands, as much of this historic street survives intact.

Owen Finnigan Cooper, Eugene Reid, John Ramsay, Emerson Reed, Doris Moore, Anna Jones: World War II and Patriotic Service

The Portsmouth Naval Shipyard in Kittery, Maine, is a defense facility and is not generally open to the public. It is best viewed from Prescott Park. From this vantage the viewer sees mostly buildings constructed in the twentieth century. The Navy Yard houses an interesting museum of its history. (Open by appointment.)

Rosary Broxay Cooper: Migration, Career Options, Patriotic Service

The Cooper house still stands at 171 Washington Street. Not long after Rosary's death in 1997 the house was sold and gentrification/ renovation commenced. Asbestos siding, twin Victorian-era bay windows, interior partitions, and the little wing on the left that housed Rosary's hairdressing shop were removed. New clapboards, window sashes, and paint transform the house beyond any similarity to its appearance during the Coopers' ownership. (Private residence.)

Chapter 6. Civil Rights

Lost Boundaries, Broken Barriers

The Rockingham Hotel still stands at 401 State Street. In the late twentieth century it was converted to condominiums, with careful attention to preserving many of its historic details. It has two front doors. The left-hand front door leads into the original lobby (private entrance for condo owners). The right-hand entrance led into parlors and a public dining room. This section of the building functions as a restaurant today, enabling the visitor to get a sense of the setting in which the film crew and cast stayed, and of rooms in which the NAACP met. (The east door accesses commercial property open for business.)

The Wentworth-by-the-Sea Hotel still stands in the south part of New Castle, on Great Island in the mouth of the Piscataqua River. In the 1980s most of this enormous multiera building was demolished, leaving only the earliest sections, which were gutted. Following twenty years of abandonment the surviving fragment was renovated and enlarged with new wings in 2001–3 (Commercial property open for business.)

Thomas Cobbs: Making a Living, Making a Difference

The NAACP met in the Rockingham Hotel, described above. Thomas Cobbs's house on Deer Street was swept away by urban renewal in the 1960s.

Legislating Destruction: Government Policy and the Black Experience

Urban Renewal in Portsmouth removed two-thirds of the buildings in an area now comprising Strawbery Banke Museum. "The project," as it was called (even forty years into its history as a museum), was bounded by Hancock, Washington, Court, and Marcy Streets. The city's next urban renewal project was approximately bounded by High, Hanover, and Bridge Streets, and the southern bank of the North Mill Pond, with various adjustments to its perimeter to include or exclude certain lots. The area is readily recognizable today by its extensive parking lots and large, flat-roofed, warehouse-style buildings. (The streets are public ways.)

Working Together, Seeking Understanding: The Seacoast Council on Race and Religion

Saint John's Church Parish Hall, where SCORR members met, stands on Chapel Street, next to Saint John's Church. It continues as a working facility. (Open for church functions and by applying to the church office.)

Chapter 7. Living with Diversity

The Martin Luther King Day Annual Breakfasts continued into the twenty-first century at Yoken's Restaurant on Route 1 (Lafayette Road) at the corner of Peverly Hill Road. (Commercial property open for business.)

New Hope Baptist Church is on Peverly Hill Road. (The sanctuary is open for Sunday services.)

The Seacoast African-American Cultural Center meets in the Connie Bean Center, which stands on Daniel Street at the corner of Chapel Street. The building is open most days of the week. (The center is open intermittently for exhibits and programs and by appointment.)

NOTES

❧

Chapter 1. *The Seaport*

1. Mclish, *Disowning Slavery*, 2–3.
2. United States Census Bureau website, http://fact finder.census.gov/. New Hampshire's 2000 population was 1.6% Latin, 1.3% Asian, 0.7% Black, and 0.2% Native American. A few Pacific Islanders and others make up the remainder of the state's population.
3. A country by country survey of the Americas shows that people of African descent, mixed European and African descent, or mixed Black and Native descent when combined are, in most countries, recurrently the major population by percentage. People of Native ancestry are the next largest group (particularly in western Central and South America), with people of solely European descent the majority in only a handful of American countries. By contrast 12–13% of United States residents are Black. A state by state survey shows higher or lower concentrations in some states. The combined nonwhite populations in the United States comprise a considerably higher percentage and are expected to exceed the white population within a generation. United States State Department website, www.state.gov, and United States Census Bureau website, http:// factfinder.census.gov/.
4. The status of greatest percentage seems to have migrated to nearby Exeter in the 1790s, about the time that town served as New Hampshire's state capital. Portsmouth's undulating fraction had brought its Black population to 2.1%, while Exeter was 4.8% Black. This was comprised of 81 Black people in Exeter and 102 Black people in Portsmouth. See Tuveson, "People of Color," 25.
5. *Portsmouth Herald*, March 6, 2003, 1, reports a recent survey finding 4,950 employees at Pease International Tradeport.
6. Melish, *Disowning Slavery*, 165–183.

Chapter 2. *Colonists*

1. Schwartz, "Adaptation," 6, citing Miers and Kopytoff's *African Slavery*.
2. Piersen, *Black Yankees*, 7–8.
3. Mintz, Viola, and Margolis, "Pleasure," 121.
4. Piersen, *Black Yankees*, 7–8.
5. Piersen, *Black Legacy*, 6.
6. Piersen, *Black Yankees*, 6–11, 58, 103, 144–145.
7. For a highly emotive nineteenth-century depiction of this practice see J. M. W. Turner's 1840 painting *The Slave Ship* in the Museum of Fine Arts, Boston, Massachusetts.
8. Biblical citations in defense of slavery occurred with extreme rarity in the mid–eighteenth century. The practice did not become common until a century later on the eve of the American Civil War.
9. Melish, *Disowning Slavery*, 27.
10. Piersen, *Black Yankees*, 160 and chapters 7–10.
11. Dagenais, "The Black," 5–6, citing 1865 published *Provincial Papers of the Governor and the Company of Massachusetts Bay, 1642–1644*, vol. 5, 1–7, and vol. 1, 180; Greene, *Negro in Colonial New England*, 18, n17.
12. Dagenais, "The Black," 9.
13. Greene, *Negro in Colonial New England*, 23.
14. Greene, *Negro in Colonial New England* 23, n47.
15. Dagenais, "The Black," 11.
16. Dagenais, "The Black," 11.
17. Clark and Eastman, *Portsmouth Project*, 20, citing a manuscript at New Hampshire Historical Society, Concord, New Hampshire.
18. *New Hampshire Gazette*, July 28, 1758; Dagenais, "The Black," 28.
19. Dagenais, "The Black," 13, citing *New Hampshire Gazette*, July 28, 1758.
20. Dagenais, "The Black," 13, citing *New Hampshire Gazette*, August 8, 1758.

21. Dagenais, "The Black," 13.

22. Petition to the New Hampshire Legislature, 1779, in *New Hampshire Gazette,* July 15, 1780.

23. Piersen, *Black Yankees,* 40–42; Piersen, *Black Legacy,* 161.

24. *New Hampshire Gazette,* December 12, 1775.

25. Piersen, *Black Yankees,* 16–17.

26. Salzman, Smith, and West, *Encyclopedia of African-American Culture and History,* 1987.

27. Sammons, *Strawbery Banke Guidebook,* 69–70. James Stoodley built the tavern in 1761 on Daniel Street to replace his earlier tavern, which had burned. In 1966 the tavern was moved to Hancock Street to make way for a new federal office building. The tavern's ground floor had been gutted by two centuries of changing commercial use and its second floor heavily changed; its third floor (with ballroom) survives mostly intact.

28. Sammons, *Strawbery Banke Guidebook,* 69–70.

29. *New Hampshire Gazette,* July 2, 1762; Dagenais, "The Black," 28.

30. *New Hampshire Gazette,* April 17, 1767; Dagenais, "The Black," 29.

31. *New Hampshire Gazette,* November 21, 1760; December 10, 1760.

32. Dagenais, "The Black," 28–29.

33. Dagenais, "The Black," 29.

34. Piersen, *Black Yankees,* 10–11.

35. Piersen, *Black Yankees,* 8–9.

36. Dagenais, "The Black," 67.

37. Garvin and Garvin, *On the Road,* 132.

38. Garvin and Garvin, *On the Road,* 129–132. During most of the colonial period New Hampshire's General Assembly met in Portsmouth taverns. The most favored meeting place in the first half of the eighteenth century was Packer's Tavern on Pleasant Street at the corner of Court Street (burned in 1813). In the 1750s the government favored Horney's Tavern on the northwest corner of Court and Atkinson Streets, where Aldrich Park is today (demolished c. 1914). They occasionally met in other taverns. Not until 1762 was the new capitol or statehouse in the middle of Market Square ready for occupancy.

39. Dagenais, "The Black," 5–6, citing 1867 published *Provincial Papers,* vols. 1–7, vol. I, 180, and *Records of the Company of Massachusetts Bay, 1642–1644;* Greene, *Negro in Colonial New England,* 18, n17.

40. Clark, *Eastern Frontier,* 349, citing Laws of N.H., II, 292.

41. Dagenais, "The Black," 61, citing N.H. Acts and Laws, 101.

42. Tuveson, "People of Color," 5.

43. Nash, *Red, White And Black,* 198–199.

44. Dagenais, "The Black," 58, citing N.H. Acts and Laws, 40–41.

45. Dagenais, "The Black," 55, citing N.H. Acts and Laws, 53.

46. Dagenais, "The Black," 55, citing N.H. Acts and Laws, 52.

47. Dagenais, "The Black," 55–56, citing *New Hampshire Gazette,* November 11, 1764.

48. *New Hampshire Gazette,* October 18, 1771.

49. Garvin and Garvin, *On the Road,* 129.

50. *New Hampshire Gazette,* December 30, 1774, and January 1, 1775.

51. Dagenais, "The Black," 12.

52. Banks, *History of Maine,* 242.

53. Dagenais, "The Black," 16, citing Portsmouth Town Records, I-76.

54. Dagenais, "The Black," 48–49, citing Portsmouth Town Records, I-76.

55. Dagenais, "The Black," 61; for a contrast of West African and American law, and the adaptation of the latter to the enslaved, see Schwartz, "Adaptation."

56. New Hampshire, Rockingham County, Probate Court Records, Vol. 12, 500, 1214, Joseph Sherburne Estate inventory, August 8, 1745.

57. Piersen, *Black Yankees,* 25–48.

58. A glebe is land set aside by a town or parish for the support of the church. The Portsmouth church had subdivided part of its inner glebe and issued parcels on long-term leases to increase revenue.

59. The Sherburne House is part of Strawbery Banke Museum, where it stands on Puddle Lane at the corner of Horse Lane.

60. The site was excavated by Strawbery Banke Museum, which sometimes displays some of the findings.

61. Brewster, *Rambles,* vol. 2, 219.

62. Piersen, *Black Yankees,* 100–101.

63. Botanical information from the website of the California Rare Fruit Growers, Inc. The plant's botanical name is *tamarindus indica Leguminosae* (*Fabaceae*).

64. Piersen, *Black Yankees,* 101.

65. Brewster, *Rambles,* vol. 2, 219.

66. DuPré, *Wheelwright House,* N-10. In 1752 Jeremiah sued Archibald Smith, mariner of Somersworth, for £200 because an enslaved man named Cato, sold by Smith to Wheelwright, was not in good health. Apparently Wheelwright had paid in trade with a Negro woman, Jenny, plus £100 worth of shingles. Cato was sold as healthy and able-bodied, but Wheelwright found him un-

sound and unable to work. The court record describes Cato as "greatly disordered in his body by an Hernies [*sic*] or Burstness & unfit for Service." Some sailors attested that he was in good health "until after he was sold sum time." These witnesses and Cato's previous ownership by a mariner suggest that Cato was previously a sailor. The court found in favor of Smith.

67. Sammons, *Strawbery Banke Guidebook.* Son John Wheelwright sailed in the Revolution, remained a mariner, and eventually married. After his wife's death sixteen years later in 1784, he acquired the Wheelwright house from his parents' estate, and he and his young new wife Martha apparently demolished it and built a new house on its site.

68. DuPré, *Wheelwright House,* appendix, photocopy of 1768 probate of Jeremiah Wheelwright.

69. Sammons, *Strawbery Banke Guidebook,* 49.

70. *Portsmouth Directory,* 1821.

71. Tuveson, "People of Color," 9. Alternate spellings of Cheswell include Cheswill, Chiswell, Chiswil, Caswell, Chiswoll, Chesewell, Cherwell. Hopestill's son signed his will Cheswell (Tuveson, 4, n6).

72. Garvin and Grigg, *Historic Portsmouth,* 93–94; Tuveson, "People of Color," 10.

73. Brewster, *Rambles,* vol. 2, 339–340.

74. Tuveson, "People of Color," 10, citing Shupe, "Portsmouth Furniture Craftsmen," 80, ms at Portsmouth Athenaeum.

75. To save it from demolition in the 1950s, Samuel Langdon's house was acquired by Old Sturbridge Village museum in Massachusetts, which moved it there and partially restored it. As it is not a rural building consonant with that museum's mission, it is set apart from the museum's other historic exhibit buildings. It is used as administrative offices.

76. Tuveson, "People of Color," marriage 11–12, son 11–41.

77. *New Hampshire Gazette,* January 21, 1757.

78. Garvin, *Historic Portsmouth,* 65; *New Hampshire Gazette,* May 19, 1791, Primus Fowle's obituary, announcing his funeral at the home of the printer.

79. Brewster, *Rambles,* vol. 1, 210. The *Oxford English Dictionary* reports that "Jade" is an archaic term that had several variant meanings: (a) a contemptuous term for an inferior or worn-out horse; (b) to exhaust or wear out by driving or working too hard; (c) to become tired or worked out. In any sense, Primus was insulting Daniel Fowle.

80. Brewster, *Rambles,* vol. 1, 210–211.

81. Brighton, *They Came to Fish,* 65. Moore, *Printers, Printing, Publishing,* 162–166.

82. Brewster, *Rambles,* vol. 1, 359.

83. Garvin, *Historic Portsmouth,* 65. The United States Census, 1790, lists in John Melcher's household one "other free person" but no slaves. This may have been any of the inherited Black people, now free but remaining with the family. Reminiscences describe Primus living with printer Robert Fowle, who also lived on the west side of Market Street in this period. Robert Fowle's household was overlooked in the census, leaving no way of verifying Primus's location. As Melcher's and Fowle's houses were so close to one another, Primus may have moved freely between them and been perceived by an outsider as belonging to Robert Fowle rather than to John Melcher. This is especially likely given Primus's long association with the Fowle family.

84. Brewster, *Rambles,* vol. 1, 299, quoting an 1853 reminiscence letter by the widow of Captain William Brewster. The dwelling house and new shop were swept away with the rest of inner Market Street in an extensive fire in 1802.

85. *New Hampshire Gazette,* May 19, 1791, 3.

86. *New Hampshire Gazette,* May 26, 1791.

87. The training of enslaved women to perform culinary and textile arts in eighteenth-century Portsmouth is not directly documented but is implicit in their turning to these trades for survival in freedom, a subject explored in the next chapter.

88. Melish, *Disowning Slavery,* 14–15.

89. Advertisements by John Stavers for a slave auction at his tavern, *New Hampshire Gazette,* November 21, 1760 and December 10, 1760.

90. Riley, "John Stavers," 5.

91. Riley, "John Stavers," 4, citing New Hampshire Provincial Court records, files 22971 and 28656.

92. Brewster, *Rambles,* vol. 1, 194, the source of the oral tradition about James hiding in the barrel. Brewster's telling of the riot incident has several errors and is much more elaborated than the eyewitness depositions in the New Hampshire Committee of Safety records at the New Hampshire State Archives.

93. New Hampshire, Court of Session Papers, box 430153, numbers 4102 and 4103.

94. This wording appears in both complaints regarding 1777 and in the 1778 conviction.

95. Schwartz, "Adaptation," passim.

96. Schwartz, "Adaptation," 19–20.

97. *New Hampshire Gazette,* October 5, 1764.

98. The burial ground is behind the parsonage of Christ Episcopal Church on Lafayette Road. It has no historical association with this church, which was not founded until the mid–nineteenth

century and did not relocate to this site until the mid–twentieth century.

99. Langdon Papers, Strawbery Banke, box 1, folder 2, series 2. Purchased for £30.

100. Langdon Papers, Strawbery Banke, box 1, folder 2, series 2, Capt. Tobias Langdon's Personal Papers. Purchased from J. Wentworth for £36.

101. Langdon Papers, Strawbery Banke, box 1, folder 2, series 2, Capt. Tobias Langdon's Personal Papers.

102. Langdon Papers, Strawbery Banke, box 1, folder 3, series 3. Purchased for £150.

103. Langdon/Elwyn Papers, New Hampshire Historical Society, 1981-111, box 3, folder 6, Business Accounts, 1777-18-789. Each purchase of shoes cost two shillings.

104. New Hampshire, Rockingham County, Deeds, vol. 69, 267–268.

105. Langdon Papers, Strawbery Banke, box 1, folder 3, series 3. Annual payments of £4/5/0 were to begin in August of 1774. This was done with the provision that if she should die before the payments were complete the debt would die with her.

106. NB: "a house in town" does not refer to the mansion of John Langdon Jr. on Pleasant Street, which was not built until after the Revolution. Junior did, however, grow up here on his father's farm.

107. John Langdon Sr. Papers (1895-1 v), folder 10, New Hampshire Historical Society(?). Langdon rented out Pomp with the oxen for two days at £14, two more days at £20, one day for £12, one more day for £12, then rented Pomp without the oxen for two days for "a holang of dong" for £24. No further tasks were specified, nor was the months of Pomp's rental to Clarkson named.

108. Brewster, *Rambles*, vol. 1, 212.

109. *New Hampshire Provincial Papers*, ed. Boulton, vol. 18, 705–707.

110. The market house was below the junction of Ceres, Bow, and Market Streets, near the present tugboat pier. Another market house was later built on Market Square.

111. Clark and Eastman, *Portsmouth Project*, 24.

112. Clark and Eastman, *Portsmouth Project*, 24.

113. *Portsmouth Freeman's Journal*, June 8, 1776.

114. Piersen, *Black Yankees*, 26.

115. Schwartz, "Adaptation," passim.

116. Melish, *Disowning Slavery*, 16–18, comparing interpretations by Lorenzo Greene, Edgar J. McManus, Jackson Turner Main, Henry Cabot Lodge, John Daniel, etc.

117. Quamino was mistakenly remembered as Namino in a newspaper account 150 years later.

118. Names from Richard Candee citing Warner Family Papers. Of the several spellings of Macpheadris, this is the one he himself used when signing his will, per Joyce Volk of Warner House Association.

119. Piersen, *Black Yankees*, 7; Wade, "Shining in Borrowed Plumage," 174.

120. J. & S. Wentworth owned ships in the African trade (Dagenais, "The Black," 11); J. Wentworth sold Hannah to Captain Tobias Langdon (Langdon Papers, Strawbery Banke, box 1, folder 2, series 2, Capt. Tobias Langdon's Personal Papers); a John Wentworth owned slaves (John Wentworth's Will, 1774); Ensign Paul Wentworth of Dover (Inventory of John Wentworth, Portsmouth, June 3, 1774, 3); a branch of the family in Somersworth, New Hampshire (Portsmouth Marriage Records, Pomp Spring to Candace Wentworth, 1793); Major Andrew Wentworth of Berwick, Maine (*Portsmouth Directory*, 1851); and of course Archibald Macpheadris's wife Sarah Wentworth. For genealogical relationships see Wentworth, *Wentworth Genealogy*, vol. I, 215.

121. Per 1998 conversation with Jim Garvin and e-mail of May 2002: Tradition holds that Wentworth's private papers, where evidence of slave ownership might appear, were destroyed after his death, and his state papers do not address his domestic life. Not surprisingly, then, there is no documentary evidence of Wentworth owning slaves. A rumored receipt recording Wentworth's payment for inoculation of a Negro girl against smallpox hints at the possible presence of at least one Black person in Wentworth's household, a person he valued enough to provide for her health care. Her status is unknown; payment of the bill by Wentworth would suggest she was a minor or he owned her. A parallel case occurred when Portsmouth minister Ezra Stiles had "my negro servant Newport" inoculated on May 9, 1778 (Estes and Goodman, in *Changing Humors*, transcribe Stiles's diary description of the process of inoculation). Other documents show that Wentworth employed local white farm women.

122. Perkins, *Once I Was Very Young*. As an elderly woman Mary Coolidge Perkins (1881–1962) published reminiscences that describe her childhood summers living with her parents in the old Wentworth mansion at Little Harbor. Like the owners of the house before them—the

Perkins and especially the Israel families—the Coolidge family was acutely aware of the history of the house and, like previous owners, gave tours of the old mansion to visitors and guests. When the Coolidge children conducted these tours they sometimes knowingly included fanciful stories of their own invention and other times perpetuated local oral tradition, misinterpretations, inaccuracies, and perhaps facts the origins of which are now lost. In these published reminiscences Perkins says they interpreted certain small bedchambers as the slaves' rooms. Whether this was sheer invention or an echo of fact is unknown.

123. Jonathan Warner married Mary Macpheadris, daughter of Archibald, who built the house. In May 1740, when Mary was an adolescent, the late George Plummer of Portsmouth bequeathed to her a gold watch, a ring, and "my negro boy named Juba" (Last Will & Testament of Benjamin Plummer, May 7, 1740, microfilm at Strawbery Banke Museum library). Mary's father Archibald had died in 1729. In 1738 her mother Sarah Wentworth Macpheadris married widower George Jaffrey II (Brewster, *Rambles*, vol. 2, 69), who lived in an adjacent mansion. The youthful Mary likely moved with her mother into the new household, so Juba might have entered the Jaffrey household. Later Mary married Bostonian John Osborne and moved there. When widowed, Mary returned to Portsmouth, married Jonathan Warner in 1760, and they moved into the brick house of her childhood. Juba's plight through all this is unknown; he may have gone into the Jaffrey household. Whether Mary took him to Boston and back to Portsmouth to enter the Warner household is unknown.

124. John Langdon, Letter Book #3, September 10, 1779, microfilm, Strawbery Banke Museum library.

125. North Church Records, marriages.

126. *Greenland Historical Society Newsletter*, 1971; New Hampshire, Rockingham County, Deeds.

127. Around 1815–20 (by which time slaves were no longer in the Warner household) the wooden ell was moved to make room for a new brick kitchen wing. The wooden ell was moved one block to the corner of Sheafe and Chapel Streets to a lot left clear by an immense fire in 1813. On this new site the ell was enlarged into a small house. The moved and altered building survived long enough to be photographed. The old photograph provides a rare glimpse, if atypical and altered, of the housing of enslaved people in early Portsmouth. The altered and relocated ell was demolished in the 1890s. This story is relayed in a 1890s news clipping in the Warner House collection. The relocated ell is depicted in a glass plate negative (#657) in the Strawbery Banke Museum library collection. Direct correspondence with Richard Candee regarding Warner family papers, inventory, and archaeological evidence relates that an inventory of 1814 suggests the old wooden ell, when still attached to the brick mansion, encompassed a kitchen and scullery downstairs (and possibly a china room too) with two rooms above. The inventory combines the contents of these two upper rooms without distinction: 3 maple chairs, 2 tables, 1 old chest of drawers, 1 looking glass, and 3 bedsteads with 3 beds and bedding. Such spare fittings might have served Cato, John Jack, and Peter until they were freed, apparently before Warner's death in 1814. In Agnes Austin Aubin, *A Warner House Biography* (Boston, 1935, reprinted 1977) a descendant is quoted as recalling her grandmother's "telling me how she was taken out to Uncle Warner's farm at Greenland, where the Negro servants he had freed lived in little cabins on the estate, some tilling the soil, others working in Blacksmith or carpenter shops."

128. Cupolas were lined up in a row on the Macpheadris and Sherburne mansions, the capitol, and at least one surviving mansion on Islington Street. Cupolas were also features of some churches.

129. These names are drawn from a single document, the enslaved signers of a 1779 petition for abolition of slavery in New Hampshire.

130. Bed canopies reduced drafts but were powerless to retain warmth in New England's subfreezing indoor temperatures. Their impractical presence in the South affirms their role as status symbols. Pulpit canopies were wooden and misinterpreted in the twentieth century as sounding boards, but all documentary references call them canopies, confirming their symbolic function.

131. For their outlook in their own wording see the slaves' petition for freedom, quoted in full elsewhere in this book.

132. Banks, *History of Maine*, 107–108, quoting Charles E. Banks, *History of York, Maine* (Boston: Murray Printing Company, 1935), vol. 2, 228–244. Asked why he did not kill himself instead, Tony said that would be wicked. At his execution (at the county seat in York, the next

town north of Kittery) white record keepers reported with satisfaction that Tony "Behaved very penitently."

133. Members of Saint John's were sorely taxed in their wish to be generous to the poor. A year earlier a major fire had swept the waterfront, destroying the wooden church dating to the colonial period, and they were in the process of constructing the new brick church that stands there today.

134. Brewster, *Rambles*, vol. 1, 201–205, 208–209, describes white poverty on the edges of the compact part of Portsmouth and in the rural outlands of Portsmouth.

135. Prince Whipple, who lived at the Moffatt-Ladd house in the late eighteenth century, was described by nineteenth-century antiquarians as coming from royal lineage back in Africa. Nothing has come to light to clarify whether this is a legitimate derivation, or if this tale originated in authorial sentiment, or can be attributed to the enslaving owner's self-aggrandizement.

136. Joseph Sherburne Estate Probate inventory, August 8, 1745; vol. 12, 500, Concord Probates #1214, shows that Joseph Sherburne of Puddle Lane, merchant and mariner, owned a pew in the North Church and that he also owned an enslaved man and woman whom he may have brought to church with him. Dagenais, "The Black," 67, cites tavern keeper James Stoodley as owning pews in North Church for himself and his enslaved Frank and Flora. North Church marriage records record how, after the Revolution, in 1781, the minister married Prince Whipple to Dinah Chase, and in 1786 married Peter Warner to Dinah Pearn. At that date weddings in New England's Reformed religious tradition were not conducted in houses of worship. The wedding probably occurred in their own or their owners' home, or possibly in the home of the minister.

137. The few pulpit canopies that survive today are often mistakenly called sounding boards, acoustical properties they may incidentally have lent. Typical pulpit ornaments included richly painted woodwork, a tasseled scarlet desk cushion on which to rest the Bible, an arched window to light it, and sometimes scarlet or green window curtains.

138. Assigning pews by rank was a complicated affair involving age, office, landownership, and other determinants. Assignments were necessarily revised from time to time to accommodate passing and maturing generations and newcomers. Ownership emerged gradually through the eighteenth century; in this phase pews were private personal estate and were deeded from owners to heirs. From 1790 to 1840 ownership was gradually displaced by annual rental; in this system pews were distributed at annual auctions and reflected Americans' tendency to define rank in terms of fluid cash wealth. From about 1830 to 1930 old systems were displaced by free and open seating except for Negro pews, which lingered to the 1950s and '60s.

139. Dagenais, "The Black," 67.

140. Dagenais, "The Black," 67.

141. Piersen, *Black Yankees*, 50–51.

142. George Mason University website quotes an article that reports an interview with the elderly Ona Judge, who had escaped from George Washington's wife to Portsmouth. She said that "she never received the least mental or moral instruction of any kind while she remained in Washington's family. The stories of Washington's piety and prayers, so far as she ever saw or heard while she was his slave, have no foundation. Card-playing and wine-drinking were the business at his parties, and he had more of such company Sundays than on any other day."

143. Dagenais, "The Black," 67.

144. Piersen, *Black Yankees*, 102, citing early-eighteenth-century Boston selectmen.

145. Piersen, *Black Yankees*, 103.

146. Piersen, *Black Yankees*, chapters 5, 6, 7.

147. Examples of slaves in Portsmouth with names drawn from scriptural sources include Adam Marshall, James Stavers, John Jack Warner, Peter Warner, Peter Frost, Hannah Langdon, Samuel Wentworth, Rebecca Chase, and the ironically named Pharaoh Rogers. The latter was named for the Egyptian kings who kept the Israelites in bondage. We are left to wonder if he somehow chosen his own name as a subtle act of resistance or if his master was acknowledging that the pharaohs were African.

148. *New Hampshire Gazette*, December 31, 1773.

149. Piersen, *Black Yankees*, 51.

150. Dagenais, "The Black," 67.

151. Piersen, *Black Yankees*, 69–70.

152. Dagenais, "The Black," 66–68.

153. Animism prevailed in sub-Saharan Africa, but Islam extended well into that area, and some Muslims may well have been among colonial Portsmouth's Black population, though stripped of their original culture and religion as captive children.

154. Piersen, *Black Yankees*, 69–70.

155. Piersen, *Black Yankees*, 69.

156. Brewster, *Rambles*, vol. 1, 360n-361n.

157. *New Hampshire Gazette,* October 26, 1770.

158. Candee, *Building Portsmouth,* 80.

159. DuPré, *Wheelwright House,* Wheelwright Probate Inventory, 1768.

160. Dagenais, "The Black," 69–70.

161. Piersen, *Black Yankees,* 49–61.

162. Piersen, *Black Yankees,* 57.

163. *New Hampshire Mercury,* April 19, 1786.

164. Wade, "Shining in Borrowed Plumage," 171.

165. Piersen, *Black Yankees,* chapter 10.

166. Brewster, *Rambles,* vol. 1, 212–213.

167. Garvin and Garvin, *On the Road,* 18–19.

168. Wade, "Shining in Borrowed Plumage," 171.

169. Piersen, *Black Yankees,* chapters 10–11.

170. Aldrich, "An Old Town by the Sea," 1883.

171. After slavery ended some Black people transformed the equation into a ranking system based on the social status of one's white employer. This continued into the twentieth century, noticeably among domestic workers.

172. Piersen, *Black Yankees,* 120.

173. Alexander Pope, *The Rape of the Lock,* circa 1714. Canto III: "Mean while, declining from the Noon of Day / The Sun obliquely shoots his Ray; / The hungry Judges soon the sentence sign, / And Wretches hang that Jury-men may dine."

174. Wade, "Shining in Borrowed Plumage," 173.

175. Piersen, *Black Yankees,* chapters 10–11.

176. Wade, "Shining in Borrowed Plumage," introduction, 175.

177. Piersen, *Black Yankees,* 124.

178. Advertisement for Cromwell as runaway from Henry Sherburne Jr., *Boston Gazette,* October 22, 1754, quoted in Dow, *Arts and Crafts,* vol. 1, 200.

179. Advertisement for Jean Paul, a French Creole, as runaway, Dagenais, "The Black," 57, citing *New Hampshire Gazette,* August 31, 1764.

180. Advertisement for Scipio as runaway from James Dwyer of Portsmouth, *Boston Gazette,* August 8, 1757, quoted in Dow, *Arts and Crafts,* vol. 1, 200.

181. Advertisement for Stephen Hall as runaway, Dagenais, "The Black," 44, citing *New Hampshire Gazette,* December 16, 1761.

182. Piersen, *Black Yankees,* 101–102.

183. Schwartz, "Adaptation," 6–11.

184. Wade, "Shining in Borrowed Plumage," 174–175.

185. Their birth in Africa is stated in the petition for the abolition of slavery they signed in 1779.

186. Piersen, *Black Yankees,* 124; Wade, "Shining in Borrowed Plumage," 172.

187. Wade, "Shining in Borrowed Plumage," 171, 178.

188. Wade, "Shining in Borrowed Plumage," 178.

189. Persistent in an inherited Calvinist tradition, the vast majority of Protestant New Englanders did not observe Christmas until they very slowly and cautiously adopted it between 1850 and 1900.

190. The twelve-acre parcel was approximately bounded by today's Pleasant and Congress Streets, the backs of the west lots on Chestnut Street, and the backs of the south lots on Court Street. The other glebe parcel was a sprawling outlying rural acreage that flanked today's outer Islington Street from approximately the Bartlett Street intersection to Portsmouth Plains. Islington Street was not extended through this parcel until nearly a century later.

191. For a copy of the glebe division map see Brewster, *Rambles,* vol. 1, 44–45.

192. Portsmouth Town Records, 1695–1779, II, July 19, 1760, refer to it as the "Negro Burying Yard" as a reference point in discussing possible locations for a proposed market house.

193. Wright, Hughes, and Hughes *Lay down Body,* 4–18.

194. Hansen and McGowan, *Breaking Ground, Breaking Silence,* provides a synoptic analysis of archaeological findings conducted at Howard University in Washington, D.C., through 1992. There were many clues to daily life in Africa and New York. After the investigation the bones were to be reinterred.

195. Dagenais, "The Black," 25n.

196. Hansen and McGowen *Breaking Ground, Breaking Silence,* includes an analysis of nutrition, health, diet, and cause of death (including disease, accident, and violence) among a community of enslaved Africans in eighteenth-century New York, in regard to the African Burial Ground there.

197. *New Hampshire Gazette,* April 21, 1769.

198. *New Hampshire Gazette,* January 10, 1772.

199. Estes and Goodman, *Changing Humors,* 21.

200. Darling, *Smallpox,* an online exhibit. Smallpox and measles were first distinguished from one another by Abu Bakr Muhammad Ibn Zakariya al-Razi (?850–923) or Rhazes, as he was called in the West. Latin translations of his work were published under the title *De variolis et morbillis commentarius.*

201. Piersen, *Black Yankees,* 99. Medicinet website says yaws is caused by a spirochete that enters the body through scratched or injured skin. Other characteristics of yaws are bone damage and scarring.

202. Piersen, *Black Yankees,* 40, citing Cotton Mather, *The Angel of Bethesda,* as quoted in Kittredge, "Some Lost Works of Cotton Mather," 431.

203. Estes and Goodman, *Changing Humors,* 21.

204. Estes and Goodman, *Changing Humors,* 21.

205. Greene, *Negro in Colonial New England,* 226–227, citing Drake's *History and Antiquities of Boston,* vol. 2, 562.

206. Darling, *Smallpox,* an online exhibit. Mary Wortley Montague had had one of her children inoculated in Constantinople in 1718 and had another child inoculated back in Britain in October of 1721.

207. Piersen, *Black Yankees,* 99.

208. Estes and Goodman, *Changing Humors,* 21–23; Brighton, *They Came to Fish,* vol. 2, 290, n67.

209. Estes and Goodman, *Changing Humors,* 23–24.

210. Burke, *The Day the Universe Changed,* 229–233. Until 1853 European physicians thought that cholera was spread by fog or bad smells rather than by contaminated water. The discovery of the germ in the 1860s revolutionized medicine.

211. Ulrich, *Midwife's Tale,* 49, 52–53; Piersen, *Black Legacy,* 99–117.

212. The John Samuel Sherburne house stood on the north side of today's State Street about where the Memorial Bridge approach ramps and parking lots are today.

213. Brewster, *Rambles,* vol. 2, 213–214.

214. Piersen, *Black Yankees,* 82, 85.

215. Piersen, *Black Yankees,* 85–86.

216. Piersen, *Black Yankees,* 77.

217. Piersen, *Black Yankees,* 78.

218. Piersen, *Black Yankees,* 77, citing Swift's "Oration on Domestic Slavery."

219. Piersen, *Black Yankees,* 77–78.

220. *Portsmouth New Hampshire Mercury,* April 19, 1786, obituary.

221. The Purcell house survives and since the early twentieth century has been the home of the Portsmouth Historical Society. It is often called the John Paul Jones House for a famous boarder taken in by the widowed Sarah in the 1770s and '80s.

222. Portsmouth Town Records, 1695–1779, II, July 19, 1760.

223. Brewster, *Rambles,* vol. 1, 46–48.

224. Manuscript notation on the flyleaf of Gurney's *Portsmouth Historic and Picturesque* in New York City Public Library collection, transcription by Paul Hughes of Greenland, New Hampshire, collection of Valerie Cunningham.

225. Dagenais, "The Black," 51.

226. Prince Whipple, probably Dinah Whipple, and their daughter Esther Whipple Mullinaux are buried together near Pomp and Candace Spring in the southwest corner of North Burial Ground.

227. Cunningham, "First Blacks of Portsmouth," 191, citing South Church Records.

228. Piersen, *Black Yankees,* 88–89.

229. Piersen, *Black Yankees,* 91.

230. Piersen, *Black Yankees,* 93.

231. Dagenais, "The Black," 18, citing a Portsmouth census of 1767 that counted 124 Black men and 62 Black women. A 1773 census counted 100 Black men and 60 Black women.

232. Dagenais, "The Black," 48–49, citing Portsmouth Town Records, I-76.

233. Some sources trace the term to an Arabic word for giving birth.

234. Schwartz, "Adaptation," 19.

235. Cunningham, "First Blacks of Portsmouth," 191–192.

236. Cunningham, "First Blacks of Portsmouth," 193.

237. Piersen, *Black Yankees,* 89.

238. Piersen, *Black Yankees,* 91.

239. Piersen, *Black Yankees,* 87–95 passim.

240. Piersen, *Black Yankees,* 91.

241. North Church Records.

242. Piersen, *Black Yankees,* 93.

243. Langdon Papers, Strawbery Banke, box 1, folder 3, series 3.

244. Piersen, *Black Yankees,* 92.

245. Prince and Cuffee used Whipple as their last name throughout their lives. They may at some time both have lived with William, but other records show that Cuffee was the property of William's brother Joseph. Windsor used the name Moffatt, the form in which his name appears on the abolition petition of 1779. Apparently he came into the household as part of Katherine Moffatt Whipple's estate; she and her husband William lived in her father's house. As part of settling her father's estate she paid twelve shillings for a coffin for Windsor— she spelled it Winzorr—on June 14, 1786. Perhaps Windsor was part of a cargo of slaves on John Moffatt's snow *Exeter* in Portsmouth harbor in 1755 at the time of the death of its captain, as cited earlier. Cuffee's name is rendered "Cuff" in the record of his manumission, Portsmouth Town Records, 1779–1807, vol. 3, 101B.

246. The petitioners signed the document in a slightly different order from the sequence in which their names appear in the opening of the text. The order of signatures on the petition is Seneca Hall, Peter Frost, Zebulon Gardner, Peter Warner, Prince Whipple, Quam Sherburne, Cato Warner, Nero Brewster, Samuel Wentworth, Pharaoh Shores, Pharaoh Rogers, Will Clarkson, Windsor Moffatt, Romeo

Rindge, Jack Odiorne, Garrett Colton, Cato Newmarch, Cipio Hubbard, Kittindge Tuckerman, Cesar Gerrish.

247. As Boston was alternately held by patriots, then by the British army, and then by patriots again, the enslaved there submitted three petitions to the consecutive authorities.

248. Philip Yorke, and Lord Chancellor Talbot, Lord Hardwicke, sitting as chancellors on October 19, 1749.

249. *New Hampshire Gazette,* July 31, 1772.

250. His name is sometimes rendered simply "William Murray Mansfield."

251. Davis, "Emancipation Rhetoric," 260; Medicolegal website, where the full text of Mansfield's decision is posted; United States Library of Congress, "American Memory" website, where partial texts (arguments) are posted.

252. *New Hampshire Gazette,* May 20, 1774.

253. *New Hampshire Gazette,* November 2, 1775, notes three runaways in one issue: Cato, Peter Lang, and Oliver.

254. *New Hampshire Provincial Papers,* ed. Boulton, vol. 18, 705–707. "Speaker" Langdon is John Langdon Jr.

255. Dagenais, "The Black," 84, citing United States Census of 1790.

256. Foster, *Soldier's Memorial,* 27, 100. Prince's grave was originally marked with two rough stones barely visible above the ground, stones similar to those at the Langdon slave cemetery. Later its obscure location had to be identified by Prince's grandson, John Smith.

257. Prince was one of twenty Portsmouth men who signed a petition for freedom during the Revolutionary War, in which they collectively describe themselves as "torn by the cruel hand of violence" from their mothers' "aching bosom," and "seized, imprisoned and transported" to America and deprived of "the nurturing care of [their] bereaved parent."

258. Kaplan, *Black Presence,* 46. In 1851, decades after the deaths of Prince and Cuffee, Black antiquarian William C. Nell published a pioneering history of the Black experience in America, in which he introduced a number of unsubstantiated details that have since been taken as fact, as by Kaplan. Some of Nell's details—such as the timing of Prince's emancipation—have been proven wrong. Nell wrote: "Prince Whipple was born in Amabou, Africa, of comparatively wealthy parents. When about ten years of age, he was sent by them, in company with a cousin, to America, to be educated. An elder brother

had returned four years before, and his parents were anxious that their child should receive the same benefits. The captain who brought the two boys over proved a treacherous villain, and carried them to Baltimore, where he exposed them for sale, and they were both purchased by Portsmouth men, Prince falling to Gen. Whipple. He was emancipated during the war, was much esteemed, and was once entrusted by the General with a large sum of money to carry from Salem to Portsmouth. He was attacked on the road, near Newburyport, by two ruffians; one he struck with a loaded whip, the other he shot. . . . Prince was beloved by all who knew him. He was the 'Caleb Quotem' of Portsmouth, where he died at the age of thirty-two, leaving a widow and children." "Amabou" was probably Anomabu on the Gold Coast of western Africa (Piersen, *Black Legacy,* 90). Given Prince's parents' supposed wealth, prince may have been Prince's African status as well as his American name. No documents have ever come to light to substantiate the highwayman story. If it derived from oral histories and was true of some enslaved individual, whether or not Prince, the tale suggests a surprising liberty of movement and responsibility sometimes accorded to slaves.

259. The mansion still stands on Market Street and is known as the Moffatt-Ladd House. It is maintained by the Colonial Dames, who open it to the public seasonally.

260. Special thanks to Barbara McLean Ward, director of the Moffatt-Ladd House museum, and Andy Melville for sharing their research, still in progress, on Cuffee Whipple.

261. Seacoast New Hampshire website, letter from Blaine Whipple of Whipple Organization.

262. Whipple Organization website. Mevers, *Josiah Bartlett,* 139 ff. General Whipple's presence in Baltimore is confirmed by two letters from him to Josiah Bartlett dated at Baltimore December 23 and December 31, just before and just after the Battle of Trenton. In the latter he refers to "a successful Enterprise at Trenton," providing general information but not indicating that he (or Prince) was there.

263. Seacoast New Hampshire website, letter from Blaine Whipple of Whipple Organization.

264. Whipple Organization website.

265. Brewster, *Rambles,* vol. 1, 154–155, incorrectly states that as William prepared to depart he promised Prince immediate freedom if he would accompany the general cheerfully.

266. Cunningham, "First Blacks in Portsmouth," 198, citing Portsmouth Town Records, vol. 3, 95.

267. Seacoast New Hampshire website, letter from Blaine Whipple of Whipple Organization.

268. Dinah's ownership: Brewster, *Rambles,* vol. 1, 155. Marriage: North Church Records.

269. Brewster, *Rambles,* vol. 1, 155.

270. Sully's painting is at the Museum of Fine Arts in Boston. Leutze's painting is at the Metropolitan Museum of Art in New York. In 1853, M. Knoedler published an engraving of Leutze's painting, and many copies were made; see Metropolitan Museum of Art website for more detail on the proliferation of this image.

271. Beth A. Marchese, "Revolutionary Cemetery," *Fitchburg (Massachusetts) Sentinel and Enterprise,* August 23, 1992. The claim for Estabrook gains plausibility from the presence of two regiments from Lexington at the crossing of the Delaware.

272. Kaplan, *Black Presence,* 44–46; Burgoyne, *The Trenton Commanders,* 1–7.

273. Information on the service of New Hampshire Black men in the Revolution from Professor Robert Dishman, University of New Hampshire, public lecture on preliminary research findings, Portsmouth Athenaeum.

274. Kaplan, *Black Presence,* 232.

275. Dagenais, "The Black," 16, citing Portsmouth Town Records, I-76.

276. Cunningham, "First Blacks of Portsmouth," 185, citing Boulton, *Probate Records,* I, 1635–1717.

277. Dagenais, "The Black," 84.

278. Cunningham, "First Blacks of Portsmouth," 184, citing Rindge Family Papers, New Hampshire Historical Society, box 1, folder 1.

279. Cunningham, "First Blacks of Portsmouth," 184.

280. Cunningham, "First Blacks of Portsmouth," 186.

281. Cunningham, "First Blacks of Portsmouth," 187, citing Portsmouth Town Records, III, 16, and North Church Records, marriages, October 1, 1799.

282. United States Treasury website. Oliver Wolcott (b. 1760 at Litchfield, Connecticut, died 1833 at New York City), was second secretary of the treasury, serving 1795–1800.

283. Jackson, *Diaries of George Washington;* Fitzpatrick, *Writings of George Washington;* Adams, essay in *Granite Freeman,* May 1845; *Portsmouth Journal,* May 3, 1803; *Portsmouth Journal,* March 7, 1857. Ona's story is also told in Kirkland, Morgan and Nocholls, "Slave Flight." Ona's story is documented in letters between George Washington and Secretary of the Treasury Oliver Wolcott and Portsmouth collector of customs Joseph Whipple, as well as in an 1845 interview with the elderly Ona. The official Mount Vernon website describes the incident as follows: "Oney Judge had worked as Martha Washington's maid since childhood and was an expert seamstress, a skill that would support her as a free woman. In 1796, Oney ran away from the presidential mansion and settled in New Hampshire where she married and had a child. The Washingtons tried to persuade her to come back once they learned of her whereabouts, but Oney never returned to Mount Vernon. Many years later, she told reporters that she had no misgivings about leaving the Washingtons who had always treated her well. Despite her many hardships in New Hampshire, she would never regret her freedom."

284. Cunningham, "First Blacks of Portsmouth," 186, citing Portsmouth Town Records, II, 154A.

285. Abraham Dearborn, March 25, 1778, Portsmouth Town Records.

286. Portsmouth Town Records, vol. I, 5, June 9, 1778. Estes and Goodman, *Changing Humors,* relay that the previous spring the Reverend Ezra Stiles had taken his wife, three children, and household including "my negro servant Newport" to be inoculated against smallpox by Dr. Hall Jackson; a daughter's household members and Newport were inoculated on May 9, 1778. Sammons, *Strawbery Banke Guidebook,* tells that Deacon Samuel Penhallow lived on the southeast corner of Pleasant and Court Streets in the eighteenth century. In 1862 his house was moved to Washington Street, where it still stands. Penhallow, as a justice of the peace, was empowered to record the manumission or free status of colonial Portsmouth's free Black people, as well as to hear minor legal cases.

287. Portsmouth Town Records, May 28, 1777.

288. Piersen, *Black Yankees,* 4.

289. Portsmouth Town Records, book of marriages, 10.

290. Portsmouth Town Records, VI-4.

291. Cunningham, "First Blacks of Portsmouth," 195, citing North Church Records, funerals, 1818.

Chapter 3. Early Americans

1. Lexis Nexis website; Chronicle of Slavery website.

2. Public Broadcasting System website. This case began with a routine domestic incident of white violence against a slave, Elizabeth Freeman, then known as Mum Bett (1742–1829). She intercepted a blow with a hot kitchen shovel di-

rected at her sister by their owner's wife. Bett walked out on her owners. Ashley turned to the law for Bett's recovery. Bett and Brom turned to the law for protection, engaging a local lawyer, Theodore Sedgewick of Stockbridge, to represent them. The county court heard the case in Great Barrington, and the jury upheld the argument that the status of enslavement violated the new state constitution. The court ordered Ashley to pay thirty shillings to Bett and Brom plus court costs. Bett and Brom were the first to gain their freedom under Massachusetts's new constitution. Among Bett's grandchildren was W. E. B. DuBois, born in nearby Great Barrington, Massachusetts.

3. Public Broadcasting System website. Variant spellings of Quock Walker's name include Quock, Quacks, Quaco, Quack, Quork, and Quork.

4. Melish, *Disowning Slavery,* 65–83.

5. Public Broadcasting System website.

6. Public Broadcasting System website; Melish, *Disowning Slavery,* 96–97.

7. Connecticut Freedom Trail website.

8. Rhode Island Black Heritage Society website.

9. Melish, *Disowning Slavery,* 66; Dagenais, "The Black," 86.

10. Melish, *Disowning Slavery,* 66.

11. United States Census, 1840. Inter-University Consortium for Political and Social Research (ICPSR) Ann Arbor, Michigan, website.

12. Melish, *Disowning Slavery,* 66.

13. United States Census, 1790, Inter-University Consortium for Political and Social Research (ICPSR), Ann Arbor, Michigan, website. Vermont was enumerated for the United States Census, 1790, though not formally admitted to the Union until the following year. In 1790 New Hampshire's distribution of slaves by county was Cheshire 18; Grafton 21; Hillsborough 0; Rockingham 97; Strafford 21.

14. Sammons, "Cold," *Encyclopedia of New England Culture;* Fagan, *The Little Ice Age.* The unseasonable frosts were due to short-term climatic change caused by volcanic ash in the stratosphere from the eruption of Mount Tambora in the Sumatra archipelago of Indonesia, the largest volcanic eruption in historic time. Referencing that year of misery, Yankees occasionally refer to 1816 as "eighteen-hundred-and-frozen-to-death."

15. New England's small ports—such as Portsmouth, New Hampshire; Newburyport, Salem, and Marblehead, Massachusetts; and Newport, Rhode Island—had up to this time been roughly equal to the ports that outstripped them. The small ports' slower recovery and lesser subsequent growth minimized the large-scale rebuilding enabled by the prosperity of larger ports. Hence the small ones are admired today as well-preserved historic towns.

16. Piersen, *Black Yankees,* 18.

17. Cunningham, "First Blacks of Portsmouth," 195.

18. Melish, *Disowning Slavery,* 164–183.

19. Melish, *Disowning Slavery,* 140–162.

20. Piersen, *Black Yankees,* 46.

21. Piersen, *Black Yankees,* quoting Alexis de Tocqueville.

22. Public Broadcasting System website.

23. Tuveson, "People of Color," 1, 22.

24. *Portsmouth Daily Morning Chronicle,* March 27, 1854.

25. United States Census, 1830, Rockingham County, New Hampshire, ms, 149; nine people out of twenty-eight.

26. United States Census, 1790, Rockingham County, New Hampshire, ms, 81–82.

27. *Portsmouth Directory,* 1821, 1827, 1834, 1839, 1851; Dagenais, "The Black." The numbers of Black households in Portsmouth in the second quarter of the nineteenth century were 1821, 28; 1827, 40; 1834, 25; 1839, 27; 1851, 14.

28. United States Census, 1850, 1860.

29. United States Census, 1790. The names and numbers of people in the household in the first cluster are Caesar Hodgedon (2 people); Peter Adams (2); Nanny (possibly Nanny Langdon, 2); Mercy (2); Peter Warner (2); William Simonds (2); Pharaoh Shores (4); Juba (4); Myrtilla (possibly Matilday, who married William Clarkson in 1798 and was later a widow at Sheafe's Pasture [*Portsmouth Directory,*1821], 3); Jock Odiorne (4); Romeo (probably Romeo Rindge, 2). The second cluster of names is comprised of Prince Whipple (5); Cuff Whipple (2); Caesar Gerrish (6); Caesar Hart (6). A few in the first cluster can be located at rural places like Sagamore Creek, the Plains, Sheafe's Pasture, etcetera. In the second cluster, the Whipples lived together with their wives and children in one house on High Street. White Gerrishes and Harts lived on Deer Street; the two Caesars may also have lived there or nearby on High Street.

30. United States Census, 1790, Rockingham County, New Hampshire, microfilm at Strawbery Banke Museum library.

31. Brewster, *Rambles,* vol. 1, 201–205, 208–209, provides detailed descriptions of the lives of poor whites living on the edge of the compact part of town and in rural parts of Portsmouth.

32. *Portsmouth Directory,* 1821. United States: Federal Direct Tax, 1798, B List.

33. United States Federal Direct Tax, 1798, B List.

34. *Portsmouth Directory,* 1839.

35. Tuveson, "People of Color," 34–35.

36. *Portsmouth Directory,* 1821: laborer, 2 barbers, truckman (remaining 24 unidentified); 1827: 2 laborers, clothes cleaner, mason, hostler at stable; hairdresser; 2 barbers, truckman (remaining 31 unidentified); 1834: 4 laborers, 5 mariners, hairdresser, clothes cleaner, truckman (remaining 13 unidentified); 1839: 9 mariners, laborer, clothes renovator, farmhand, 2 laborers, ostler, seamen's boardinghouse (remaining 11 unidentified); 1851: 4 laborers, 4 mariners, laundress, barber (remaining 4 unidentified).

37. Piersen, *Black Yankees,* 47.

38. New Hampshire, Rockingham, County Probate Records, John Wentworth will, 1774.

39. New Hampshire, Rockingham County Probate Records, Inventory of John Wentworth, Portsmouth, June 3, 1774, 3. For genealogical relationships see Wentworth, *Wentworth Genealogy,* vol. I, 215. John Wentworth inherited Tom and Dinah in 1748.

40. New Hampshire, Rockingham County, Deeds, vol. 69, 267–268.

41. Brewster, *Rambles,* vol. 1, 127.

42. Brewster, *Rambles,* vol. 1, 127. The first almshouse stood at the corner of Chestnut and Porter Streets, site of today's Music Hall, from 1716 to 1756. The second was built three blocks away, where the Court Street fire station now stands, and stood from 1756 to 1834.

43. Cunningham, "First Blacks of Portsmouth," 195; Dagenais, "The Black," 106.

44. Dagenais, "The Black," 107.

45. Dagenais, "The Black," 110.

46. Brewster, *Rambles,* vol. 1, 201–205, 208–209.

47. *Portsmouth Directory,* 1821. This pasture might have been on Sheafe's Road, near the Newington border at the north edge of town.

48. Portsmouth Town Records, III, 95.

49. Dagenais, "The Black," 186, appendix 7; undated letter from Dagenais to Michael Gowell of Kittery, Maine.

50. *Portsmouth Journal of Literature and Politics,* February 22, 1846, Dinah's obituary. The house was replaced sometime after 1832, when Dinah ceased living there. Though the present house is old, it is not the building in which the Black Whipples lived.

51. *Portsmouth Journal of Literature and Politics,* February 22, 1846, Dinah's obituary.

52. Brewster, *Rambles,* vol. 1, 155.

53. The *New Century Cyclopedia of Names,* vol. 3. The opera *Caleb Quotem* was not successful, but the character Caleb Quotem was reused in an eighteenth-century publication called *The Review* by "the younger Colman." Evidently this was successful, remained popular, and was read widely enough that even in the mid–nineteenth century the reference to Prince as a Caleb Quotem was understood.

54. Brewster, *Rambles,* vol. 1, 176–177.

55. Goodwin "Pleasant Memories"; Brewster, *Rambles,* vol. 1, 176–177.

56. Garvin, "Academic Architecture," 257.

57. *Portsmouth Journal of Literature and Politics,* February 22, 1846, Dinah's obituary.

58. Kaplan, *Black Presence,* 46, estimates that Prince died at the age of thirty-two. This implies Prince was born in 1765. This date of birth seems highly implausible because it would make Prince eleven years old when and if he accompanied William Whipple to Philadelphia, twelve and thirteen when he accompanied William in the campaigns at Saratoga and Rhode Island, fourteen when he signed the petition to end slavery, sixteen when he married twenty-one-year-old Dinah, and nineteen when manumitted. A boy so young would surely have been more of a burden than an aid in military settings. It seems unlikely the Black elders would have included a fourteen-year-old youth in their petition. Dinah would not likely have married a lad five years younger than herself. As manumission laws took shape, most specified ages in the early to midtwenties, suggesting a white cultural sense of appropriate age for this act. William would have been going against this cultural norm if he manumitted Prince at age nineteen. Kaplan's estimate of Prince's age is probably off by a decade or more.

59. Barbara McLean Ward, director of the Moffatt-Ladd House museum, is researching Cuffee Whipple and postulates that Cuffee may not have signed the petition for any of several reasons. He may simply have been away with his owner, Joseph, who at that time was fairly often in northern New Hampshire looking after his extensive landholdings there. He may not have been a native of Africa, a status indicated in the petition's text and perhaps a requirement of those who created the petition. He may not have signed it because he didn't feel the petition represented his outlook.

60. Portsmouth Town Records, 1779–1807, vol. 3, 101B; typed transcript.

61. A new Gregorian calendar, designed to correct

an error in the old Julian calendar, was promulgated by the Vatican in 1582 and displaced the old practice of measuring the new year from the Feast of the Annunciation on March 26 with a neoclassical January 1 date for the New Year. Protestant and insular Britain and its colonies did not adopt the Gregorian calendar until 1751, when eleven days were dropped from the calendar and a new New Year's Day adopted. Dates of British events falling between January and March 26 in the years between 1582 and 1751 are sometimes annotated "old style" or "new style," "o.s." or "n.s." or with a slash, e.g., March 2, 1741/42.

62. Brewster, *Rambles,* vol. 1, 176–177. Garvin "Tour of the Wentworth-Coolidge Mansion," 21–22. Michael Wentworth's love of music was legendary. He had married the widow of the late Governor Benning Wentworth and had a harpsichord that survives in their house, the Wentworth-Coolidge Mansion in the Little Harbor neighborhood of Portsmouth.

63. Brewster, *Rambles,* vol. 2, 88.

64. Piersen, *Black Yankees,* 104.

65. Brewster, *Rambles,* vol. 1, 212; Piersen, *Black Yankees,* 124.

66. Piersen, *Black Yankees,* 77.

67. Piersen, *Black Yankees,* 105.

68. Piersen, *Black Yankees,* 104, 124.

69. Mazzari, "African American Music."

70. Brewster, *Rambles,* vol. 2, 324. The school play was in a brick schoolhouse that stood on the rocky knoll beside today's Temple Israel on State Street.

71. Taylor, Howard, et al., *Foster,* 13; "Who Writes Our Songs," unsigned *New York Evening Post* article, reprinted in *Dwight's Journal of Music,* Boston, May 14, 1859, posted at Harriet Beecher Stowe Center, *Uncle Tom's Cabin* website.

72. Railton, *Mark Twain* website.

73. For recent scholarship in this area see Lott, *Love and Theft;* Cockrell, *Demons of Disorder;* and Mahar, *Behind the Burnt Cork Mask.*

74. *Portsmouth Daily Morning Chronicle,* September 1, 1852: "Smith's Real Ethiopian African Serenaders, Would respectfully announce to the ladies and gentlemen of this city and vicinity, that they will give their Last Concert This Evening, at the Temple, where they have been greeted by crowded house. This is the only real Ethiopian Band now travelling, and is composed of superior Musicians. Doors open at 7, to commence at 8 precisely. Tickets 12½ cents."

75. Brewster, *Portsmouth Jubilee,* 14.

76. Mazzari, "African American Music."

77. Mazzari, "African American Music."

78. *Portsmouth Herald,* May 20, 2002.

79. Brewster, *Rambles,* vol. 1, 155.

80. *Portsmouth Journal of Literature and Politics,* February 14, 1846, obituary.

81. *Portsmouth Journal of Literature and Politics,* February 14, 1846, obituary.

82. Portsmouth went on to build a series of schoolhouses. These included one on South Street (established in 1708); one on State Street (operating privately before 1735 and taken over by the town in that year); one in Christian Shore (established in 1737); and one just off High Street behind the Moffatt-Ladd garden (established in 1751).

83. Brewster, *Rambles,* vol. 1, 303–305. Hitherto, girls' public school attendance was limited to the summer term, before and after the boys' school day, from 6:00 to 7:00 A.M. and 5:00 to 6:00 P.M., four days a week.

84. Chronology pieced together from Brewster, *Rambles,* vol. 1, 78–85, 156, 228–229, 299–306; vol. 2, 316, 322; Garvin, *Historic Portsmouth,* 72; Garvin, "Academic Architecture," 467. In 1780 Benjamin Dearborne opened a private school admitting boys and girls in his house in Market Street, a short distance from Dinah's school. Soon there were additional private schools admitting girls. In 1784 the town of Portsmouth at last opened a school for girls aged eight and upward, which met in rented space in a house on Market Square. It operated only eighteen months, and the experiment was not repeated for thirty years. About the year 1790 Portsmouth rebuilt the State Street School in brick, with a cupola and bell on its roof.

85. *Boston Gazette,* October 22, 1754.

86. *New Hampshire Gazette,* December 11, 1772, courtesy Elizabeth Nowers.

87. Tuveson, "People of Color," 39, n227, citing Piersen, *Black Yankees,* 29.

88. Mars, *Life of James Mars.*

89. Sammons, "Schools, Scholars, and Society," 5; Sammons, "Myths and Methods."

90. Garland Patch Collection of Glass Plate Negative Photographs, Strawbery Banke Museum.

91. The note is from Dinah's impoverished old age and requests a gift of firewood.

92. Public Broadcasting System website.

93. Public Broadcasting System website. Philadelphia's Black charitable societies distributed $7,000 a year in 1832 and $14,000 yearly by 1837.

94. Horton and Horton, *Black Bostonians,* 28.

95. *Portsmouth Oracle,* July 18, 1807, obituary.

96. Tuvesen, "A People of Color," 44, citing *Exeter Watchman,* August 12, 1817.

97. Cunningham, "First Blacks of Portsmouth," 199, citing Horton and Horton, *Black Bostonians,* 56–66; Piersen, *Black Yankees,* 59.

98. Dagenais, "The Black," 70, citing grant of $130 from city to school in 1853, recorded in Portsmouth City Records, in City Book for 1853.

99. *Portsmouth Journal of Literature and Politics,* February 14, 1846, obituary.

100. North Church Records. Amos Tappan was also paid for supplying the communion table for nine months.

101. North Church Records, gifts to the poor, 1825.

102. North Church Records, Wardens of the North Parish Account Current with Josiah Webster, March 4, 1828.

103. North Church, Records, receipt, March 1, 1829; *Portsmouth Directory,* 1821, 1827 (spelled Jenness), 1834, 1839.

104. United States Census, 1830, Rockingham County, New Hampshire, microfilm, Strawbery Banke Museum library.

105. United States Census, 1830, Rockingham County, New Hampshire, microfilm, Strawbery Banke Museum library. Dinah's Black neighbors included mariners John Ross and William Smith, and a widow Webb. The latter was possibly Phoebe Webb, who in 1830 had a little girl, two teenage girls, a teenage boy, and a young man in her household. She was likely related to William Webb, a Black man who kept a boardinghouse for mariners in State Street in the same decade.

106. North Church Records.

107. North Church Records, gifts to poor, 1825, 1844, 1846.

108. *Portsmouth Journal of Literature and Politics,* February 14, 1846, obituary; *Portsmouth Directory,* 1839.

109. That Rebecca stayed with Dinah is implicit in the wording of a gift to the two of them from North Church in 1825.

110. Alternate spellings or renditions of his name, as recorded by others than himself, include Cyrus de Bruce and Silas Bruce.

111. From a manuscript at the New Hampshire Historical Society, Concord.

112. Garvin, "Academic Architecture," 192, 246–247. The Packer house stood on the northeast corner of Pleasant and Court Streets. Packer's forebears operated a tavern in the house, when it was frequently the place of the legislature's sessions in the first half of the eighteenth century. The building was destroyed in the fire of 1813

and soon replaced by the brick Ann Treadwell mansion, which stands there still.

113. Brewster, *Rambles,* vol. 1, 210.

114. Langdon Papers, Strawbery Banke, series 4, box 2, folder 8, Business Records of John Langdon, 1784–1789. Two are marked on the back "S. Hardy's Bill against Siras de Bruce" and "Mr. S. Hardy's bill for work done for Siras de Bruce." The obverses of these bills itemize expenses from October 23 1783 to July 1784, charged to John Langdon Esq. for clothing "for his Negro man Siras." Expenditures on the first bill add up to £3/12/2 and include a coat, a surtout (overcoat) with pockets and lined sleeves, a lined waistcoat, and lined breeches. Fabrics include buckram, shalloon, and linen; notions include silk twist (thread), two dozen coat buttons, two dozen breast buttons, thirteen metal buttons, and stays. The second bill, for £1/11/7, adds to the wardrobe a waistcoat with a lined back, pockets, and buttons, a "Suit" at £1/4/0, and "altering a pair of white Breeches."

115. Cunningham, "First Blacks of New Hampshire," 183n.

116. Dated 1779; Dagenais, "The Black," 67.

117. The original back ell was replaced at the turn of the twentieth century with a much larger ell in a revival style matching the original front section of the house, magnifying its size well beyond that known by Langdon and Siras.

118. NB: These small brick buildings were mercantile offices, not slave cabins. Freestanding slave quarters were not normal housing of New England's enslaved, as they were in parts of the South. In such a hierarchical era, southern slave cabins usually stood to the side or back of the owner's house.

119. Brewster, *Rambles,* vol. 1, 256, quoting Washington's diary, November 2, 1789.

120. Cleary, "Langdon," citing ms no. 2.13 in the New Hampshire Historical Society, Concord, New Hampshire. Abner Blaisdel built the brick house for Langdon.

121. Gurney, *Portsmouth Historic and Picturesque,* 113. Canoe Creek once connected Puddle Dock and South Mill Pond. It ran along the boundary between the Langdon and Thomas Thompson mansions. The creek had been bridged since 1727; in 1786 Langdon rebuilt the bridge and presented it to the town. The creek was filled around 1800. The 1813 map of Portsmouth shows two small houses—one brick and one wood—sharing a lot on Washington Street be-

side the site of the filled Canoe Creek. The long narrow lot ran parallel to the creek to the back of the Langdon mansion's barn and back door-yard. The site of these two houses is vacant today, occupied by a romantic woodland garden created by early-twentieth-century owners. A low brick wall that divides this woodland garden is reputed in local oral tradition to be a fragment of the brick house built for Langdon in 1797.

122. Langdon Papers, Strawbery Banke, series 4, box 2, folder 9, Business Records of John Langdon, 1799–1819.

123. *Portsmouth Oracle,* July 18, 1807, obituary. Birth year calculated from age at his death.

124. Pomp's obituary doesn't mention his place of birth. His mother's name, Phyllis, is found in probate records related to the settling of Pomp's estate.

125. New Hampshire, Rockingham County, Deeds, vol. 154, 402, deed of May 7, 1799.

126. Portsmouth Town Records, marriages.

127. New Hampshire, Rockingham County, Probate Court Records, Last Will and Testament, Pomp Spring, January 20, 1804.

128. New Hampshire, Rockingham County, Probate Court Records, Petition of Caesar Whidden to the Court of Probate, November 8, 1807.

129. The Fyals may have been named for an original home in Fyal/Fayal in the Portuguese Azores but more likely took their name from owners of Scottish ancestry, where Fyal is a recurrent surname.

130. Horton and Horton, *Black Bostonians,* 28.

131. Cunningham, "First Blacks of Portsmouth," 199, citing Horton and Horton, *Black Bostonians,* 56–66; Piersen, *Black Yankees,* 59.

132. This area was part of the ancient glebe that had been divided in 1705 and developed to increase the support of North Church.

133. New Hampshire, Rockingham County, Deeds, vol. 157, November 10, 1800.

134. Such compacted buildings are still visible on nearby Gate Street and other old streets in Portsmouth's Puddle Dock and South End neighborhood.

135. While Church Lane's original name survives in its current appellation of Church Street, the lane that crossed it has been renamed many times, including Prison Lane in the eighteenth century, Warren Street by 1850, and Porter Street today.

136. New Hampshire, Rockingham County, Probate Court Records, Petition of Caesar Whidden to the Court of Probate. Caesar was appointed executor.

137. *Portsmouth Oracle,* August 14, 1807, 4. "Average" ages of death given for that period seem to correspond to modern middle age. They are however skewed by inclusion of childhood deaths in an era of high infant and early childhood mortality. Those who reached adulthood could expect to live well beyond modern middle age, perhaps to sixty, and many individuals lived considerably longer.

138. *Portsmouth Oracle,* July 18, 1807.

139. *Portsmouth Oracle,* November 14, 1807.

140. The louvered exterior shutters, formerly called "blinds," popularly associated with New England today were just coming into use in the region and were not yet widespread.

141. Bushman, *Refinement of America.*

142. Garvin, *Historic Portsmouth,* 59.

143. Brewster, *Rambles,* vol. 2, 280.

144. Brewster, *Rambles,* vol. 2, 281.

145. Piersen, *Black Yankees,* 100–102.

146. Garvin, "Academic Architecture," 253.

147. Goodwin, "Pleasant Memories."

148. Dagenais, "The Black," 155, citing North Church Records.

149. Goodwin, "Pleasant Memories."

150. Garvin, "Academic Architecture," 500–502.

151. North Church Records, funerals, February 10, 1825.

152. *Portsmouth Journal,* June 19, 1830.

153. Pecor, *The Magician,* 70.

154. Brewster, *Rambles,* vol. 2, 209. The hotel was adapted from an old brick house once belonging to the Captain Benjamin Sherburne family. The house, the pier behind it, and the long row of warehouses that stood on the pier were destroyed in the fire of 1813.

155. Massachusetts, Roxbury, Vital Records, September 15, 1808; banns of marriage intentions also recorded.

156. Price, *Magic,* 54. Date of birth calculated from age at time of death.

157. Public Broadcasting System website. Prince Hall and others had tried to join white Masonic lodges in the late eighteenth century but had been refused. So they turned to a British military lodge, no. 441, garrisoned at Fort Independence in Massachusetts. Prince and fourteen other Black men were initiated into membership on March 6, 1775. Within a few months these Black men received a qualified permit for

an independent lodge, and on July 3, 1775, they organized African Lodge no. 1 and chose Prince Hall as their grand master. The lodge met at "the Golden Fleece," where Hall conducted his catering and leather-dressing business. Receipt of an official charter was delayed by the Revolution. The African Lodge received an official charter from London on May 6, 1787, and was renumbered 459. With Hall's help other lodges were organized in Philadelphia and in Providence, Rhode Island. Forty years later, when Richard Potter was a member of this lodge, it would gain independence from its British parent lodge.

158. Charles, "America's First Negro Magician," 77.

159. Andover, New Hampshire, Town Records, vol. I, 464, May 31, 1824.

160. Charles, "America's First Negro Magician," 77.

161. Known locales of Potters performances include Plaistow, New Hampshire, in 1814; Greenfield, Massachusetts, in 1819; Northampton, Massachusetts, in 1818; and repeated performances in Boston.

162. The Philadelphia painter Thomas Sully painted portraits of a number of actors and performers; his account books indicate he painted a Richard Potter in the 1810s, possibly the "celebrated ventriloquist." But the sitter and whereabouts of this painting too are unknown (per Robert Olson, Old Sturbridge Village Museum), nor has such a painting been located by the National Portrait Gallery's American Portraits project.

163. Brewster, *Rambles*, vol. 2, 209.

164. *Poetry of Vermont,* University of Vermont Press.

165. *Saratoga Sentinel,* August 12, 1828.

166. Per Robert Olson, Old Sturbridge Village Museum.

167. Additional Sources on Richard Potter: *Baltimore American & Commercial Daily Advertiser,* February 29, 1817; *Hampshire Gazette* (Massachusetts), September 18, 1818; Nell, *Colored Patriots;* Robert Lund, "Reports," *Abra* no. 905, June 1, 1963; Eastman, *History of Andover,* 425–427. All sources on Potter courtesy of research files of Robert Olson, Old Sturbridge Village Museum.

168. Some biographers propose that Potter was considerably older at his death.

169. Price, *Magic,* 54.

170. Metalious, *Peyton Place,* 11–12, 102, etc.

171. Dagenais, "The Black," 38, citing Boulton's edition of *New Hampshire Provincial Papers,* vol. IV, 442.

172. Riley, "John Stavers," 1, citing New Hampshire, Provincial Court Records (NHPCR), files 22971 and 28656. The ship's mate, John Stavers, beat the Black man, for which Warner took Stavers to court.

173. John Langdon Jr. Papers, New Hampshire Historical Society, 1895–1 V, box 1, folder 24. One of Langdon's notations records "3 Negroes [for] working on board ye ship £0/6/9 on January 21." Langdon's rentals continued at the rate of two, three, or four people per day for two weeks, with no rentals on every seventh day, presumably Sundays. Another bill from the same group of family papers enumerates expense for meals and drink to William Turlonge, plus "cash paid negros 12/ & two bowls yesterday." These were either free laborers or enslaved men whose owner had allowed them independent work for pay. Whether they worked as stevedores or were doing skilled repair work was not specified.

174. Morgan, *Documents of the American Revolution,* Vol. 9, 80. He was cruising the New England coast on the fourteen-gun sloop *Satisfaction,* enlisting seamen for the dangerous undertaking of privateering, or legally licensed piracy against British shipping. He wrote a letter to men named Cushing and White, presumably investors in the undertaking. In his letter Wheelwright casually mentions his purchase between comments on provisions and well wishes for his patrons. Wheelwright doesn't mention the joint owner of the slave.

175. Winslow, *Wealth and Honor,* 26, citing *New Hampshire Gazette,* October 5, 1776.

176. For example, Samuel Welles wrote from Natick, Massachusetts, that he was loaning or renting a man to Captain Hector McNeill of the Continental Navy: "I have Conveyed Caesar to you. He is an Artful Fellow. I must Request you Prevent his taking up his Wages more than what are absolutely Necessary. His Wages you will keep for me & his Prize Money, which I hope you will [have] such Success as to have a Prosperous Cruise. . . . P.S.—You will find him a very good Seaman, and conduct towards him as if he was your own, and on your Return Please to keep him on Board, for if he gets on Shore [I] am afraid of his running away." Winslow, *Wealth and Honor,* 27.

177. Winslow, "Wealth and Honour," 27; *Portsmouth Oracle,* April 5, 1800.

178. Bolster, "Black Seamen," 1174, 1177–1178, 1181, 1184–1185.

179. Bolster, "Black Seamen," 1179.

180. Bolster, "Black Seamen," 1183.

181. Bolster, "Black Seamen," 1180, 1184.

182. Bolster, "Black Seamen," 1183.

183. Bolster, "Black Seamen," 1184.

184. Bolster, "Black Seamen," 1184.

185. Bolster, "Black Seamen," 1185.

186. Bolster, "Black Seamen," 1192.

187. Bolster, "Black Seamen," 1188.

188. Bolster, "Black Seamen," 1194.

189. Bolster, "Black Seamen," 1196.

190. Brewster, *Portsmouth Jubilee,* 19.

191. Bolster, "Black Seamen," 1194–1196.

192. *Portsmouth Chronicle,* November 24, 1862.

193. Abrams, *Tall Ships of Newburyport,* 16. The *Montana* sailed with an all-Black crew under all-white officers. Ownership of the vessel was divided among six people, among whom John N. and William Cushing provided working direction. They were part of a prominent Newburyport shipping family and brothers of Caleb Cushing, secretary of state to President Franklin Pierce.

194. Those born in the Piscataqua basin were born in Exeter, Durham, Newington, Berwick, Kittery, Portsmouth, and New Castle.

195. United States, National Archives, Record Group 41, no. 2270, Portsmouth, New Hampshire, "Abstracts of Registers, Licenses, Enrollments, 1801–1805," Book D, 26, 32; Book E, 13, "Records of Registers, Licenses, Enrollments." These manuscript volumes were compiled by Portsmouth customs officer J[oseph] Whipple (a relation of the Whipples who owned Prince Whipple) and include a "Register of American Seamen in the District of Portsmouth in the State of New Hampshire pursuant to the Act entitled An Act for the relief & protection of American Seamen commencing the 1st July and ending the 30th September 1801." Whipple lists mariners who were given papers proving citizenship. These papers were meant as protection from impressment into foreign navies. These documents describe complexion using the terms "light," "dark," "molatto," "negro," "brown," and "black," as well as one each of "fair," "florid," and "dark/Indian." "Light" and "dark" seem to have been meant as variants of Caucasian complexions; "negro" and "black" were certainly individuals of African ancestry. "Brown" apparently was a variant of African ancestry too, as all cases have the last names of local and regional Anglo families, many of whom were slave owners in the eighteenth century.

196. *Portsmouth Directory,* 1821.

197. *Portsmouth Directory,* 1834. These included Robert Carman (lived on Dennett Street), Jacob Morris (on State Street), John Ross and William Smith (on Pleasant Street), and Isaac Webb (on South Street).

198. *Portsmouth Directory,* 1839. The nine mariners were Mark Ash Baker (who lived on Water Street, now Marcy Street); George Ball (State Street); James Ball (Sifton Street); Prince Champion (State Street at the same address as George Ball); Samuel Harmon (Daniel Street); George Hitchings (Bow Street); Joseph Jackson (Hancock Street); John Long (Penhallow Street); Joseph Stevens (Walden Lane).

199. *Portsmouth Directory,* 1827; *Portsmouth Directory,* 1834.

200. Bolster, "Black Seamen," 1190–1191. Statistical studies in the port of Providence, Rhode Island, show this to be the case there, and it was likely the pattern in most New England seaports.

201. Bolster, "Black Seamen," 1187. W. Jeffrey Bolster has published more research on Black mariners in *Black Jacks.*

202. Brewster, *Rambles* vol. 2, 293; Gurney, *Portsmouth Historic and Picturesque,* 135–136.

203. *Portsmouth Directory,* 1851. Curiously only one of the four mariners listed in 1851 was living close to the water: John T. Brown, who lived on Washington Street, two blocks from the river. James Wentworth, a mariner, lived with laborer Job Wentworth on Tanner Street, eight blocks from the river. Considerably farther inland on Wibird Street (probably the house on the south corner of today's Wibird and Chauncey Streets) Black mariners David and John Long (and laborer Charles Long) boarded.

204. *Portsmouth Directory,* 1821. In 1821 there were eight Black heads of household among these lanes and possibly more on adjacent Water Street. The eight Black households were those of Elvinia Cornelius (on Walden Lane); Philip Mizze, or Muzze, and Jason Sankee (Holmes Lane); Titus Folsom, Archilus Jamison, Dolly Simmons, and Dinah Wear (Partridge Lane); and Silvia Gerrish (Pray Lane). Black people known to have lived on Water (Marcy) Street may have been at this end of the street, adding to the numbers of Black people within a short distance of one another.

Portsmouth Directory, 1827. Six years later, in 1827, four of these households had moved away, four were still there (though one had moved only a block or two, remaining in the neighborhood), and six new ones had joined in, for a total of ten Black households. Elvinia Cornelius continued on Walden Lane, and now counted Dinah Barney and Jacob Morris, and Abraham Webb, among her neighbors. Philip Muzze still lived on Holmes Street, but Jason Sankee had moved one block to Partridge Street, where Dolly Simmons continued to live. They were joined on their street by __ Ashington, David Grant, and George Thomas. Silvia Gerrish still lived on Pray Street.

Portsmouth Directory, 1834. Seven years later, in 1834, the number of Black residents in these streets had dropped precipitously, leaving only three families, all on Walden Lane. These included Susan Ashington (probably the Ashington previously on Partridge), Andrew Barnet, and Pamelia Whipple.

Portsmouth Directory, 1839. Five years later, in 1839, there were still two Black households, again both on Walden Street. Laborer Andrew Barnet still lived on Walden Street, as well as a Black mariner, Joseph Stevens.

Portsmouth City Directories; Dagenais, "The Black." In a dozen years the neighborhood's Black households had peaked at ten, then dropped to two, paralleling the general decline in the number of Black families in Portsmouth.

205. United States Census, 1830, Rockingham County, New Hampshire, microfilm, Strawbery Banke Museum Library. Barnet's household included five boys and one girl under 10; one male and six females between 10 and 25; a male 25–36; one male and one female 36–55; and a male over 55, probably himself. Other examples: in 1830 Jacob Morris (over 55 years of age) had a teenage girl and a young adult woman (aged 24–36) in his household. Susan Ashington (over 36 years of age) had a teenage girl in her household.

206. By 1851 Andrew Barnet had moved from Walden to Holmes Lane, and a Black barber, George Tilmon II (who worked on Water Street), boarded on Holmes.

207. Of the several spellings of her name, this is the one that appears on her tombstone.

208. Dagenais, "The Black," Appendix 5, 160–161, citing Portsmouth Town Records, marriages, and North Church Records.

209. North Church Records.

210. *Portsmouth Directory;* United States Census, 1850, Rockingham County, New Hampshire, microfilm, Strawbery Banke Museum Library.

211. Prince, North Church Records, 1801; Anna, South Church Records, 1813; Elizabeth, North Church Records, 1828; Richard, North Church Records, 1828, Horace William, North Church Records, 1831; Nan, North Church Records, 1801.

212. *Portsmouth Directory*, 1834, 1839.

213. North Church Records, gifts to poor, January 1844, February 1844, February 1846.

214. *Portsmouth Directory*, 1851.

215. New Hampshire, Rockingham County, Deeds, vol. 425, 95. Deed of September 17, 1851. The deed of sale from her estate to Leonard Cotton on December 28, 1868, incorrectly cites her date of purchase as September 20, 1851.

216. Karnan, "Untold Tales," 10–12.

217. New Hampshire, Rockingham County, Probate Court Records, 1868.

218. Sammons, *Strawbery Banke Guidebook,* 37. Cotton was a sixty-eight-year-old merchant who lived on Washington Street in a large white hip-roofed house that still stands on the corner of Richmond Street. It was old-fashioned when Cotton bought it. Cotton recognized the economic need for rental properties in Portsmouth and the advantages of being a landlord. He had been investing in lots and tenant houses since he was in his thirties. By the time of his death in 1872 he owned more than forty properties in Portsmouth. One of these was Esther Mullinaux's house in Walden Lane.

Chapter 4. Abolition

1. Public Broadcasting System website.

2. Public Broadcasting System website. Representatives of the Society for the Abolition of the Slave Trade traveled to Liverpool and Bristol, Britain's two major slave ports, where they interviewed people with direct experience of the trade. Armed with the knowledge they gained there, they approached Member of Parliament William Wilberforce, who agreed to present their arguments to Parliament.

3. Chronicle of Slavery website.

4. Britannia History website. In that same year members of an ever conservative Parliament, frightened by the revolutions that had rocked Paris in 1789 and again in 1830, encouraged an additional reform to avoid a buildup of revolutionary pressure in their own country. They passed the Factory Act forbidding employment of children under nine and limiting the length of the workday for children in textile mills.

5. Colin Nickerson, "Quiet Protest to Mark Rest-

ing Place: Quebecer Aims for Recognition of Slave Cemetery," *Boston Sunday Globe,* June 16, 2002, A6.

6. Haiti shares the Greater Antilles island of Hispaniola with the country of the Dominican Republic. Haiti occupies the western third of the island.

7. Encarta website.

8. Public Broadcasting System website.

9. *Kalamu Magazine* web magazine.

10. Smithsonian Institution website.

11. United States Constitution, Article I, Section 9.

12. Legislative narrative from Crowley, "A Zeal for the Cause."

13. United States Constitution, Article I, Section 2, which mandates a decennial census by which representatives are apportioned.

14. *Portsmouth Directory,* 1834, 96.

15. Public Broadcasting System website. The society's organizers included Finley's brother-in-law Elias B. Caldwell (clerk of the Supreme Court), Francis Scott Key, George Washington's nephew Bushrod (who became first president of the society), Henry Clay, and Richard Rush (son of Benjamin Rush). Although Andrew Jackson was listed, it was without his consent, and he objected to colonization.

16. The 1830s saw a proliferation of special-audience periodical publications. This development was encouraged by several factors. The extension of voting rights to nonlandowners splintered economic and political interests. Steam presses and increased numbers of paper manufacturers made production more efficient and affordable. Literacy increased. Nationalist, evangelical, and scientific zeal encouraged self-improvement of every kind. Specialty periodicals included ones dedicated to farming, horticulture, mechanical trades, missionary ventures, and other types of activities.

17. The lyceum movement came to America in the mid-1820s, and by the 1830s there were hundreds of these self-improvement clubs in America, offering lectures on every conceivable practical subject and often on philosophical subjects too.

18. Blassingame, *Frederick Douglass Papers,* 23–24.

19. Garrison *filii, Garrison,* vol. 2, 126, n3.

20. Blassingame, *Frederick Douglass Papers,* 23.

21. Blassingame, *Frederick Douglass Papers,* 23–24.

22. William Ladd file, Moffatt-Ladd Collection, Portsmouth Athenaeum.

23. Portsmouth *Directory,* 1839.

24. William Ladd file, Moffatt-Ladd House Collection, Portsmouth Athenaeum.

25. Public Broadcasting System website.

26. Tuveson, "People of Color," 1. Wentworth Cheswell had died three years earlier after a prominent career in public offices including Committee of Safety member, assessor, auditor, coroner, selectman, and justice of the peace in nearby Newmarket, New Hampshire.

27. Bolster, "Black Seamen," 1192.

28. Garrison *filii, Garrison,* vol. 1, 517. Six Mississippians offered $20,000 for William Lloyd Garrison's assassination.

29. Borden and Graham, *Portrait of a Nation,* 209–210.

30. The annexation of Texas and vast additional territories (now New Mexico, Arizona, Utah, Colorado, and California) originated Mexico's long-term ill will toward the United States.

31. Fillmore later headed the anti-immigrant (Know-Nothing) Party, opposed Lincoln, and supported Johnson during Reconstruction.

32. Handbill, April 24, 1851, facsimile, African Meetinghouse Museum, Boston.

33. Voices of Maine—Visible Black History website.

34. This would be an alternate route to a southern railroad route recently made possible by the Gadsden Purchase from Mexico for $10 million of what are now southern Arizona and New Mexico. From synoptic Peirce biography at United States White House website.

35. Melish, *Disowning Slavery,* 76.

36. Melish, *Disowning Slavery,* 3.

37. Brewster, *Rambles,* vol. 1, 230; Candee, *Building Portsmouth,* 99–101. Prior to 1798 customs functions took place at the home of Eleazer Russell on Market Street in the vicinity of today's Sheraton Hotel. Sometime after 1802 customs duties were collected in an office on Market Street in Merchant's Row, the long row of contiguous buildings backing onto Ceres Street. Then import duties were collected by Colonel Joseph Whipple in an office adjoining his residence on State Street. In 1817 the federal government purchased as the first permanent home for the Portsmouth customs office a brick structure recently erected on a site cleared by the great fire of 1813. It still stands on Penhallow Street at the corner of Daniel Street. Captains or supercargoes reported imports to officers in a large room occupying the entire second floor. This new customhouse, now called the Old Custom House, was succeeded in the 1850s by a new granite federal office building housing a post office on the first floor, a series of rooms for the customs office on the second floor, and the federal district court on the third. This building served for a century and

still stands on Pleasant Street at the corner of State Street. It is known locally as the Old Post Office building. Since 1913, when the Portsmouth customs district was absorbed into a larger regional district, only representative agents of that district have been stationed in Portsmouth.

38. Candee, *Building Portsmouth,* 69 ff., 114. Carley, *Cuba,* 80: In the early nineteenth century the Spanish monarchy continued the loosening of trade restrictions in Cuba initiated by the Bourbon monarchy, increasing sugar cultivation, introducing coffee cultivation, commencing railroad construction, and bringing a flood of new slaves. With these developments came an increased export of mahogany, soon much used in New England furniture manufacturing. Jobe, *Portsmouth Furniture,* passim. The next generation of Portsmouth furniture makers included William Badger, Charles Colcord, William G. Nowell, J. H. and W. Pickering, Eldridge Remick, Joseph C. Somerby, and others.

39. Later the house's furnishings were much augmented as descendants inherited from other early-nineteenth-century Portsmouth households. The house survives as the Rundlett-May House and is opened to the public seasonally by its owner, the Society for the Preservation of New England Antiquities.

40. Penrose, *Goodwin,* 13, 26; Candee, *Building Portsmouth,* 148.

41. Sammons, *Strawbery Banke Guidebook.* Goodwin's house stood on Islington Street. To save it from demolition it was moved a few blocks to a corner of the Strawbery Banke Museum grounds, where it is open to the public seasonally, furnished and interpreted to represent the mid-nineteenth century.

42. Legislative and African Squadron narrative from Crowley, "A Zeal for the Cause"; *Portsmouth Journal,* June 21, 1851; *U.S. Nautical Magazine,* vol. 3 (1855–56), 9–10, by Griffiths; the latter two transcribed in Maritime History Virtual Archives website. Gateway to Maine website, Eliot page; sales correspondence at E-History website. Capture narrative in Banks, *History of Maine,* 242, reprint of William H. Rowe's *Maritime History of Maine* (New York: W. W. Norton & Co., 1948, 166–187); and at Houghton Mifflin College Division, *Ships of the World* website. A painting of the capture of the *Nightingale* appears at National Museums and Galleries on Merseyside Marine Paintings website. The *Nightingale* was launched in June of 1851 from Samuel Hanscom Jr.'s yard in South Eliot, Maine, on Portsmouth

Harbor. September 6 of that year it was sold at auction in Boston for $43,500 to Davis & Co. It sailed for Sampson & Tappan's Pioneer Line of Australian Packets. After many voyages carrying tea and passengers it was sold in Salem in 1860. On July 6, 1861, the seized vessel was sold at a United States marshal's sale by virtue of a writ of *venditioni exponas* to the United States government for $13,000 and refitted as a coal and store ship. Later it was sold and reentered private commercial trade. "Prince of Slavers" Francis Bowen later commanded the side-wheeler *Virginius* as a gunrunner.

43. Melish, *Disowning Slavery,* 3, citing Benedict Anderson.

44. Candee, *Building Portsmouth,* 103. The Temple stood on the northwest corner of Chestnut and Porter Streets. It was built within the shell of an earlier Protestant house of worship and carried over the name "temple" from that function. In 1876 it was replaced by an opera house now called Music Hall. The one-thousand-seat auditorium called the Temple opened in 1844. It was owned by a group of businessmen who rented or loaned it for lectures, religious services, and concerts. Since the mid-1820s and through the '30s and '40s Americans had founded self-improvement societies that pursued their goals through guest lectures, scientific demonstrations, and debates, typically convened in schoolhouses, hotels, or meetinghouses. Starting in the 1830s the topic of slavery cropped up in the oratory of all these oratorical contexts. Many of the leading abolitionists, Black and white, spoke in the Temple. Abolition and Lyceum societies alike brought guest orators to many New England towns. Their programs added to an established oratorical tradition related to holidays, centennials, and elections.

45. *Portsmouth Directory,* 1834. The Portsmouth Lyceum was founded in 1833.

46. *Portsmouth Journal of Literature and Politics,* July 2, 1841. Kelly later lectured under her married name, Abigail Kelly Foster.

47. Thayer, *Story of a Religious Democracy,* 34.

48. Blassingame, *Frederick Douglass Papers,* itinerary, xciii.

49. Blassingame, *Frederick Douglass Papers,* itinerary, xciii.

50. Quarles, *Black Abolitionists,* 63

51. Blassingame, *Frederick Douglass Papers,* 26.

52. *Portsmouth Daily Morning Chronicle,* September 7, 1852.

53. Encyclopedia Americana website.

54. *Portsmouth Daily Morning Chronicle,* October 21,

1852 (no speaker named); October 30, 1852 (names Horace Mann). Horace Mann was described as a convincing but sedate speaker. The *Chronicle* blandly reported that "his style of speaking was partly argumentative, and when so, it was strong and to the point; but he is not a wit, and his attempts in this line were generally failures. The main drift of his discourse was to expose and oppose the Fugitive Slave Act—and to lash Mr Fillmore and the Whig party severely for upholding and submitting to it, —not forgetting to bring in the Democratic party, and allude to Gen. Pierce's New Boston speech."

55. *Portsmouth Morning Chronicle*, February 23, 1853.

56. *Portsmouth Daily Morning Chronicle*, February 28, 1853.

57. *Portsmouth Daily Morning Chronicle*, April 19, 1853.

58. *Portsmouth Daily Morning Chronicle*, June 25, 1853.

59. Spartacus Educational website.

60. Quarles, *Black Abolitionists*, 26.

61. Quarles, *Black Abolitionists*, 181.

62. Quarles, *Black Abolitionists*, 56.

63. Quarles, *Black Abolitionists*, 57.

64. Quarles, *Black Abolitionists*, 58.

65. Quarles, *Black Abolitionists*, 133–134.

66. Ignatiev in his 1995 book *How the Irish Became White*.

67. *New Hampshire Gazette*, March 24, 1864; Takaki, *A Different Mirror*, 149–154.

68. Quarles, *Black Abolitionists*, 174; Public Broadcasting System website.

69. Quarles, *Black Abolitionists*, 218–219.

70. Quarles, *Black Abolitionists*, 202.

71. *Portsmouth Morning Chronicle*, February 1, 1854.

72. Quarles, *Black Abolitionists*, 166.

73. Quarles, *Black Abolitionists*, 168.

74. *Portsmouth Daily Morning Chronicle*, February 10, 1854.

75. *Portsmouth Daily Morning Chronicle*, February 14, 1854.

76. *Portsmouth Daily Morning Chronicle*, March 29, 1854.

77. Garrison *filii*, *Garrison*, vol. 1, 517. Six Mississippians offered $20,000 for Garrison's assassination.

78. *Portsmouth Daily Morning Chronicle*, March 31, 1854.

79. Melish, *Disowning Slavery*, 76. United states Census, 1840, 1850. Inter-University Consortium for Political and Social Research (ICPSR) website. The 1840 census lists a slave in New Hampshire; the 1850 census lists none.

80. Public Broadcasting System website.

81. Quarles, *Black Abolitionists*, 224.

82. Quarles, *Black Abolitionists*, 233.

83. Borden and Graham, *Portrait of a Nation*, 216–231. For information on Civil War soldiers, both Black and white, see the National Park Service's website database.

84. Quarles, *Black Abolitionists*, 63.

85. Quarles, *Black Abolitionists*, 56.

86. Quarles, *Black Abolitionists*, 58.

87. *Portsmouth Chronicle*, March 15, 1862.

88. *Portsmouth Chronicle*, March 17, 1862; October 11, 1862; October 17, 1862; October 20, 1862; November 11, 1862; November 24, 1862.

89. Public Broadcasting System website.

90. Public Broadcasting System website.

91. Quarles, *Black Abolitionists*, 15.

92. Quarles, *Black Abolitionists*, 61.

93. Quarles, *Black Abolitionists*, 62, 66. Printing musical notation was a specialized trade; most songbooks included only words and named suitable familiar tunes without printing the music. Tunes were published in separate volumes called tune books.

94. Quarles, *Black Abolitionists*, 94.

95. Rorabaugh, *Alcoholic Republic*, passim.

96. Quarles, *Black Abolitionists*, 149.

97. Quarles, *Black Abolitionists*, 227.

98. Quarles, *Black Abolitionists*, 134–135.

99. Quarles, *Black Abolitionists*, 137.

100. Quarles, *Black Abolitionists*, 137.

101. Quarles, *Black Abolitionists*, 135.

102. *Portsmouth Chronicle*, October 11, 1862.

103. Brighton, *They Came to Fish*, 160–162.

104. Brighton, *They Came to Fish*, 163–164.

105. Brighton, *They Came to Fish*, 162–163.

106. Brighton, *They Came to Fish*, 162.

107. Garvin, *Historic Portsmouth*, 132.

108. Public Broadcasting System website.

109. Garvin, *Historic Portsmouth*, 252, n43.

110. Public Broadcasting System website.

111. Garvin, *Historic Portsmouth*, 132.

112. *Portsmouth Daily Evening Times*, December 29, 1881; Maine, York County, Probate Court Records, Austin Will, 1871, probated March 1878; *Portsmouth Directories*. Austin had long lived on Court Street behind the Unitarian South Church.

113. *Portsmouth Daily Evening Times*, December 29, 1881.

114. *Portsmouth Daily Evening Times*, January 3, 1882.

115. *Kalamu Magazine*, web magazine. Carley, *Cuba*, 50, 80. Slavery had a long presence in Cuba but burgeoned in 1762 during a brief British occupancy, which temporarily broke the Spanish trade monopoly and connected the island to the British slave trade. Administrative changes origi-

nating with the Spanish Bourbon monarchy and continuing at the turn of the nineteenth century would cause a tremendous expansion of sugar and coffee plantations and an increasing demand for slaves.

116. *Portsmouth Herald,* January 2, 1923. By the sixtieth anniversary of emancipation in 1923 the program had moved to the rooms of the Granite State Glee Club. The expanded program included national songs, solo anthems, orchestral music, an invocation, and three addresses. The addresses were given by the mayor, the commander of the local Grand Army of the Republic (Civil War veterans), and local Black community leader Hayward Burton, who spoke on the "doings and progress" made by Portsmouth's Black population 1863–1923. Orations were followed by more music, then a collation of sandwiches, coffee, ice cream, and cake, continuing late into the evening.

117. The 1958 celebration was held in the Ladies' Auxiliary Hall, a large public room on the third floor above 64 Market Street.

118. The Austin-Lincoln fund remains intact, and the passage of time has allowed it to grow a bit. Its interest has been used in recent years by Portsmouth's New Hope Baptist Church to fund a Juneteenth celebration (a gospel music concert at the Music Hall) and by the Portsmouth Black Heritage Trail, Inc., to pay for its first bronze site marker on the waterfront. The fund is managed by the City of Portsmouth Trustees of Trust Funds.

Chapter 5. Community

1. Lemann, *Promised Land,* chapter 1, passim.
2. Oral history interview of Frances Tilley Satchell (1910–92) by Valerie Cunningham.
3. *Africana.com* web magazine.
4. Loewen, *Lies across America,* 136–143.
5. Steven G. Vegh, "Exhibit Includes Black Maine Bishop," 9B–10B, citing the Reverend Albert S. Foley, "Bishop Healy: Beloved Outcast," a biography. Healy was born in Georgia of an enslaved woman and an Irish Catholic father. State law did not recognize their interracial marriage, so they lived as common-law spouses. Technically the father owned his wife and their ten children, but they chose to live as a free family.

   James was sent to Quaker schools in New York and New Jersey, then to the Jesuit school Holy Cross in Worcester, Massachusetts. He then studied for the priesthood at the Sulpician Seminary in Montreal and at the Saint Sulpice seminary in Paris, where he was ordained at Notre Dame in 1854.

   He was assigned to a parish in Boston when relations between Black residents and Irish immigrants were tense as they vied for work in a place and time when white Yankees scorned and marginalized both groups. Healy had much to endure in bigoted New England. He was considered Black, legally illegitimate, the son of a slave owner in a region that was hesitantly accepting abolition, and Roman Catholic in a region that was overwhelmingly radical Protestant and overtly anti-Catholic.

   Healy was consecrated bishop of Portland in 1875. A few days later Yankee bigots burned Saint Joseph's Church in East Machias, Maine. By the end of his first summer Healy had zigzagged thirty thousand miles across Maine and New Hampshire visiting Roman Catholic Acadian, French Canadian, Indian, and Irish families and parishes. He established 60 new churches, 68 missions, 18 convents, and 18 schools while bishop. There were about 300 Black Roman Catholics in Maine.

   Growing numbers of Roman Catholics in New England necessitated dividing the Diocese of Portland; in 1884 New Hampshire was set off from Portland as a new diocese. In the decade between his consecration in 1875 and the division of the diocese in 1884 Healy probably visited Immaculate Conception Parish in Portsmouth for confirmation and other important church activities.

6. Kaplan, *Black Presence,* 75, 76, and 78.
7. Kaplan, *Black Presence,* 88–89.
8. Kaplan, *Black Presence,* 90–92.
9. Public Broadcasting System website. Jones's response was issued on August 12, 1794.
10. Kaplan, *Black Presence,* 90–92.
11. New Hampshire, Rockingham County, Deeds, vol. 90, 519–520.
12. "A Testament to Maine's Black History," *Boston Sunday Globe,* February 8, 1998, B1.
13. *Portsmouth Chronicle,* December 24, 1879.
14. People's Baptist Church, Sunday bulletin, fiftieth anniversary celebration, September 26, 1943.
15. At that time the Middle Street Baptist Church met for worship in a brick church that stood across the street from their present location. It stood on the southwest corner of State and Middle Streets, a site now occupied by a gas station soon to be replaced by condominiums.

16. People's Baptist Church, Sunday bulletin, fiftieth Anniversary celebration, September 26, 1943.

17. *Portsmouth Herald,* January 14, 1921, January 17, 1921.

18. *Portsmouth Herald,* obituary, January 19 and 22, 1920.

19. Candee, *Building Portsmouth,* 146.

20. Peterson, "Boston University," reports that Boston University, founded in 1867 by Methodists, was among the region's leaders in integration as an extension of its dedication to equality of opportunity in education. It was the first Massachusetts institution to admit Black students and to graduate a Black woman with an M.D. degree.

21. People's Baptist Church, Sunday bulletin, October 26, 1952, fifty-ninth anniversary celebration, *Portsmouth Herald,* October 28, 2002. Ministers down to the fiftieth anniversary of People's Baptist Church were James R. Randolph, 1893–95; George O. Bullock, summer 1896; James O. Cornish, 1896–98; Robert L. Harris, 1899–1904; William H. McLean, 1905; W. A. Burch, 1906; L. G. Nichols, 1907–9; John L. Davis, 1912–17; James R. Randolph, 1918–22; James B. Riley, 1923–25; J. R. Custis, 1925–27; L. G. Nichols, 1928–30; Henry B. Harris, 1930–37; Davis S. Klugh, 1939–41; E. E. Thompson (supply), 1942; Charles R. McCreary, 1943–?

22. Candee, *Building Portsmouth,* 139; *Portsmouth Directories.* This old building stood at 215 Hanover Street. It was built in 1853 by the Advent Christian Church, which in 1946 had just moved to a new church on Summer Street. The old church was on the north side of Hanover Street between Vaughan and Bridge Streets (roughly where Maplewood Avenue now crosses Hanover).

23. Hyde, "Property of the African Methodist Episcopal Zion Church."

24. Christian, *Black Saga,* 429–437.

25. "History of New Hope Baptist Church."

26. The United Baptist Convention of New Hampshire is now known as the American Baptist Convention of Vermont and New Hampshire.

27. "History of New Hope Baptist Church." The succession of ministers and spiritual leaders at New Hope Baptist Church from its founding to 2002 is Reverend Raymond Hailes, Reverend Soloman Stith, Deacon Walter Johnson, Reverend Ralph G. Henley, Sister Elease Gray, Reverend Willard Ashley, Reverend Foster L. Covington Jr., Reverend Frank Parker, Reverend Garth Baker-Fletcher, Deacon Nathaniel Holloway, Reverend Dr. Arthur Hilson.

28. Dr. Parsons's lot occupied the west side of Chestnut Street from Porter to State Streets (this block is now discontinued from use by cars). His house faced State Street; his office was in the rear, at 3 Chestnut Street.

29. *Portsmouth Directory,* 1896. Straughn lived at 46 Bow Street.

30. Burton's house still stands at 179 Union Street.

31. Estes and Goodman, *Changing Humors,* 214. The hospital was on Junkins Avenue. In the last quarter of the twentieth century the hospital moved to a suburban site, and the city bought the old and much expanded building and adapted it for use as a city hall.

32. Valerie Cunningham, oral histories collected from Portsmouth's Black elders, and personal reminiscence.

33. Garvin and Grigg, *Historic Portsmouth,* 115.

34. *Portsmouth Herald,* February 3, 1919.

35. *Portsmouth Herald,* February 13, 1919. *Portsmouth Directory,* 1920. From the combined evidence of newspaper accounts and *Portsmouth Directories,* it appears that Grace's drugstore was at 14 Market Square and the door to the staircase to the rooms above it was numbered 16. Even today the commercial space at street level and the door to the stairway have different street numbers. Another upstairs tenant at the time of the Comfort Club was A. J. McKnight's office, also at number 16. A photo (c. 1920) in the Strawbery Banke Museum collection shows the building with McKnight's advertising painted across its upper facade and a rod supporting an oversize mortar and pestle jutting diagonally from the building's corner over the intersection of Daniel and Pleasant Streets.

36. *Portsmouth Herald,* September 27, 1919.

37. *Portsmouth Herald,* March 19, 1920.

38. Order of the Knights of Pythias website. At the time of the Pythians' incorporation all the routine affairs of the District of Columbia, major and minor, were administered directly by Congress. The group applied to Congress for a charter as it would have applied to a state government had it been founded elsewhere.

39. The Kings and Reeds lived on Manning Street in the short block between Howard and Gates Streets.

40. *Portsmouth Directory,* 1926.

41. More information about Black attorneys is provided in a following chapter about Louis Gregory.

42. *Portsmouth Herald,* March 29, 1920.

43. *Portsmouth Directory,* 1881. Girouard, *Return to Camelot,* chapters 16, 17, 18, passim, and 147–149, 252, 255–257. The fraternal movement grew in

Portsmouth throughout the nineteenth century. White men founded many clubs or lodges of national and international groups (including a group of whites illogically called the "Red Men"). Portsmouth lodges (virtually all white) included several Odd Fellows lodges (founded in 1844, 1845, 1846, 1868, and 1871); Knights of Honor (1876, 1879); United Order of Pilgrim Fathers (1880); Patrons of Husbandry (Grange, 1874); the Red Men; the Royal Arcanum Alpha Council (1878); Sovereigns of Industry (1874); the United Order of the Golden Cross (1879). Portsmouth also had local lodges of veterans' and military groups, such as the Grand Army of the Republic (1878), the American Legion of Honor (1879), and others. Boys' equivalents were emerging by the opening of the twentieth century. This gave rise to such groups as the Boy Scouts, Boys' Brigade, and Chivalrous Boys in Britain and America. Women joined the impulse through ladies' auxiliaries or undertook charitable and social work in their own societies. For example Portsmouth had eight temperance societies (when Portsmouth had fifty-five saloons). Turn-of-the-twentieth-century Portsmouth also had many musical societies, bands, sports clubs, gyms, and other voluntary associations. Men's groups favored quasi-medieval titles: commander, generalissimo, prelate, warden, standard bearer, sword bearer, master, hospitaler, almoner, grand master, steward, chaplain, scribe, orator, guide, dictator, guardian. Other groups used thematic titles: veterans used military titles; the Pilgrim Fathers used colonial-revival titles like governor, lieutenant governor, master-at-arms, and sergeant-at-arms; while the Red Men's officers were sachem, sagamore, sentinel, prophet, keeper of wampum, etcetera. These groups enjoyed great popularity; membership in each of Portsmouth's groups ranged from 100 to 300 members, with most at 100–150 members. This is the context in which the Comfort Club, Black Pythians, the Colored Citizens League, and the Ku Klux Klan were founded.

44. *Portsmouth Herald,* November 16, 1922.
45. Fifteenth Amendment: "The right of citizens of the United States to vote shall not be denied or abridged by the United States or by any State on account of race, color, or previous condition of servitude."
46. *Portsmouth Directory,* 1881, 203–205.
47. Price, *Magic,* 54, in re: Richard Potter.
48. *Portsmouth Herald,* June 19, 1926.
49. Bedford and Colbourn, *The Americans,* vol. 2, 237.

50. Bedford and Colbourn, *The Americans,* vol. 2, 371–372.
51. *Portsmouth Herald,* November 12, 1925.
52. *Portsmouth Herald,* June 1, 1926.
53. *Portsmouth Herald,* July 12, 1926.
54. *Portsmouth Herald,* August 28, 1926.
55. *Portsmouth Directory,* 1920, 1923, 1928, 1941. Not much information on Charles H. Partridge has come to light. Among the city directories, a Charles H. Partridge (and wife Florence) appears only in 1928. They lived on Chapel Street on the south corner of Chapel Court, opposite Saint John's Church. He is listed as a machinist and as having a telephone. He is not listed in Rye from 1920 to 1941, where many of the local Klan activities took place. Apparently he had a short but active residence in Portsmouth.
56. The city hall at that time occupied a converted Victorian high school building on Daniel Street at the corner of Chapel Street, almost back-to-back with Charles H. Partridge's 1928 residence a block away. Councilman Donovan objected. Mayor Dale, Frederickson, Payne, Matthews, Rand, Littlefield, Harmon, and Burkhart voted to approve. Councilman Hersey was absent.
57. At this meeting all but two councillors (Hersey and Harmon) voted to rescind the permit. Mayor Dale's vote was not published.
58. *Portsmouth Herald,* March 16, 1927, March 19, 1927.
59. *Portsmouth Herald,* July 13, 1927. Evidently the city council didn't wish to repeat its March experience. They denied permits for the parade and field day (with minority votes in favor cast by councilmen Harmon, Hersey, and Littlefield). The fireworks permit request was tabled. The city council's reversals on permitting may represent lack of legal grounds for denial or personal approval of the Klan.
60. *Portsmouth Herald,* September 6, 1927.
61. By the 1920s the Black community had been part of Portsmouth for a little less than three centuries. A Roman Catholic congregation had been part of Portsmouth for nearly a century. Jews had been part of the local community for fifty years and had had a temple for about twenty years.
62. *Portsmouth Herald,* March 21, 22, 23, 1928.
63. Brown, "Genesis of the Negro Lawyer," in *Making a Living,* 389–397. Black people began to practice law in America when Macon B. Allen was admitted to the bar of Portland, Maine, in 1844. Allen was subsequently admitted to the Massachusetts bar, which became the principal locus of Black lawyers in nineteenth- and early-twentieth-century America. As recently as 1950

there were only forty Black lawyers in all of New England.

64. *Louis G. Gregory.*

65. The Gregorys lived at 47 South Street in a house that backs onto South Mill Pond.

66. Gregory's legacy and memory are preserved in a Baha'i institute named for him in Hemingway, South Carolina. His childhood home in Charleston has recently opened as a museum.

67. They first moved to a house on Washington Street near the corner of Court, approximately where the Temple Israel parking lot is now, then moved to Hunking Street in 1914.

68. This longer-term home was on Washington Street opposite today's Strawbery Banke Museum grounds.

69. Still on Washington Street, they now lived in an apartment near their earlier Washington Street residence.

70. Alberta now lived on Court Street west of Washington Street, a block away from her previous residence.

71. Henrietta lived on Liberty Street, which is now absorbed into Strawbery Banke Museum. The museum has reverted to Liberty Street's eighteenth-century name of Horse Lane.

72. Virgil's longest and final residence was at 50 Brewster Street (off Islington Street) in the West End, opposite the western terminus of Hanover Street.

73. Oral history interview of Elizabeth Virgil by Valerie Cunningham; "A Reception in Honor of Ms. Elizabeth Virgil."

74. Oral history interview of Elizabeth Virgil by Valerie Cunningham; Casanave, "Learning to Look at Racism."

75. Diggins, *Proud Decades*, 28.

76. Oral histories and reminiscences collected by Valerie Cunningham.

77. Doris recalls enlisting the same day as Eileen Dondero, who later, as Eileen Dondero Foley, served several terms as Portsmouth's mayor.

78. Diggins, *Proud Decades*, 29.

79. Diggins, *Proud Decades*, 27–28.

80. Nelson, *Posters That Won the War*, 77, citing Arthur Upham Pope's book *America Organizes to Win the War.*

81. Candee, *Building Portsmouth*, 188–190.

82. Oral histories and reminiscence collected by Valerie Cunningham.

83. Diggins, *Proud Decades*, 29–31.

84. Today the Portsmouth Naval Shipyard no longer builds. It specializes in repair and refitting of nuclear-powered submarines.

85. Interview with Jim Dolph, curator, Portsmouth Naval Shipyard Museum. Navy Yard employment statistics were not kept in a way that recorded race. War-era employment records are on file in Saint Louis, where they are sealed to nonfamily members because they include social security and other private information. For security reasons photography was kept to a minimum during the war. As a result information about wartime Black employees of the Navy Yard remains anecdotal rather than statistical.

86. Interview of Hazel Sinclair by Valerie Cunningham.

87. Oral History interview of Doris Moore by Valerie Cunningham. V-E Day, Victory in Europe Day, was May 8, 1945, the day of the Nazi surrender.

88. When integration was required after the war, the navy proved particularly resistant and became the least favored branch of service for Black men, though there were still many in its ranks.

89. This commercial laundry stood approximately where the Prescott Park test flower beds are today.

90. Oral History interviews of Anna Jones by Valerie Cunningham, March 28, 1996.

91. Nelson, *Posters That Won the War*, 78–79, 81.

92. *Portsmouth Directory*, 1943. Portsmouth's USO halls were at 143 Congress and 135 Daniel Streets, and its club was at 53 Market Street near the corner of Commercial Alley.

93. Local oral tradition, collected by Valerie Cunningham.

94. People's Baptist Church, Sunday bulletin, February 1, 1953.

95. Eatonville, Florida, was also home to author Zora Neale Hurston (1891–1960).

96. They lived on Hanover Street for a while and then on Gate Street. Biographical details from oral history interview of Rosary Broxay Cooper by Valerie Cunningham.

97. Diggins, *Proud Decades*, 15.

98. Sitkoff, "American Home Front," 51.

99. Oral history interview of Rosary Broxay Cooper by Valerie Cunningham.

100. Salzman, Smith, and West, *Encyclopedia of African-American Culture and History*, vol. 4, 1792.

101. Leavitt, *Florence*, 137; McCarthy, *Florence*, 28–30. When the head of a statue from the destroyed Santa Trinita Bridge was missing, rumors flew that it had been retrieved and taken by a Black solider. The head was eventually recovered from the riverbed, where the rest of the

statue had been found amid the bridge rubble. Racism remains widespread among fair northern Italians toward darker southern Italians, an unresolved by-product of unification in the 1860s and '70s. The assumption that one of the Black American soldiers took the sculpture was an expression of this racism. Americans are not unique.

102. This house is on the east side of Washington Street between Gates and Hancock Streets. They bought it circa 1948.

103. People's Baptist Church, Sunday bulletin, February 1, 1953, homage to Rosary Cooper.

104. Portsmouth city hall was then housed in a former high school built of red brick in the 1850s on Daniel Street at the corner of Chapel Street.

105. People's Baptist Church, Sunday bulletin, February 1, 1953.

106. Diggins, *Proud Decades,* chapter 1, passim.

107. Twenty years later, identical arguments successfully discouraged President Clinton from allowing Gay Americans to serve in the armed forces.

108. Salzman, Smith, and West, *Encyclopedia of African-American Culture and History,* vol. 4, 1793–1794.

Chapter 6. Civil Rights

1. John Staudenmaier, University of Detroit-Mercy, lecture for Portsmouth Community Forum, March 22, 1996.

2. *Africana.com* web magazine.

3. Georgia flag: *Boston Sunday Globe,* March 2, 2003, A13; South Carolina flag: ABC News website.

4. Age discrimination against those over forty, reportable to the Equal Employment Opportunity Commission (EEOC), was barred by a separate Age Discrimination Employment Act (ADEA) passed in 1967.

5. Bedford and Colbourn, *The Americans,* vol. 2, 453–456, 486–491.

6. *Africana.com* web magazine.

7. White, *Lost Boundaries.*

8. Local Black residents who appeared in the film included Mrs. Idella Cooper, her daughter and son-in-law Jane Cooper Faust and Leon Faust, and their children Earl, Judith, and Owen. Also in the film were Clayton and Hazel Sinclair, Richard Johnson, Jane, Marjorie, and Harry Jones Sr., and others.

9. The Reverend Mr. Robert Hayes Dunn was minister of the Episcopal church. Oral histories, interviews, reminiscences collected by Valerie Cunningham.

10. *Portsmouth Directories,* 1950s. Cobbs's new house was at 149–151 Deer Street.

11. Thomas Cobbs in newsletter *NAACP Reports,* June 1965.

12. Personal reminiscences by Valerie Cunningham and Jean Potter.

13. Story assembled from taped interview with Emerson Reed (January 10, 1991, by Valerie Cunningham), written reminiscence by Jean Potter (letter to "Uncle Sy," January 2003), and phone interview with Jean Potter (February 2003).

14. Thomas Cobbs in newsletter *NAACP Reports,* June 1965.

15. Thomas Cobbs in newsletter *NAACP Reports,* June 1965.

16. Undated report in SCORR Papers, circa 1965.

17. Warner, *Urban Wilderness,* 239–246, 37–52, 270–271.

18. Jacobs, *Death and Life,* passim.

19. Sammons, *Strawbery Banke Guidebook,* passim. In the 1950s Puddle Dock was about half Anglo-American and half Americans of other ethnic descent, most in the second or third generation. It was sometimes perceived as a Jewish neighborhood because this portion of its population had peaked in the early twentieth century at about 10–15% of the neighborhood, and the temple stood (and remains) one block away. Two streets and about sixty buildings were taken out. The outdoor history museum was able to preserve about forty buildings on their original sites amid this much disrupted and garbled landscape. The museum is called Strawbery Banke, reviving a name used briefly in the seventeenth century for what is now the downtown area of the British colonial settlement.

20. The North End was popularly viewed as the Italian district in reference to a prominent part of its population. Like the Puddle Dock neighborhood, its makeup with ethnically diverse. Preservationists were dismayed to see numerous eighteenth-century buildings demolished by urban renewal. A band of history-minded people saved several buildings, moving them to a parcel on a knoll within the urban renewal district, where they were renovated into a kind of history theme park/office complex called "The Hill."

21. Bedford and Colbourn, *The Americans: A Brief History,* Vol. 2, 470, 475–476, 486–491.

22. Christian, *Black Saga,* 429, quoting a book by Carmichael and Charles Hamilton delineating the meaning of Black Power.

23. Christian, *Black Saga,* 429–430.

24. SCORR papers; Letter, Helen Ebbeson to members, September 11, 1964.

25. SCORR papers; Letter, Helen Ebbeson to members, September 11, 1964.

26. SCORR papers; Letter, Helen Ebbeson to members, September 11, 1964.

27. SCORR papers; Undated brochure, "What Is SCORR?"; undated 1965 and 1966 newsletters; *Portsmouth Periscope,* 1965; *The SCORR Card* newsletter, January 1966; *Portsmouth Herald,* April 1967; *Portsmouth Herald,* April 20, 1967; *Portsmouth Herald,* May 1968.

28. Candee, *Building Portsmouth,* 190.

29. *Portsmouth Herald,* July 8, 1965.

30. Wording from Article 34 of the Universal Code of Military Justice, for the violation of which Harvey and Daniels were convicted.

31. SCORR papers; copy of Letter, the Reverend John D. Swanson of Christ Church Portsmouth to his congregation (n.d., probably spring 1969), quoting Murray Polner in *Commonweal* magazine, March 28, 1969, issue. Personal reminiscence, Valerie Cunningham.

32. *The SCORR Card* newsletter, July 1967.

33. *The SCORR Card* newsletter, November 1965.

34. *The SCORR Card* newsletter, April 1967.

35. SCORR papers; *Portsmouth Herald,* news clippings, May, July, 1968.

Chapter 7. Living with Diversity

1. E-mail correspondence, Valerie Cunningham to Mark Sammons, Thursday, June 3, 1999.

2. Equal Employment Opportunity Commission website; General Service Administration, "Civil Liberties, Civil Rights, Equal Opportunity, and Discrimination" webpage. Protections based on age were added in 1965 and 1975, and based on disabilities in 1990. An Age Discrimination in Employment Act was passed in 1967.

3. Official Kwanzaa website. Kwanzaa is observed December 26 through January 1.

4. *Africana.com* web magazine. In the early 1970s, after the considerable success with Black audiences of the independent film *Shaft,* some two hundred Black-themed movies were released between 1971 and 1975. Hollywood jumped in feet-first, directing about forty films a year toward Black audiences in a short, three-year period. Then the industry lost interest and dropped its production to an average of six or seven Black-themed movies per year through the remainder of the century, even though Black audiences comprise an estimated 25 percent of the Hollywood's national audience.

5. *Boston Sunday Globe,* June 16, 2002, A12, citing radio address by President George W. Bush (Sr.).

6. *Boston Sunday Globe,* June 16, 2002, A12–A13. One article told the story of a cemetery for slaves taken by their owner into Canada when fleeing the American Revolution. Another article summarized a radio address by President George W. Bush (Sr.) on a proposal to make home ownership more affordable to Black and Hispanic Americans. The third article told of the Smithsonian Institution's breaking ground for an Underground Railroad Museum in Cincinnati, a city convulsed by race riots less than a year earlier and currently boycotted by Black public figures.

7. *Portsmouth Herald,* February 20, 2003.

8. Center for Equal Opportunity, an antiquota group, website.

9. Randall, "Seabrook," Gowell, "Clamshell," and Dudley, "Defeating," all in Bolster, *Cross-Grained and Wiley Waters,* 18–22, 157–159.

10. In 1990 Portsmouth had a population of about 25,000 residents; two years later it had about 20,000 because of the departure of most of the base's 5,000 personnel and their families. By 2000 it was approximately 21,000.

11. Interview of University of New Hampshire Admissions Department staff member Eric Weinhold by Mark Sammons, 1992.

12. Candee, *Building Portsmouth,* 103.

13. Chronology from National Association for the Advancement of Colored People website.

14. Findarticles.com website and ABC News website. In 2003 Georgia debated whether or not to continue using the Confederate flag as its state flag, an emblem adopted by that state in 1956 in resistance to the civil rights movement.

15. Kwanza, Inc., spells its name with one *a* at the end; the holiday is spelled Kwanzaa.

16. Sammons interview with Kwanza cofounder Gerry Copeland, June 2002.

17. Collected mostly between September 1990 and December 1991.

18. Blues Bank Collective website.

19. The House passed it 338–90 and the Senate passed it 78–22, notwithstanding attempts by Senator Jesse Helms to derail it. Seattle Times website.

20. Blassingame, *Frederick Douglass Papers,* 23.

21. Sammons, eyewitness, January 1990.

22. Martin Luther King, Jr., Day website. Several other states have holidays with hybrid names: "Martin Luther King/Human Rights Day" in

Utah; "Martin Luther King, Jr., Wyoming Equality Day" in Wyoming; "Martin Luther King, Robert E. Lee, Stonewall Jackson Day" in Virginia; and "Martin Luther King, Jr.–Civil Rights Day" in Arizona. In Louisiana, the governor issues an annual executive order declaring the holiday in fulfillment of legislation that specifically names an approved Martin Luther King, Jr., Day.

23. Sammons, "Gay and Lesbian."

24. Martin Luther King, Jr., Day website; Learning Network website.

25. With some 250 members in its House of Representatives alone the New Hampshire legislature is among the largest legislative bodies in the world. Local oral tradition reports that its numbers are surpassed only by the United States Congress and Britain's Parliament, a widely circulated, oft repeated, characteristically undocumented, and ultimately meaningless claim.

26. Sammons, eyewitness, January 1990.

27. The right of free public assembly clashed with sensibilities of tolerance in 1978 when neo-Nazis applied for a permit to march in heavily Jewish Skokie, Illinois. The issue of permitting became a lightning rod, drawing national attention and comment.

28. Sammons, "Black History Trails."

Appendix

1. Garvin, "Academic Architecture," 192.
2. Candee, *Building Portsmouth*, 103.
3. Candee, *Building Portsmouth*, 67.

BIBLIOGRAPHY

⦿⟨ᘿ⟩⦿

The following bibliography is clustered by type of resource. These are (1) published sources, (2) unpublished and manuscript sources, and (3) consultations and interviews.

Published Souces

ABC News website. http://abcnews.go.com/sections/us/DailyNews/flag000413.html.

Abrams, Freda Morrill, editor. *Tall Ships of Newburyport: The "Montana," the "Whittier," the "Nearchus," as Remembered by George W. Goodwin, Mate.* Yellow Springs, Ohio: The Free Wind Press, 1989.

Adams, Rev. T. H. Essay describing interview with Oney Judge Staines. *Portsmouth (New Hampshire) Granite Freeman,* May 1845.

Africana.com web magazine. http://www.africana.com.

Aldrich, Thomas Bailey. "An Old Town by the Sea," 1883. In *Works of Thomas Bailey Aldrich.* Volume 8. Boston(?): Houghton Mifflin Company, 1911.

Banks, Ronald F. *A History of Maine: A Collection of Readings on the History of Maine, 1600–1974.* Dubuque, Iowa: Kendall/Hunt Publishing Company, n.d.

Barnhart, Clarence L., editor. *The New Cyclopedia of Names.* New York: Appleton-Century-Crofts, n.d.

Bedford, Henry F., and Trevor Colbourn. *The Americans: A Brief History since 1865.* New York: Harcourt Brace Jovanovich, 1972.

Blassingame, John W., editor. *The Frederick Douglass Papers.* Series one: *Speeches, Debates, and Interviews. Volume 2: 1847–54.* New Haven, Connecticut: Yale University Press, 1979.

Blues Bank Collective website. http://www.bluesbankcollective.org.

Bolster, Jeffrey W. *Black Jacks: African American Seamen in the Age of Sail.* Cambridge, Massachusetts: Harvard University Press, 1997.

———. "Business in Great Waters: Black Seamen in the Age of Sail." *Reunion,* February 1995. (Sudbury, Massachusetts: Published by Frank D. Lucas.)

———. "'To Feel Like a Man': Black Seamen in the Northern States, 1800–1860." *Journal of American History,* volume 76, no. 4, March 1990.

Borden, Morton, and Otis L. Graham, Jr., with Roderick W. Nash and Richard E. Oglesby. *Portrait of a Nation: A History of the United States.* Lexington, Massachusetts: D. C. Heath and Company for University of California, 1973.

Boston (Massachusetts) Gazette. October 22, 1754.

Boston (Massachusetts) Sunday Globe. June 16, 2002, March 2, 2003.

Brewster, Charles. W. *The Portsmouth Jubilee: The Reception of the Sons of Portsmouth Resident Abroad, July 4, 1853.* Portsmouth, New Hampshire: C. W. Brewster, 1853.

———. *Rambles About Portsmouth.* 1859; 1873 edition. Reprint, Somersworth, New Hampshire: New Hampshire Publishing Company, 1971.

Brighton, Ray. *They Came to Fish.* 1979 edition. Portsmouth, New Hampshire: Peter E. Randall Publisher, 1973.

Britannia History website. www.britannia.com/history/naremphist6.html.

Brown, Charles Sumner. "The Genesis of the Negro Lawyer in New England, Part I." *Negro History Bulletin,* April 1959. Reprinted in *Making a Living: The Work Experience of African Americans in New England, Selected Readings.* Boston: New England Foundation for the Humanities, 1995.

Burgoyne, Bruce E. *The Trenton Commanders: Washington and Rall as Noted in Hessian Diaries.* Bowie, Maryland: Heritage Books, 1997.

Burke, James. *The Day the Universe Changed.* Boston: Little, Brown and Company, 1985.

Bushman, Richard L. *The Refinement of America: Per-*

sons, Houses, Cities. New York: Random House, Vintage Books, 1992–93.

California Rare Fruit Growers, Inc., website. www .crfg.org.

Candee, Richard, editor. *Building Portsmouth: The Neighborhoods and Architecture of New Hampshire's Oldest City.* Portsmouth, New Hampshire: Portsmouth Advocates, 1992.

Carley, Rachel. *Cuba: 400 Years of Architectural Heritage.* New York: Watson-Guptil Publications, Whitney Library of Design, 1997.

Casanave, Suki. "Learning to Look at Racism." *Campus Journal,* March 2, 1995. (Durham, New Hampshire: University of New Hampshire).

Center for Equal Opportunity website. http://www .ceousa.org.

Charles, Mary Grant. "America's First Negro Magician." *Negro Digest,* December 1949.

Christian, Charles M. *Black Saga: The African American Experience.* Boston: Houghton Mifflin Company, 1995.

Chronicle of Slavery © by Richard E. Irby, Jr., 1994, website. www.geocities.com/Athens/Acropolis/ 2691/COS2.

Clark, Charles E. *The Easter Frontier: The Settlement of Northern New England, 1610–1763.* Hanover, New Hampshire: University Press of New England, 1983.

Clark, Charles, and Eastman W. Eastman, Jr., editors. *The Portsmouth Project: An Exercise in Inductive Historical Scholarship.* Somersworth, New Hampshire: New Hampshire Publishing Company, 1974.

Cleary, Barbara Ann. "John Langdon." *Old-Time New England,* volume 69, nos. 1–2, 1978. (Boston: Society for the Preservation of New England Antiquities.)

Cockrell, Dale. *Demons of Disorder: Early Blackface Minstrels and Their World.* Cambridge, England: Cambridge University Press, 1997.

Connecticut Freedom Trail website. www.ctfreedom trail.com.

Cox, Stephen L. "Abolitionism." In *Encyclopedia of New England Culture.* New Haven, Connecticut: Yale University Press, 2003.

Crowley, Charlotte. "A Zeal for the Cause: The Navy's Role in Stopping Illegal Slave Trade." Posted January 2002 in Sea Services Weekly web magazine, *The Waterline.* http://www.dcmilitary .com/navy/ seaservices/7_2/national_news/13153–1.html.

Cunningham, Valerie. "The First Blacks of Portsmouth." *Historical New Hampshire,* winter 1989. (Concord, New Hampshire: New Hampshire Historical Society.)

Darling, Louise M. *Smallpox.* An Online Exhibit. History and Special Collections Biomedical Library, UCLA. Copyright 2000, the regents of the University of California, website. www.library.ucla .edu/libraries/biomed/smallpox/.

Davis, Thomas J. "Emancipation Rhetoric, Natural Rights, and Revolutionary New England: A Note on Four Black Petitions in Massachusetts, 1773–1777." *New England Quarterly,* volume 62, no. 2, June 1989.

Diggins, John Patrick. *The Proud Decades: America in War and in Peace, 1941–1960.* New York: W. W. Norton and Company, 1989.

Dow, George, with Adolf K. Placzek, editors. *Arts and Crafts of New England, 1704–1775.* 1927. Reprint, New York: DaCapo Press, 1967.

Dudley, Dudley. "Defeating the Onassis Refinery." In *Cross-Grained and Wiley Waters: A Guide to the Piscataqua Maritime Region.* W. Jeffrey Bolster, editor. Portsmouth, New Hampshire: Peter E. Randall Publisher, 2002.

Eastman, John R. *The History of Andover, N.H. 1751–1906.* Concord, New Hampshire, 1910.

E-History website. http://www.ehistory.com/uscw/ library/or/116/0004.cfm.

Encarta website. http://encarta.msn.com/find/concise .asp?mod51&ti5761576153&page55#s57.

Encyclopedia Americana website. http://gi.grolier .com/presidents/ea/side/freesoil.html.

Equal Employment Opportunity Commission website. http://www.eeoc.gov/laws/vii.html.

Estes, J. Worth, and David M. Goodman. *The Changing Humors of Portsmouth: the Medical Biography of an American Town, 1623–1983.* Boston: Francis A. Countway Library of Medicine, 1986.

Fagan, Brian M. *The Little Ice Age: How Climate Made History, 1300–1850.* New York: Basic Books, 2000.

Feintuch, Burt, and David Watters, editors. *Encyclopedia of New England Culture.* New Haven, Connecticut: Yale University Press, 2003.

Findarticles.com website. http://www.findarticles.com/ cf_dls/m1077/6_55/61619023/p1/article.jhtml.

Fitchburg (Massachusetts) Sentinel and Enterprise. August 23, 1992.

Fitzpatrick, John C., editor. *The Writings of George Washington.* Washington, D.C.: U.S. Government Printing Office, 1931–44.

Foster, Joseph. *The Soldier's Memorial, 1893–1923.* Tercentenary edition. Portsmouth, New Hampshire: Storer Post No. 1, Grand Army of the Republic, n.d. (c. 1923).

Franklin, John Hope, and Alfred A. Moss, Jr. *From*

Slavery to Freedom: A History of Negro Americans. Sixth edition. New York: Alfred A. Knopf, 1988.

Garrison (*filii*). *William Lloyd Garrison: The Story of His Life as told by his Children.* Boston: Houghton, Mifflin & Co., 1894.

Garvin, James L. *Historic Portsmouth: Early Photographs from the Collections of Strawbery Banke, Inc.* Somersworth, New Hampshire: New Hampshire Publishing Company, 1974.

Garvin, James L., and Donna-Belle Garvin. *On the Road North of Boston: New Hampshire Taverns and Turnpikes, 1700–1900.* Concord, New Hampshire: New Hampshire Historical Society, 1988.

Garvin, James L., and Susan Grigg, editors. *Historic Portsmouth: Early Photographs from the Collections of Strawbery Banke.* Second edition. Portsmouth, New Hampshire: Peter E. Randall Publisher, 1995.

Gateway to Maine Chamber of Commerce website. Town of Eliot page. http://www.gatewaytomaine.org/ehist.htm.

General Service Administration. "Civil Liberties, Civil Rights, Equal Opportunity, and Discrimination" webpage. http://www.legal.gsa.gov/legal6.htm.

Girouard, Mark. *The Return to Camelot: Chivalry and the English Gentleman.* New Haven, Connecticut: Yale University Press, 1981.

Gowell, Michael. "The Clamshell Alliance." In *Cross-Grained and Wiley Waters: A Guide to the Piscataqua Maritime Region.* W. Jeffrey Bolster, editor. Portsmouth, New Hampshire: Peter E. Randall Publisher, 2002.

Greene, Lorenzo Johnston. *The Negro in Colonial New England.* 1942. Reprint, New York: Athenaeum Press, 1968.

Greenland (New Hampshire) Historical Society Newsletter. Greenland, New Hampshire, 1971.

Gurney, C. S. *Portsmouth Historic and Picturesque.* 1902 edition. Reprint, Portsmouth, New Hampshire: Peter E. Randall Publisher for Strawbery Banke, 1981.

Hansen, Joyce, and Gry McGowan. *Breaking Ground, Breaking Silence: The Story of New York's African Burial Ground.* New York: Henry Holt and Company, 1998.

Harriet Beecher Stowe Center, Hartford, with Stephen Railton and the University of Virginia. *Uncle Tom's Cabin and American Culture—a Multi Media Archive* website. http://www.iath.virginia.edu/utc/minstrel/miar46ft.html.

Henriques, Prof. Peter, George Mason University, Fairfax, Virginia, website. http://chnm.gmu.edu/courses/henriques/hist615/gwandreligion.htm.

Horton, James Oliver, and Lois E. Horton. *Black Bostonians: Family Life and Community Struggle in the Antebellum North.* New York: Holmes & Meier Publishers, 1979.

Houghton Mifflin College Division. *Ships of the World: An Historical Encyclopedia* website. http://college.hmco.com/history/readerscomp/ships/html/sh_064500_nightingale.htm.

Ignatiev, Noel. *How the Irish Became White.* New York: Routledge Press, 1996.

Inter-University Consortium for Political and Social Research (I.C.P.S.R.), Ann Arbor, Michigan, website. http://fisher.lib.virginia.edu/census.

Ireland, Georgia E., and Mary Yeaton. *The Underground Railroad in New England.* American Revolution Bicentennial Administration, Region 1, n.d.

Jackson, Donald, editor. *The Diaries of George Washington.* Charlottesville, Virginia: University Press of Virginia, 1976–79.

Jacobs, Jane. *The Death and Life of Great American Cities.* 1961. Reprint, New York: Vintage Books, 1992.

Jobe, Brock. *Portsmouth Furniture: Masterworks from the New Hampshire Seacoast.* Hanover, New Hampshire: University Press of New England for the Society for the Preservation of New England Antiquities, 1993.

Kalamu Magazine: The Pen of African History web magazine. http://www.kalamumagazine.com/abolition_of_slavery.htm.

Kaplan, Sidney. *The Black Presence in the Era of the American Revolution 1770–1800.* Exhibit catalogue for the National Portrait Gallery, Smithsonian Institution. New York: New York Graphic Society, 1973.

Kinkor, Kenneth J. "From the Seas! Black Men under the Black Flag." *American Visions: The Magazine of Afro-American Culture,* April/May 1995.

Kwanzaa and the Organization Us website. www.officialkwanzaawebsite.org.

Learning Network website. http://www.infoplease.com/spot/mlkhistory1.html.

Leavitt, David. *Florence: A Delicate Case.* New York: Bloomsbury, 2002.

Lemann, Nicholas. *The Promised Land: The Great Black Migration and How It Changed America.* New York: Random House, Vintage Books, 1991.

Lester, Julius, editor. *To Be a Slave.* New York: E. P. Dutton, Scholastic, Dial Books, 1968.

Lexis Nexis website, Constitution of Vermont. http://198.187.128.12/vermont.

Litwack, Leon F. *North of Slavery: The Negro in the Free States, 1790–1860.* Chicago: University of Chicago Press, 1961.

Loewen, James W. *Lies across America: What Our Historic Sites Get Wrong.* New York: New Press, 1999.

Lott, Eric. *Love and Theft: Blackface Minstrelsy and the American Working Class.* Oxford, England: Oxford University Press, 1993.

Louis G. Gregory, Champion of Racial Harmony. Pamphlet. Nation Spiritual Assembly of the Bahá'ís of the United States, 1995.

Mahar, William J. *Behind the Burnt Cork Mask: Early Blackface Minstrelsy and Antebellum American Culture.* Chicago: University of Illinois Press, 1999.

Maritime History Virtual Archives website, Larz Bruzelius. http://pc-78-120.udac.se:8001/WWW/Nautica/Maritime_History/New_Ships/PortsmJ281851-06-21%29.html.

Mars, James. *Life of James Mars, a Slave Born and Sold in Connecticut.* Hartford, Connecticut: Press of Case and Lockwood and Co., 1868.

Martin Luther King, Jr., Day website, by Arnie Alpert with Craig Werth and Dan Gordon. http://pubpages.unh.edu/~cw/mlk-nh/holback.html.

Mazzari, Louis. "African American Music." In *Encyclopedia of New England Culture.* New Haven, Connecticut: Yale University Press, 2003.

McCarthy, Mary. *The Stones of Florence.* New York: Harcourt, Brace and Company, n.d.

Medicinenet website. http://www.medicinenet.com.

Medicolegal website. http://downloads.members.tripod.com/medicolegal/somersetvstewart.htm.

Melish, Joanne Pope. *Disowning Slavery: Gradual Emancipation and "Race" in New England, 1780–1860.* Ithaca, New York: Cornell University Press, 1998.

Metalious, Grace. *Peyton Place.* New York: Simon & Schuster, 1956.

Mevers, Frank C., editor. *The Papers of Josiah Bartlett.* Hanover, New Hampshire: University Press of New England for the New Hampshire Historical Society, 1979.

Mintz, Sidney W., Herman J. Viola, and Carolyn Margolis, editors. "Pleasure, Profit, and Satiation." In *Seeds of Change: Five Hundred Years since Columbus.* Washington, D.C.: Smithsonian Institution Press, 1991.

Moore, John W. *Historical, Biographical, and Miscellaneous Gatherings, in the Form of Disconnected Notes relative to Printers, Printing, Publishing, and Editing of Books, Newspapers, Magazines and other Literary Productions. . . .* Concord, New Hampshire: Republican Press Association, 1886.

Morgan, Philip D., and Michael L. Nicholls. "Slave Flight: Mount Vernon, Virginia, and the Wider Atlantic World." In *Runaway Slaves in Eighteenth Century Virginia: A New World Perspective.* Charlottesville, Virginia: University of Virginia Press, 2002.

Morgan, William James, editor. *Documents of the American Revolution.* Volume 9. Washington, D.C.: Government Printing Office for Naval Historical Center, Department of the Navy, 1986.

Mount Vernon Ladies' Association website. www.mountvernon.org. (Including Morgan's *Runaway Slaves in Eighteenth-Century Virginia.*)

NAACP Reports. June 1965 ff. (Portsmouth, New Hampshire, Branch of the National Association for the Advancement of Colored People.)

Nash, Gary B. *Red, White, and Black: The Peoples of Early America.* Englewood Cliffs, New Jersey: Prentice-Hall, 1974.

National Association for the Advancement of Colored People website. http://www.naacp.org/past_future/naacptimeline.shtml.

National Museums and Galleries on Merseyside Marine Paintings website. http://www.nmgm.org.uk/maritime/paintings/burke.html.

National Park Service. Civil War soldier web database. www.itd.nps.gov/cwss.

Nell, William C. *The Colored Patriots of the American Revolution.* Boston: Published by Robert E. Wallcut, 1855.

Nelson, Derek. *The Posters That Won the War: The Production, Recruitment, and War Bond Posters of WW II.* Osceola, Wisconsin: Motorbooks International, 1991.

New Century Cyclopedia of Names. Volume 3.

New Hampshire Gazette (Portsmouth). Published 1756–1942.

New Hampshire Martin Luther King Day website, by Craig Werth and Dan Gordon. http://pubpages.unh.edu/~cw/mlk-nh/holback.html.

New Hampshire Provincial Papers. Edited by Nathaniel Boulton. Inventory of the Polls and Estates of Portsmouth, 1727, 1767.

Order of the Knights of Pythias website. www.pythians.org.

Palmer, R. R., and Joel Colton. *A History of the Modern World since 1815.* Fourth edition. New York: Alfred A. Knopf, 1971.

Pecor, Charles Joseph. *The Magician on the American Stage, 1752–1874.* Washington, D.C.: Emerson and West, n.d.

Penrose, Charles. *Ichabod Goodwin, 1794–1882.* New York: Newcomen Society in North America, 1956.

Perkins, Mary Coolidge. *Once I Was Very Young.* 1960. Reprint, Portsmouth, New Hampshire: Peter E. Randall Publisher, 2000.

Peterson, Barbara Bennett. "Boston University." In *Encyclopedia of New England Culture.* New Haven, Connecticut: Yale University Press, 2003.

Pickett, Gertrude M. *Portsmouth's Heyday in Shipbuilding.* Portsmouth, New Hampshire: Privately published by Joe Sawtelle, 1979.

Piersen, William D. *Black Legacy: America's Hidden Heritage.* Amherst, Massachusetts: University of Massachusetts Press, 1993.

————. *Black Yankees: The Development of an Afro-American Subculture in Eighteenth-Century New England.* Amherst, Massachusetts: University of Massachusetts Press, 1988.

Polner, Murray. *Commonweal Magazine,* March 28, 1969.

Portsmouth (New Hampshire) Chronicle (including *Daily Morning Chronicle*). Published 1852–98.

Portsmouth (New Hampshire) Daily Evening Times. Published 1868–86.

Portsmouth (New Hampshire) Directory. 1821, 1827, 1834, 1839, 1851, 1861, 1864, 1867, 1869, 1873, 1881, 1918, 1920, 1923, 1928, 1941.

Portsmouth (New Hampshire) Freeman's Journal. Published 1776–78.

Portsmouth (New Hampshire) Herald. Published 1884–present.

Portsmouth (New Hampshire) Journal (including *Journal of Literature and Politics*). Published 1821–1903.

Portsmouth New Hampshire Mercury. Published 1784–88.

Portsmouth (New Hampshire) Oracle, 1807.

The Portsmouth Periscope. Newsletter of the Portsmouth Naval Shipyard. Kittery, Maine, 1965.

Price, David. *Magic: A Pictorial History of Conjurers in the Theater.* New York: Cornwall Books, n.d.

Public Broadcasting System. Africans in America on-line companion resource website. www.pbs.org/wgbh/aia.

Quarles, Benjamin. *Black Abolitionists.* New York: DaCapo Press and Oxford University Press, 1969.

Railton, Stephen. *Mark Twain in His Times.* University of Virginia, Department of English, website. http://etext.lib.virginia.edu/railton/huckfinn/minstrl.html.

Randall, Peter E. "Seabrook and Seabrook Station." In *Cross-Grained and Wiley Waters: A Guide to the Piscataqua Maritime Region.* W. Jeffrey Bolster, editor. Portsmouth, New Hampshire: Peter E. Randall Publisher, 2002.

Rhode Island Black Heritage Society website. www.providenceri.com/RI_BlackHeritage/Historical_Highlights.html.

Rorabaugh, W. J. *The Alcoholic Republic, an American Tradition.* New York: Oxford University Press, 1979.

Salzman, Jack, David Lionel Smith, and Cornel West, editors. *Encyclopedia of African-American Culture and History.* New York: Macmillan, 1995.

Sammons, Mark J. "Black History Trails." In *Encyclopedia of New England Culture.* New Haven, Connecticut: Yale University Press, 2004.

————. "Cold." In *Encyclopedia of New England Culture.* New Haven, Connecticut: Yale University Press, 2004.

————. "Gay and Lesbian History and Culture." In *Encyclopedia of New England Culture.* New Haven, Connecticut: Yale University Press, 2004.

————, editor. *Strawbery Banke, Portsmouth, New Hampshire: Official Guidebook.* Portsmouth, New Hampshire: Peter E. Randall Publisher for Strawbery Banke, 1997.

Saratoga (New York) Sentinel.

Schwartz, Philip J. "The Adaptation of Afro-American Slaves to the Anglo-American Judiciary." Department of History, Virginia Commonwealth University. Paper prepared for presentation at the 41st Conference of the Institute of Early American History and Culture at Millersville State College, Millersville, Pennsylvania, April 30, 1981. Paper on file at Strawbery Banke Museum library, Portsmouth, New Hampshire.

Seacoast New Hampshire website. www.seacoastNH.com and www.seacoastNH.com/talkmail.

Seattle Times website. http://seattletimes.NWsource.com/mlk/holiday/holiday_time.html.

Sitkoff, Harvard. "The American Home Front." In *Produce and Conserve, Share and Play Square: The Grocer and the Consumer on the Home-Front Battlefield During World War II.* Barbara McLean Ward, editor. Hanover, New Hampshire: University Press of New England for Strawbery Banke Museum, 1994.

Smithsonian Institution. "Migrations in History" website. http://educate.si.edu/migrations/legacy/almleg.html.

Spartacus Educational website. http://www.spartacus.schoolnet.co.uk/USASremond.htm.

Takaki, Ronald. *A Different Mirror: A History of Multicultural America.* Boston: Little, Brown and Company, 1993.

Taylor, Deems, John Tasker Howard, et al. *A Treasury of Stephen Foster.* New York: Random House, 1946.

Thayer, Lucius Harrison, D.D. *The Story of a Religious Democracy: An Historical Discourse in Commemoration of the Gathering of the First Church during Two and One-Half Centuries.* Portsmouth, New Hampshire, 1921.

Ulrich, Laurel Thatcher. *A Midwife's Tale: The Life of Martha Ballard, Based on Her Diary, 1785–1812.* New York: Alfred A. Knopf, 1990.

United States Census Bureau website. http://factfinder.census.gov/.

United States Equal Employment Opportunity Commission website. http://www.eeoc.gov/laws/vii.html.

United States General Service Administration. "Civil Liberties, Civil Rights, Equal Opportunity, and Discrimination" webpage. http://www.legal.gsa.gov/legal6.htm.

United States Library of Congress. "American Memory" website. http://memory.loc.gov/.

United States: National Park Service. *Boston Black Heritage Trail.* U.S. Government Printing Office, 1992-0-601-783, 1992.

United States State Department website. www.state.gov.

United States Treasury website. www.ustreas.gov.

United States White House website. www.whitehouse.gov.

Vegh, Steven G. "Exhibit Includes Black Maine Bishop." Citing the Rev. Albert S. Foley, "Bishop Healy: Beloved Outcast,"*Portland Maine Sunday Telegram,* January 29, 1995.

Voices of Maine—Visible Black History website. http://www.visibleblackhistory.com/Freeman.htm.

Wade, Melvin. "'Shining in Borrowed Plumage': Affirmation of Community in the Black Coronation Festivals of New England, ca. 1750–1850." In *Material Life in America, 1600–1860,* edited by Robert Blair St. George. Boston: Northeastern University Press, 1989.

Warner, Sam Bass, Jr. *The Urban Wilderness: A History of the American City.* New York: Harper & Row, 1972.

Wentworth, John. *The Wentworth Genealogy: English and American.* Boston: Little, Brown and Company, 1878.

Whipple Organization website. www.whipple.org/prince/princewhipple/.

White, Shane. "'We Dwell in Safety and Pursue Our Honest Callings': Free Blacks in New York City, 1783–1810."*Journal of American History,* volume 75, September 1988.

White, William L. *Lost Boundaries: The story of Dr. Albert C. Johnston.* New York: Harcourt, Brace & World, 1947.

Winslow, Richard E., III. *"Constructing Munitions of War": The Portsmouth Navy Yard Confronts the Confederacy, 1861–1865.* Portsmouth, New Hampshire: Peter E. Randall Publisher for the Portsmouth Marine Society, 1995.

———. *"Wealth and Honour": Portsmouth during the Golden Age of Privateering, 1775–1815.* Portsmouth, New Hampshire: Peter E. Randall Publisher for the Portsmouth Marine Society, c. 1988.

Wright, Roberta Hughes, and Wilbur B. Hughes, III. *Lay down Body: Living History in African American Cemeteries.* Detroit, New York, Washington, D.C., and Toronto: Visible Ink Press, 1996.

Unpublished and Manuscript Sources

Alexander, Elise. *Blacks in Portsmouth, NH, 1750–1850: A Sourcebook.* Resource paper for Strawbery Banke Museum, May 1995. Portsmouth, New Hampshire.

"Caution!! Colored People of Boston." Handbill, April 24, 1851. Facsimile reprint from African Meeting House Museum. Boston, Massachusetts.

Dagenais, Mary Ann La Fleur. "The Black in Portsmouth, New Hampshire, 1700–1861." M.A. thesis, University of New Hampshire, 1970.

DuPré, Mary. *The Story of Wheelwright House.* Monograph for Strawbery Banke Museum, 1990. Portsmouth, New Hampshire.

Garland Patch Collection of Glass Plate Negative Photographs. Strawbery Banke Museum Research Library. Portsmouth, New Hampshire.

Garvin, James L. "Academic Architecture and the Building Trades in the Piscataqua Region of New Hampshire and Maine, 1715–1815." Ph.D. dissertation, Boston University, 1983.

———. "Outline of a Tour of the Wentworth-Coolidge Mansion, Portsmouth, New Hampshire." Monograph for New Hampshire Division of Historical Resources, 1992. Concord, New Hampshire.

Goodwin, Sarah Parker Rice. "Pleasant Memories." Manuscript essays. Strawbery Banke Museum Research Library. Portsmouth, New Hampshire.

"History of New Hope Baptist Church." Unsigned two-page essay, n.d. Cunningham collection. Portsmouth, New Hampshire.

Hyde, John L., and Associates. "Property of the African Methodist Episcopal Zion Church, 215 Hanover Street, Block no. 9, Parcel no. 14." Report for the Portsmouth Housing Authority, November 9, 1964. Portsmouth, New Hampshire.

Karnan, Robert W., D.Mn. "Untold Tales of South Church." Sermon transcript, May 28, 1989. Portsmouth, New Hampshire.

Ladd, [William], File. Moffatt-Ladd House Collection. Portsmouth (New Hampshire) Athenaeum.

Langdon Papers. Strawbery Banke Museum Research Library. Portsmouth, New Hampshire.

———. Portsmouth (New Hampshire) Athenaeum.

Langdon/Elwyn Papers. New Hampshire Historical Society. Concord, New Hampshire.

Maine: York County, Probate Court Records.

Massachusetts: Roxbury, Vital Records.

New Hampshire: Provincial Papers. See listing under published sources.

New Hampshire: Rockingham County, Probate Court Records.

New Hampshire: Rockingham County, Registry of Deeds.

New Hampshire: State Archives, Court of Session papers. Concord, New Hampshire.

North Church. Records, 1779–1835. Portsmouth (New Hampshire) Athenaeum.

People's Baptist Church. Sunday service bulletins, September 26, 1943, February 1, 1953. Portsmouth, New Hampshire.

Portsmouth, New Hampshire: Town/City Records.

Potter, Jean. Written reminiscence of Wentworth-by-the-Sea Hotel civil rights actions. Private collection.

"A Reception in Honor of Ms. Elizabeth Virgil." Printed program, March 27, 1991. University of New Hampshire, Durham, New Hampshire.

Riley, Pat. "John Stavers and the William Pitt Tavern." Research paper for Strawbery Banke Museum, n.d. Portsmouth, New Hampshire.

Saint John's Church. Records. Portsmouth (New Hampshire) Athenaeum.

Sammons, Mark J. "Abbott Store and Kitchen: Preface and Script." Paper for Strawbery Bank Museum, 1993. Portsmouth, New Hampshire.

———. "Myths and Methods: Rural Schooling in Early Nineteenth Century New England." research paper for Old Sturbridge Village, Inc., c. 1985. Sturbridge, Massachusetts.

———. "Schools, Scholars, and Society: Early New England Schooling." Resource book for teachers, Old Sturbridge Village, Inc., c. 1985. Sturbridge, Massachusetts.

Seacoast Council on Race and Religion (SCORR). Papers. African American Resource Center. Portsmouth, New Hampshire.

South Church. Records. Portsmouth (New Hampshire) Athenaeum.

Tuveson, Erik R. "A People of Color": A Study of Race and Racial Identiacation in New Hampshire, 1750–1825. M.A. thesis, University of New Hampshire, 1992.

United States: Census for Rockingham County, New Hampshire.

United States: Federal Direct Tax records. B List, 1798. Portsmouth, New Hampshire.

United States: National Archives. Abstracts of Registers, Licenses, Enrollments, 1801–5, Book E, Records of Registers, Licenses, and Enrollments. Washington, D.C.

United States: National Archives. Record Group 41, no. 2270, Portsmouth, New Hampshire. Washington, D.C.

Warner Family. Papers. Warner House Association. Portsmouth (New Hampshire) Athenaeum.

Consultations and Interviews

Bolster, Jeffrey W. Department of History, University of New Hampshire. Durham, New Hampshire.

Candee, Richard. Department of American Studies, Boston University. Boston, Massachusetts.

Copeland, Gerry. Kwanza, Inc. Portsmouth, New Hampshire.

Cunningham, Valerie. African American Resource Center. Portsmouth, New Hampshire.

———. Oral history interviews with Rosary Broxay Cooper, Anna Jones, Doris Moore, Frances Tilley Satchell, Elizabeth Virgil.

Dolph, Jim. Curator, Portsmouth Naval Shipyard Museum. Kittery, Maine.

Garvin, James L. State Architectural Historian, New Hampshire Division of Historical Resources. Concord, New Hampshire.

Heidelberg, Kenneth A. Boston African American National Historic Site. Boston, Massachusetts.

Melville, Andrew. Hampton Falls, New Hampshire.

Muscato-Lalley, Suzanne. Museum of Afro-American History, African Meeting House. Boston, Massachusetts.

Nowers, Elizabeth. Strawbery Banke Museum. Portsmouth, New Hampshire.

Olson, Robert. Old Sturbridge Village, Inc. Sturbridge, Massachusetts.

O'Toole, Dennis. Strawbery Banke Museum. Portsmouth, New Hampshire.

Potter, Jean. South Yarmouth, Massachusetts.

Volk, Joyce. Warner House Association. Portsmouth, New Hampshire.

Ward, Barbara McLean. Moffatt-Ladd House. Portsmouth, New Hampshire.

Weinhold, Eric. University of New Hampshire. Durham, New Hampshire.

INDEX

◆§◊◊

Page numbers for material found in illustrations and captions are italicized. People whose names changed through marriage, sale, or adoption of a new name are listed under the latest form of their name.

Quechee Library
P.O. Box 384
Quechee, VT 05059